Takeshi Obata

Continued from volume 8...

Even if you're missing a go stone or two, apparently it isn't really a problem because you don't use up all the stones in a game anyway.

On another note, the Shosoin Imperial Repository in Nara holds ivory go stones with carvings like the illustrations above. I want some. Even just one...

—Takeshi Obata

It all began when Yumi Hotta played a pick-up game of go with her father-in-law. As she was learning how to play, Ms. Hotta thought it might be fun to create a story around the traditional board game. More confident in her storytelling abilities than her drawing skills, she submitted the beginnings of **Hikaru no Go** to **Weekly Shonen Jump**'s Story King Award. The Story King Award is an award that picks the best story, manga, character design and youth (under 15) manga submissions every year in Japan. As fate would have it, Ms. Hotta's story (originally named, "*Kokonotsu no Hoshi*"), was a runner-up in the "Story" category of the Story King Award. Many years earlier, Takeshi Obata was a runner-up for the Tezuka Award, another Japanese manga contest sponsored by **Weekly Shonen Jump** and **Monthly Shonen Jump**. An editor assigned to Mr. Obata's artwork came upon Ms. Hotta's story and paired the two for a full-fledged manga about go. The rest is modern go history.

HIKARU NO GO VOL. 10
SHONEN JUMP Manga Edition

This manga contains material that was originally published in English from
SHONEN JUMP #51 to #55.

STORY BY YUMI HOTTA
ART BY TAKESHI OBATA
Supervised by YUKARI UMEZAWA (5 Dan)

Translation & English Adaptation/Andy Nakatani
English Script Consultant/Janice Kim (3 Dan)
Touch-up Art & Lettering/Inori Fukuda Trant
Cover & Interior Design/Courtney Utt
Additional Touch-up/Josh Simpson
Editors/Yuki Takagaki & Annette Roman

Printed in the U.S.A.

Published by VIZ Media, LLC
P.O. Box 77010
San Francisco, CA 94107

10 9 8 7 6 5 4 3
First printing, August 2007
Third printing, February 2011

www.viz.com

THE WORLD'S
MOST POPULAR MANGA
SHONEN JUMP
www.shonenjump.com

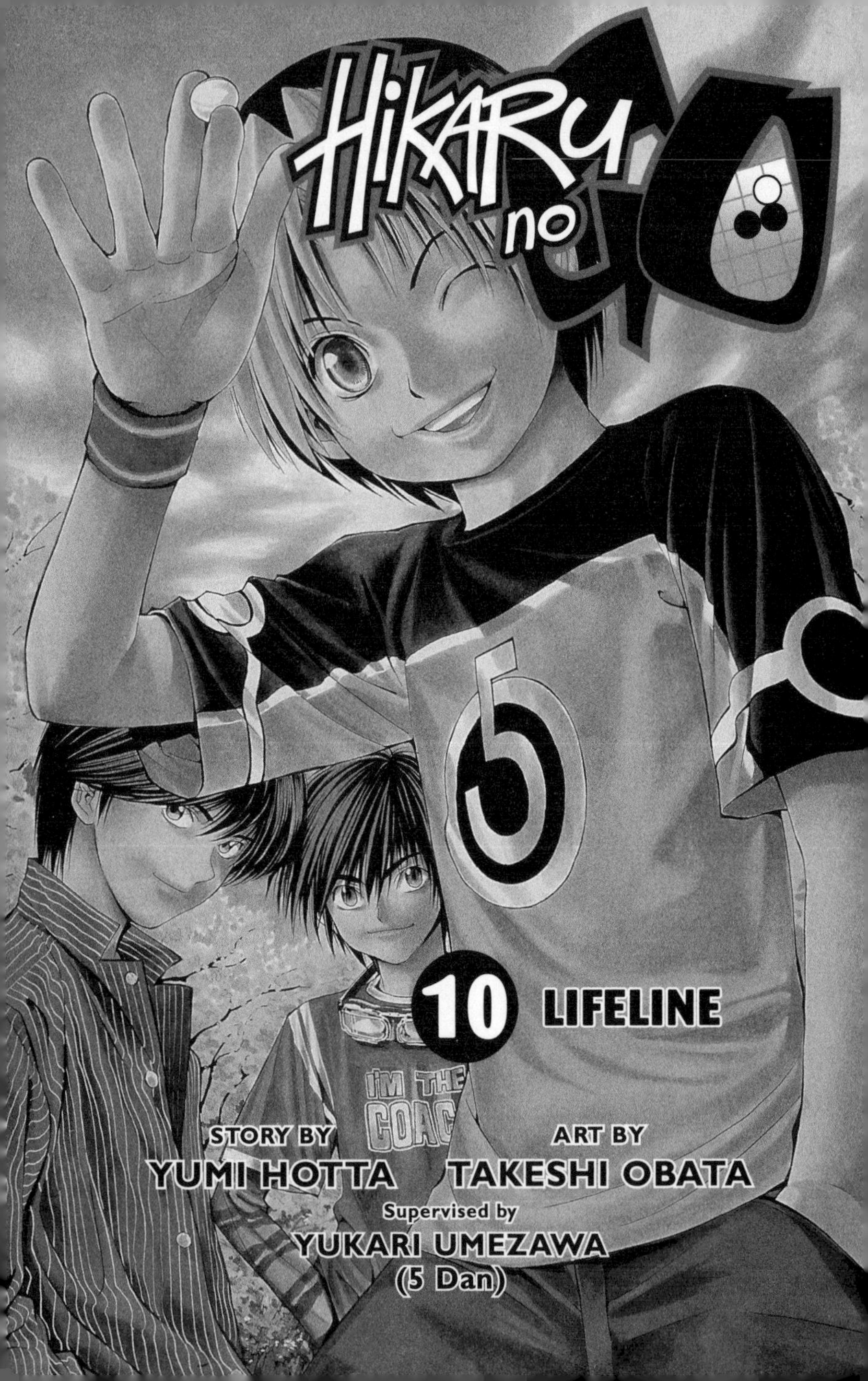
HIKARU no GO
10 LIFELINE
I'M THE COAC
STORY BY
YUMI HOTTA
ART BY
TAKESHI OBATA
Supervised by
YUKARI UMEZAWA
(5 Dan)

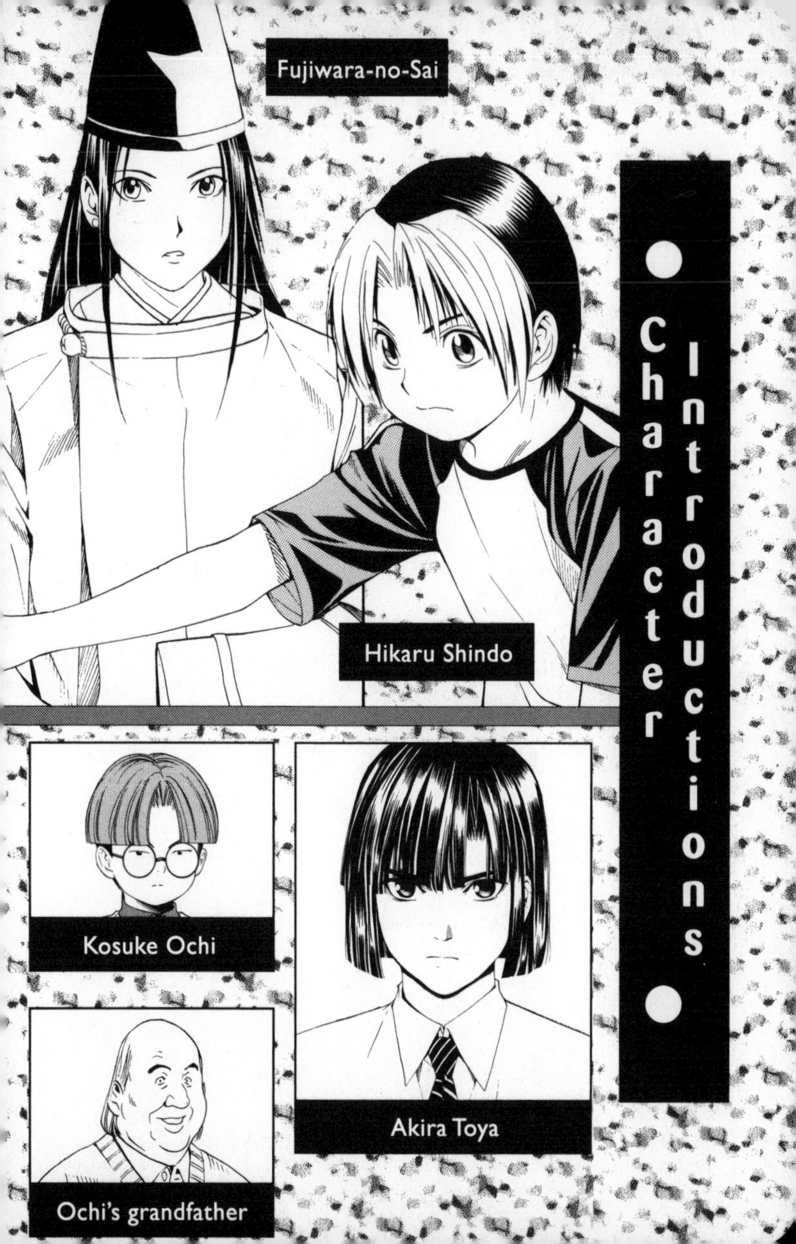
Character Introductions
Fujiwara-no-Sai
Hikaru Shindo
Akira Toya
Kosuke Ochi
Ochi's grandfather

Shinichiro Isumi

Yuta "Fuku" Fukui

Yoshitaka Waya

Ryo Iijima

Toshiro Tsubaki

Toshinori Honda

Asumi Nase

Story Thus Far

Hikaru Shindo discovers an old go board one day up in his grandfather's attic. The moment Hikaru touches the board, the spirit of Fujiwara-no-Sai, a genius go player from Japan's Heian Era, enters his consciousness. Sai's love of go inspires Hikaru, as does a meeting with the child prodigy Akira Toya—son of go master Toya Meijin. With his interest in go awakened, Hikaru now dreams of becoming a professional player.

Hikaru barely passes the preliminary rounds of the pro test because he lacks experience playing against adults. Waya and Isumi take him to some go salons to fix the problem. At one place, they meet a Korean insei named Suyong Hong. Hikaru unwittingly offends Suyong, which leads to a grudge match between them. Suyong doesn't take Hikaru seriously and ends up losing to Hikaru by one and a half points. When the final rounds of the pro test begin, Hikaru amazes his rivals by winning his first six games. Meanwhile, Akira is shocked to see Hikaru's undefeated record on the Internet. Hoping to learn more, Akira agrees to play a teaching game with Hikaru's friend and rival Ochi.

CONTENTS

10

GAME 79
Hikaru vs. Tsubaki   7

GAME 80
A Stand-in   29

GAME 81
An Important Game   51

GAME 82
An Ill-Fated Moment   71

GAME 83
The Elusive Win   91

GAME 84
Waya vs. Ochi   115

GAME 85
Lifeline   137

GAME 86
You Never Know   157

GAME 87
Who Played Black?   179

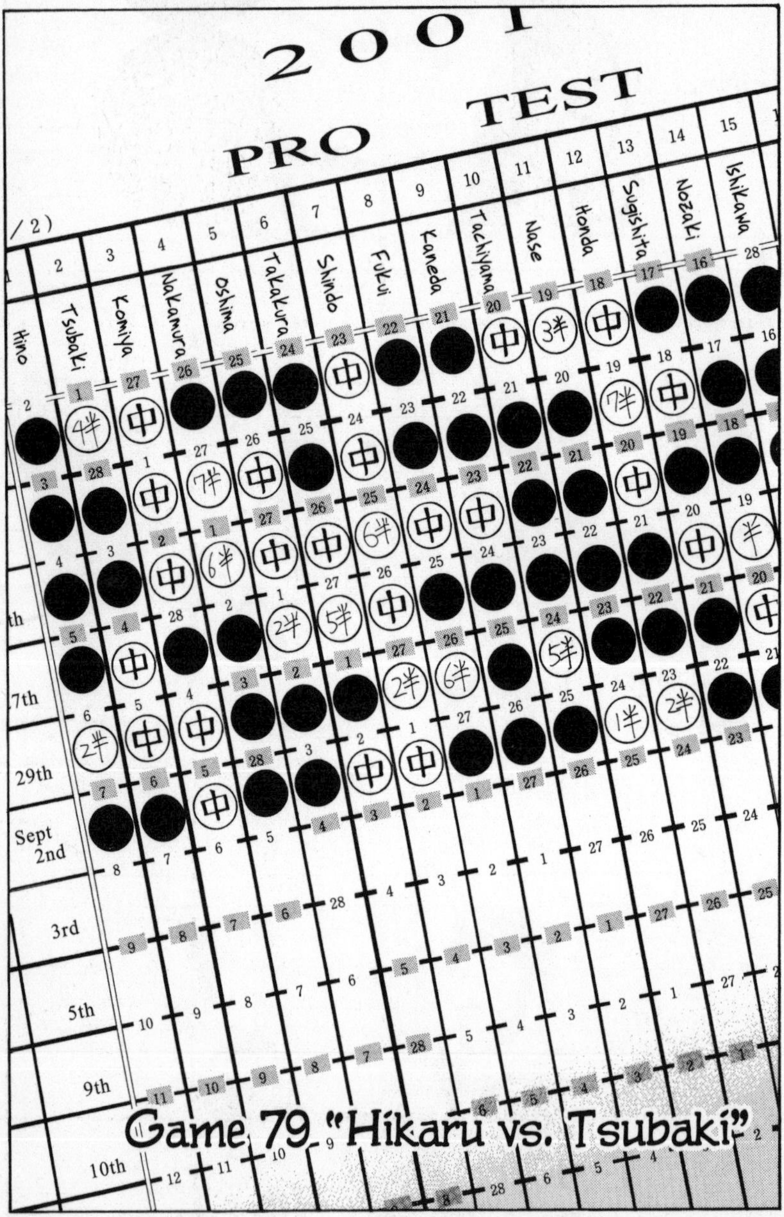
2001 PRO TEST
/2)
Hino
Tsubaki
Komiya
Nakamura
Oshima
Takakura
Shindo
Fukui
Kaneda
Tachiyama
Nase
Honda
Sugishita
Nozaki
Ishikawa
29th
Sept 2nd
3rd
5th
9th
10th

Game 79 "Hikaru vs. Tsubaki"

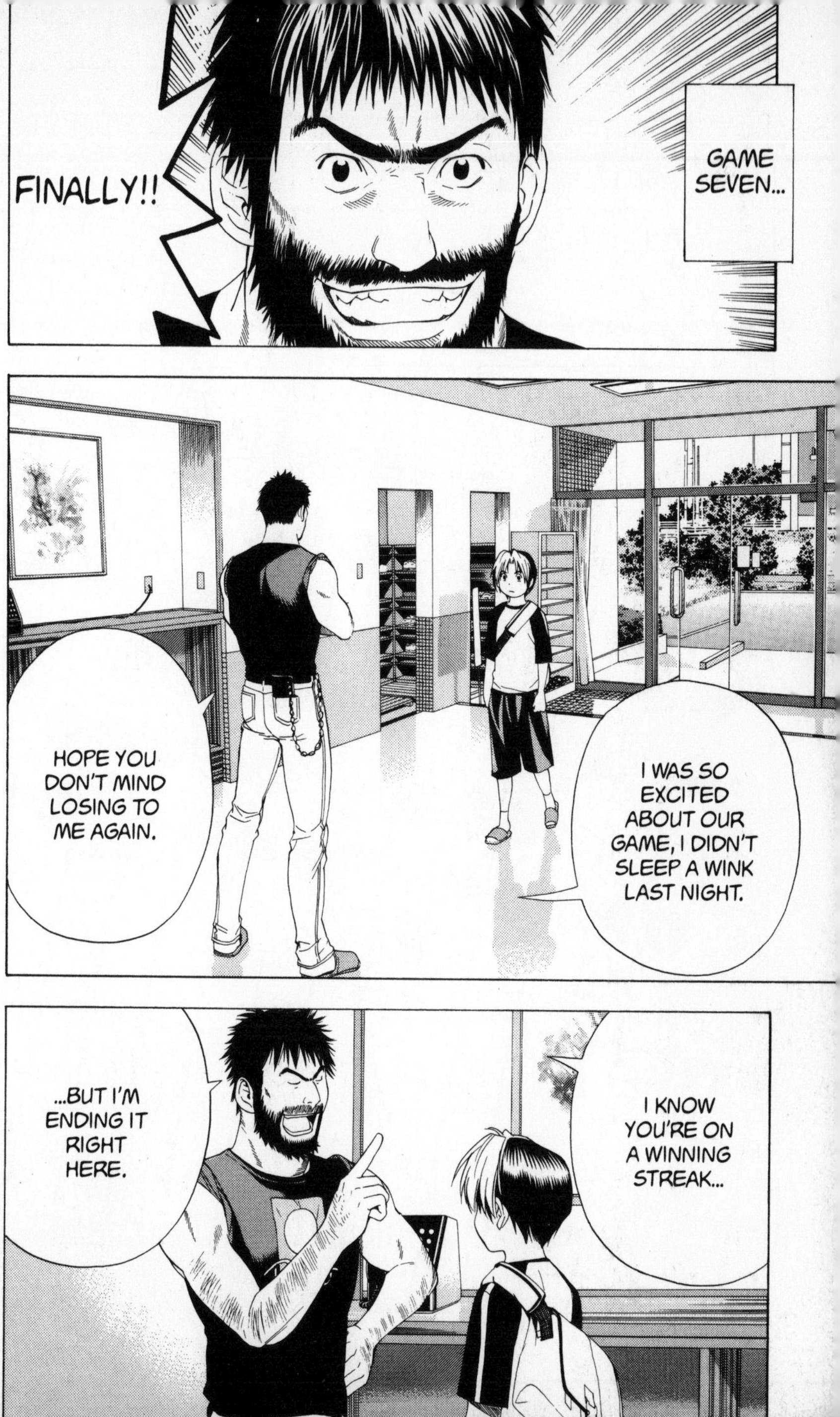
GAME SEVEN...
FINALLY!!
I WAS SO EXCITED ABOUT OUR GAME, I DIDN'T SLEEP A WINK LAST NIGHT.
HOPE YOU DON'T MIND LOSING TO ME AGAIN.
I KNOW YOU'RE ON A WINNING STREAK...
...BUT I'M ENDING IT RIGHT HERE.

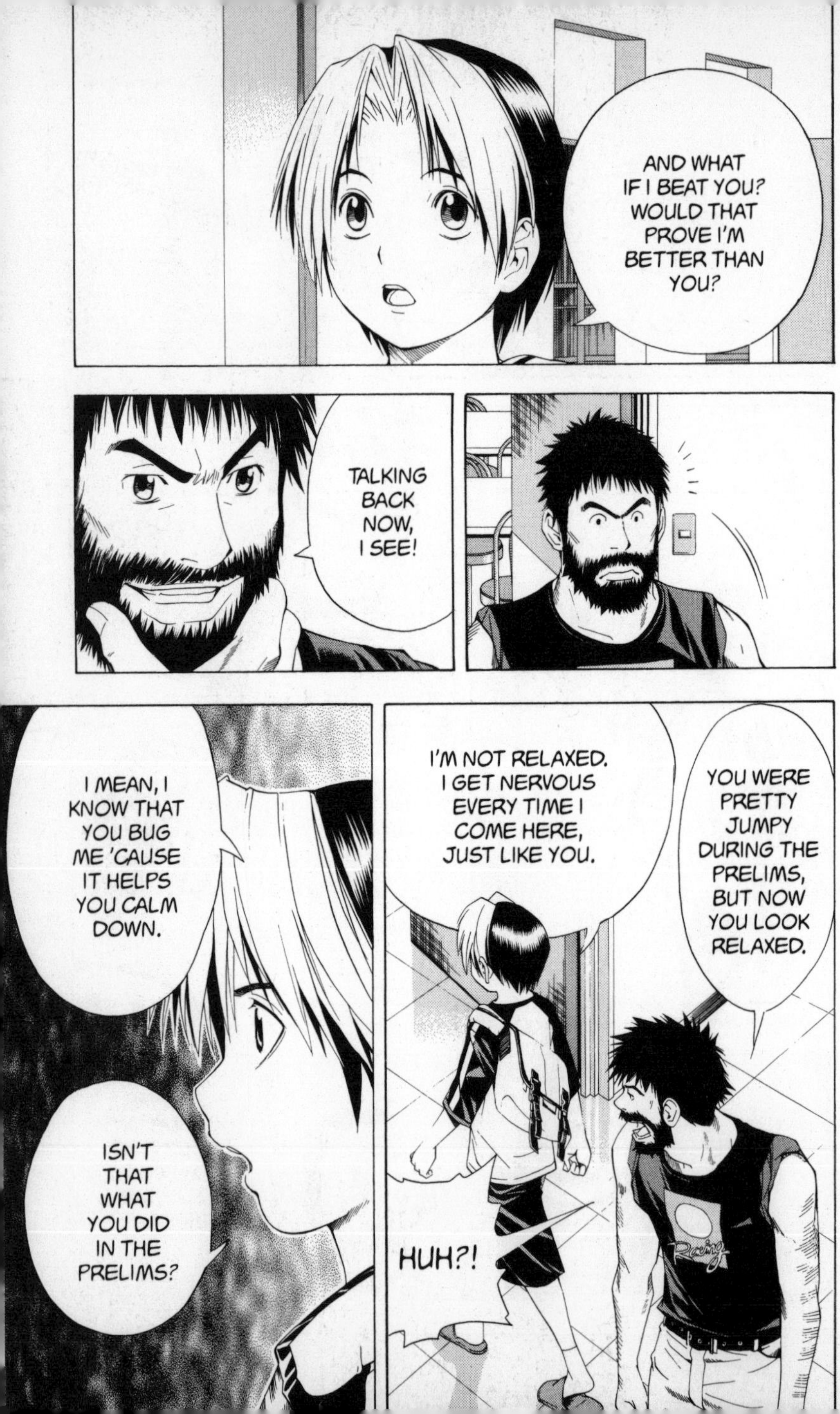
AND WHAT IF I BEAT YOU? WOULD THAT PROVE I'M BETTER THAN YOU?
TALKING BACK NOW, I SEE!
YOU WERE PRETTY JUMPY DURING THE PRELIMS, BUT NOW YOU LOOK RELAXED.
I'M NOT RELAXED. I GET NERVOUS EVERY TIME I COME HERE, JUST LIKE YOU.
HUH?!
I MEAN, I KNOW THAT YOU BUG ME 'CAUSE IT HELPS YOU CALM DOWN.
ISN'T THAT WHAT YOU DID IN THE PRELIMS?

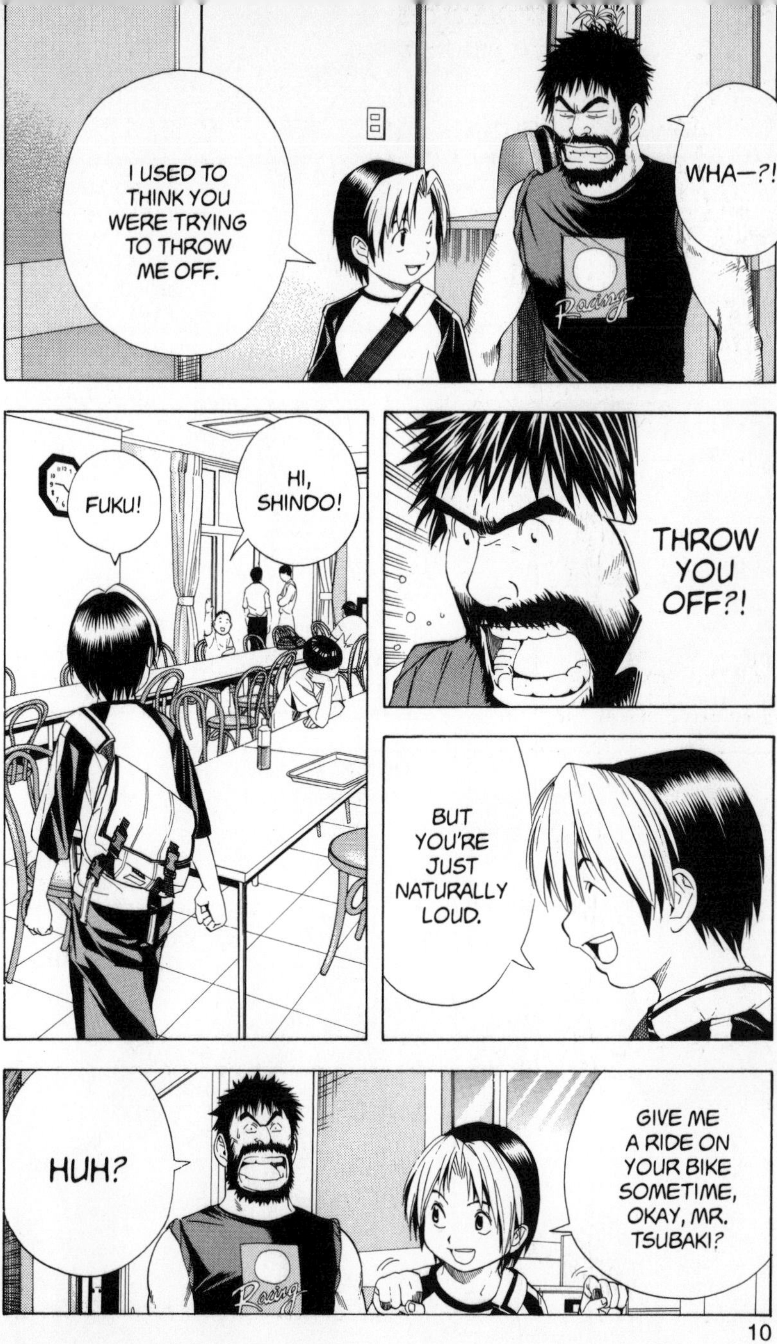
I USED TO THINK YOU WERE TRYING TO THROW ME OFF.
WHA—?!
THROW YOU OFF?!
BUT YOU'RE JUST NATURALLY LOUD.
HI, SHINDO!
FUKU!
GIVE ME A RIDE ON YOUR BIKE SOMETIME, OKAY, MR. TSUBAKI?
HUH?

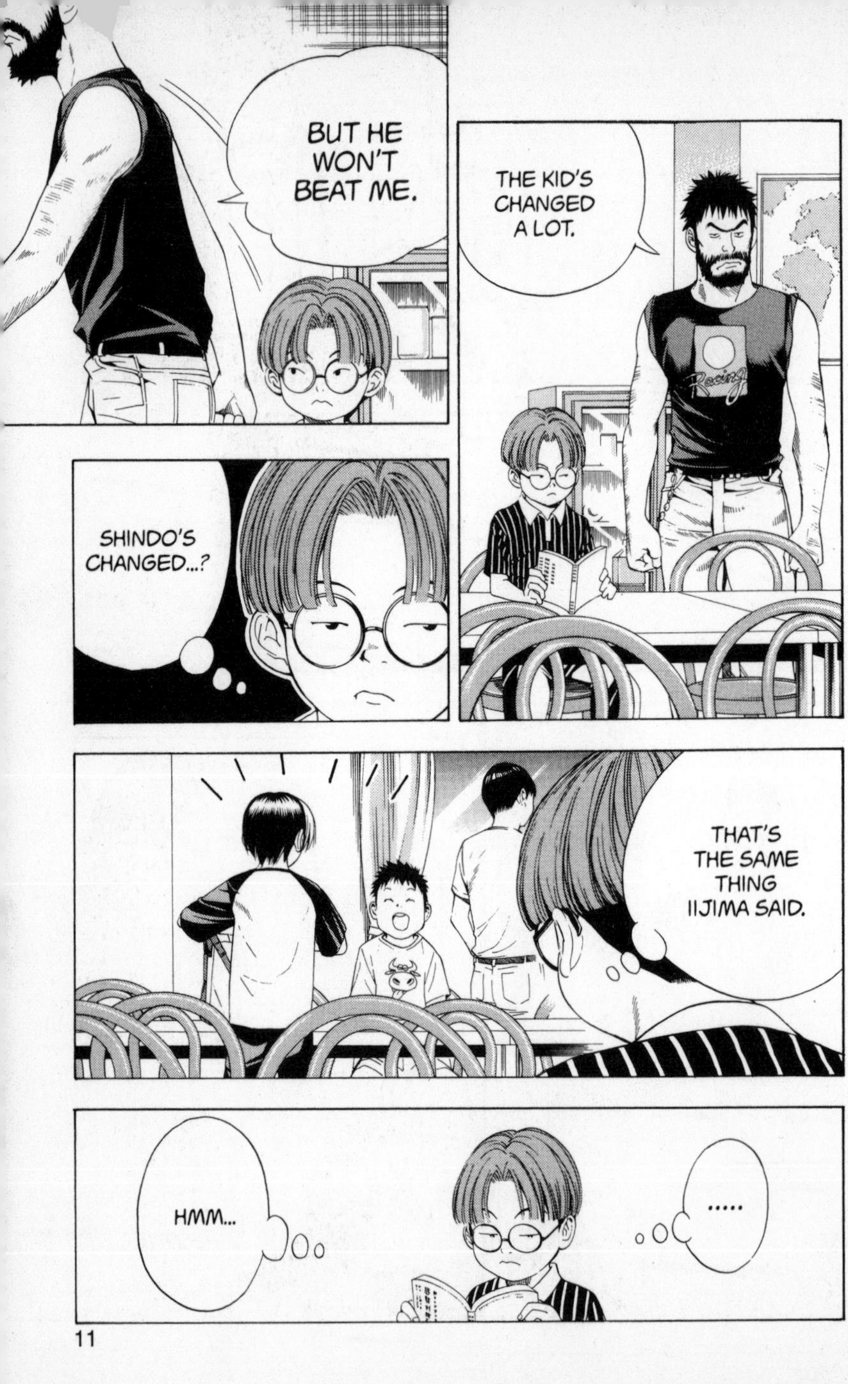
THE KID'S CHANGED A LOT.
BUT HE WON'T BEAT ME.
SHINDO'S CHANGED...?
THAT'S THE SAME THING IIJIMA SAID.
.....
HMM...

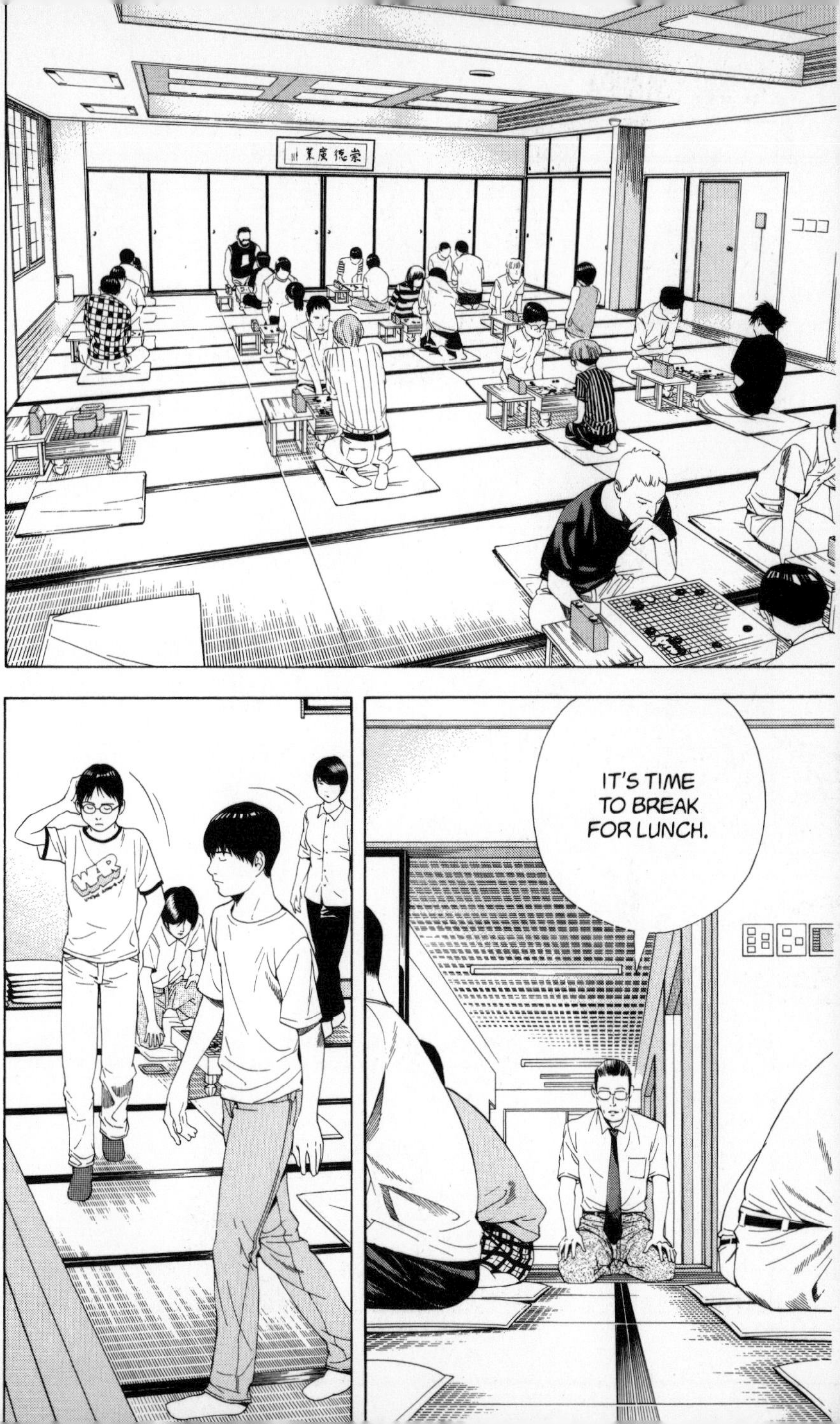
IT'S TIME TO BREAK FOR LUNCH.

READ THIS WAY

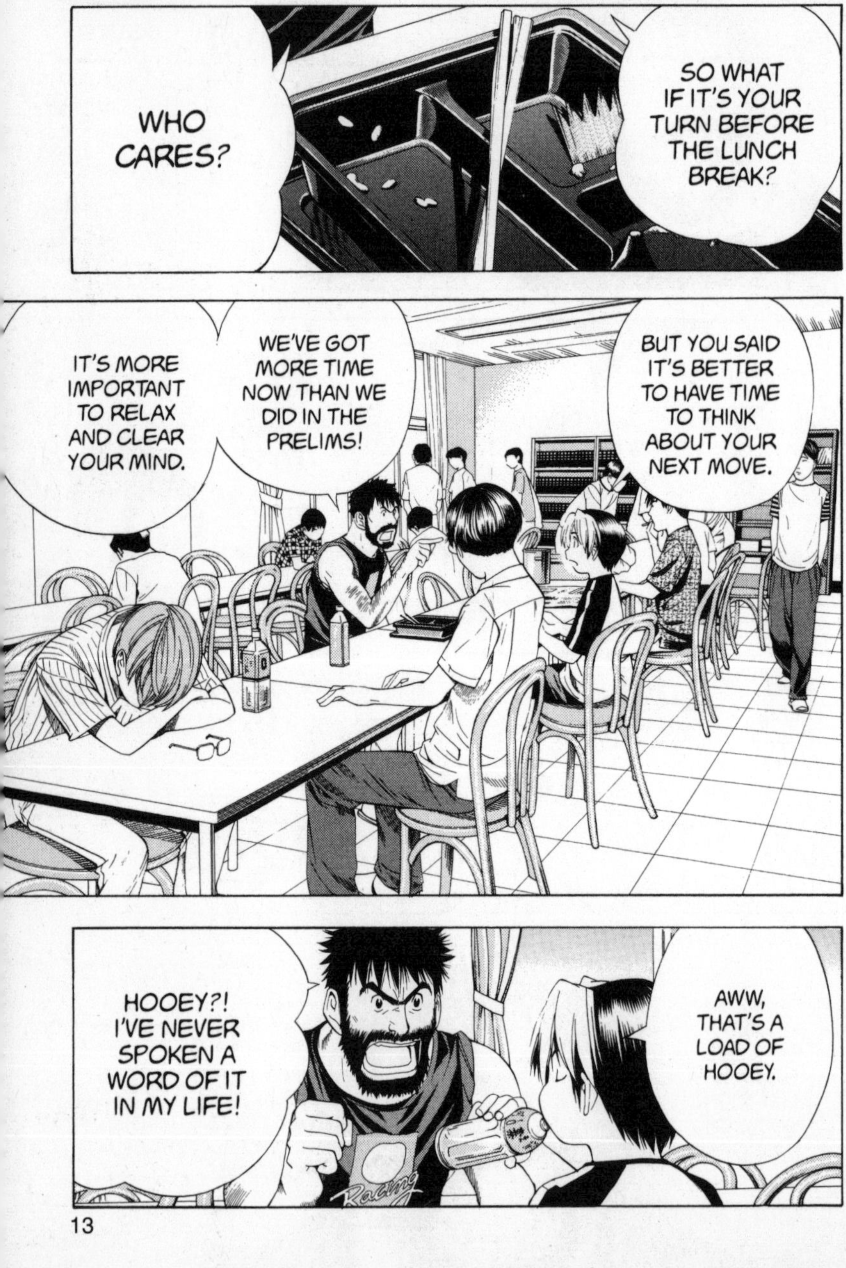
SO WHAT IF IT'S YOUR TURN BEFORE THE LUNCH BREAK?
WHO CARES?
BUT YOU SAID IT'S BETTER TO HAVE TIME TO THINK ABOUT YOUR NEXT MOVE.
WE'VE GOT MORE TIME NOW THAN WE DID IN THE PRELIMS!
IT'S MORE IMPORTANT TO RELAX AND CLEAR YOUR MIND.
AWW, THAT'S A LOAD OF HOOEY.
HOOEY?! I'VE NEVER SPOKEN A WORD OF IT IN MY LIFE!

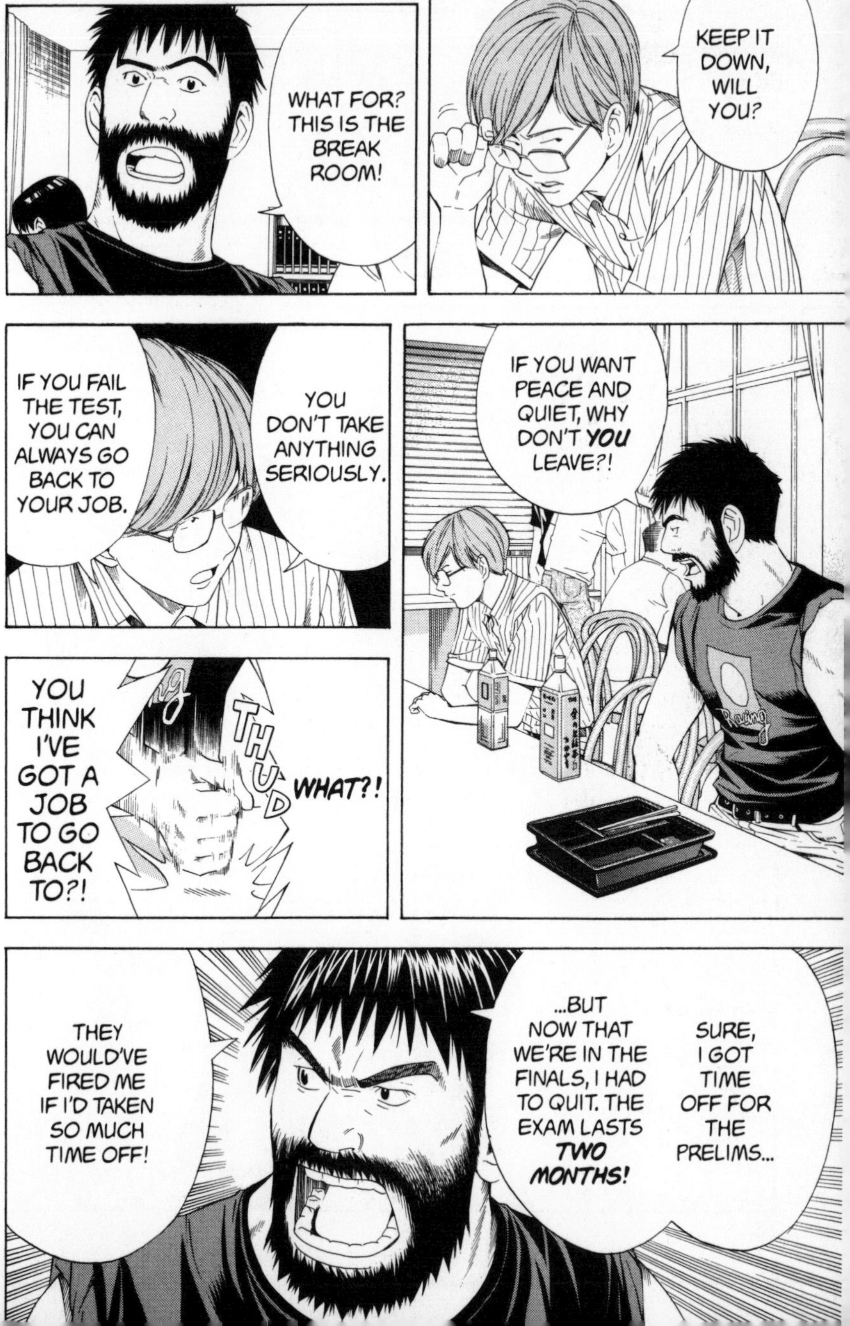
KEEP IT DOWN, WILL YOU?
WHAT FOR? THIS IS THE BREAK ROOM!
IF YOU WANT PEACE AND QUIET, WHY DON'T *YOU* LEAVE?!
YOU DON'T TAKE ANYTHING SERIOUSLY.
IF YOU FAIL THE TEST, YOU CAN ALWAYS GO BACK TO YOUR JOB.
WHAT?!
THUD
YOU THINK I'VE GOT A JOB TO GO BACK TO?!
SURE, I GOT TIME OFF FOR THE PRELIMS...
...BUT NOW THAT WE'RE IN THE FINALS, I HAD TO QUIT. THE EXAM LASTS *TWO MONTHS!*
THEY WOULD'VE FIRED ME IF I'D TAKEN SO MUCH TIME OFF!

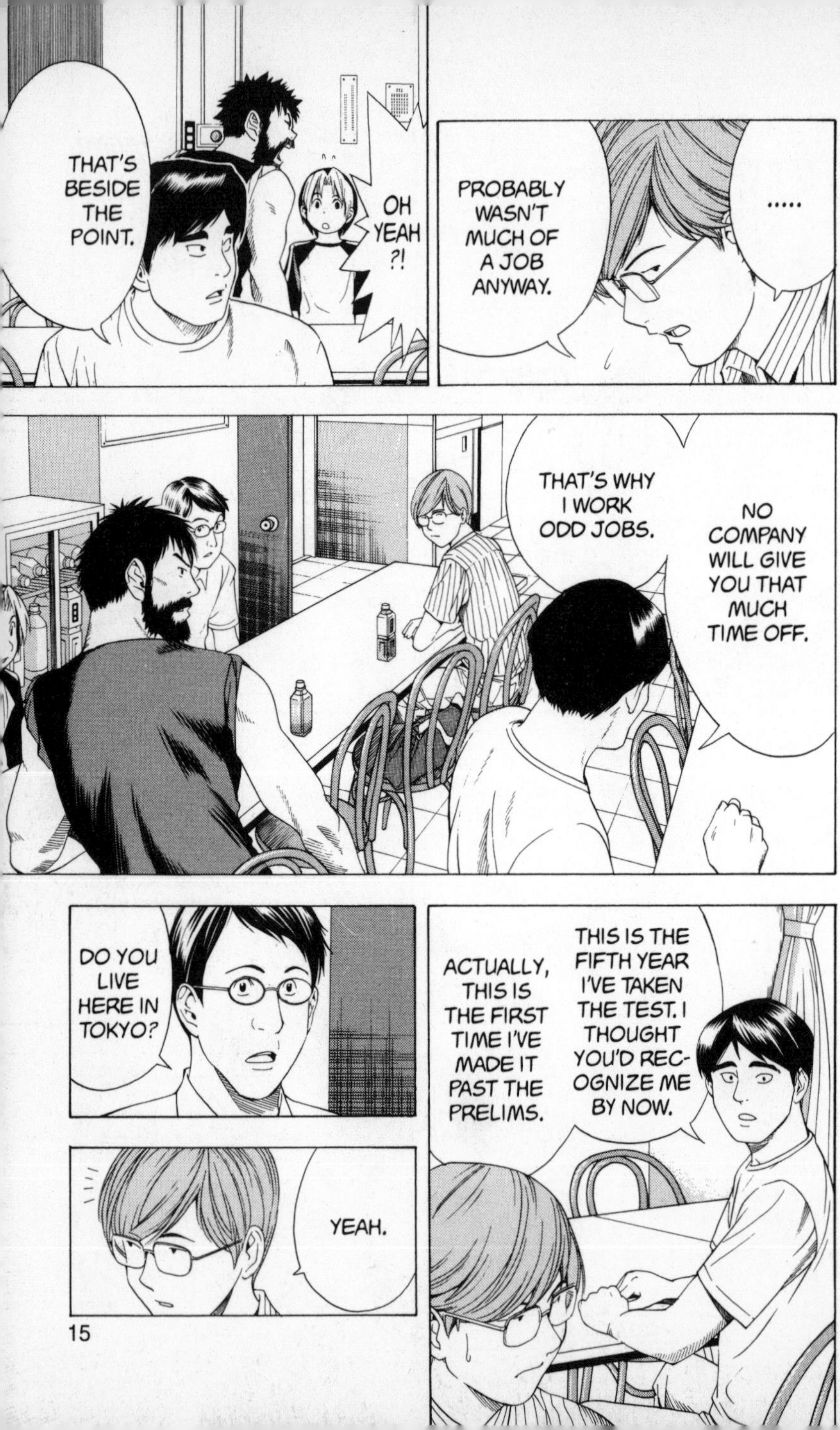
.....
PROBABLY WASN'T MUCH OF A JOB ANYWAY.
OH YEAH ?!
THAT'S BESIDE THE POINT.
NO COMPANY WILL GIVE YOU THAT MUCH TIME OFF.
THAT'S WHY I WORK ODD JOBS.
THIS IS THE FIFTH YEAR I'VE TAKEN THE TEST. I THOUGHT YOU'D REC-OGNIZE ME BY NOW.
ACTUALLY, THIS IS THE FIRST TIME I'VE MADE IT PAST THE PRELIMS.
DO YOU LIVE HERE IN TOKYO?
YEAH.

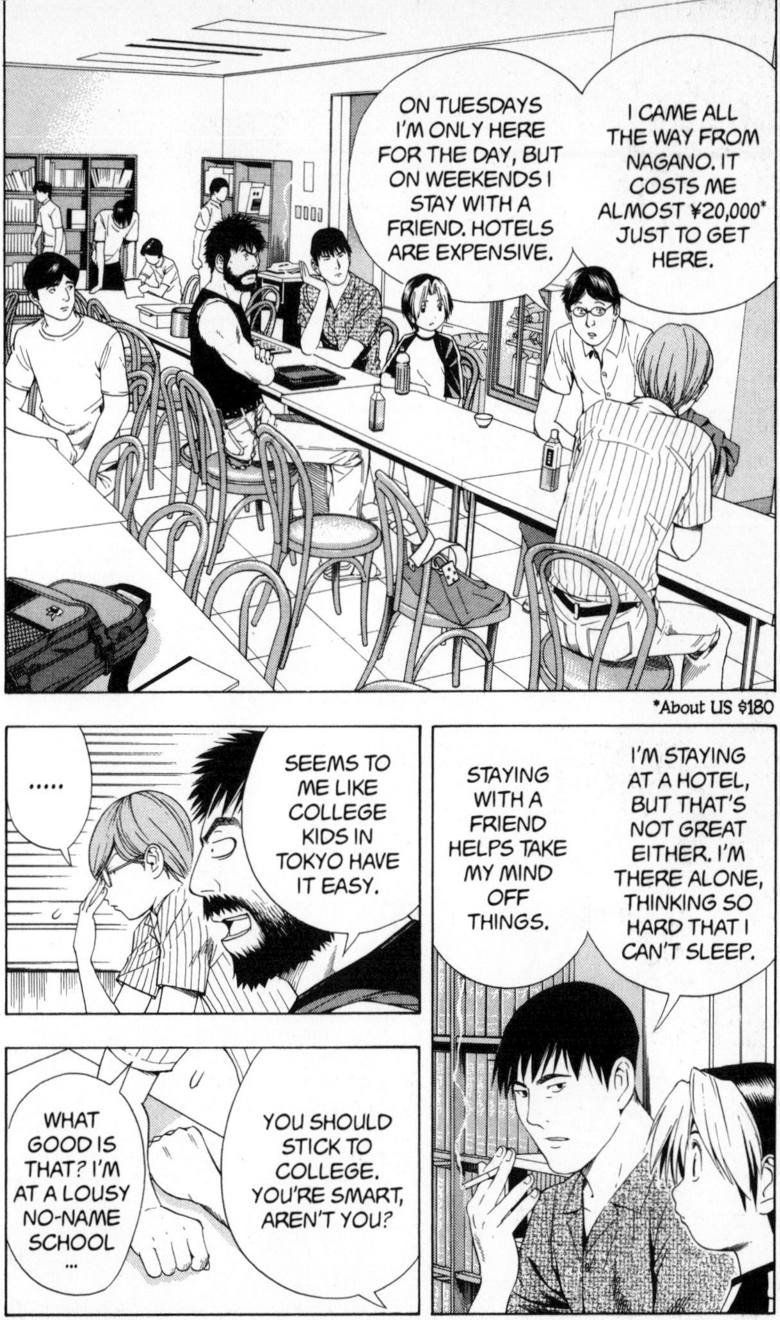
I CAME ALL THE WAY FROM NAGANO. IT COSTS ME ALMOST ¥20,000* JUST TO GET HERE.
ON TUESDAYS I'M ONLY HERE FOR THE DAY, BUT ON WEEKENDS I STAY WITH A FRIEND. HOTELS ARE EXPENSIVE.
I'M STAYING AT A HOTEL, BUT THAT'S NOT GREAT EITHER. I'M THERE ALONE, THINKING SO HARD THAT I CAN'T SLEEP.
STAYING WITH A FRIEND HELPS TAKE MY MIND OFF THINGS.
SEEMS TO ME LIKE COLLEGE KIDS IN TOKYO HAVE IT EASY.
.....
YOU SHOULD STICK TO COLLEGE. YOU'RE SMART, AREN'T YOU?
WHAT GOOD IS THAT? I'M AT A LOUSY NO-NAME SCHOOL ...

*About US $180

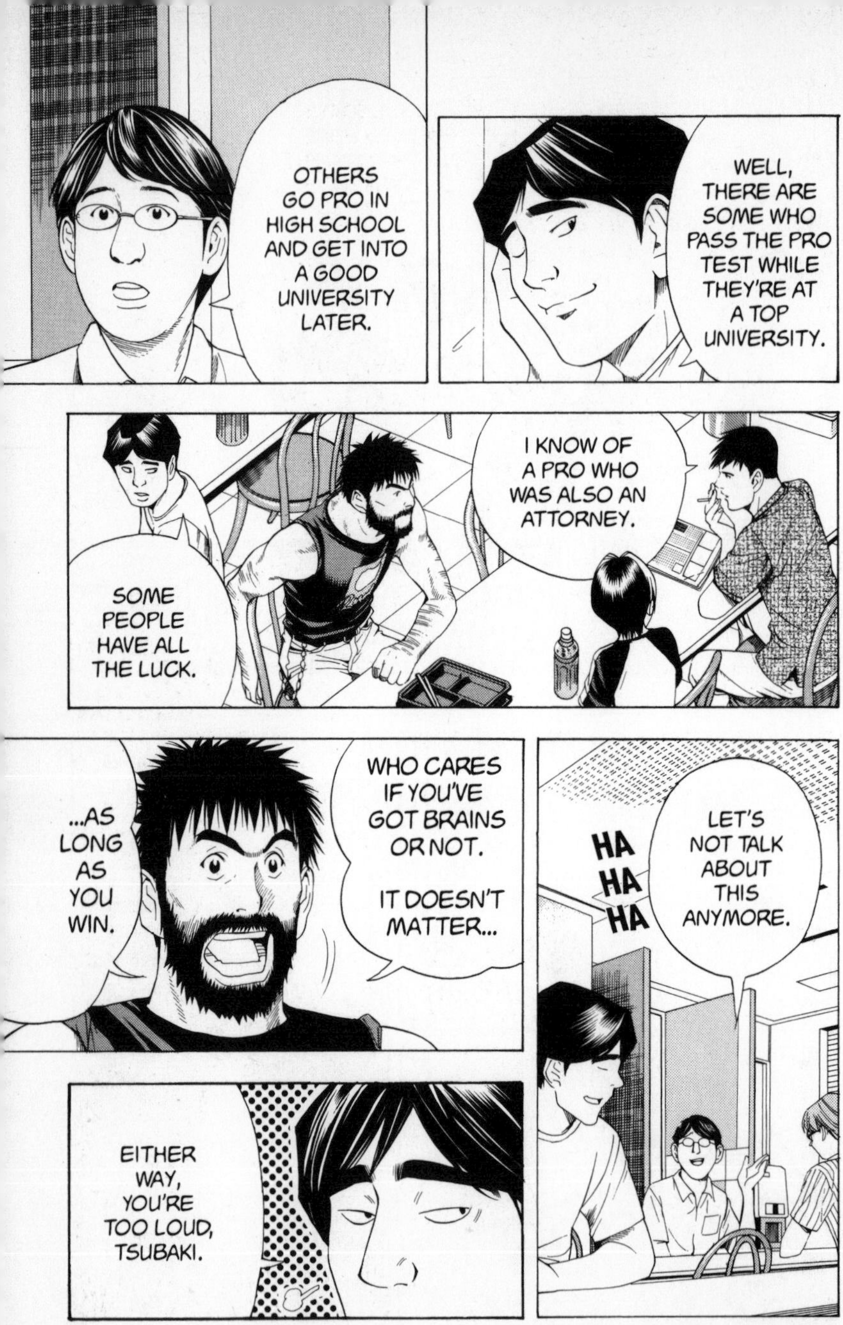
WELL, THERE ARE SOME WHO PASS THE PRO TEST WHILE THEY'RE AT A TOP UNIVERSITY.
OTHERS GO PRO IN HIGH SCHOOL AND GET INTO A GOOD UNIVERSITY LATER.
I KNOW OF A PRO WHO WAS ALSO AN ATTORNEY.
SOME PEOPLE HAVE ALL THE LUCK.
LET'S NOT TALK ABOUT THIS ANYMORE.
HA HA HA
WHO CARES IF YOU'VE GOT BRAINS OR NOT.
IT DOESN'T MATTER...
...AS LONG AS YOU WIN.
EITHER WAY, YOU'RE TOO LOUD, TSUBAKI.

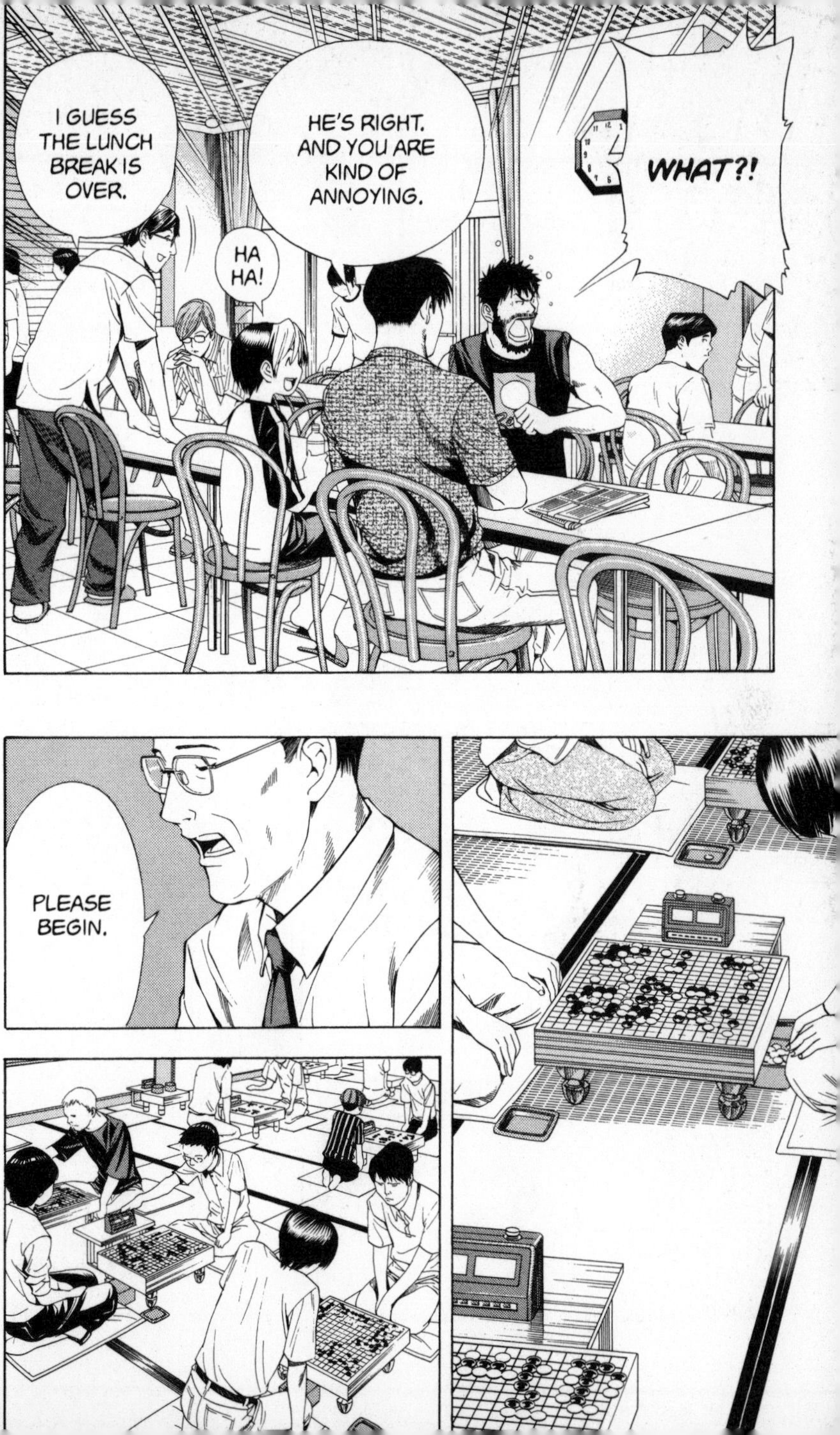
I GUESS THE LUNCH BREAK IS OVER.
HE'S RIGHT. AND YOU ARE KIND OF ANNOYING.
WHAT?!
HA HA!
PLEASE BEGIN.

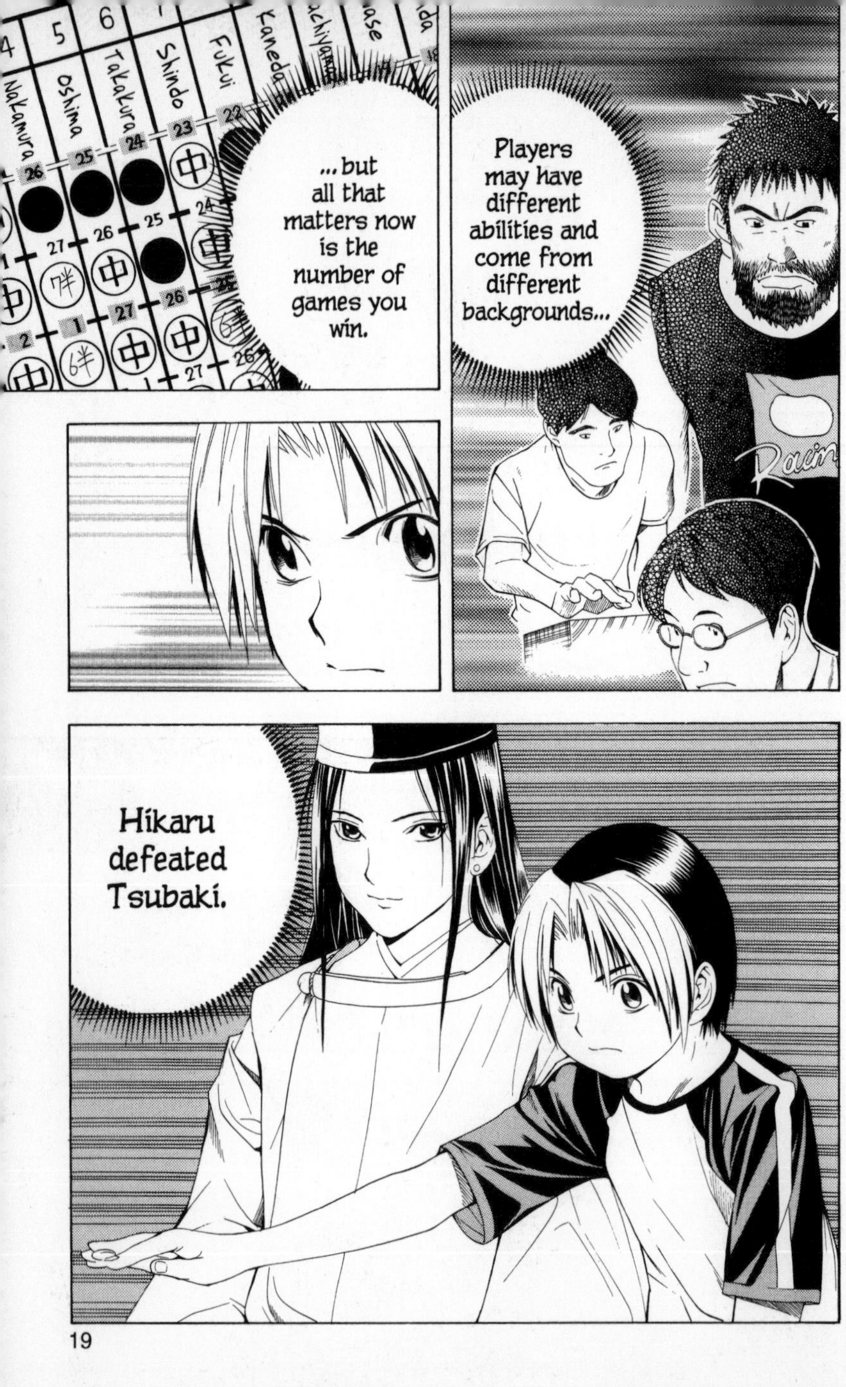
Players may have different abilities and come from different backgrounds...
Nakamura
Oshima
Takakura
Shindo
Fukui
Kaneda
...but all that matters now is the number of games you win.
Hikaru defeated Tsubaki.

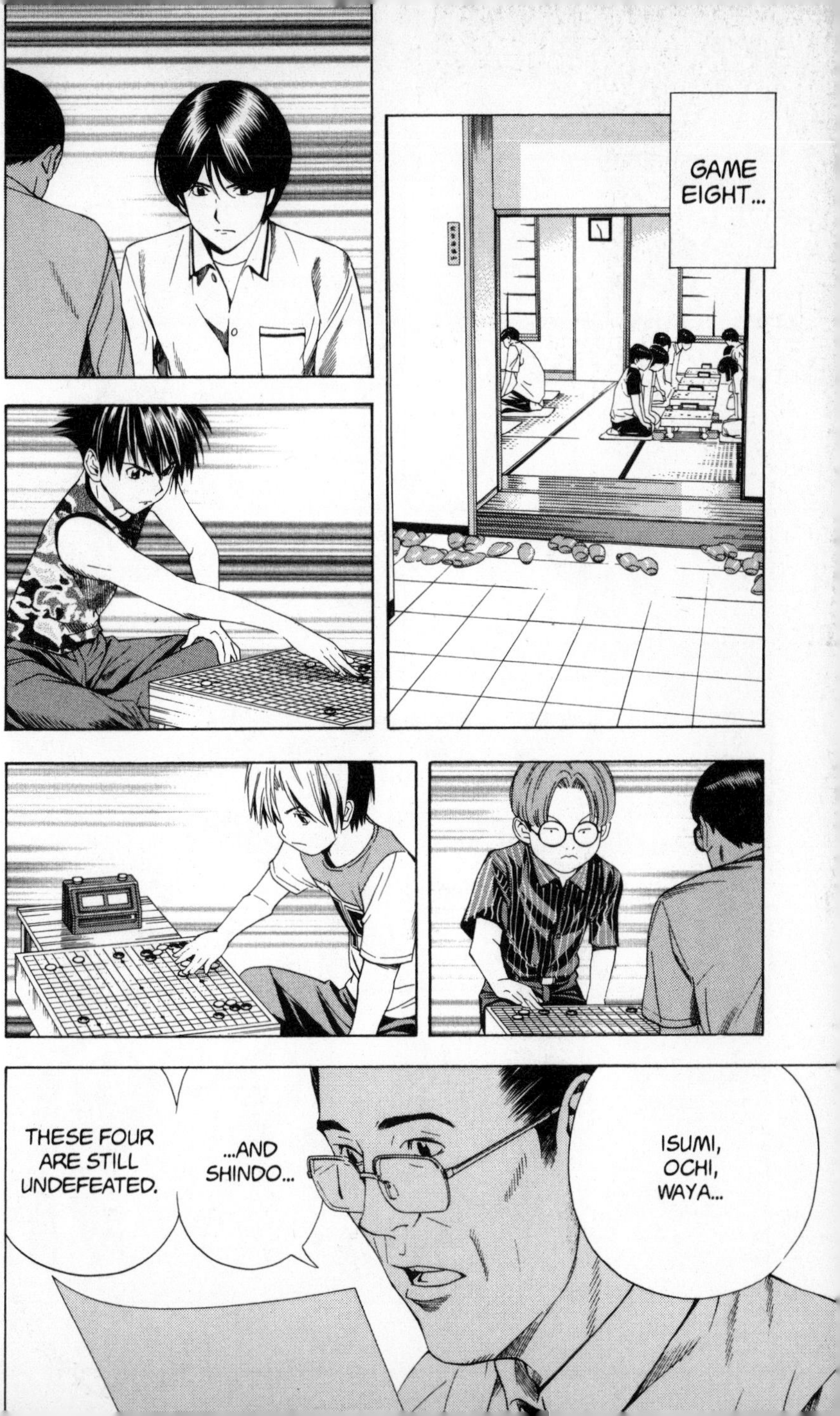
GAME EIGHT...
ISUMI, OCHI, WAYA...
...AND SHINDO...
THESE FOUR ARE STILL UNDEFEATED.

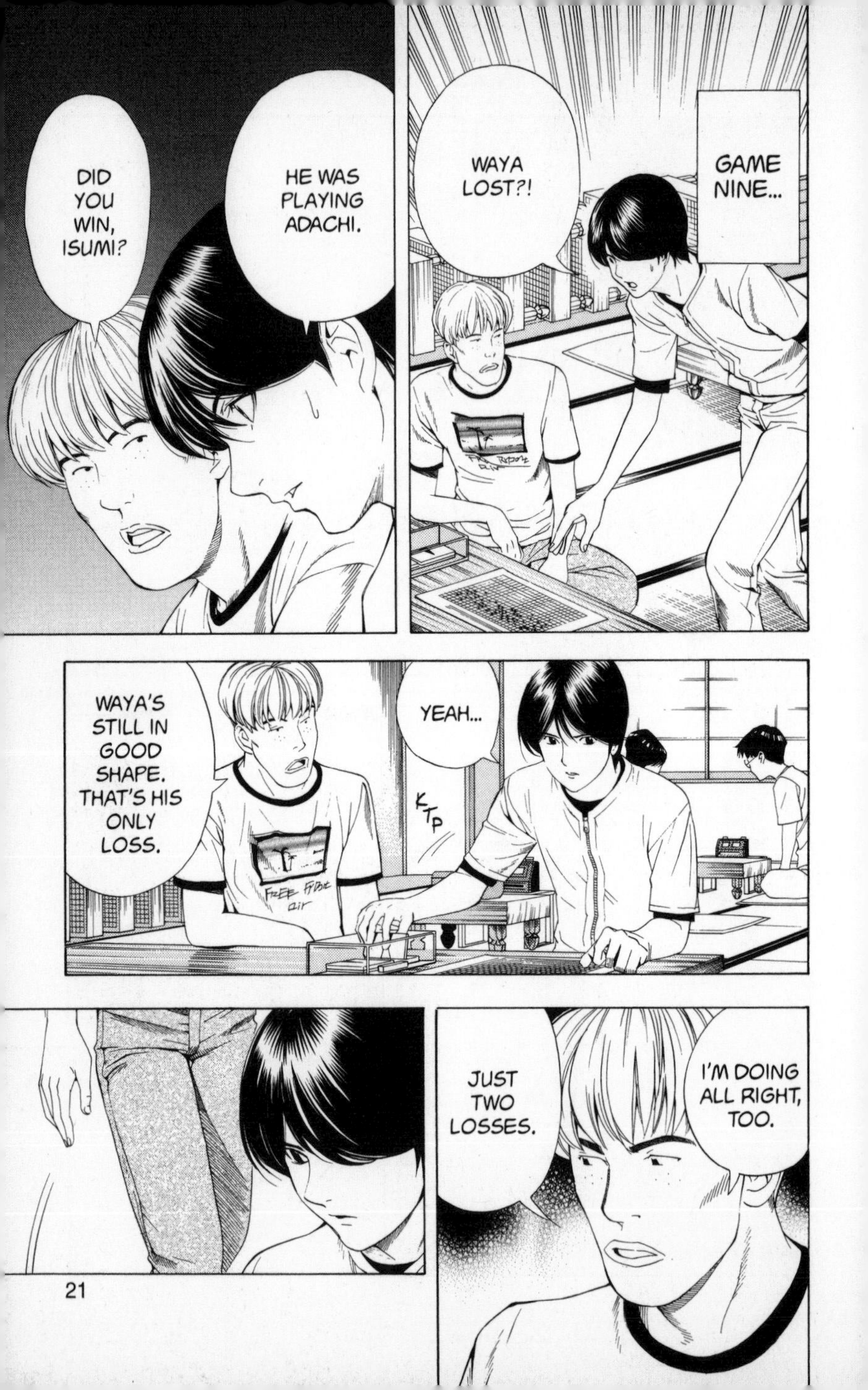
GAME NINE...
WAYA LOST?!
HE WAS PLAYING ADACHI.
DID YOU WIN, ISUMI?
YEAH...
KTP
WAYA'S STILL IN GOOD SHAPE. THAT'S HIS ONLY LOSS.
I'M DOING ALL RIGHT, TOO.
JUST TWO LOSSES.

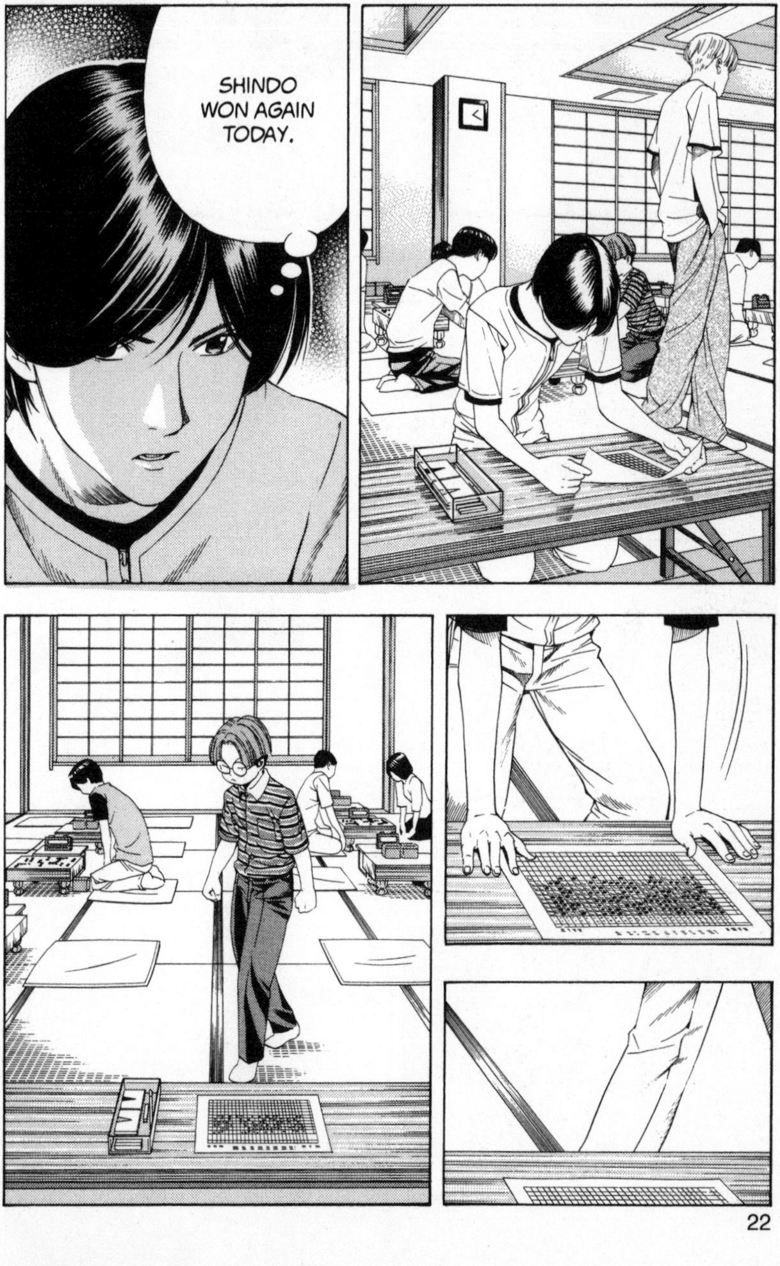
SHINDO WON AGAIN TODAY.

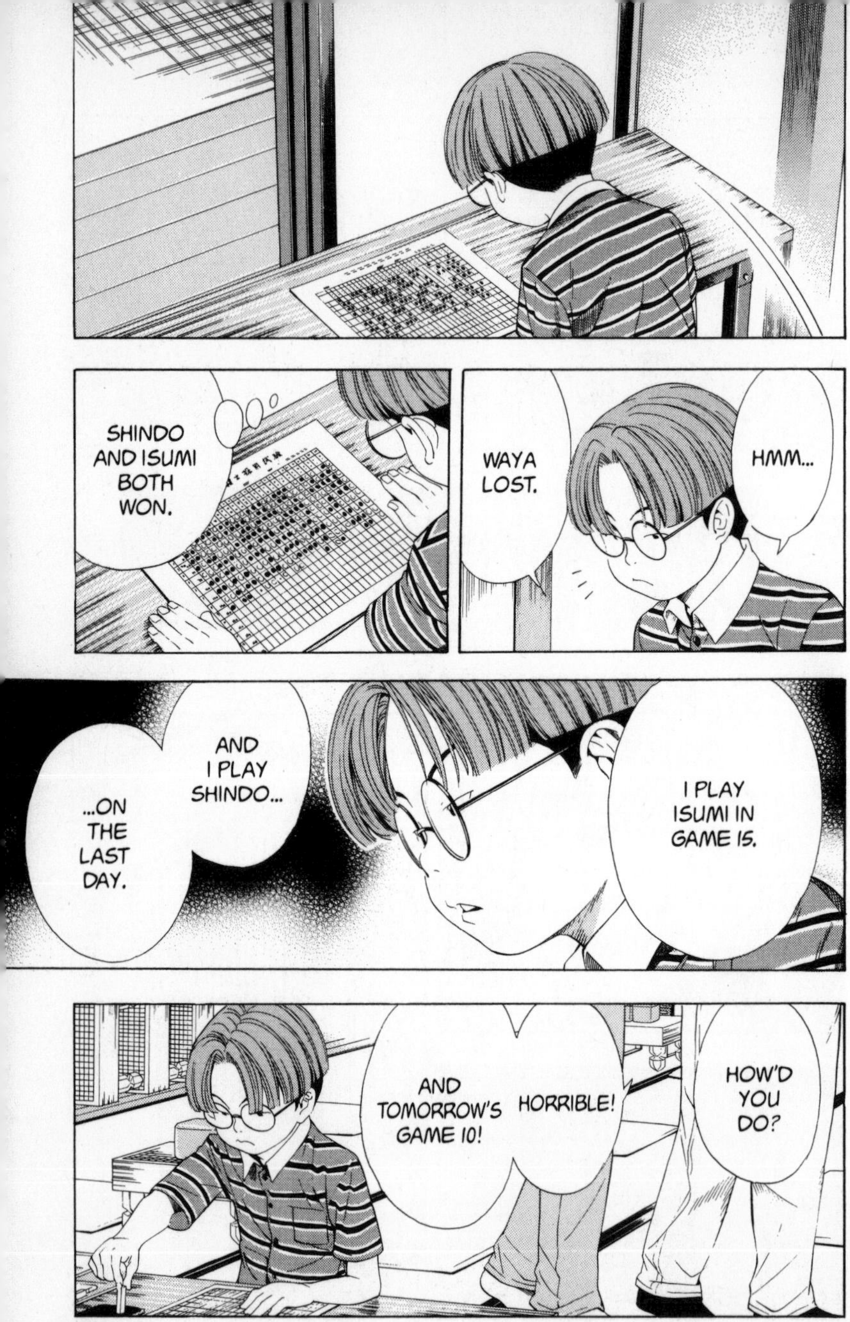
HMM...
WAYA LOST.
SHINDO AND ISUMI BOTH WON.
I PLAY ISUMI IN GAME 15.
AND I PLAY SHINDO...
...ON THE LAST DAY.
HOW'D YOU DO?
HORRIBLE!
AND TOMORROW'S GAME 10!

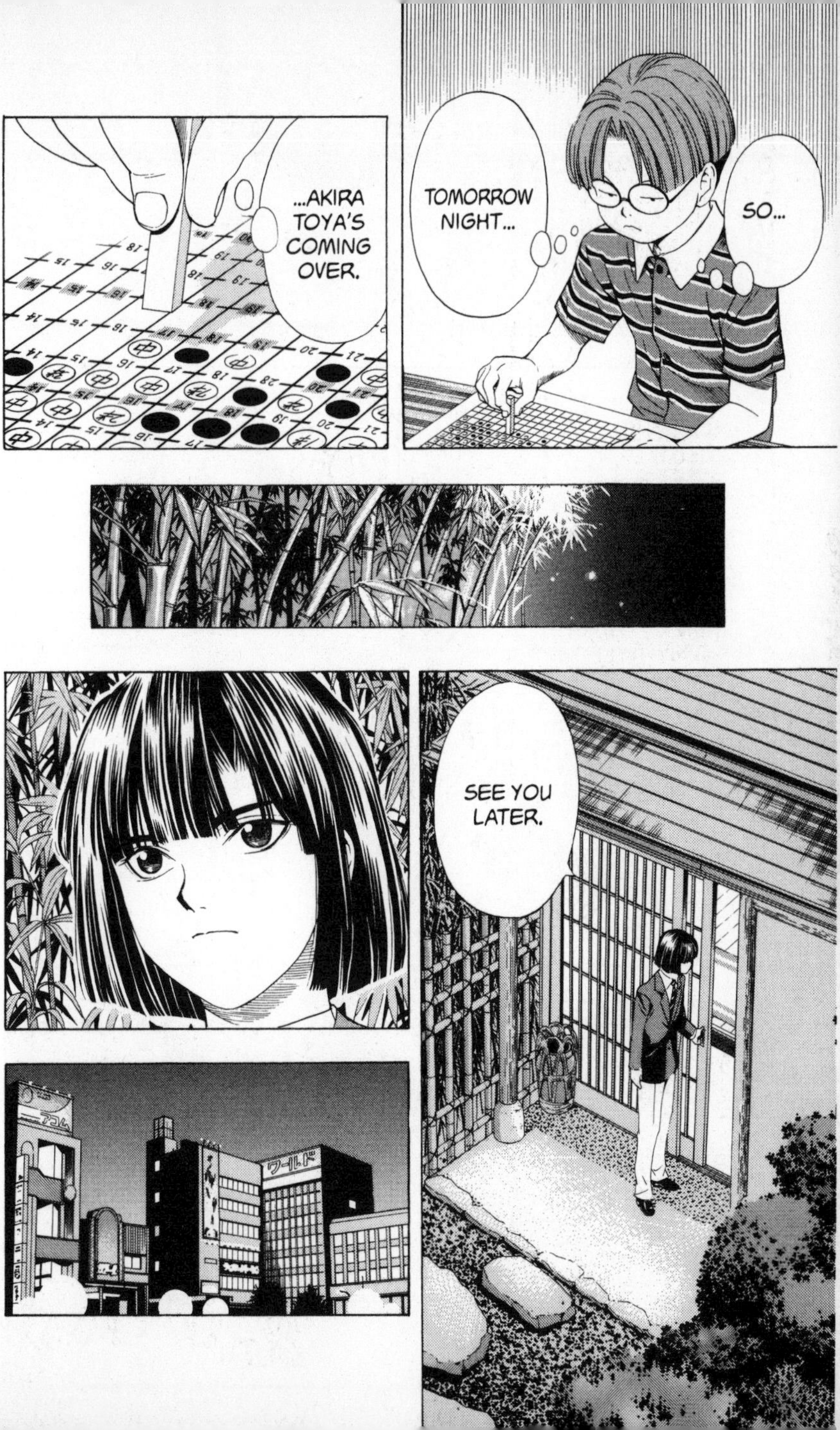
SO...
TOMORROW NIGHT...
...AKIRA TOYA'S COMING OVER.
SEE YOU LATER.
アコム
ワールド

READ THIS WAY

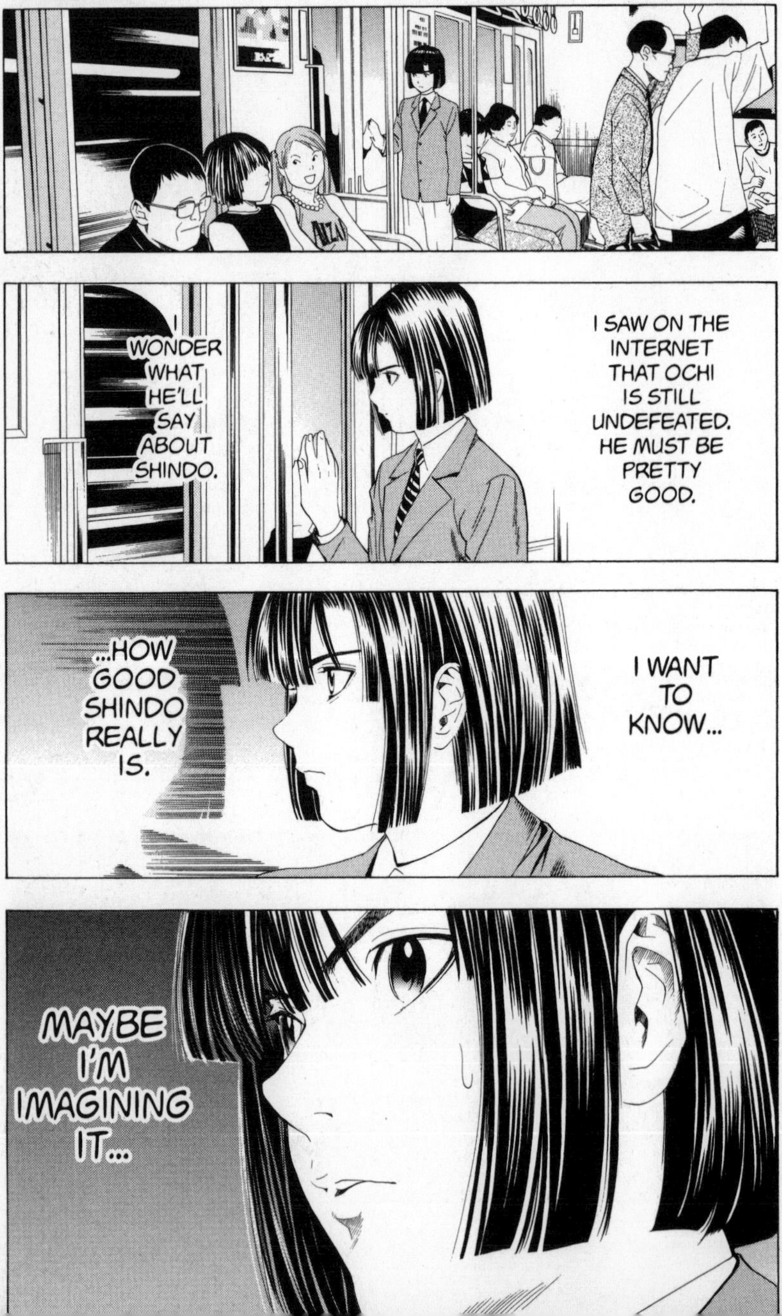
I SAW ON THE INTERNET THAT OCHI IS STILL UNDEFEATED. HE MUST BE PRETTY GOOD.
I WONDER WHAT HE'LL SAY ABOUT SHINDO.
I WANT TO KNOW...
...HOW GOOD SHINDO REALLY IS.
MAYBE I'M IMAGINING IT...

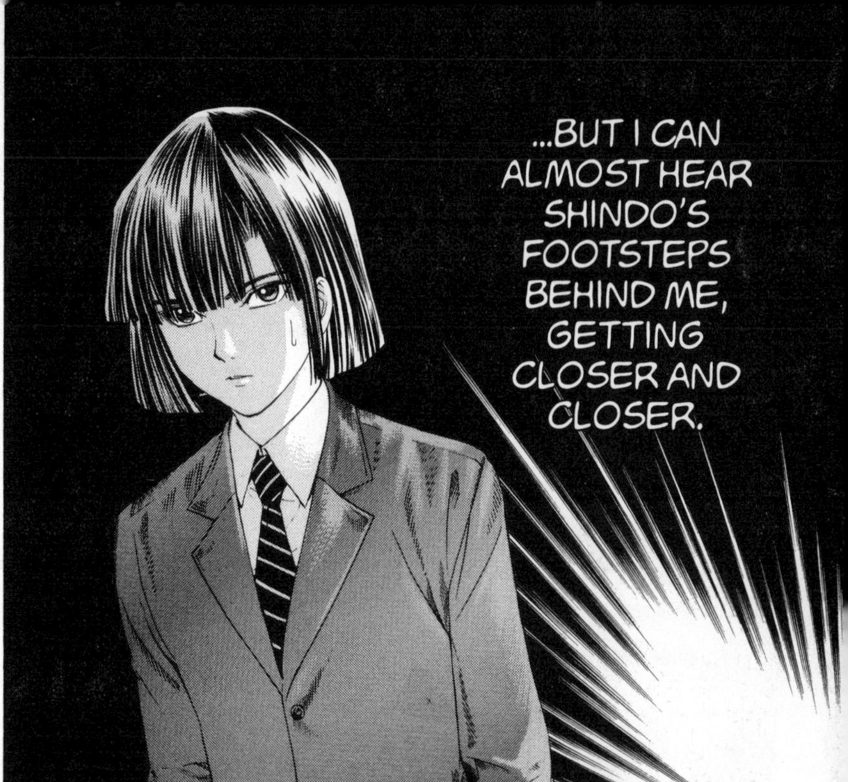
...BUT I CAN ALMOST HEAR SHINDO'S FOOTSTEPS BEHIND ME, GETTING CLOSER AND CLOSER.
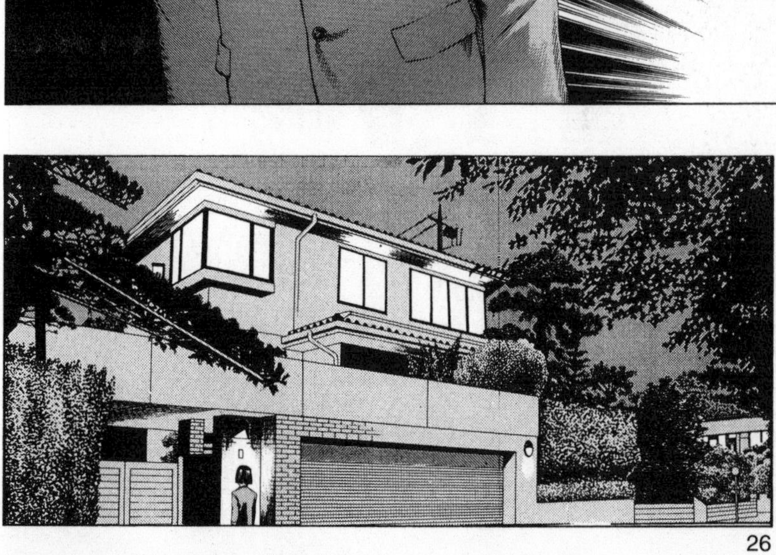

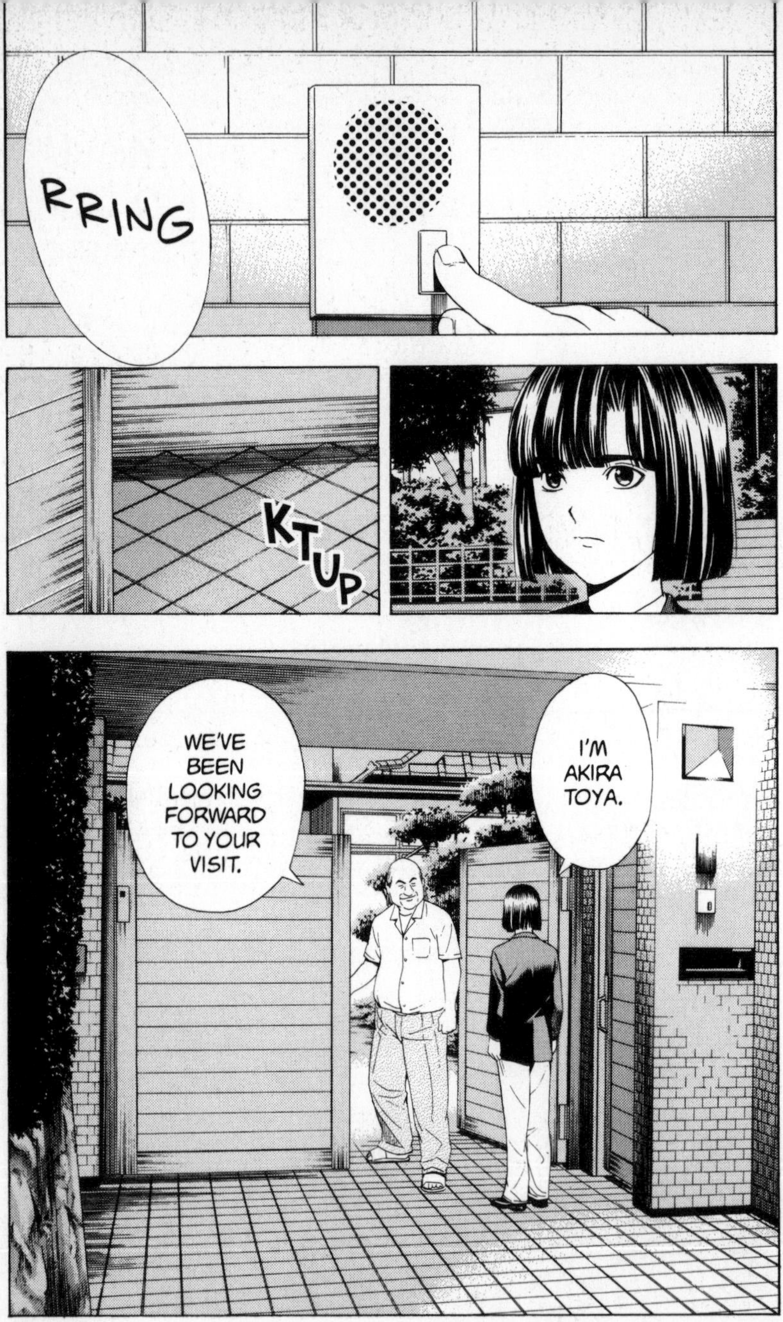
RRING
KTUP
I'M AKIRA TOYA.
WE'VE BEEN LOOKING FORWARD TO YOUR VISIT.

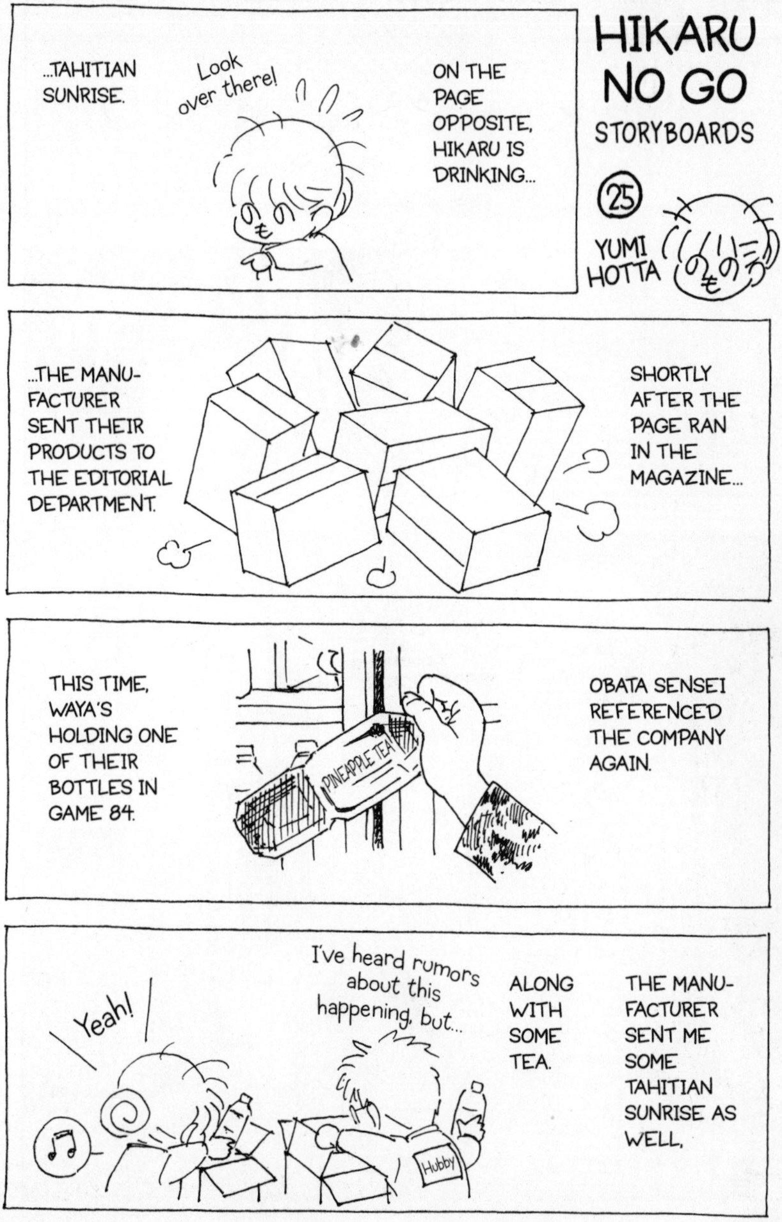
HIKARU NO GO
STORYBOARDS
25
YUMI HOTTA
ON THE PAGE OPPOSITE, HIKARU IS DRINKING...
Look over there!
...TAHITIAN SUNRISE.
SHORTLY AFTER THE PAGE RAN IN THE MAGAZINE...
...THE MANU-FACTURER SENT THEIR PRODUCTS TO THE EDITORIAL DEPARTMENT.
OBATA SENSEI REFERENCED THE COMPANY AGAIN.
PINEAPPLE TEA
THIS TIME, WAYA'S HOLDING ONE OF THEIR BOTTLES IN GAME 84.
THE MANU-FACTURER SENT ME SOME TAHITIAN SUNRISE AS WELL.
ALONG WITH SOME TEA.
I've heard rumors about this happening, but...
Hubby
Yeah!

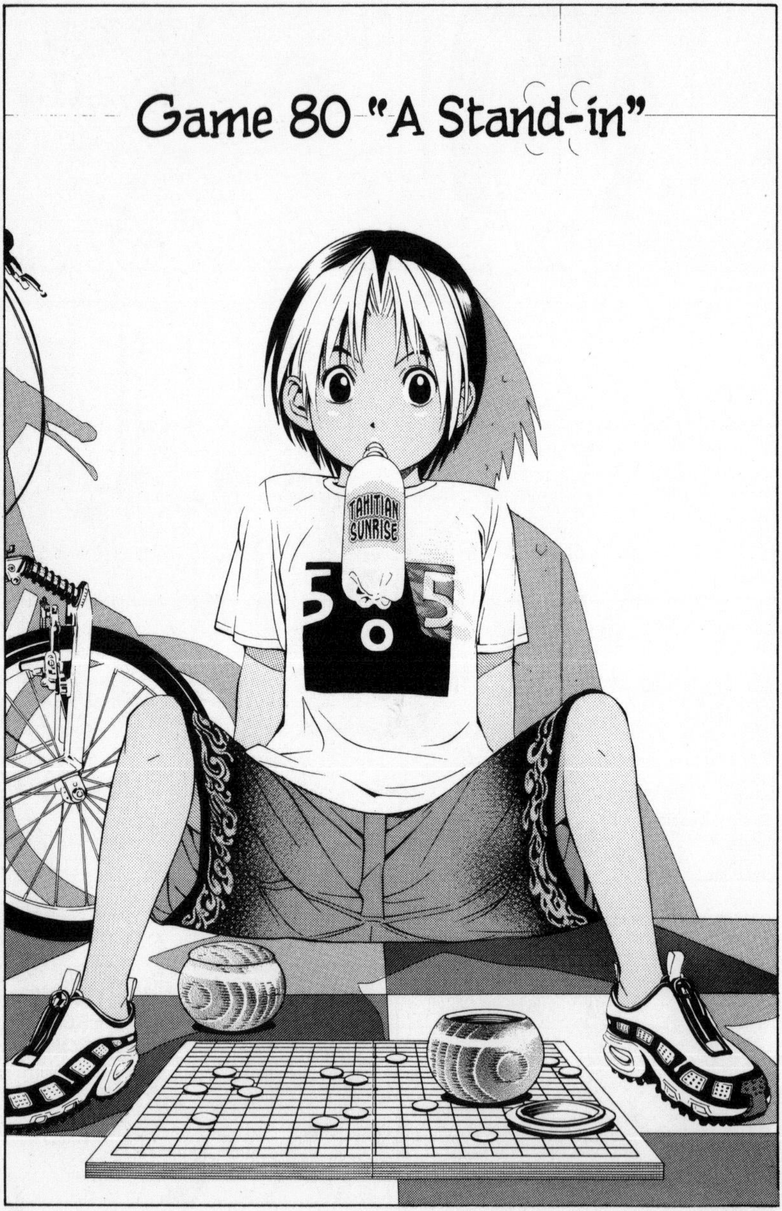
Game 80 "A Stand-in"
TAHITIAN SUNRISE

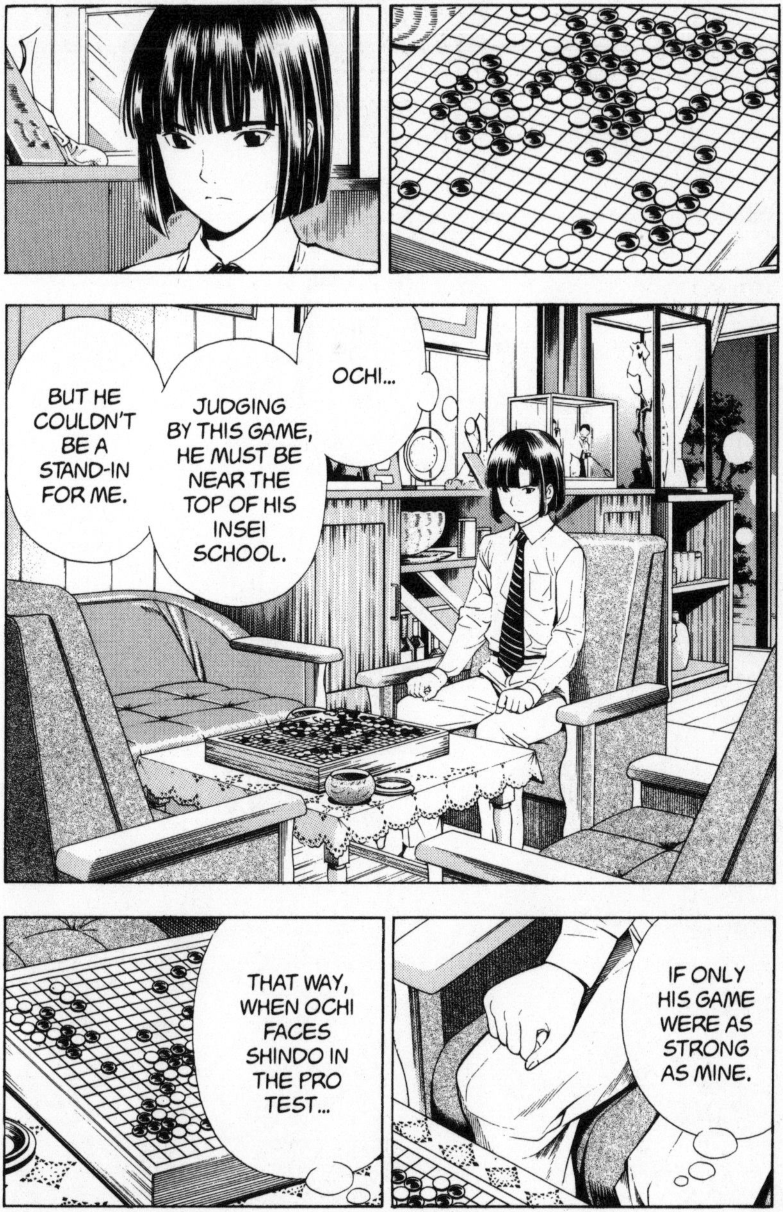
OCHI...
JUDGING BY THIS GAME, HE MUST BE NEAR THE TOP OF HIS INSEI SCHOOL.
BUT HE COULDN'T BE A STAND-IN FOR ME.
IF ONLY HIS GAME WERE AS STRONG AS MINE.
THAT WAY, WHEN OCHI FACES SHINDO IN THE PRO TEST...

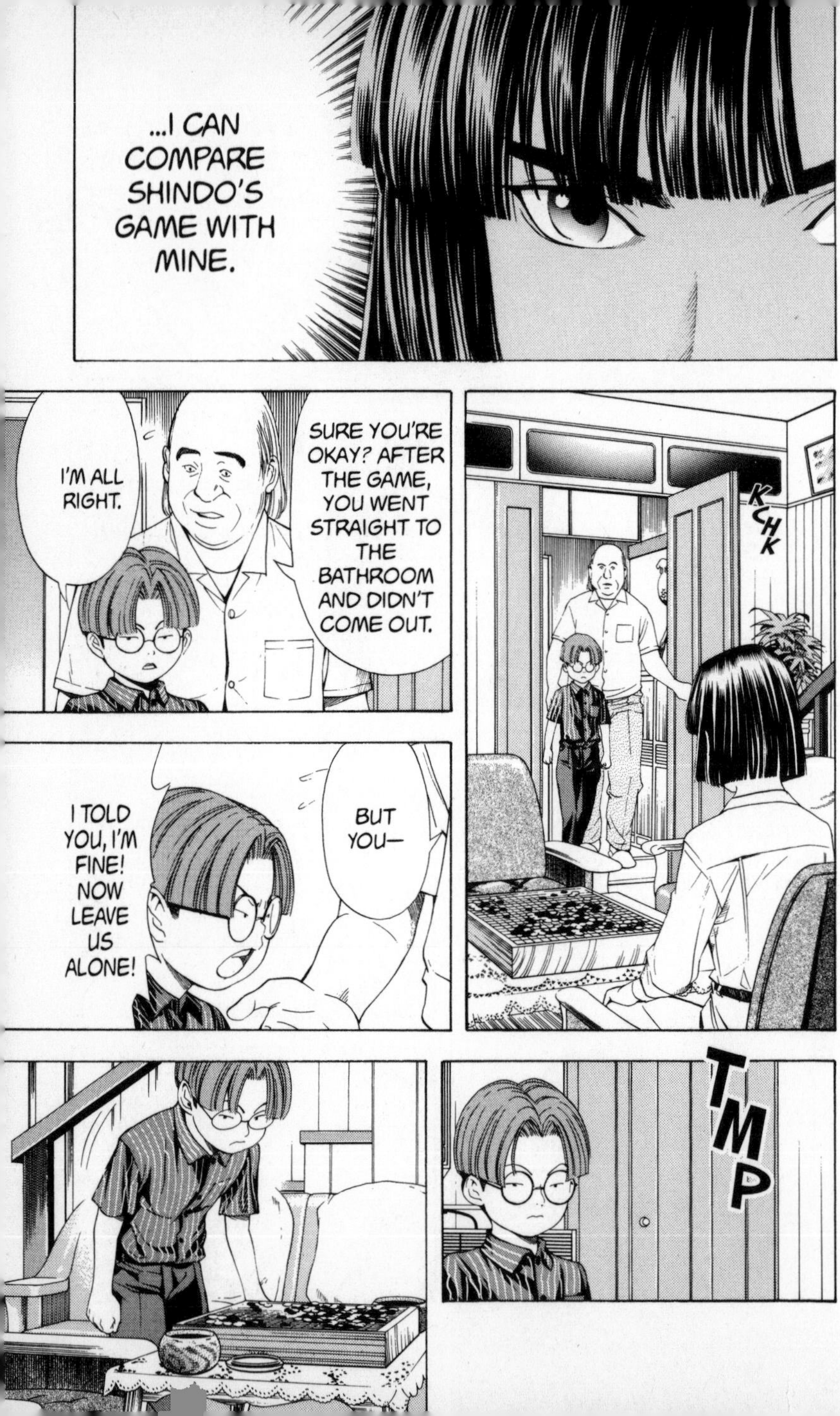
...I CAN COMPARE SHINDO'S GAME WITH MINE.
KCHK
SURE YOU'RE OKAY? AFTER THE GAME, YOU WENT STRAIGHT TO THE BATHROOM AND DIDN'T COME OUT.
I'M ALL RIGHT.
BUT YOU—
I TOLD YOU, I'M FINE! NOW LEAVE US ALONE!
TMP

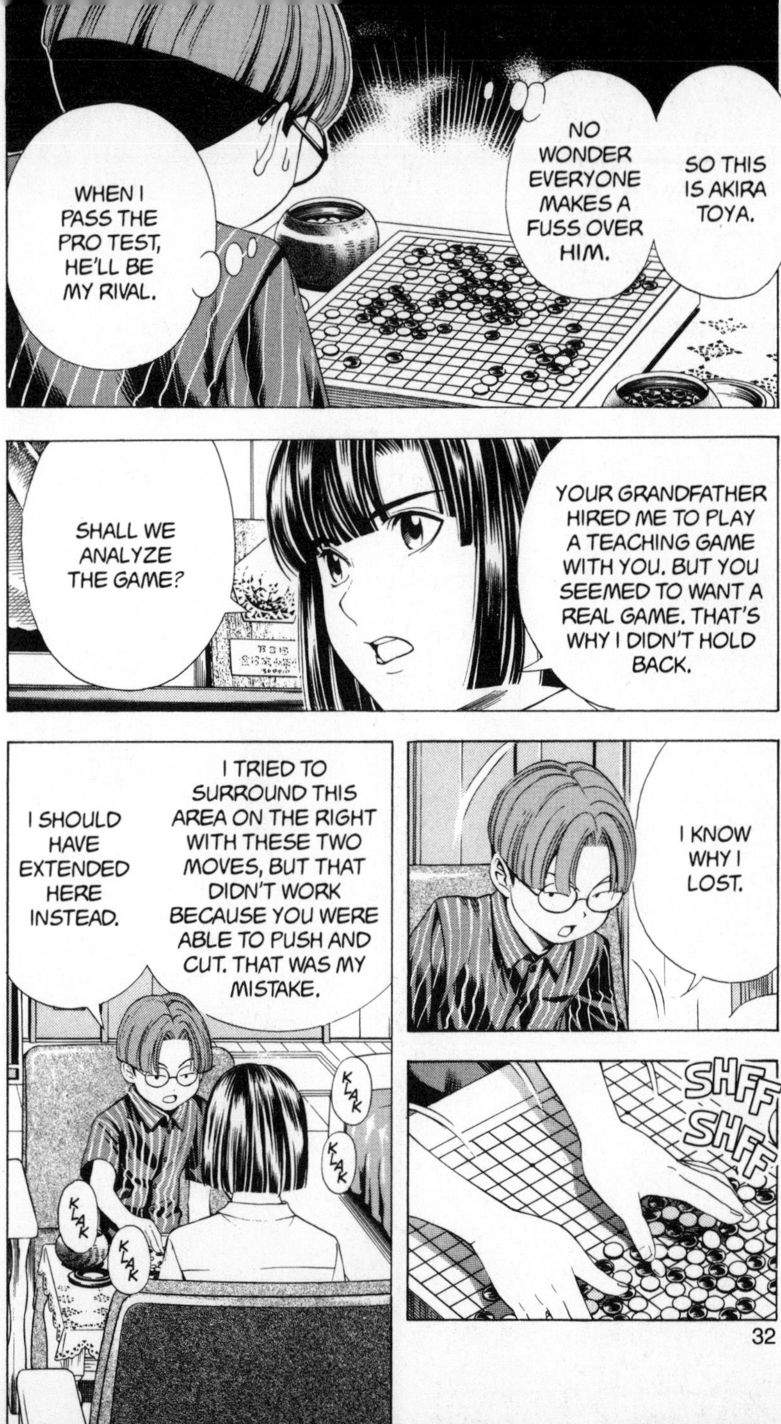
SO THIS IS AKIRA TOYA.
NO WONDER EVERYONE MAKES A FUSS OVER HIM.
WHEN I PASS THE PRO TEST, HE'LL BE MY RIVAL.
YOUR GRANDFATHER HIRED ME TO PLAY A TEACHING GAME WITH YOU. BUT YOU SEEMED TO WANT A REAL GAME. THAT'S WHY I DIDN'T HOLD BACK.
SHALL WE ANALYZE THE GAME?
I KNOW WHY I LOST.
SHFF
SHFF
I TRIED TO SURROUND THIS AREA ON THE RIGHT WITH THESE TWO MOVES, BUT THAT DIDN'T WORK BECAUSE YOU WERE ABLE TO PUSH AND CUT. THAT WAS MY MISTAKE.
I SHOULD HAVE EXTENDED HERE INSTEAD.
KLAK
KLAK
KLAK
KLAK

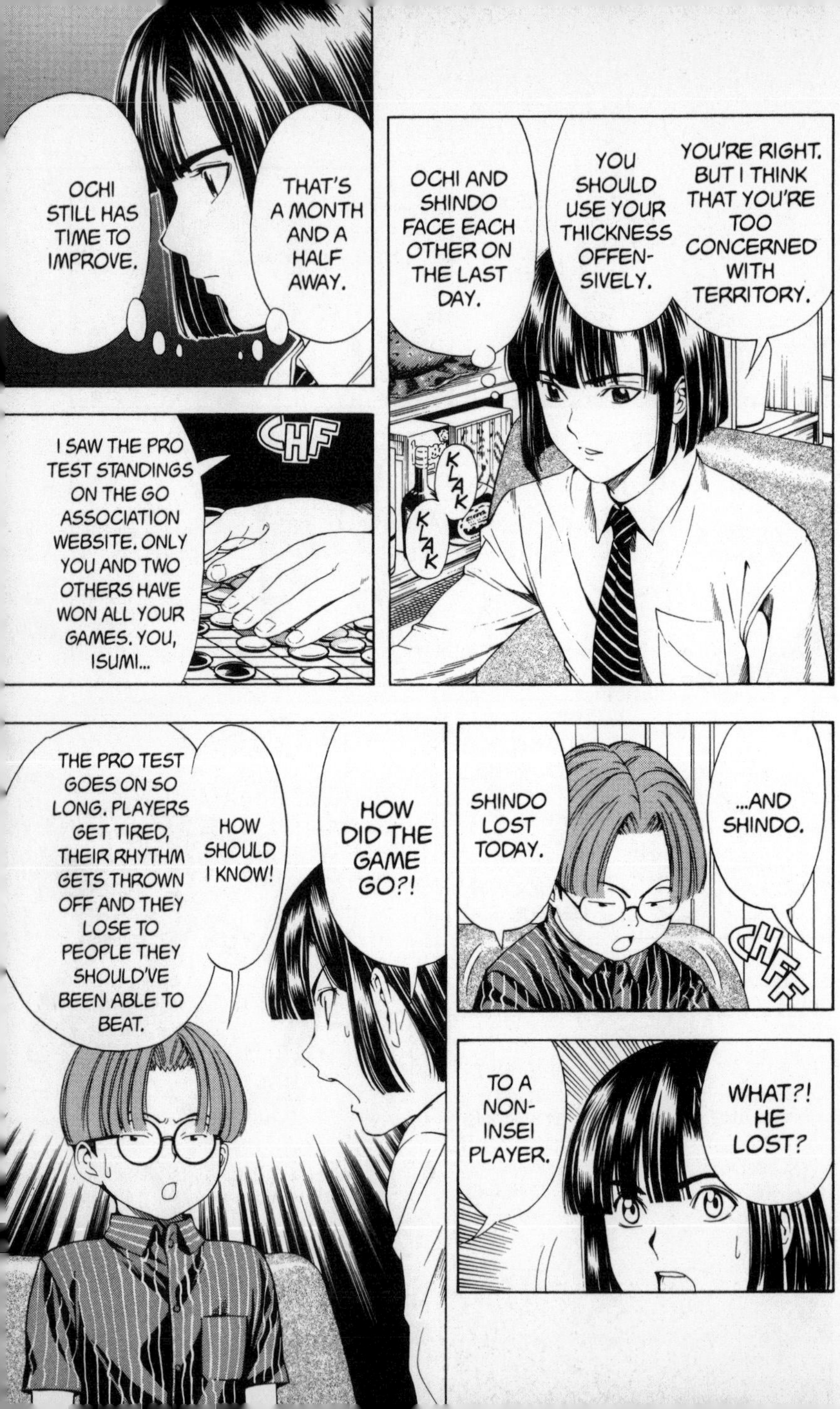
YOU'RE RIGHT. BUT I THINK THAT YOU'RE TOO CONCERNED WITH TERRITORY.
YOU SHOULD USE YOUR THICKNESS OFFEN-SIVELY.
OCHI AND SHINDO FACE EACH OTHER ON THE LAST DAY.
KLAK
KLAK
THAT'S A MONTH AND A HALF AWAY.
OCHI STILL HAS TIME TO IMPROVE.
CHF
I SAW THE PRO TEST STANDINGS ON THE GO ASSOCIATION WEBSITE. ONLY YOU AND TWO OTHERS HAVE WON ALL YOUR GAMES. YOU, ISUMI...
...AND SHINDO.
SHINDO LOST TODAY.
CHF
WHAT?! HE LOST?
TO A NON-INSEI PLAYER.
HOW DID THE GAME GO?!
HOW SHOULD I KNOW!
THE PRO TEST GOES ON SO LONG. PLAYERS GET TIRED, THEIR RHYTHM GETS THROWN OFF AND THEY LOSE TO PEOPLE THEY SHOULD'VE BEEN ABLE TO BEAT.

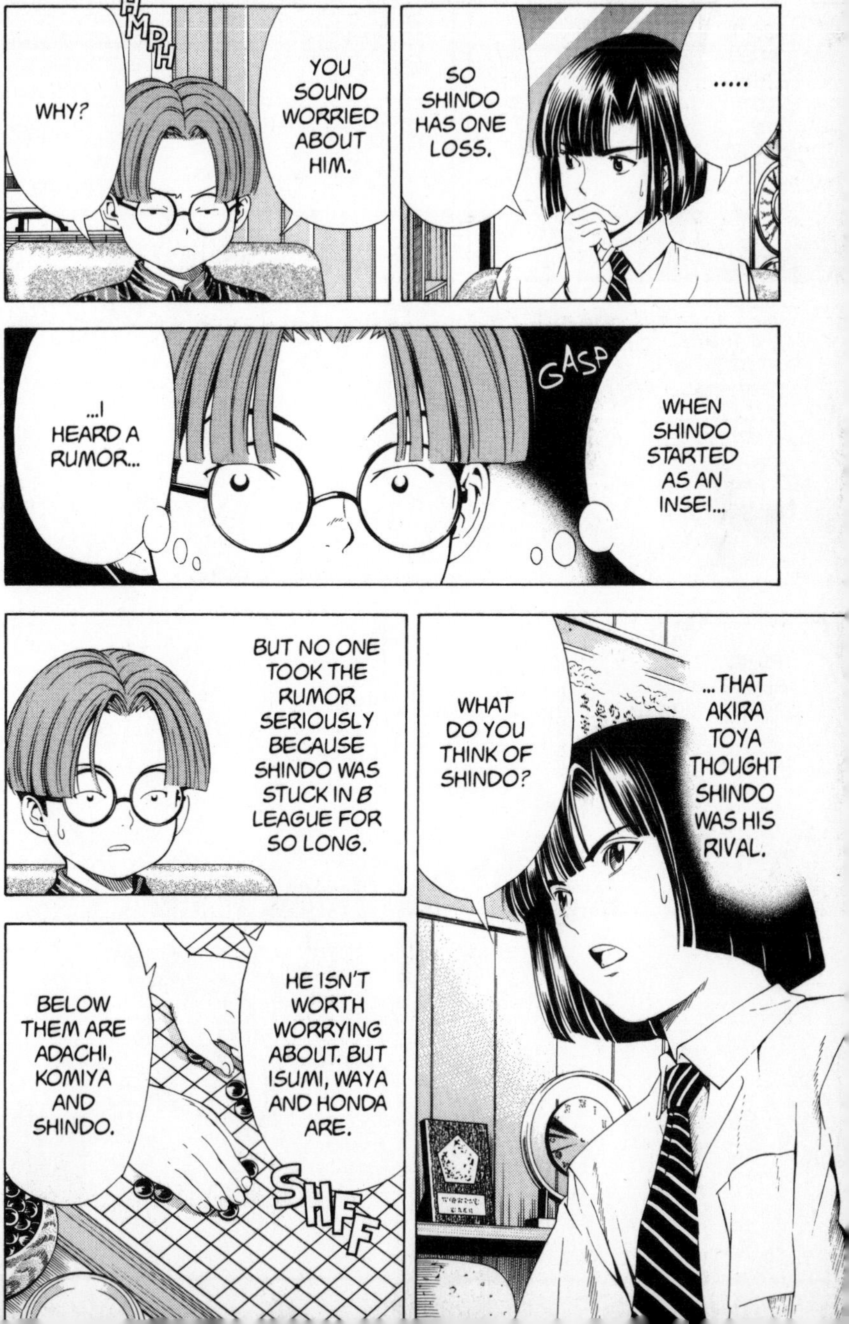
.....
SO SHINDO HAS ONE LOSS.
YOU SOUND WORRIED ABOUT HIM.
HMPH
WHY?
GASP
WHEN SHINDO STARTED AS AN INSEI...
...I HEARD A RUMOR...
...THAT AKIRA TOYA THOUGHT SHINDO WAS HIS RIVAL.
WHAT DO YOU THINK OF SHINDO?
BUT NO ONE TOOK THE RUMOR SERIOUSLY BECAUSE SHINDO WAS STUCK IN *B* LEAGUE FOR SO LONG.
HE ISN'T WORTH WORRYING ABOUT. BUT ISUMI, WAYA AND HONDA ARE.
BELOW THEM ARE ADACHI, KOMIYA AND SHINDO.
SHFF

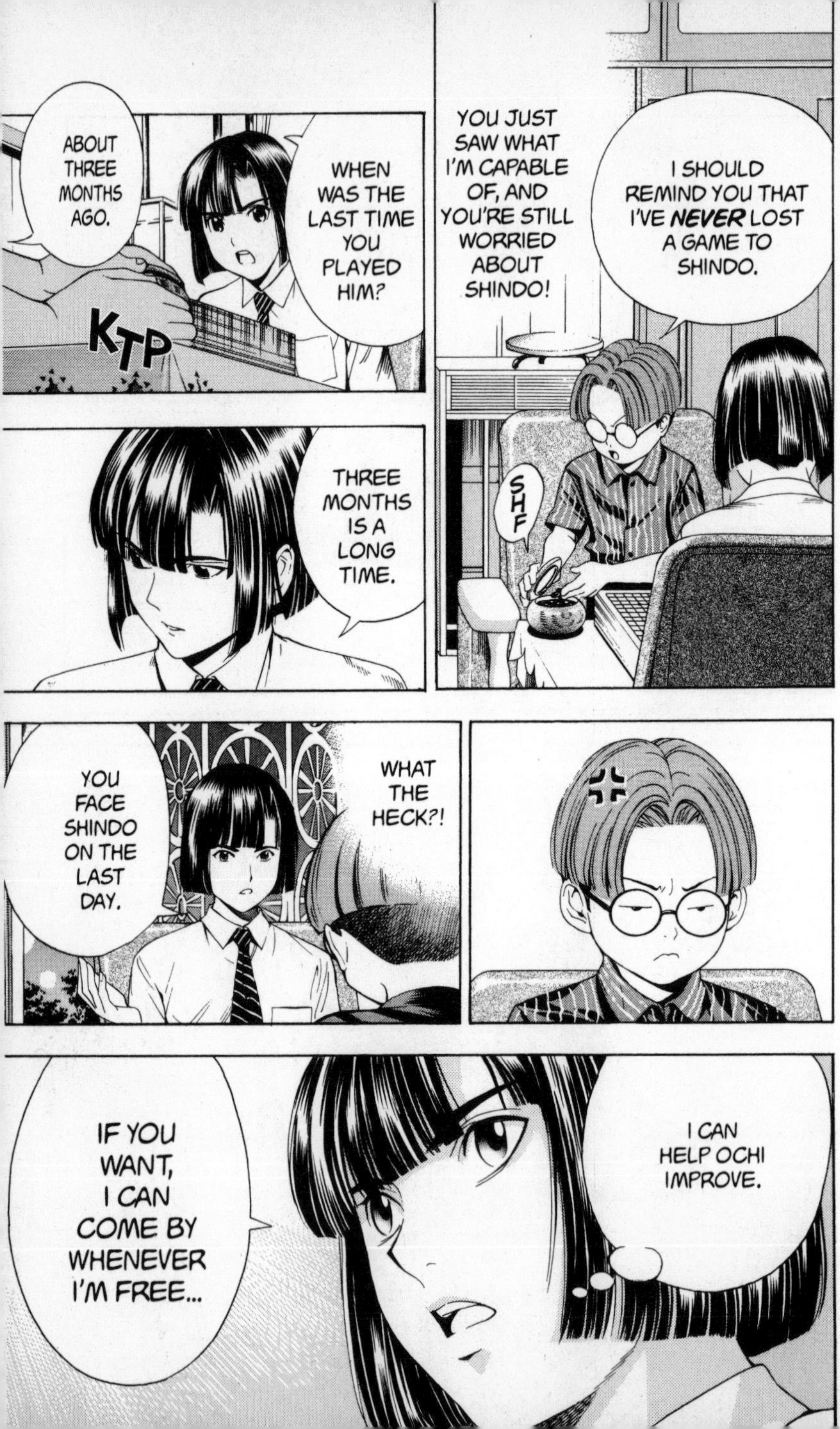
I SHOULD REMIND YOU THAT I'VE **NEVER** LOST A GAME TO SHINDO.
YOU JUST SAW WHAT I'M CAPABLE OF, AND YOU'RE STILL WORRIED ABOUT SHINDO!
SHF
WHEN WAS THE LAST TIME YOU PLAYED HIM?
ABOUT THREE MONTHS AGO.
KTP
THREE MONTHS IS A LONG TIME.
WHAT THE HECK?!
YOU FACE SHINDO ON THE LAST DAY.
I CAN HELP OCHI IMPROVE.
IF YOU WANT, I CAN COME BY WHENEVER I'M FREE...

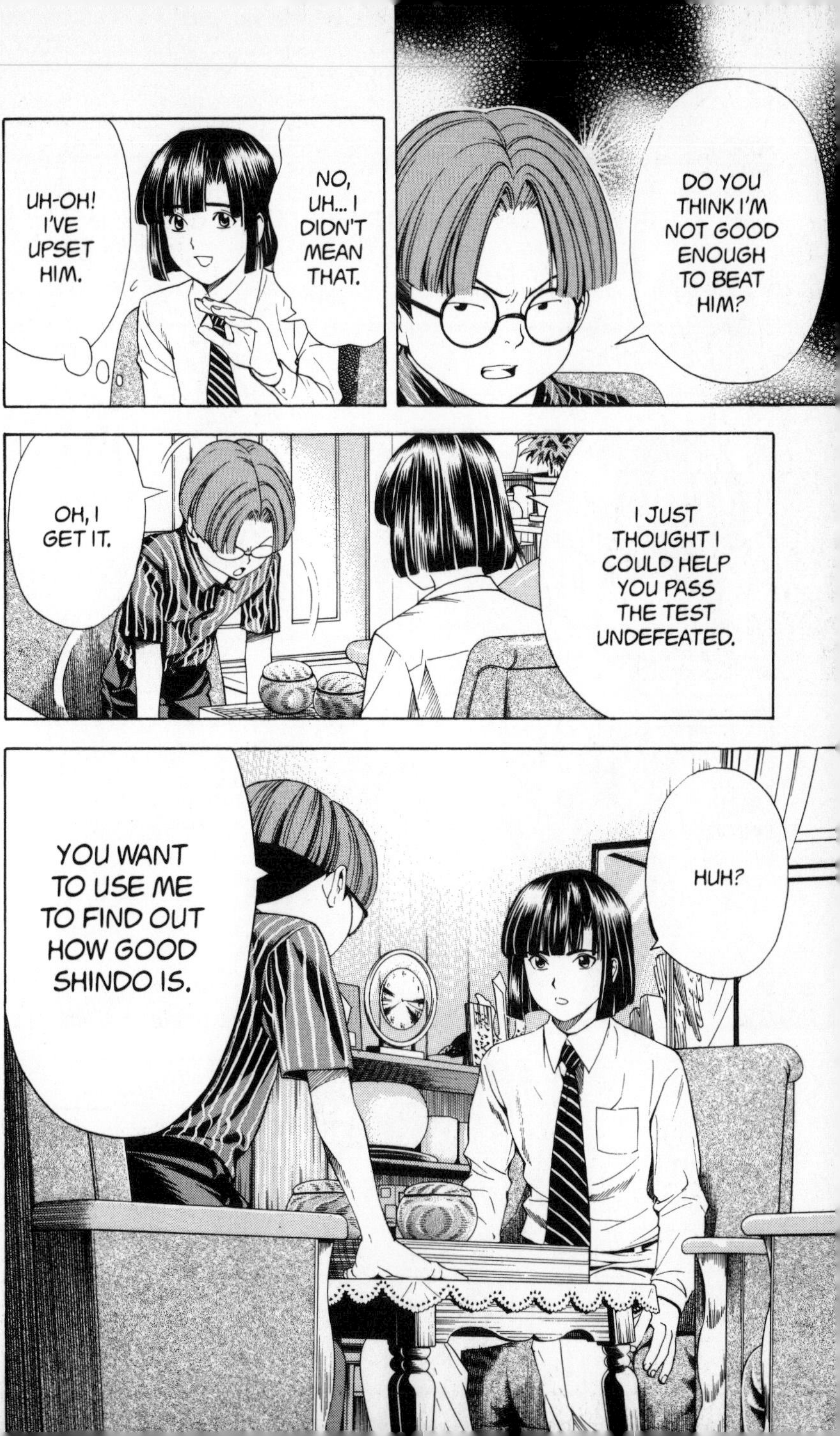
DO YOU THINK I'M NOT GOOD ENOUGH TO BEAT HIM?
NO, UH... I DIDN'T MEAN THAT.
UH-OH! I'VE UPSET HIM.
I JUST THOUGHT I COULD HELP YOU PASS THE TEST UNDEFEATED.
OH, I GET IT.
HUH?
YOU WANT TO USE ME TO FIND OUT HOW GOOD SHINDO IS.

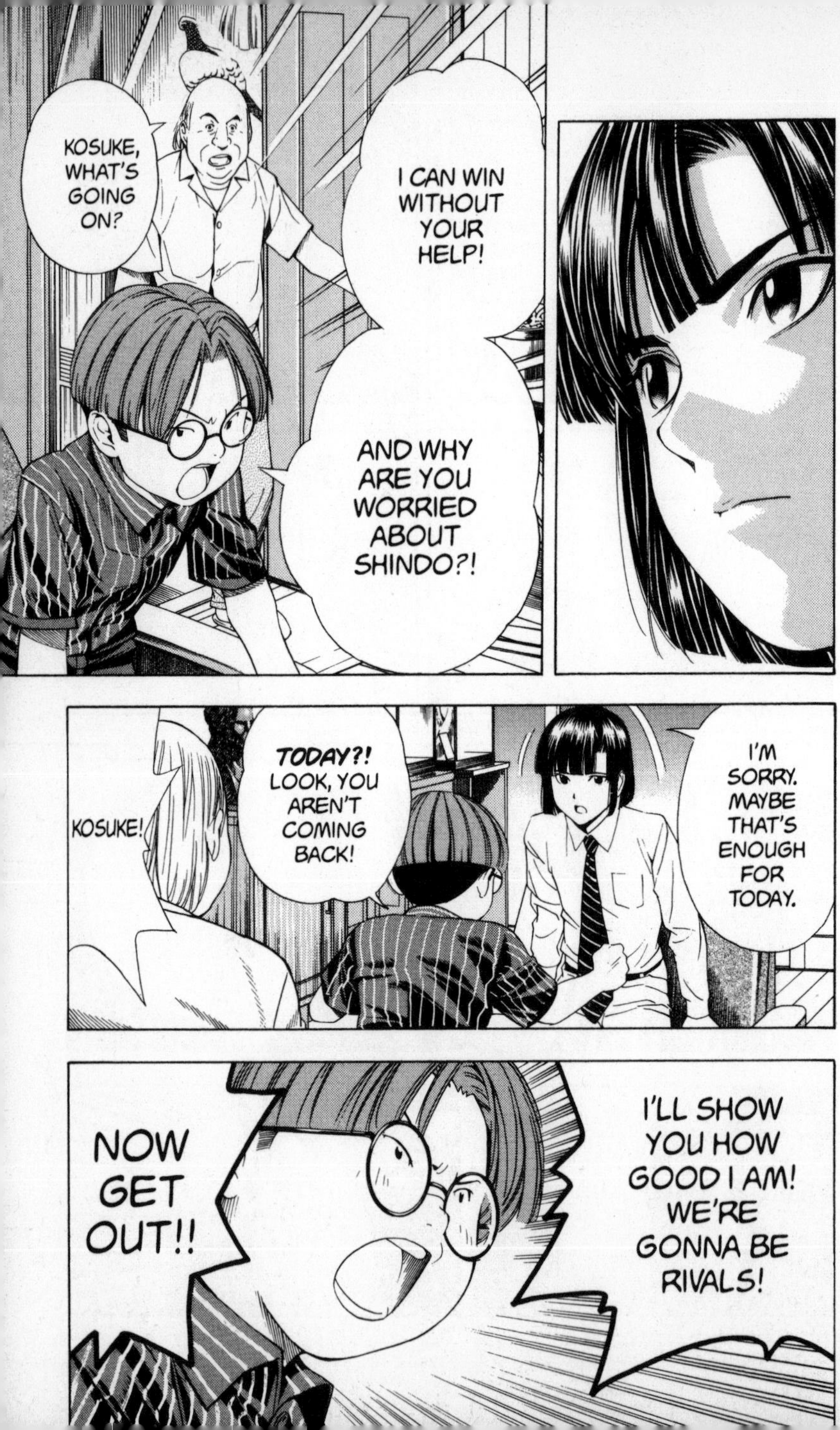
I CAN WIN WITHOUT YOUR HELP!
AND WHY ARE YOU WORRIED ABOUT SHINDO?!
KOSUKE, WHAT'S GOING ON?
I'M SORRY. MAYBE THAT'S ENOUGH FOR TODAY.
TODAY?! LOOK, YOU AREN'T COMING BACK!
KOSUKE!
I'LL SHOW YOU HOW GOOD I AM! WE'RE GONNA BE RIVALS!
NOW GET OUT!!

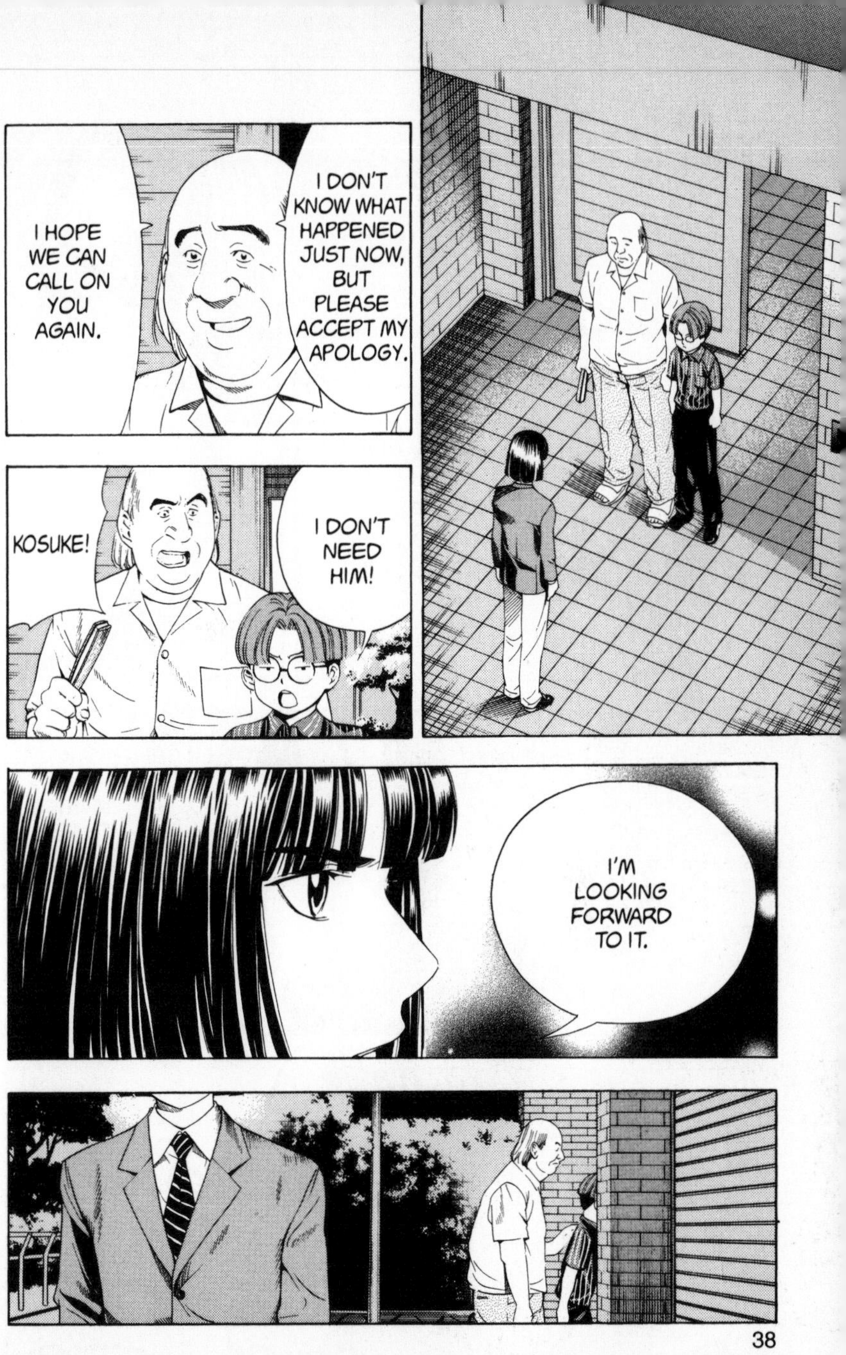
I DON'T KNOW WHAT HAPPENED JUST NOW, BUT PLEASE ACCEPT MY APOLOGY.
I HOPE WE CAN CALL ON YOU AGAIN.
I DON'T NEED HIM!
KOSUKE!
I'M LOOKING FORWARD TO IT.

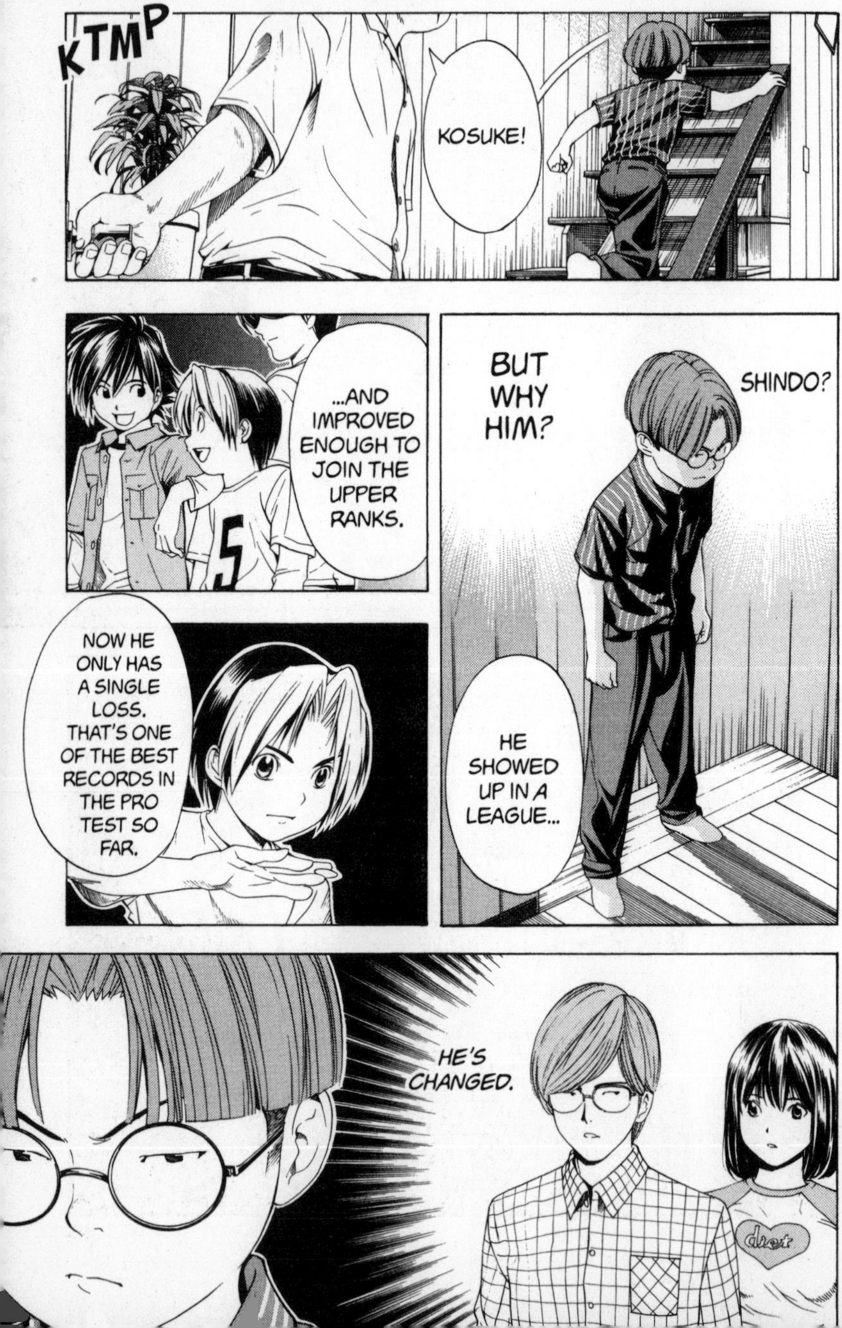
KTMP
KOSUKE!
SHINDO?
BUT WHY HIM?
HE SHOWED UP IN A LEAGUE...
...AND IMPROVED ENOUGH TO JOIN THE UPPER RANKS.
NOW HE ONLY HAS A SINGLE LOSS. THAT'S ONE OF THE BEST RECORDS IN THE PRO TEST SO FAR.
HE'S CHANGED.

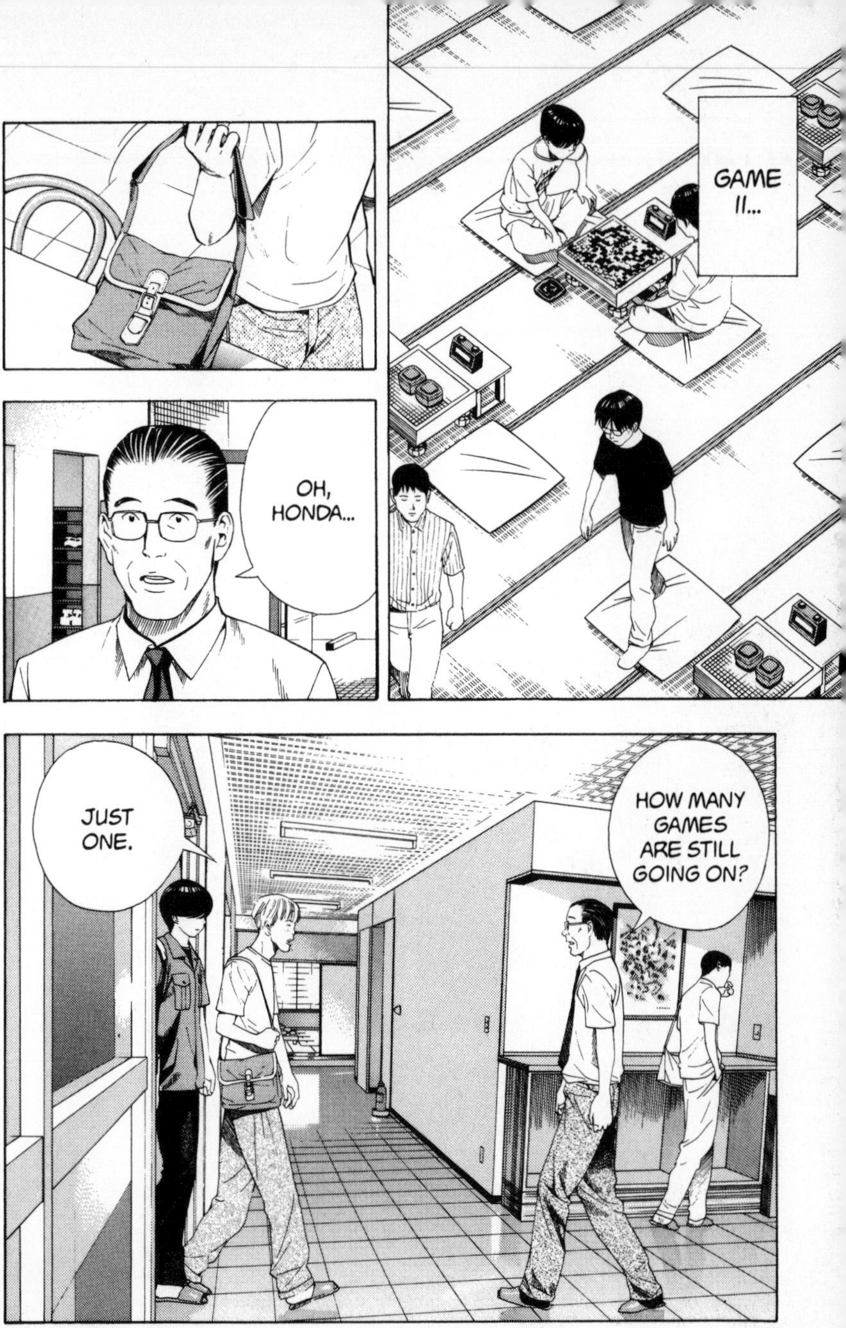
GAME 11...
OH, HONDA...
HOW MANY GAMES ARE STILL GOING ON?
JUST ONE.

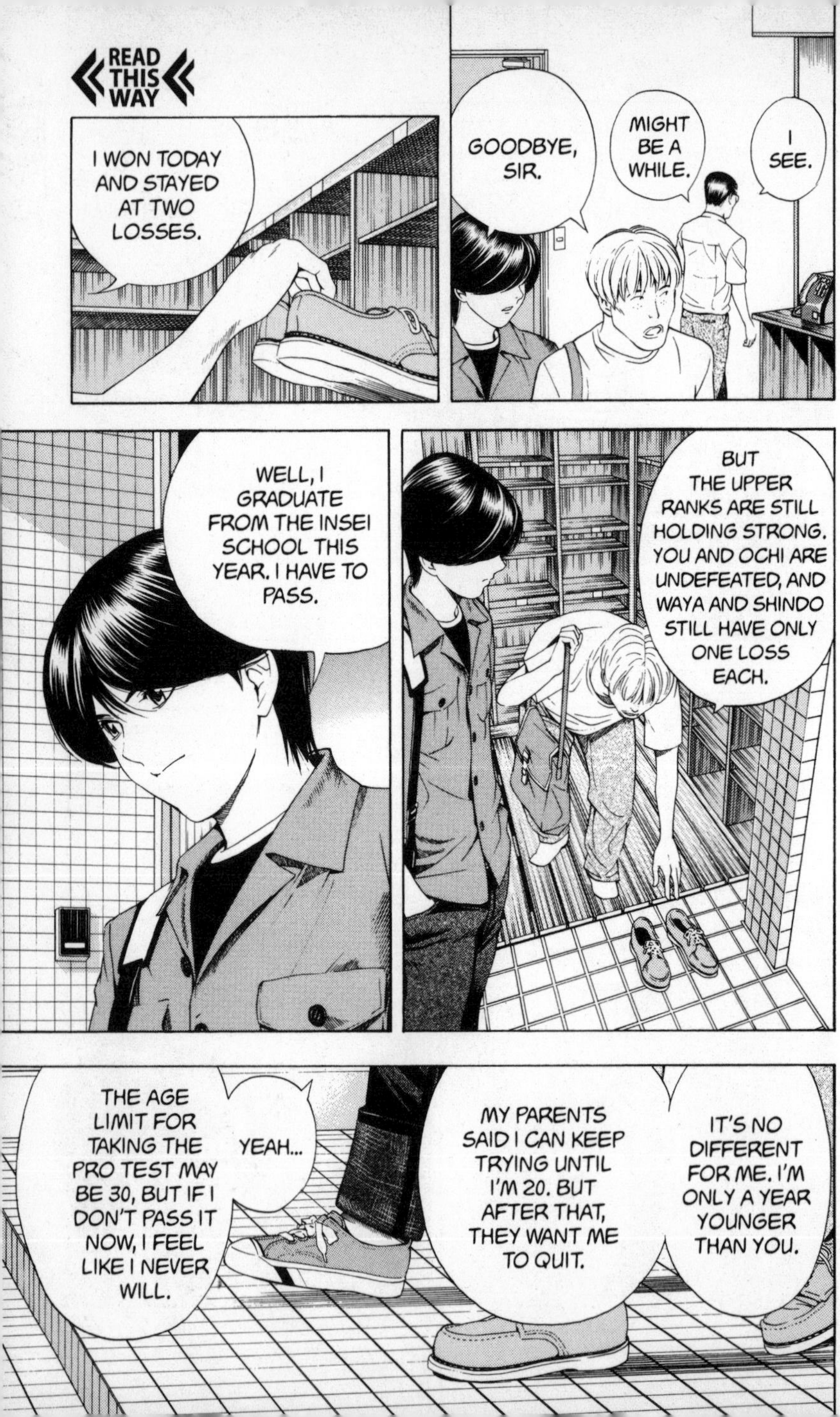
READ THIS WAY
I SEE.
MIGHT BE A WHILE.
GOODBYE, SIR.
I WON TODAY AND STAYED AT TWO LOSSES.
BUT THE UPPER RANKS ARE STILL HOLDING STRONG. YOU AND OCHI ARE UNDEFEATED, AND WAYA AND SHINDO STILL HAVE ONLY ONE LOSS EACH.
WELL, I GRADUATE FROM THE INSEI SCHOOL THIS YEAR. I HAVE TO PASS.
IT'S NO DIFFERENT FOR ME. I'M ONLY A YEAR YOUNGER THAN YOU.
MY PARENTS SAID I CAN KEEP TRYING UNTIL I'M 20. BUT AFTER THAT, THEY WANT ME TO QUIT.
YEAH...
THE AGE LIMIT FOR TAKING THE PRO TEST MAY BE 30, BUT IF I DON'T PASS IT NOW, I FEEL LIKE I NEVER WILL.

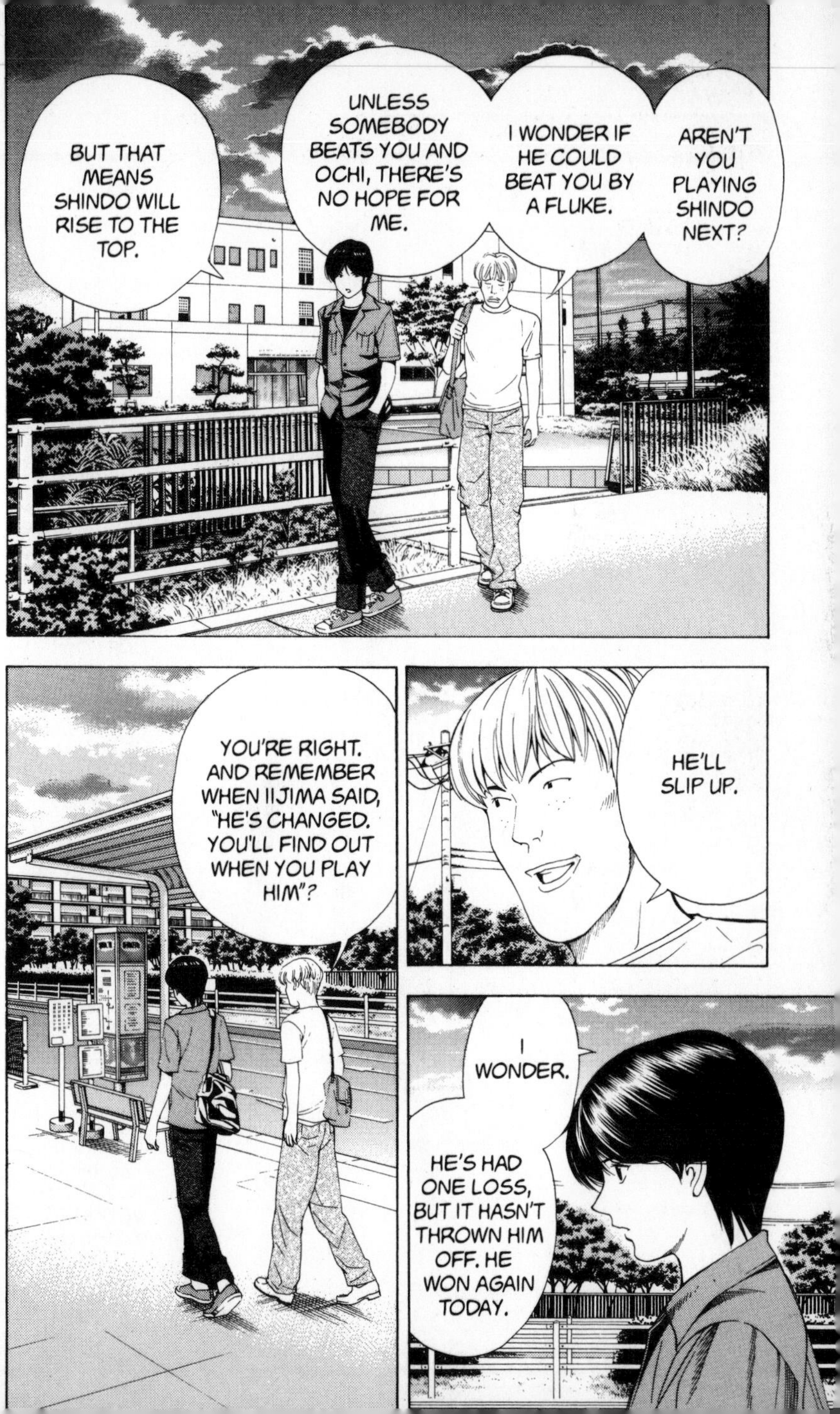
AREN'T YOU PLAYING SHINDO NEXT?
I WONDER IF HE COULD BEAT YOU BY A FLUKE.
UNLESS SOMEBODY BEATS YOU AND OCHI, THERE'S NO HOPE FOR ME.
BUT THAT MEANS SHINDO WILL RISE TO THE TOP.
HE'LL SLIP UP.
I WONDER.
HE'S HAD ONE LOSS, BUT IT HASN'T THROWN HIM OFF. HE WON AGAIN TODAY.
YOU'RE RIGHT. AND REMEMBER WHEN IIJIMA SAID, "HE'S CHANGED. YOU'LL FIND OUT WHEN YOU PLAY HIM"?

READ THIS WAY

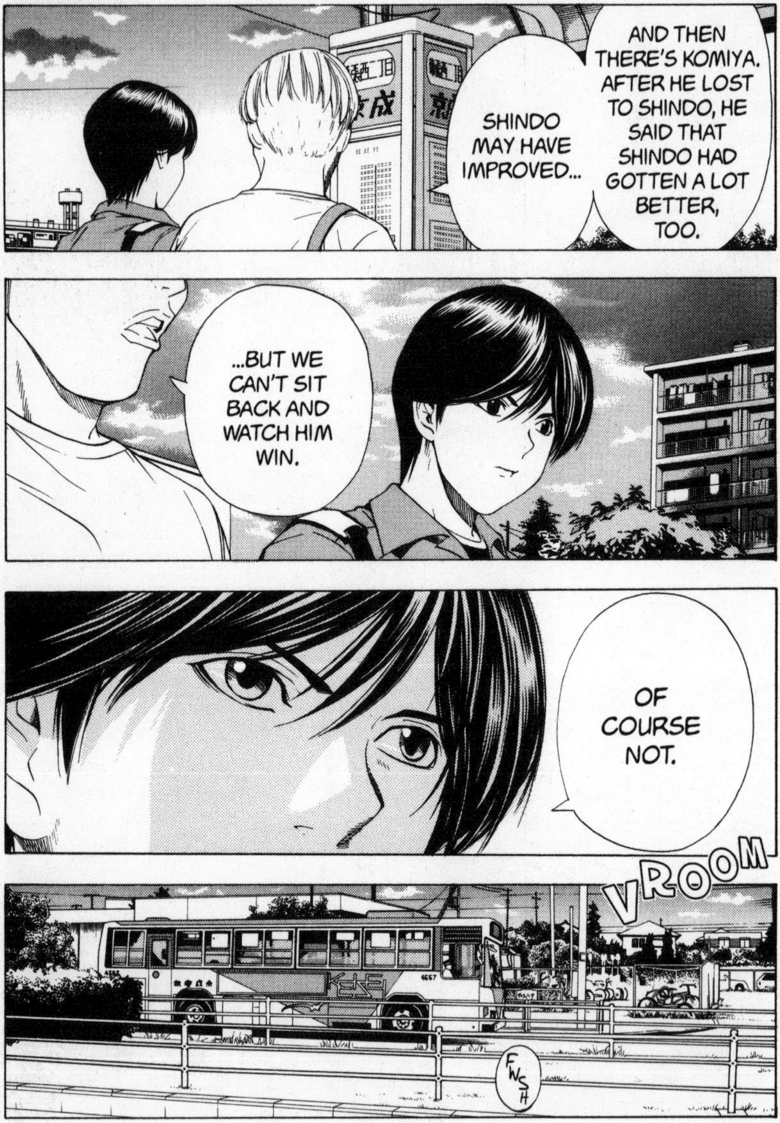
AND THEN THERE'S KOMIYA. AFTER HE LOST TO SHINDO, HE SAID THAT SHINDO HAD GOTTEN A LOT BETTER, TOO.
SHINDO MAY HAVE IMPROVED...
...BUT WE CAN'T SIT BACK AND WATCH HIM WIN.
OF COURSE NOT.
VROOM
FWSH

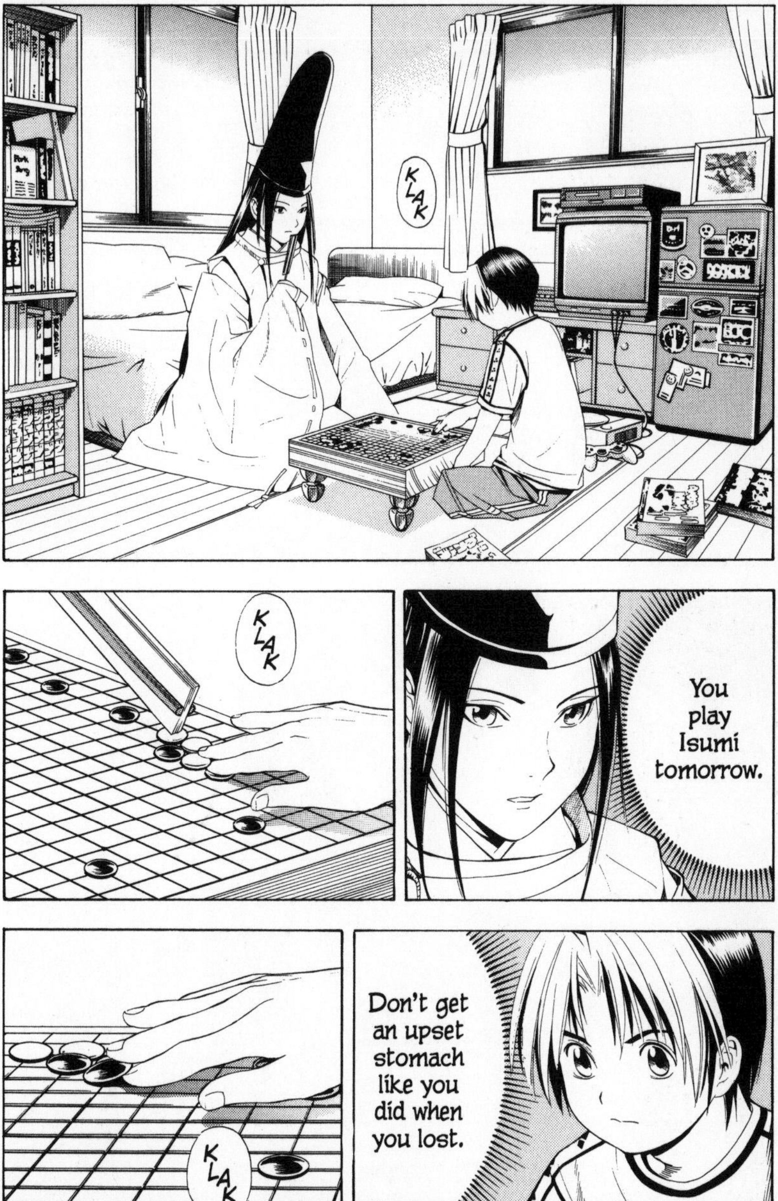
KLAK
You play Isumi tomorrow.
KLAK
Don't get an upset stomach like you did when you lost.
KLAK

READ THIS WAY

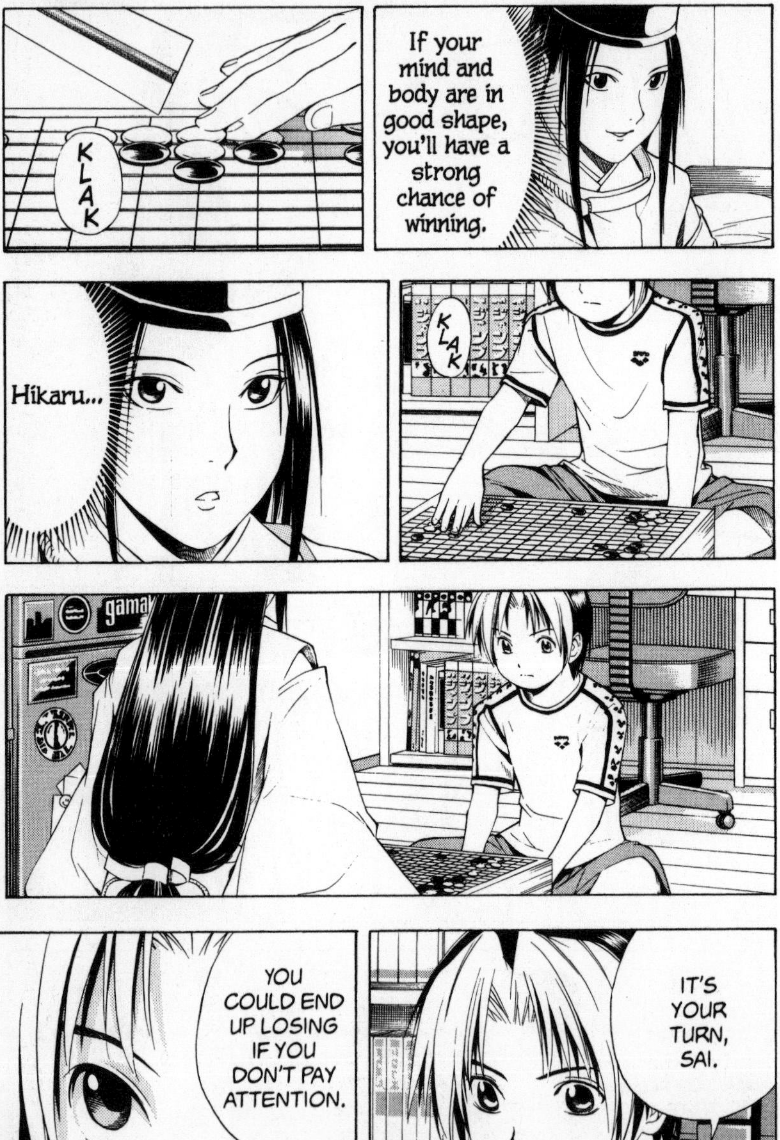
If your mind and body are in good shape, you'll have a strong chance of winning.
KLAK
KLAK
Hikaru...
IT'S YOUR TURN, SAI.
YOU COULD END UP LOSING IF YOU DON'T PAY ATTENTION.

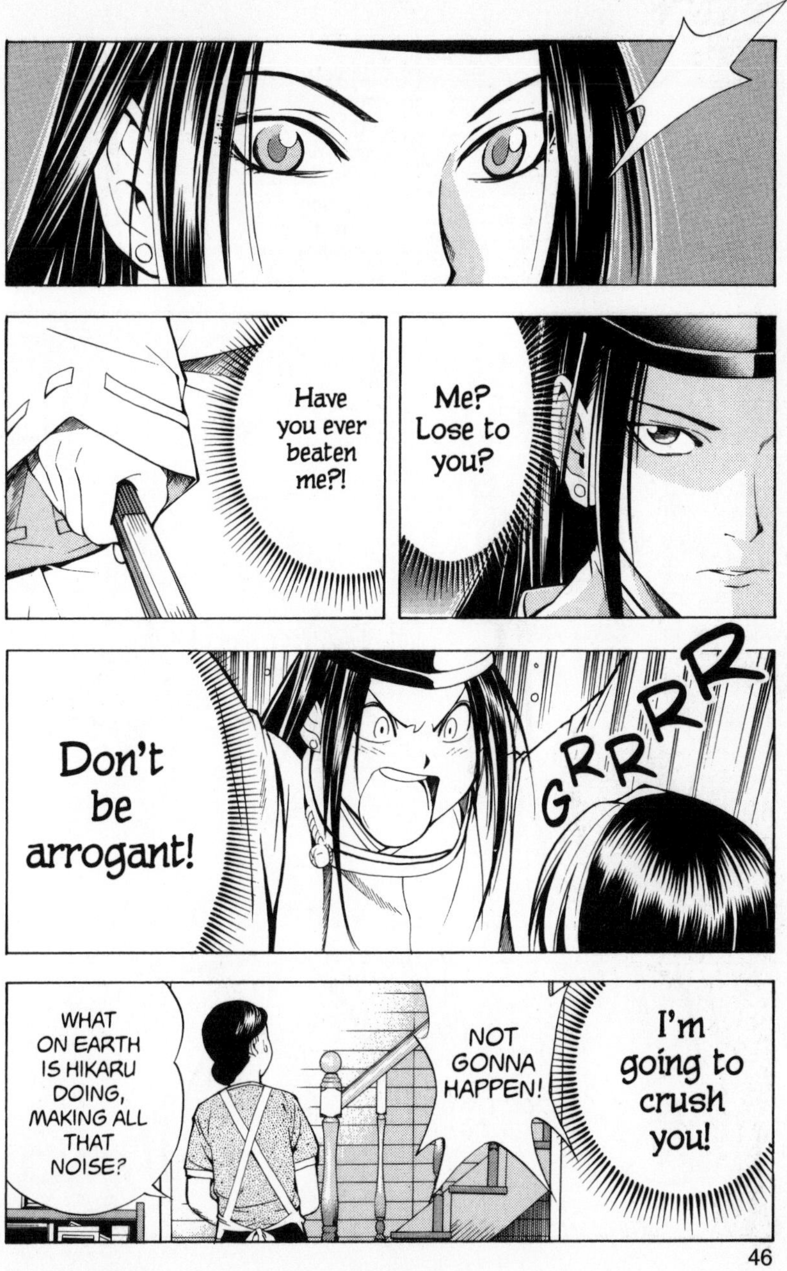
Me? Lose to you?
Have you ever beaten me?!
GRRRR
Don't be arrogant!
I'm going to crush you!
NOT GONNA HAPPEN!
WHAT ON EARTH IS HIKARU DOING, MAKING ALL THAT NOISE?

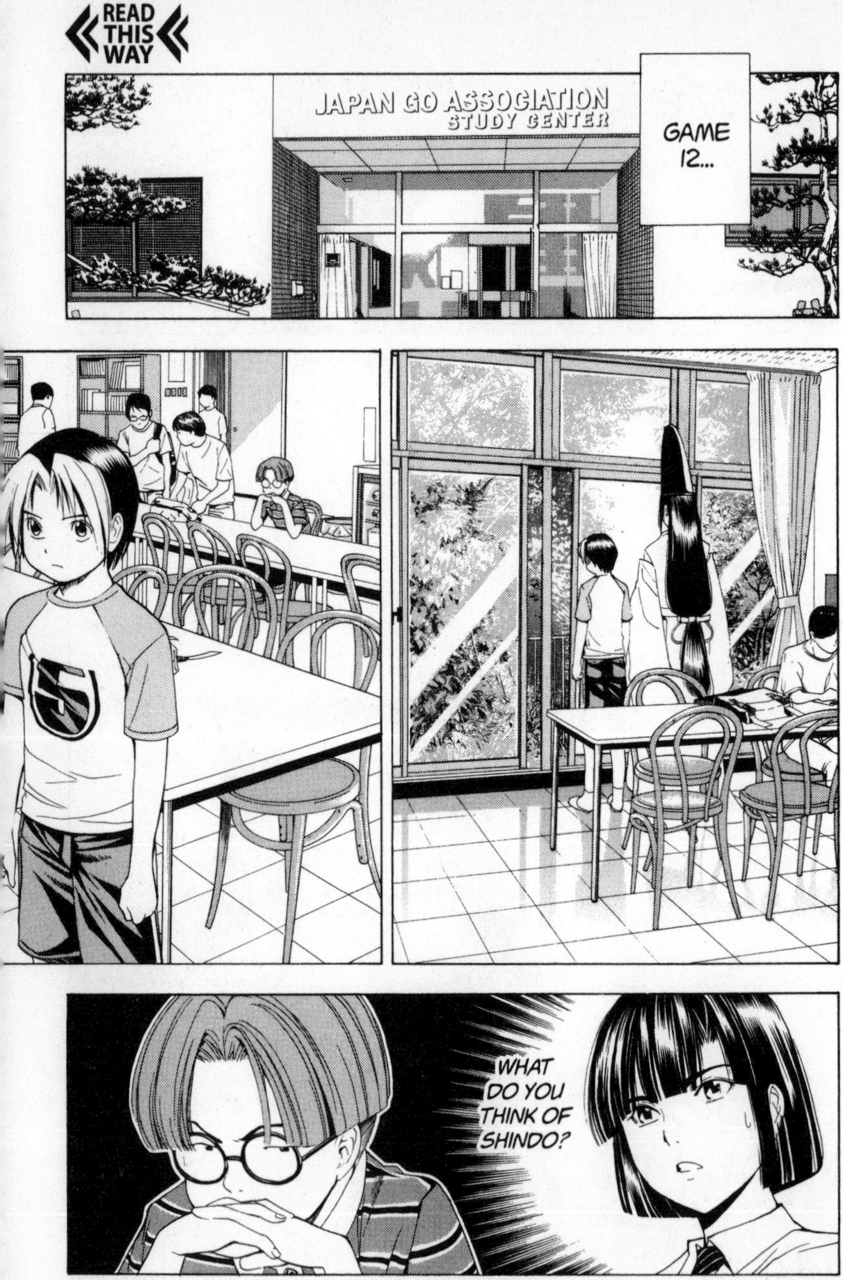
READ THIS WAY
GAME 12...
JAPAN GO ASSOCIATION
STUDY CENTER
WHAT DO YOU THINK OF SHINDO?

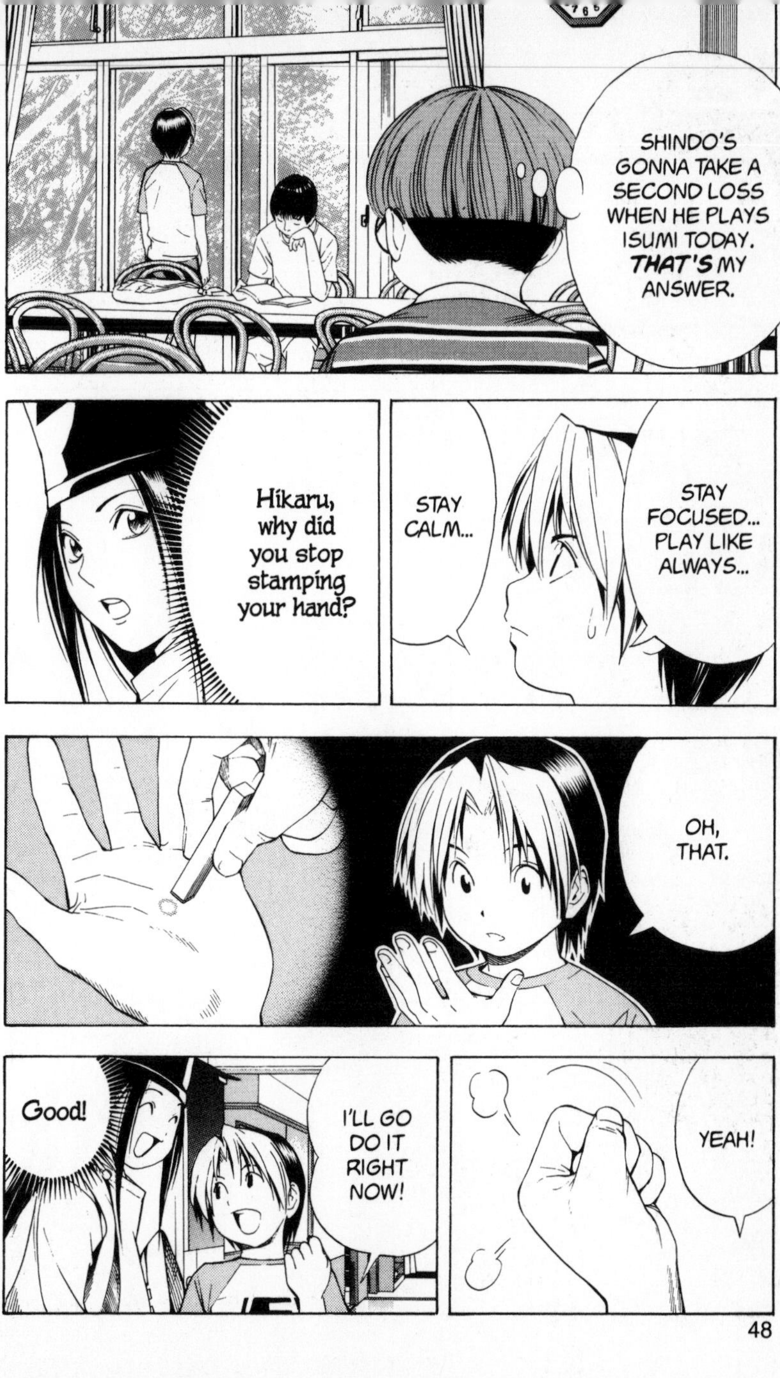
SHINDO'S GONNA TAKE A SECOND LOSS WHEN HE PLAYS ISUMI TODAY. **THAT'S** MY ANSWER.
STAY FOCUSED... PLAY LIKE ALWAYS...
STAY CALM...
Hikaru, why did you stop stamping your hand?
OH, THAT.
YEAH!
I'LL GO DO IT RIGHT NOW!
Good!

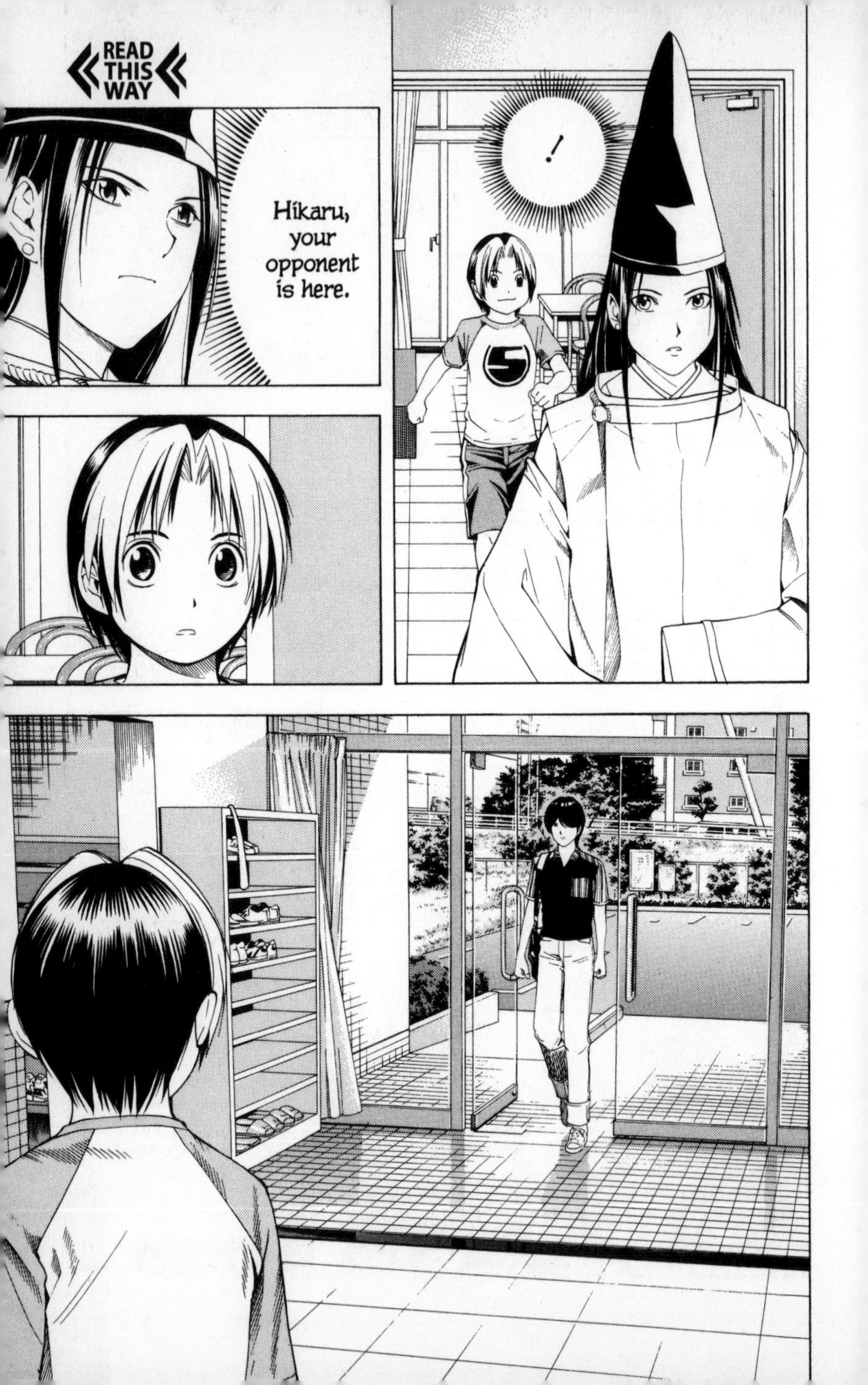
READ THIS WAY
!
Hikaru, your opponent is here.

AND NOW...

WHAT'S MY LINE?

FROM **HONG KONG**

GAME 63

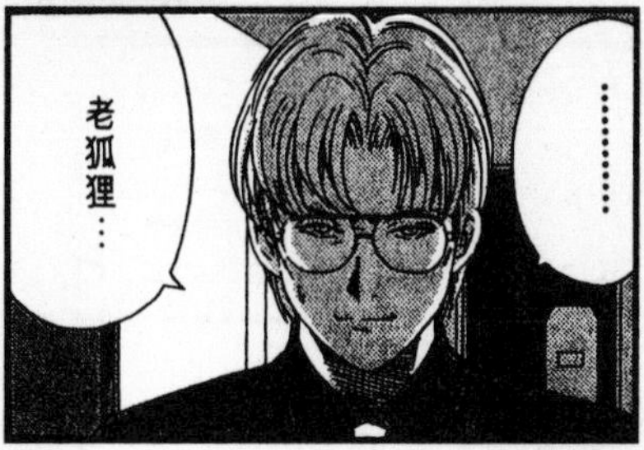
……
老狐狸…

GAME 57

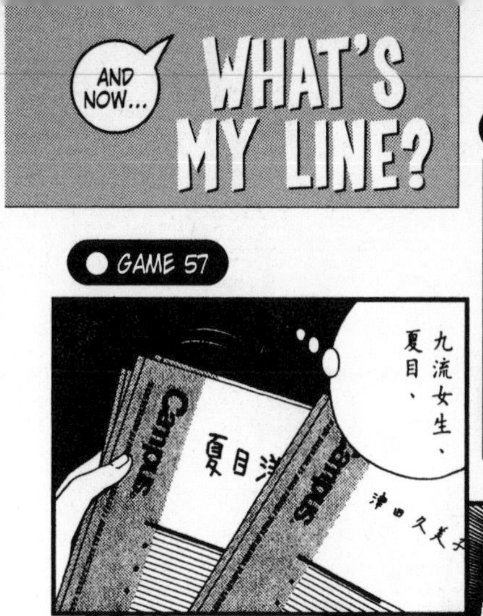
九流女生、夏目、

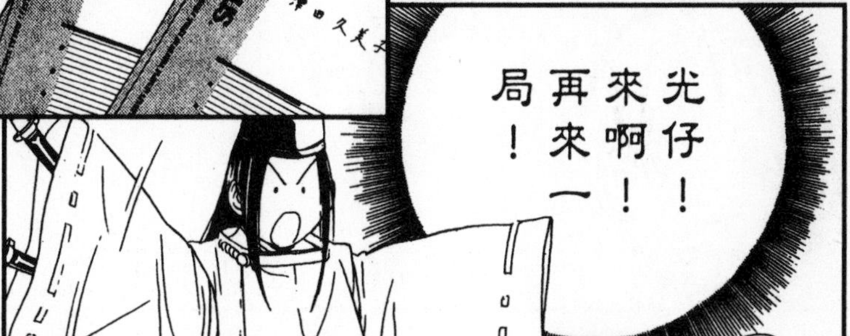
光仔！來啊！再來一局！
白痴…

GAME 54

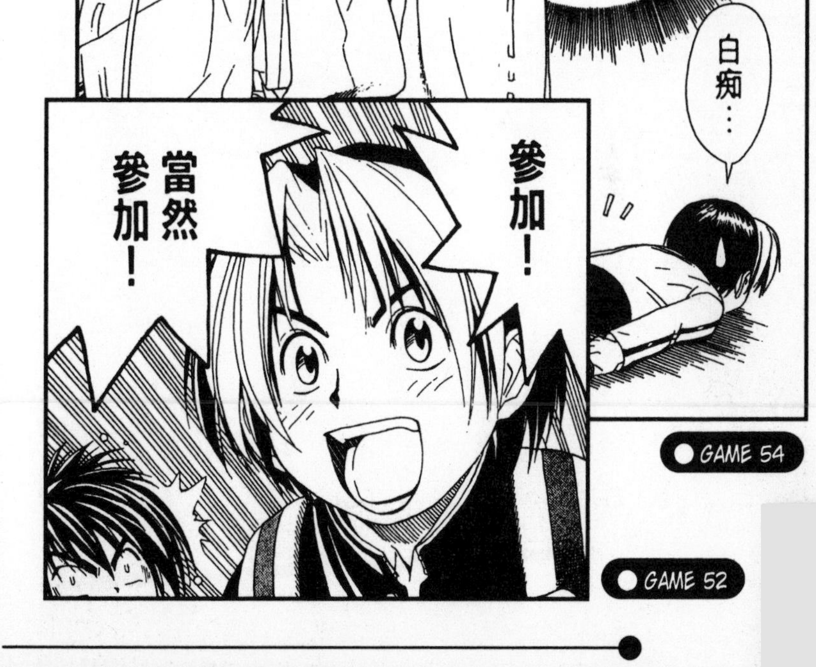
參加！
當然參加！

GAME 52

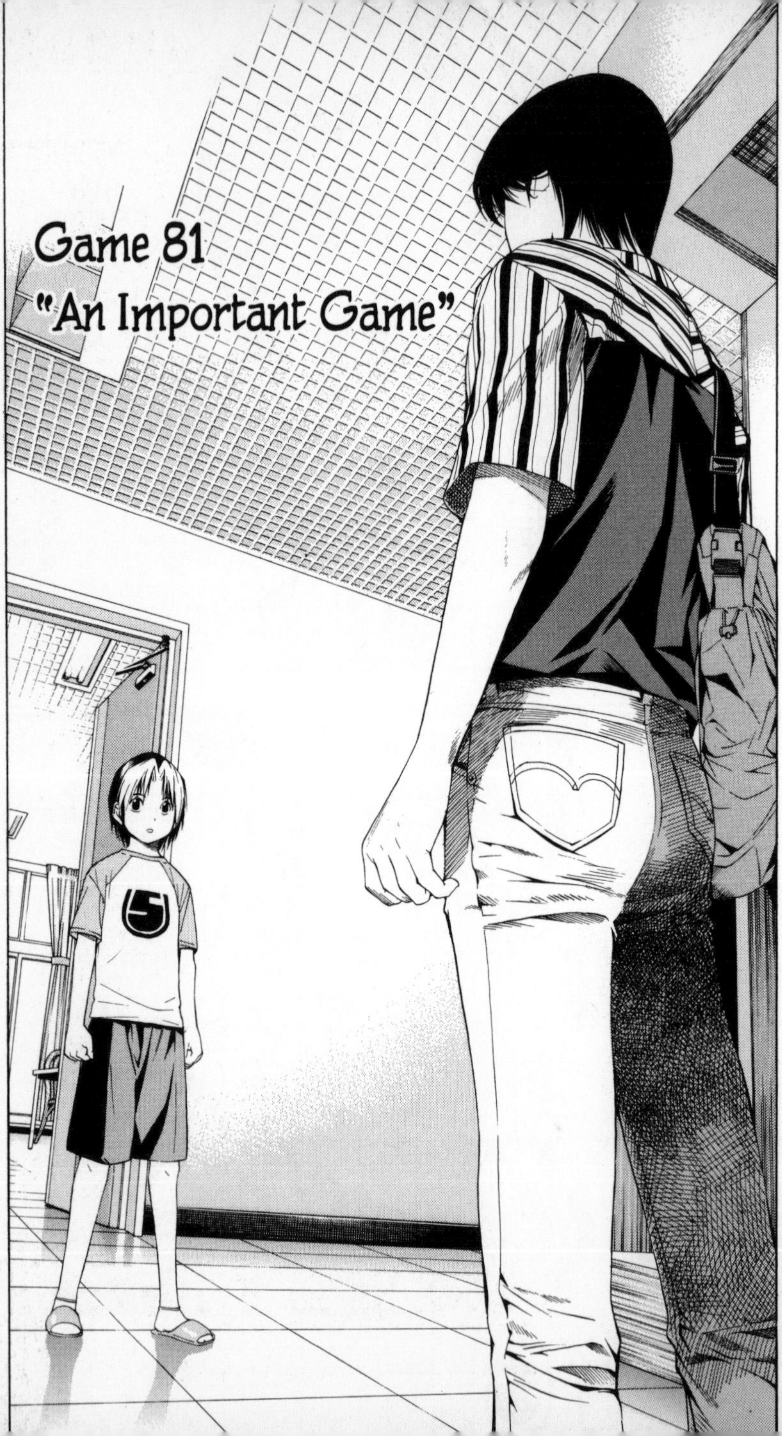
Game 81
"An Important Game"

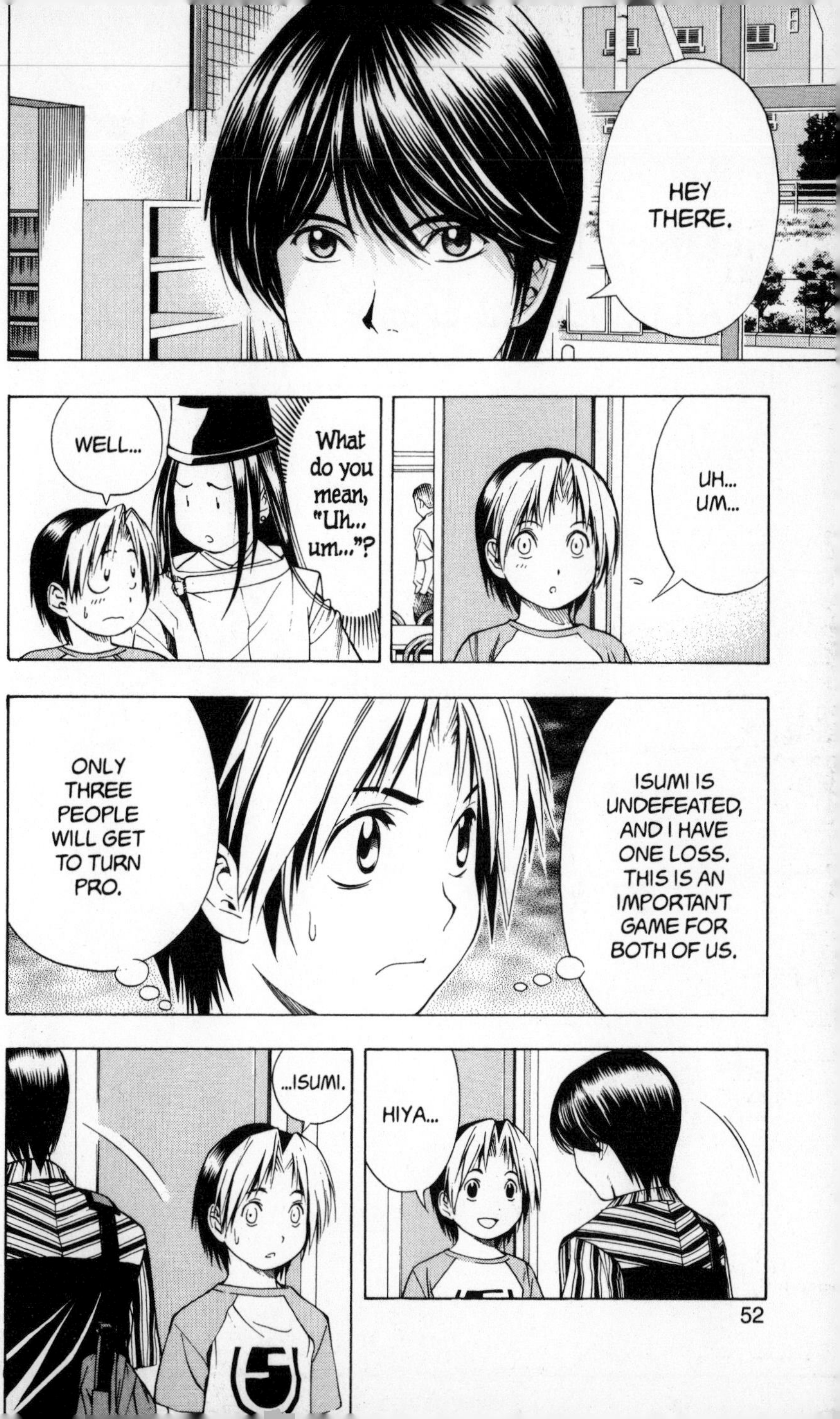
HEY THERE.
UH... UM...
What do you mean, "Uh... um..."?
WELL...
ISUMI IS UNDEFEATED, AND I HAVE ONE LOSS. THIS IS AN IMPORTANT GAME FOR BOTH OF US.
ONLY THREE PEOPLE WILL GET TO TURN PRO.
HIYA...
...ISUMI.

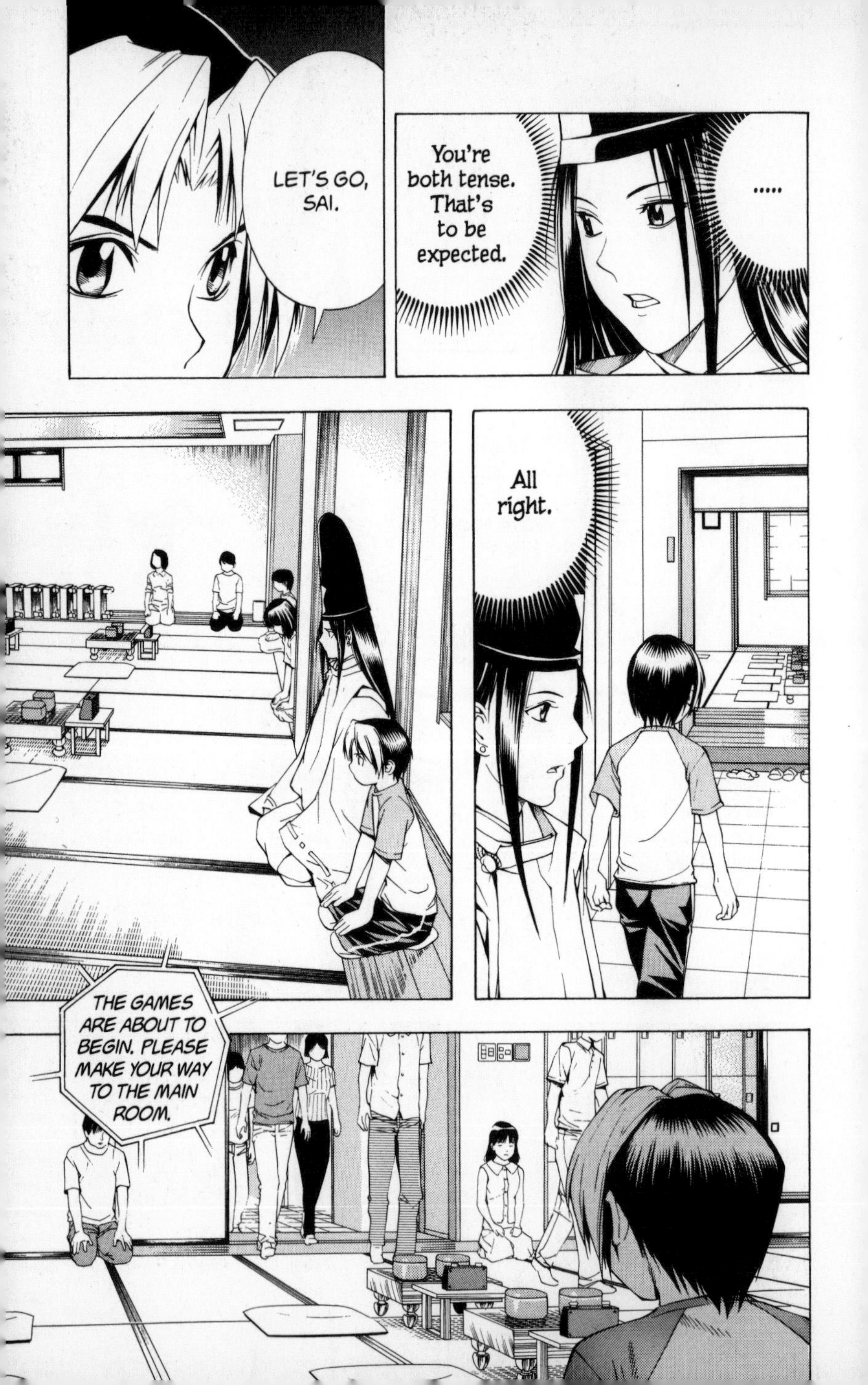
.....
You're both tense. That's to be expected.
LET'S GO, SAI.
All right.
THE GAMES ARE ABOUT TO BEGIN. PLEASE MAKE YOUR WAY TO THE MAIN ROOM.

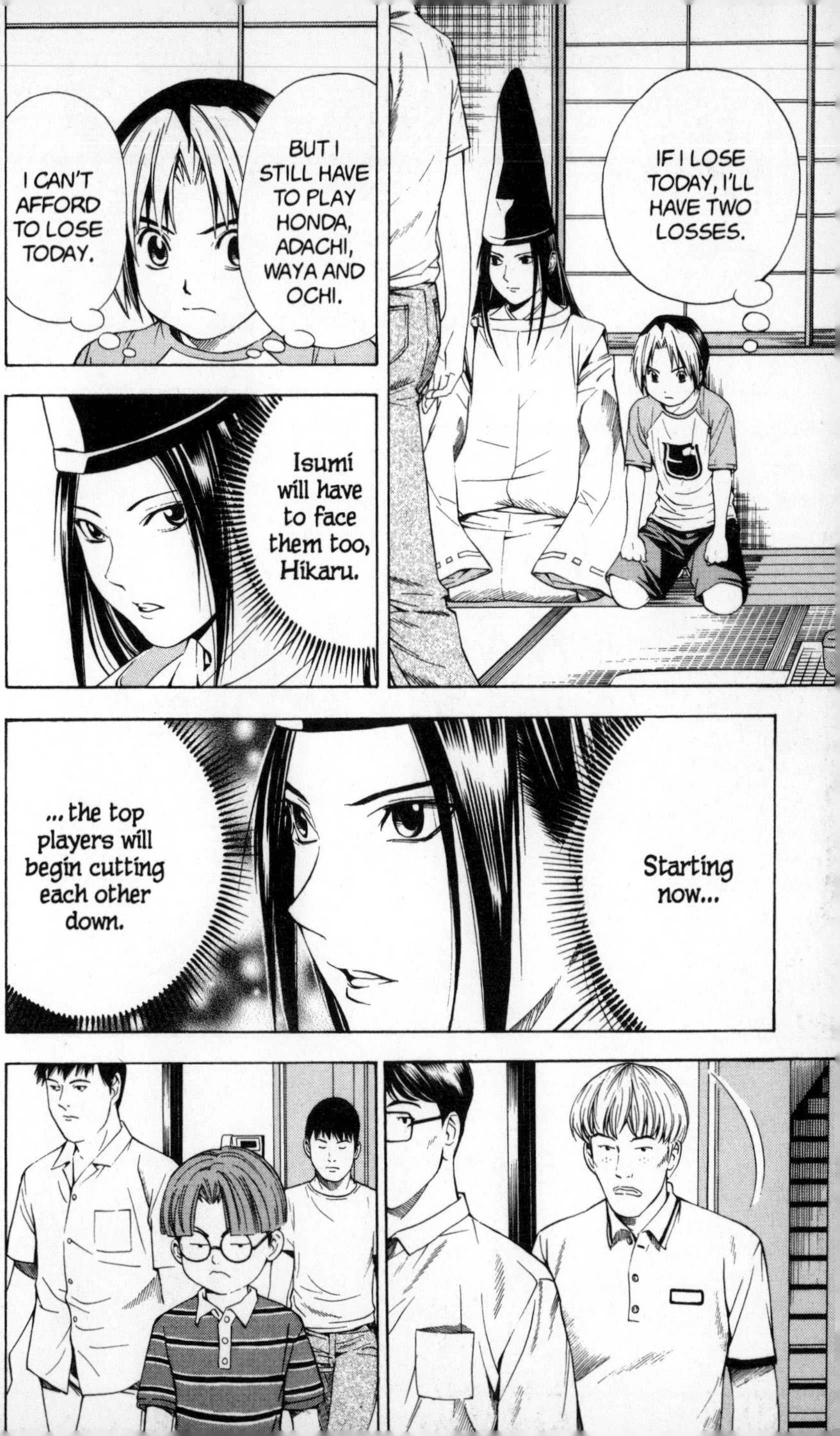
IF I LOSE TODAY, I'LL HAVE TWO LOSSES.
BUT I STILL HAVE TO PLAY HONDA, ADACHI, WAYA AND OCHI.
I CAN'T AFFORD TO LOSE TODAY.
Isumi will have to face them too, Hikaru.
Starting now...
...the top players will begin cutting each other down.

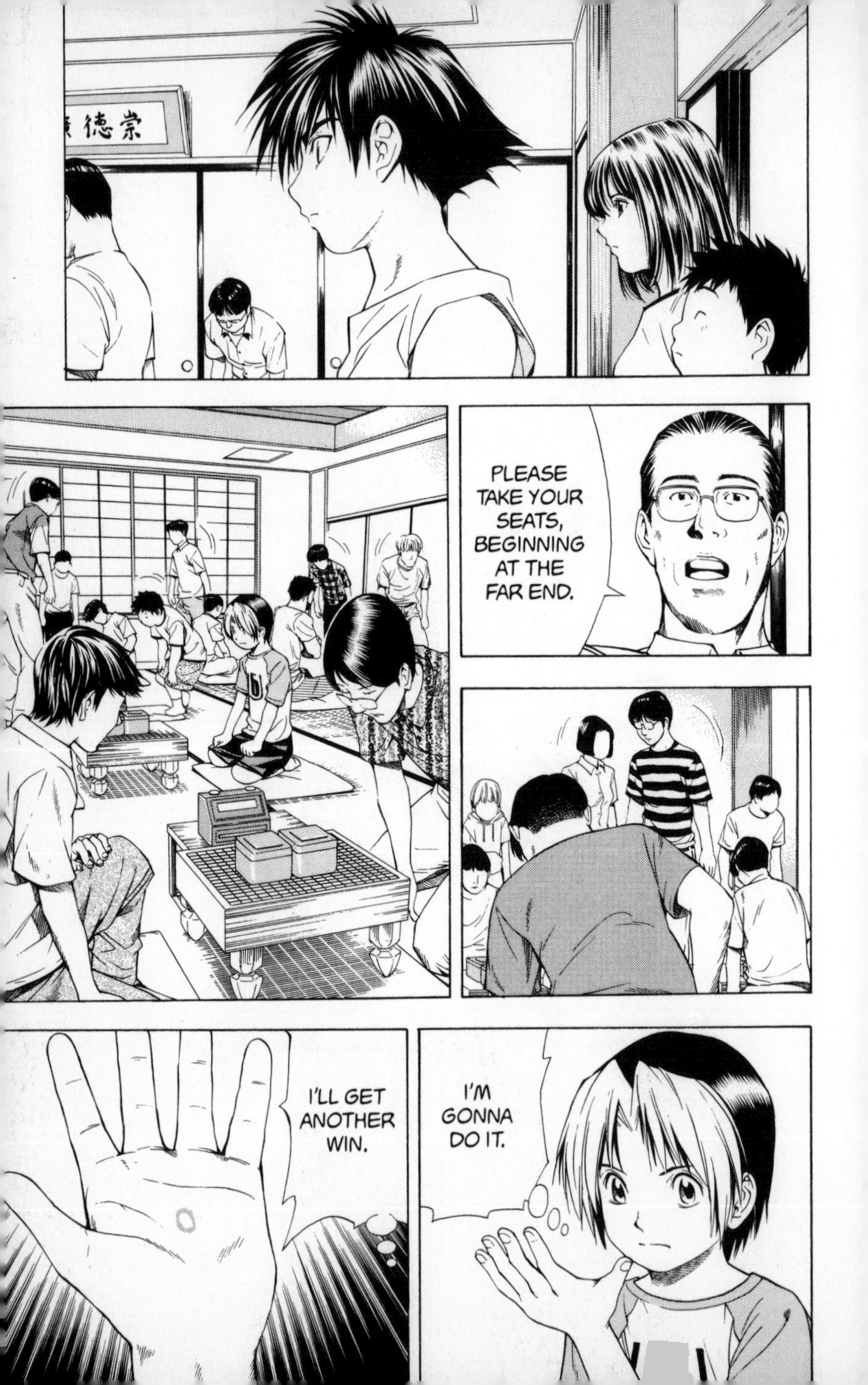

崇徳
PLEASE TAKE YOUR SEATS, BEGINNING AT THE FAR END.
I'M GONNA DO IT.
I'LL GET ANOTHER WIN.

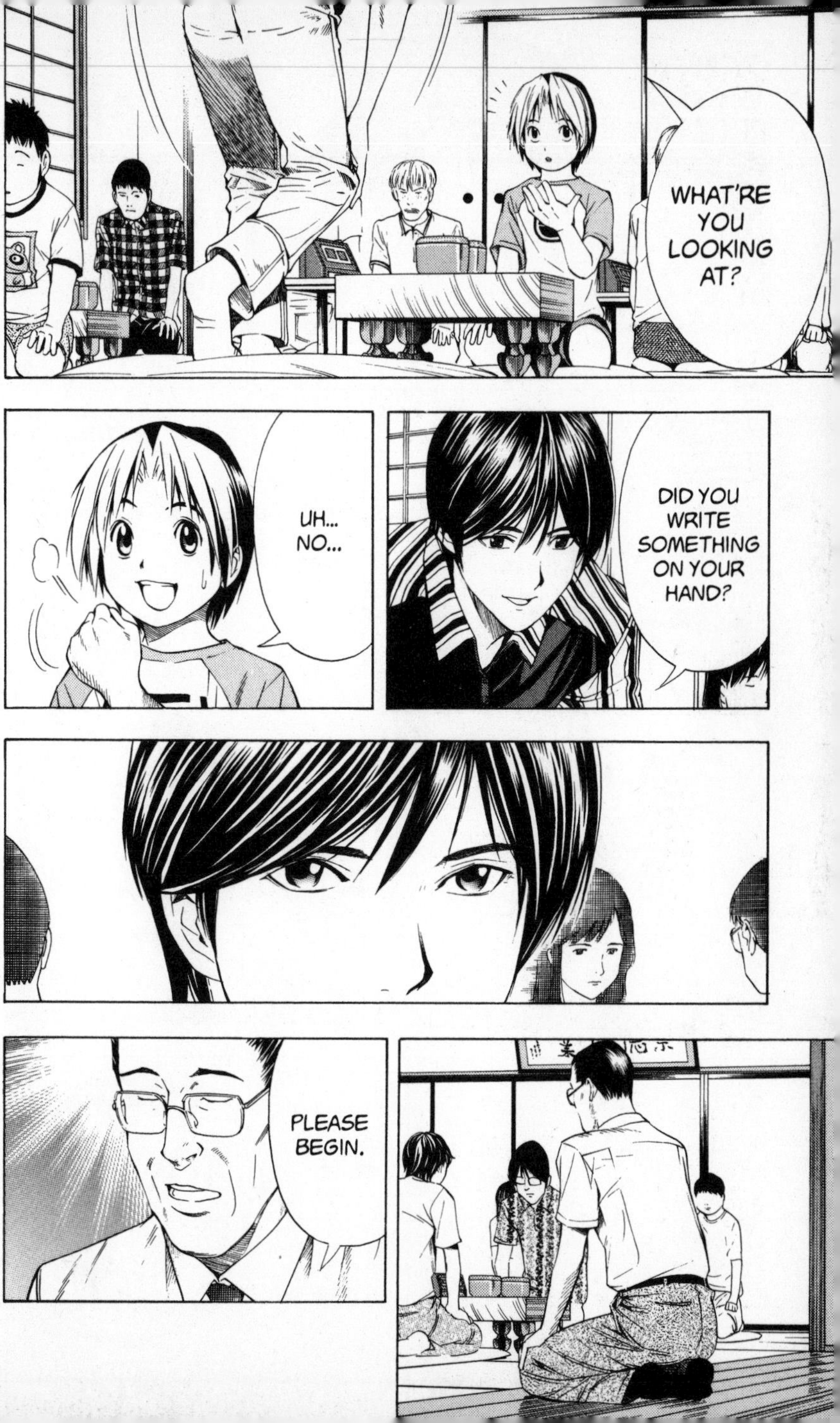
WHAT'RE YOU LOOKING AT?
DID YOU WRITE SOMETHING ON YOUR HAND?
UH... NO...
PLEASE BEGIN.

READ THIS WAY

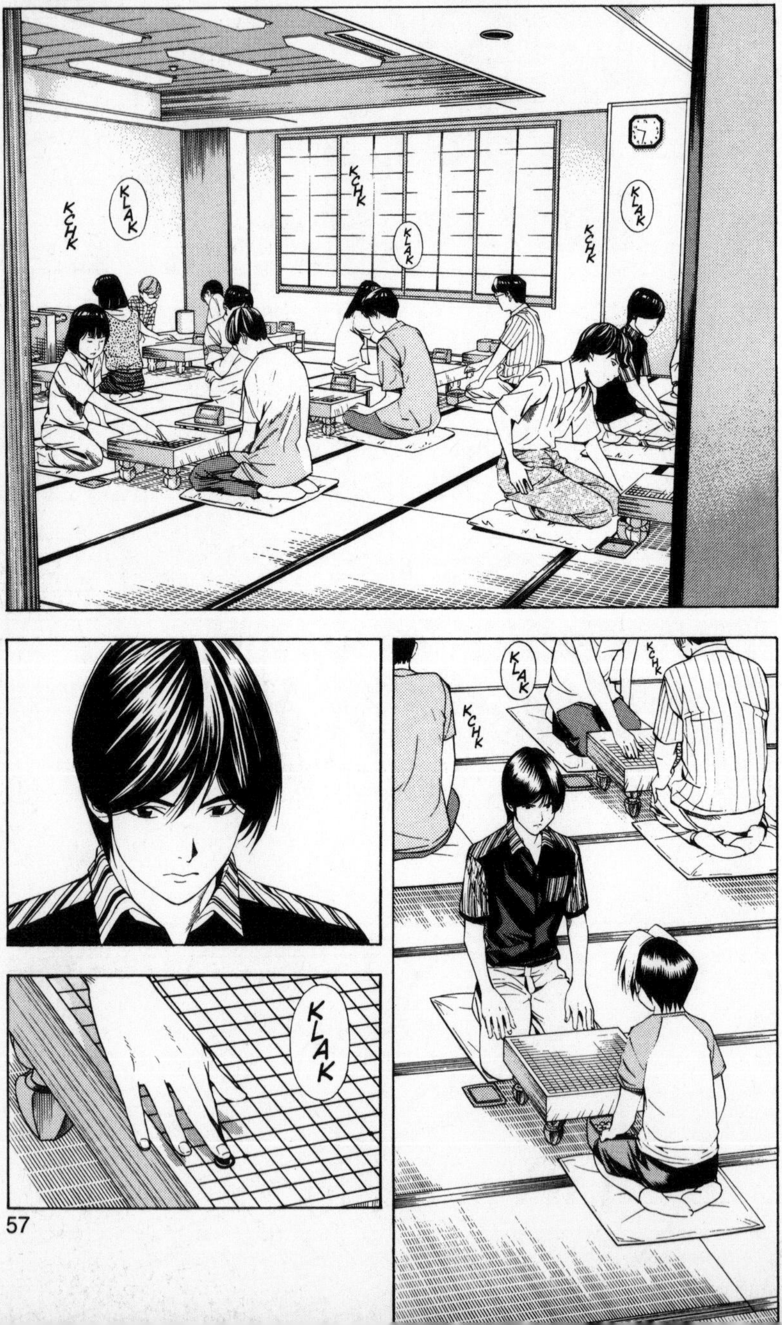
KLAK
KCHK
KLAK
KCHK
KLAK
KCHK
KCHK
KLAK
KCHK
KLAK

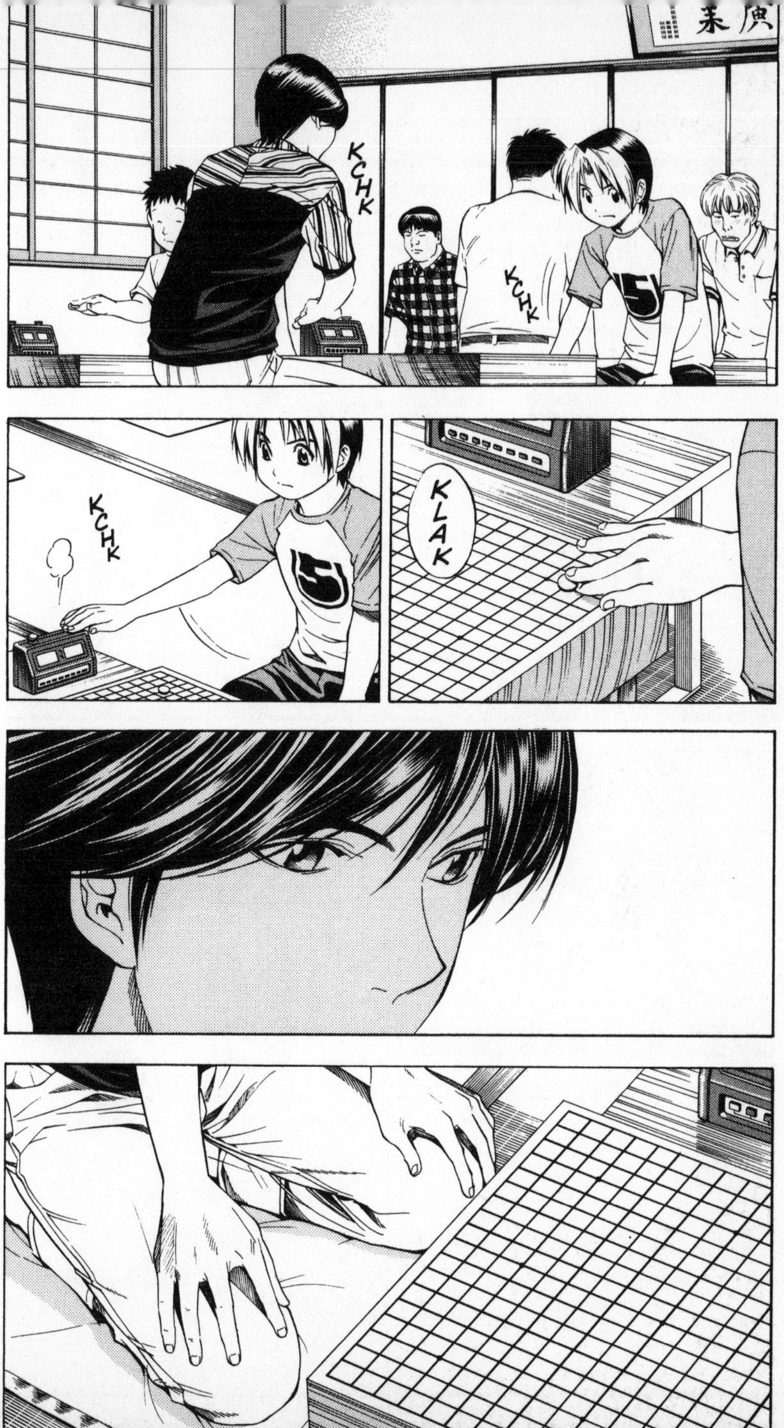
KCHK
KCHK
KLAK
KCHK

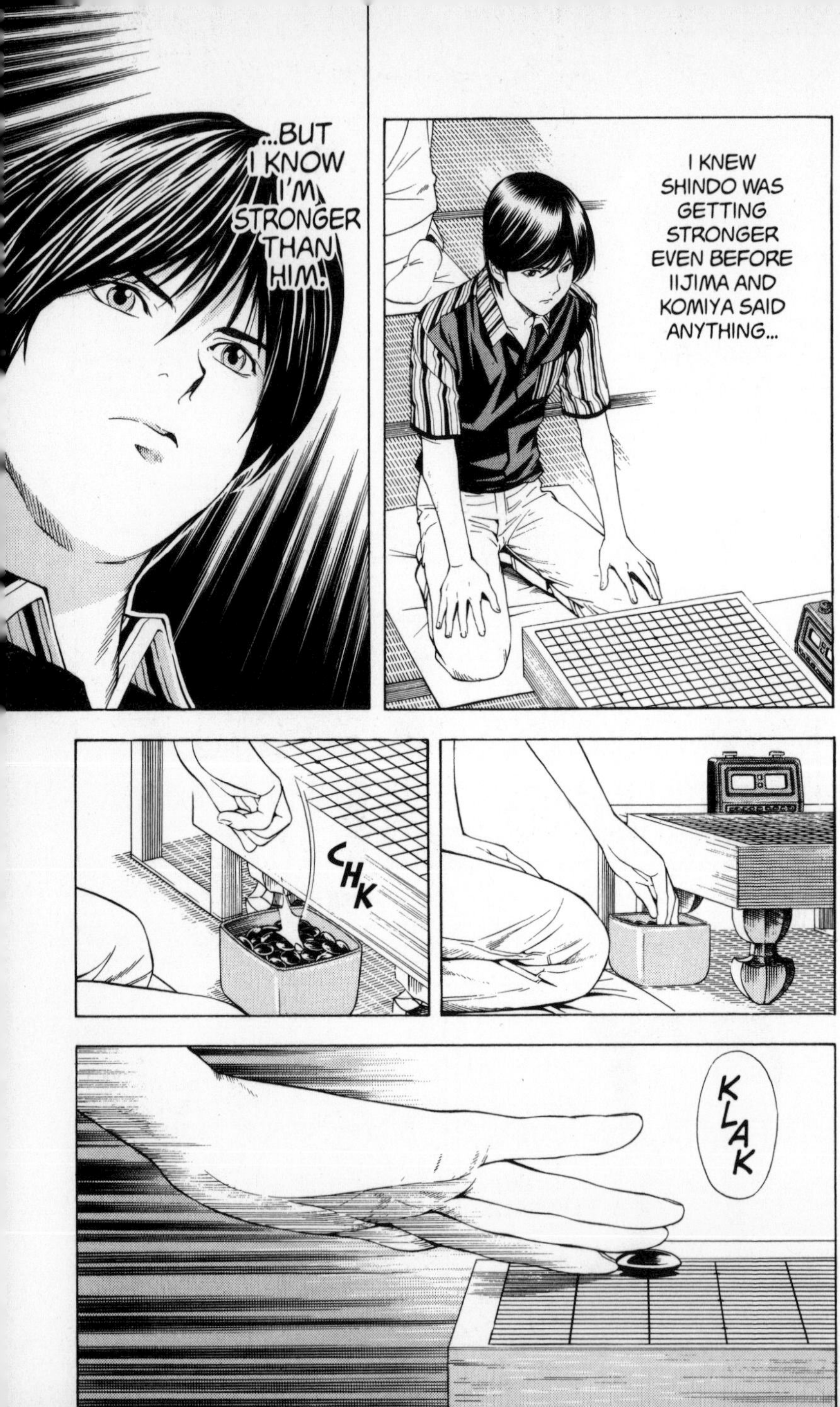
I KNEW SHINDO WAS GETTING STRONGER EVEN BEFORE IIJIMA AND KOMIYA SAID ANYTHING...
...BUT I KNOW I'M STRONGER THAN HIM.
CHK
KLAK

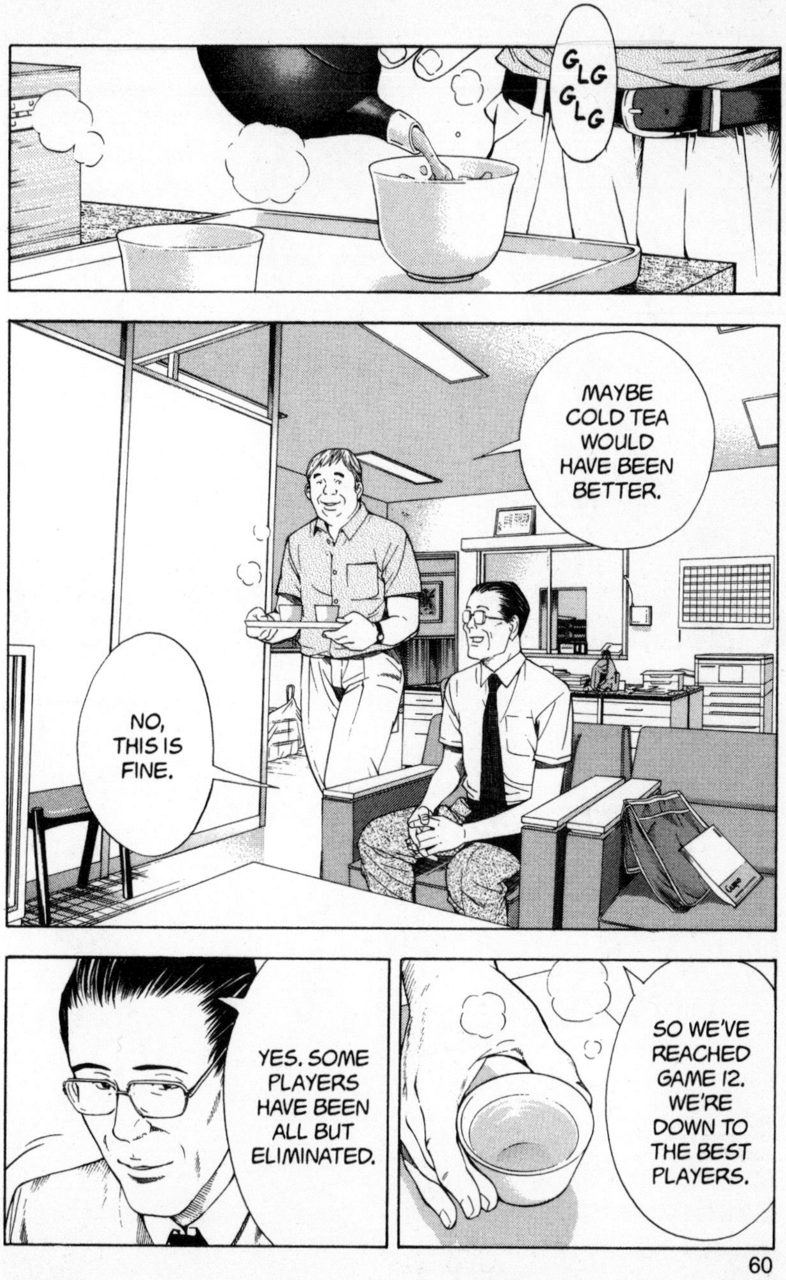
GLG GLG
MAYBE COLD TEA WOULD HAVE BEEN BETTER.
NO, THIS IS FINE.
SO WE'VE REACHED GAME 12. WE'RE DOWN TO THE BEST PLAYERS.
YES. SOME PLAYERS HAVE BEEN ALL BUT ELIMINATED.

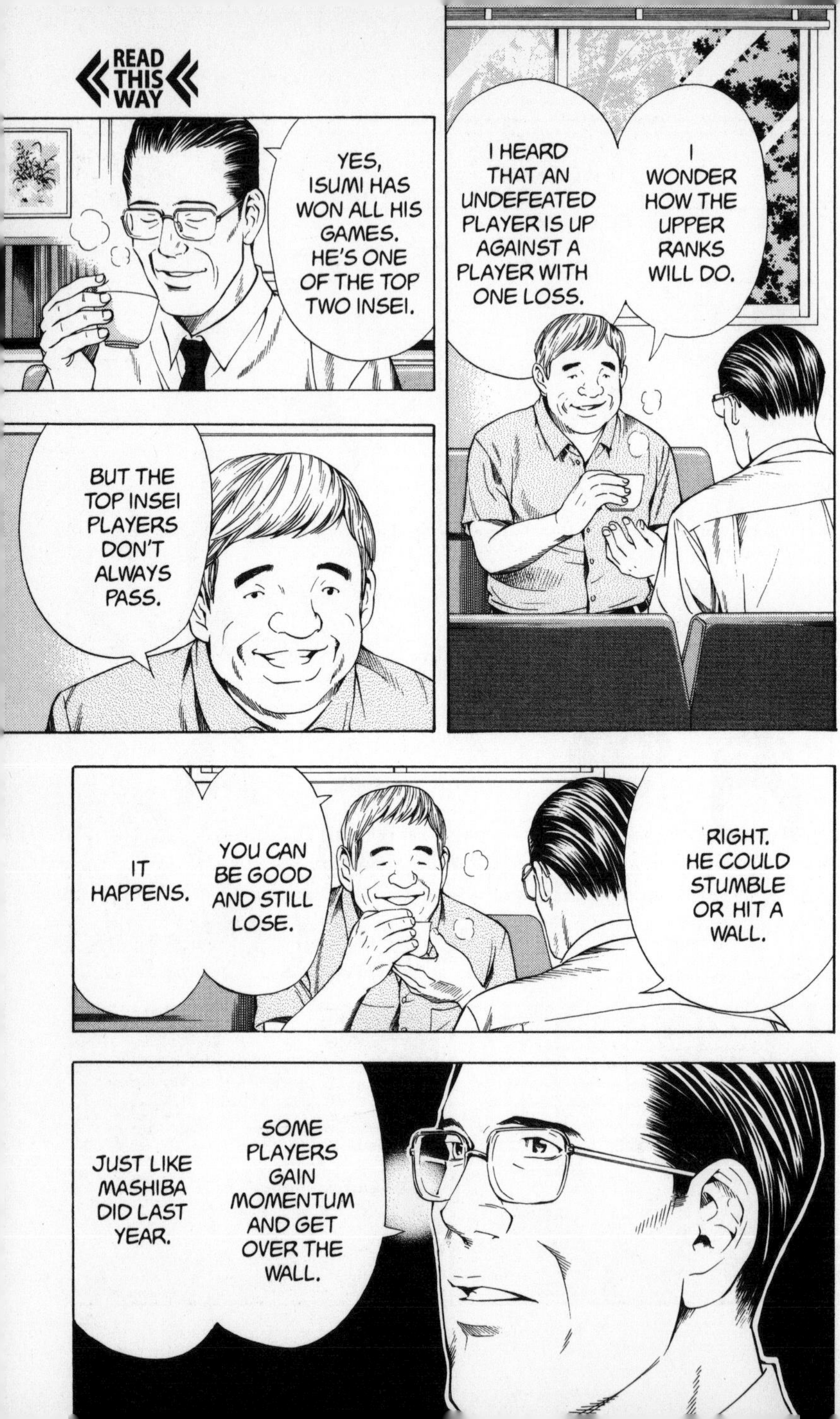
READ THIS WAY
I WONDER HOW THE UPPER RANKS WILL DO.
I HEARD THAT AN UNDEFEATED PLAYER IS UP AGAINST A PLAYER WITH ONE LOSS.
YES, ISUMI HAS WON ALL HIS GAMES. HE'S ONE OF THE TOP TWO INSEI.
BUT THE TOP INSEI PLAYERS DON'T ALWAYS PASS.
RIGHT. HE COULD STUMBLE OR HIT A WALL.
YOU CAN BE GOOD AND STILL LOSE.
IT HAPPENS.
SOME PLAYERS GAIN MOMENTUM AND GET OVER THE WALL.
JUST LIKE MASHIBA DID LAST YEAR.

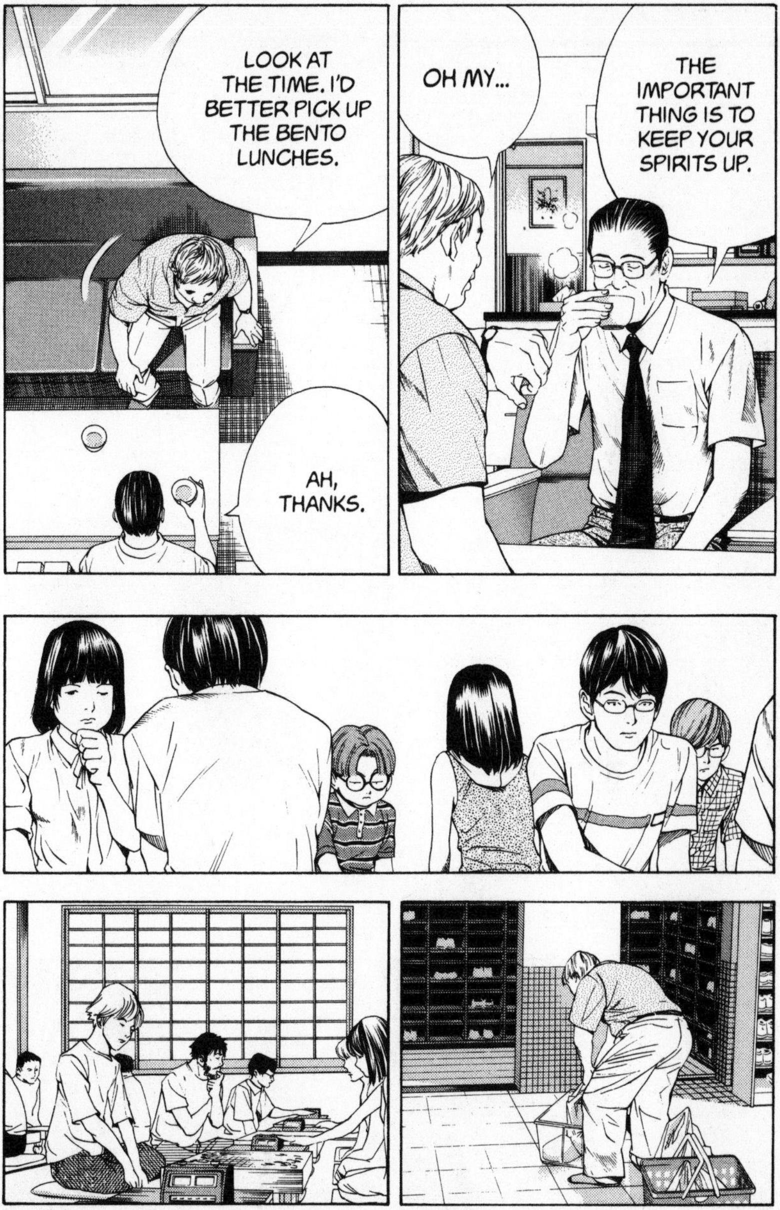
THE IMPORTANT THING IS TO KEEP YOUR SPIRITS UP.
OH MY...
LOOK AT THE TIME. I'D BETTER PICK UP THE BENTO LUNCHES.
AH, THANKS.

READ THIS WAY

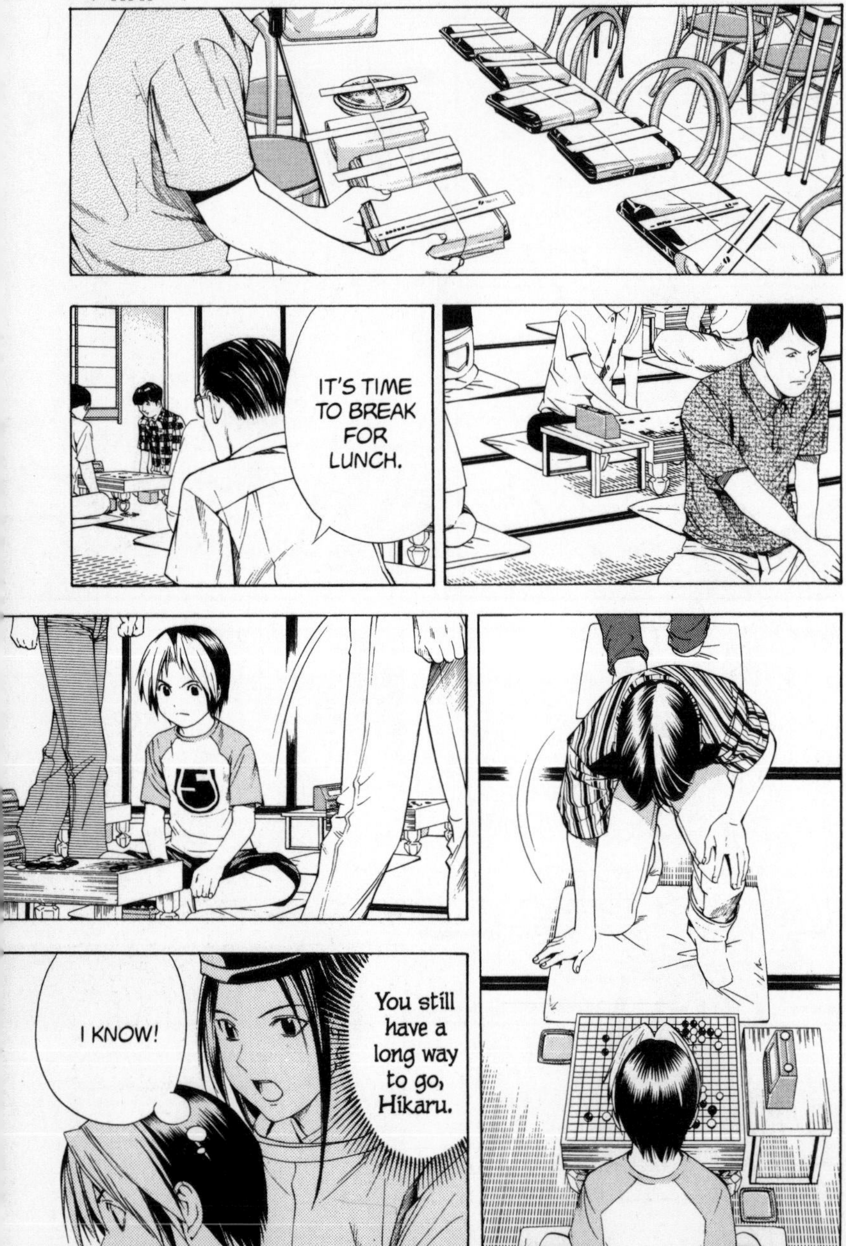
IT'S TIME TO BREAK FOR LUNCH.
You still have a long way to go, Hikaru.
I KNOW!

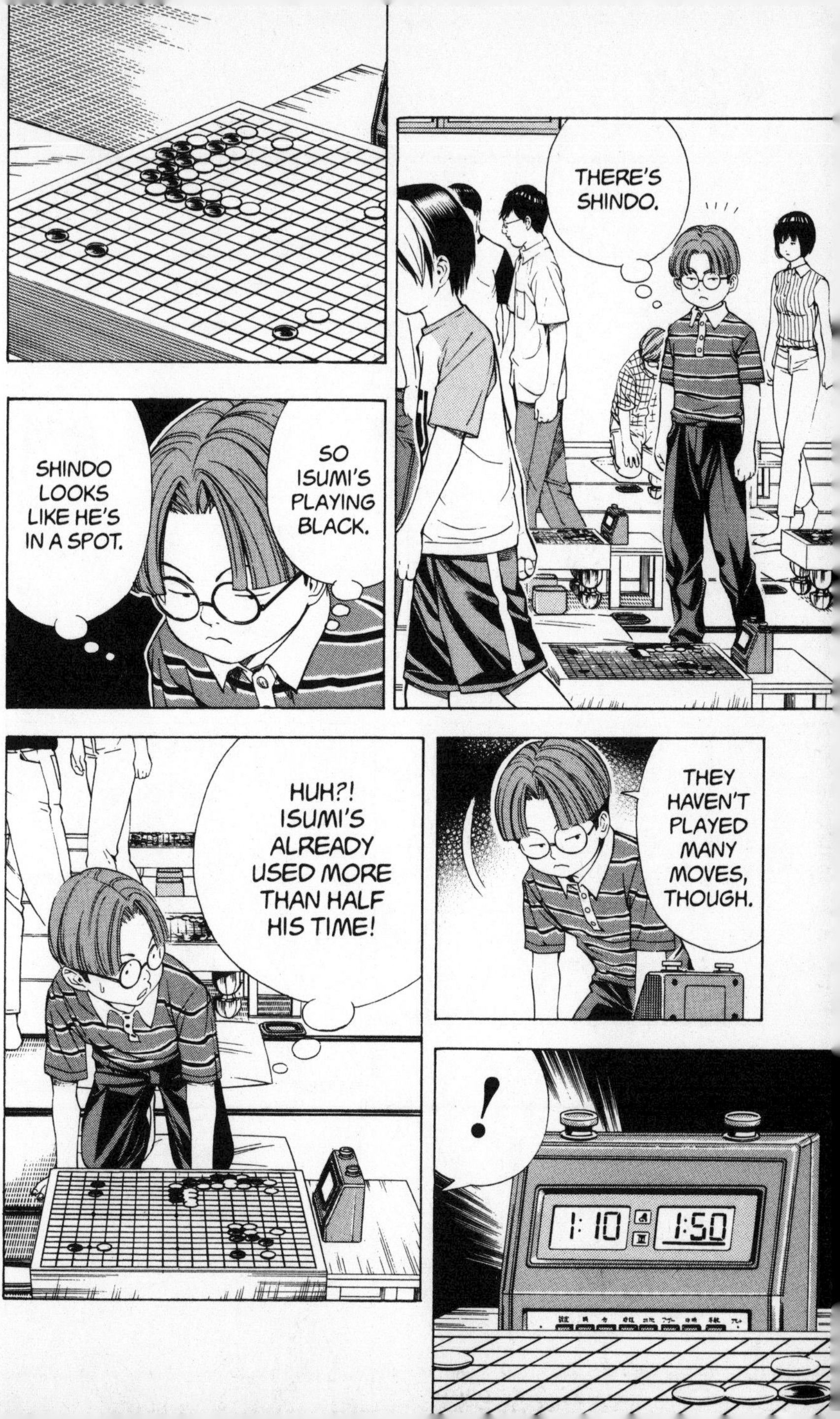
THERE'S SHINDO.
SO ISUMI'S PLAYING BLACK.
SHINDO LOOKS LIKE HE'S IN A SPOT.
THEY HAVEN'T PLAYED MANY MOVES, THOUGH.
!
1:10
1:50
HUH?! ISUMI'S ALREADY USED MORE THAN HALF HIS TIME!

READ THIS WAY

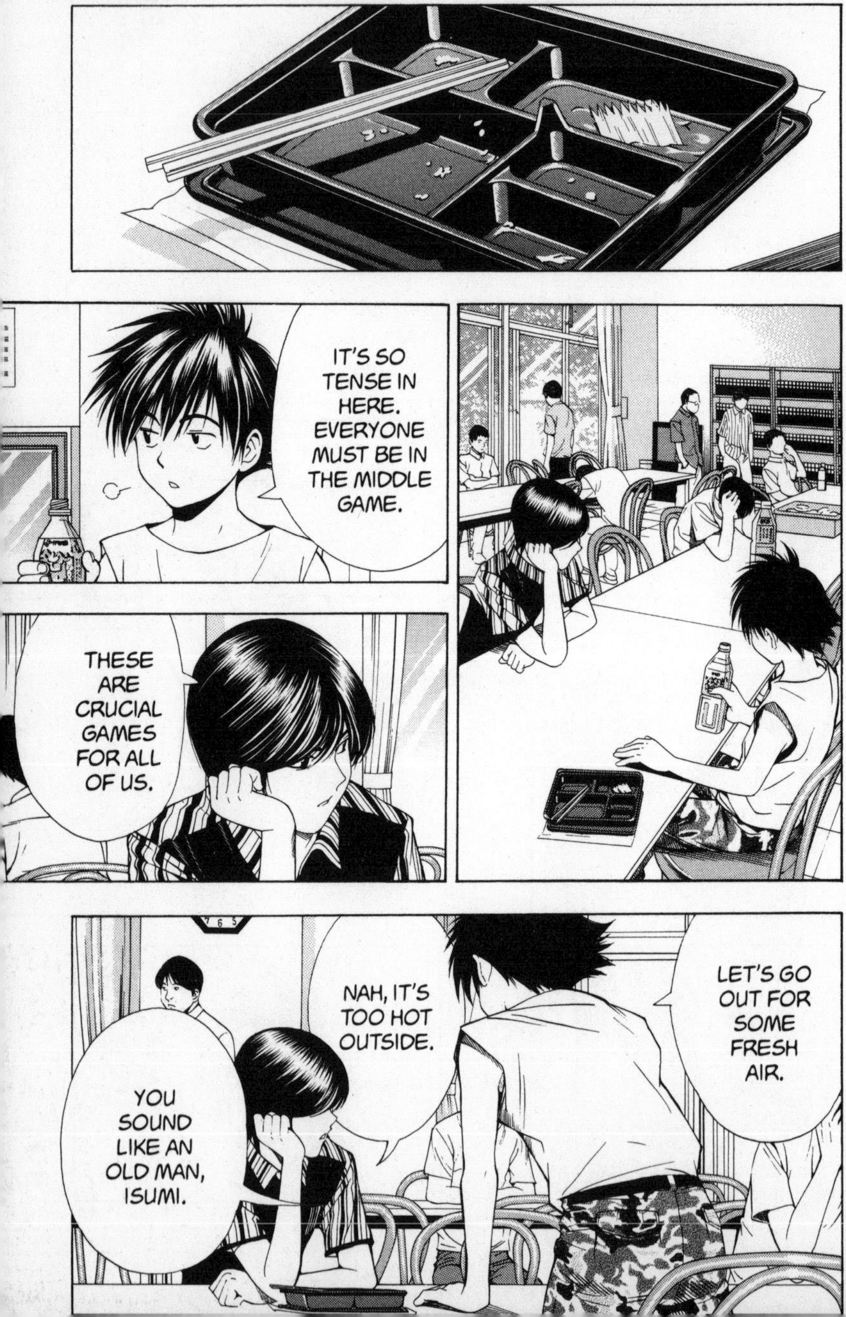
IT'S SO TENSE IN HERE. EVERYONE MUST BE IN THE MIDDLE GAME.
THESE ARE CRUCIAL GAMES FOR ALL OF US.
LET'S GO OUT FOR SOME FRESH AIR.
NAH, IT'S TOO HOT OUTSIDE.
YOU SOUND LIKE AN OLD MAN, ISUMI.

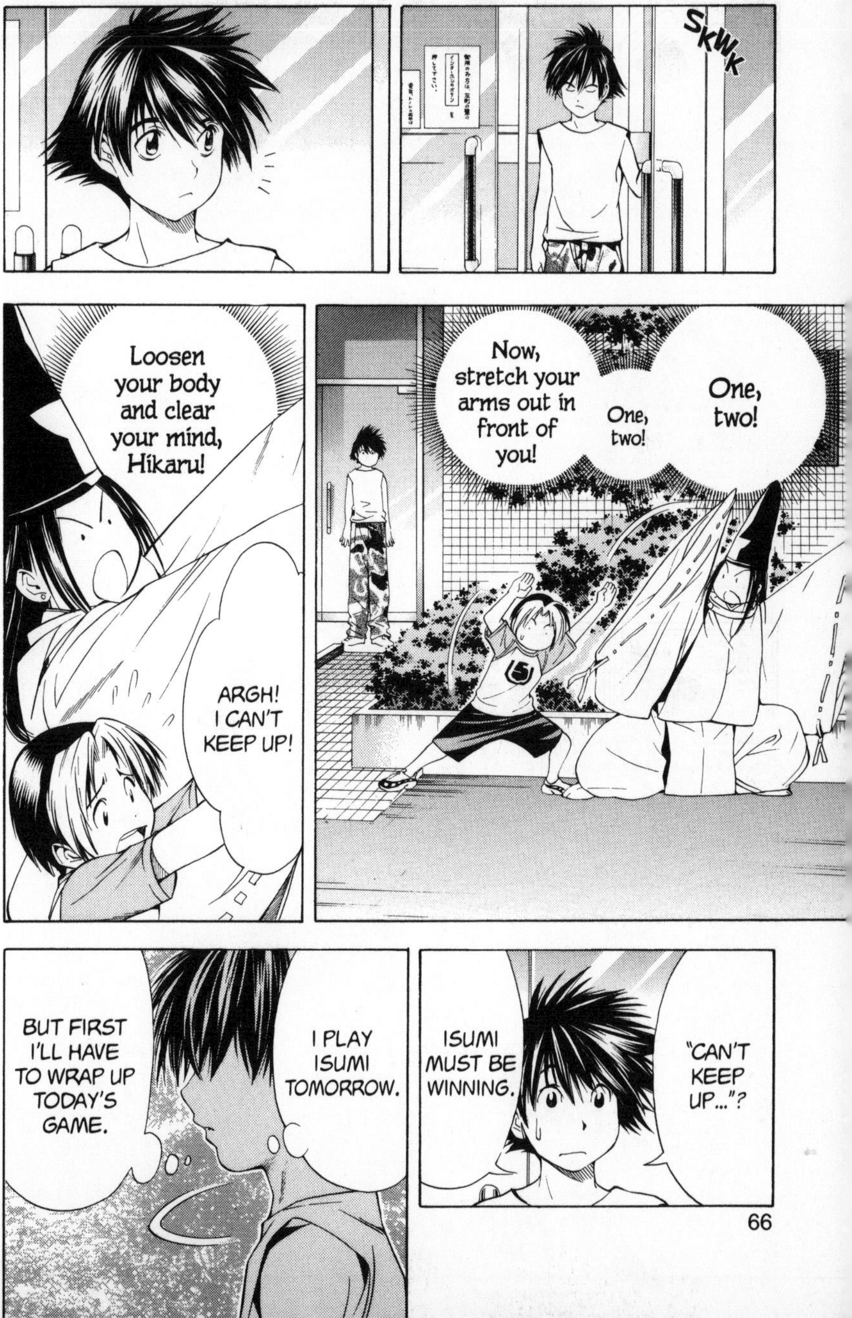
SKWK
Now, stretch your arms out in front of you!
One, two!
One, two!
Loosen your body and clear your mind, Hikaru!
ARGH! I CAN'T KEEP UP!
"CAN'T KEEP UP..."?
ISUMI MUST BE WINNING.
I PLAY ISUMI TOMORROW.
BUT FIRST I'LL HAVE TO WRAP UP TODAY'S GAME.

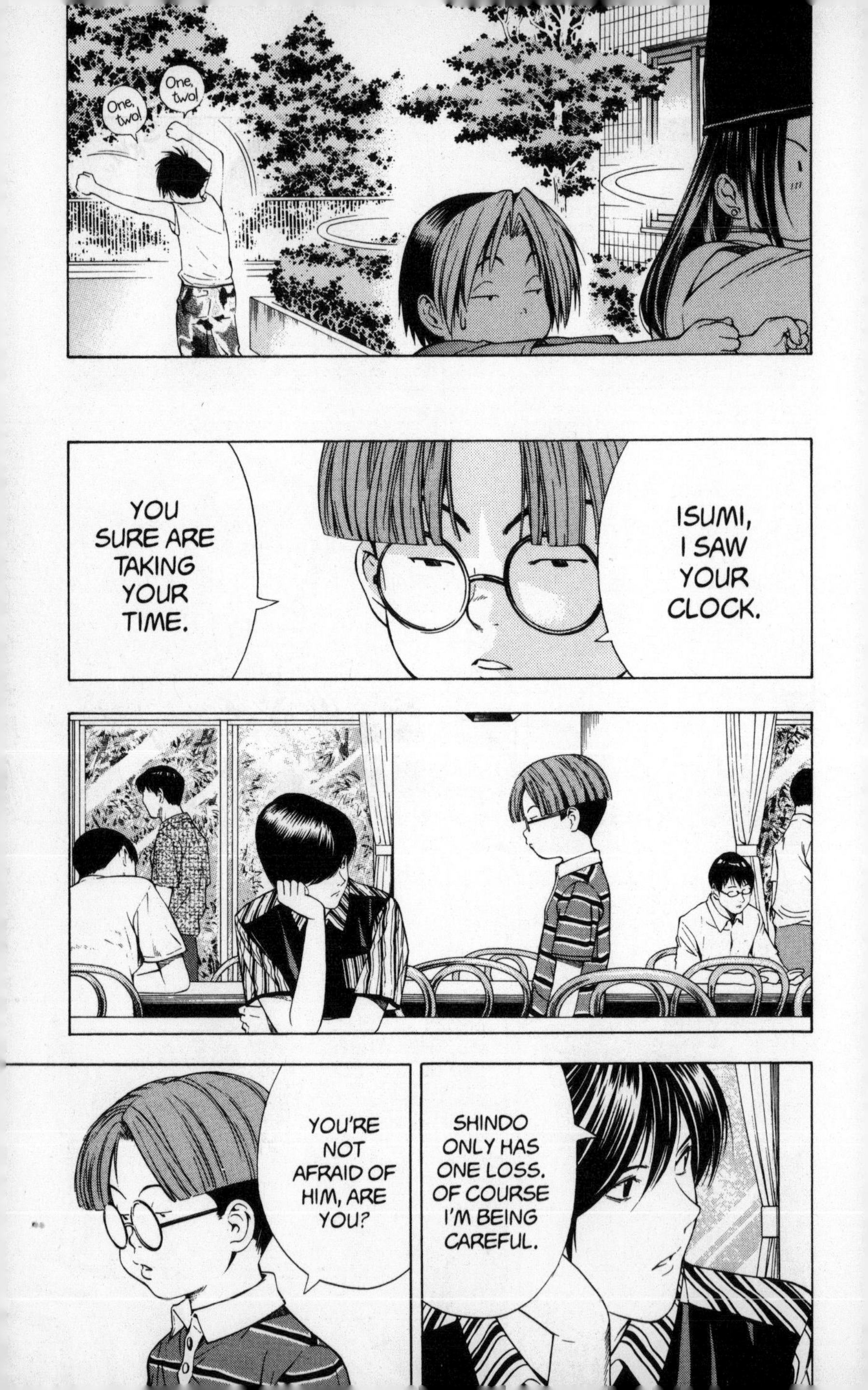
One, two!
One, two!
ISUMI, I SAW YOUR CLOCK.
YOU SURE ARE TAKING YOUR TIME.
SHINDO ONLY HAS ONE LOSS. OF COURSE I'M BEING CAREFUL.
YOU'RE NOT AFRAID OF HIM, ARE YOU?

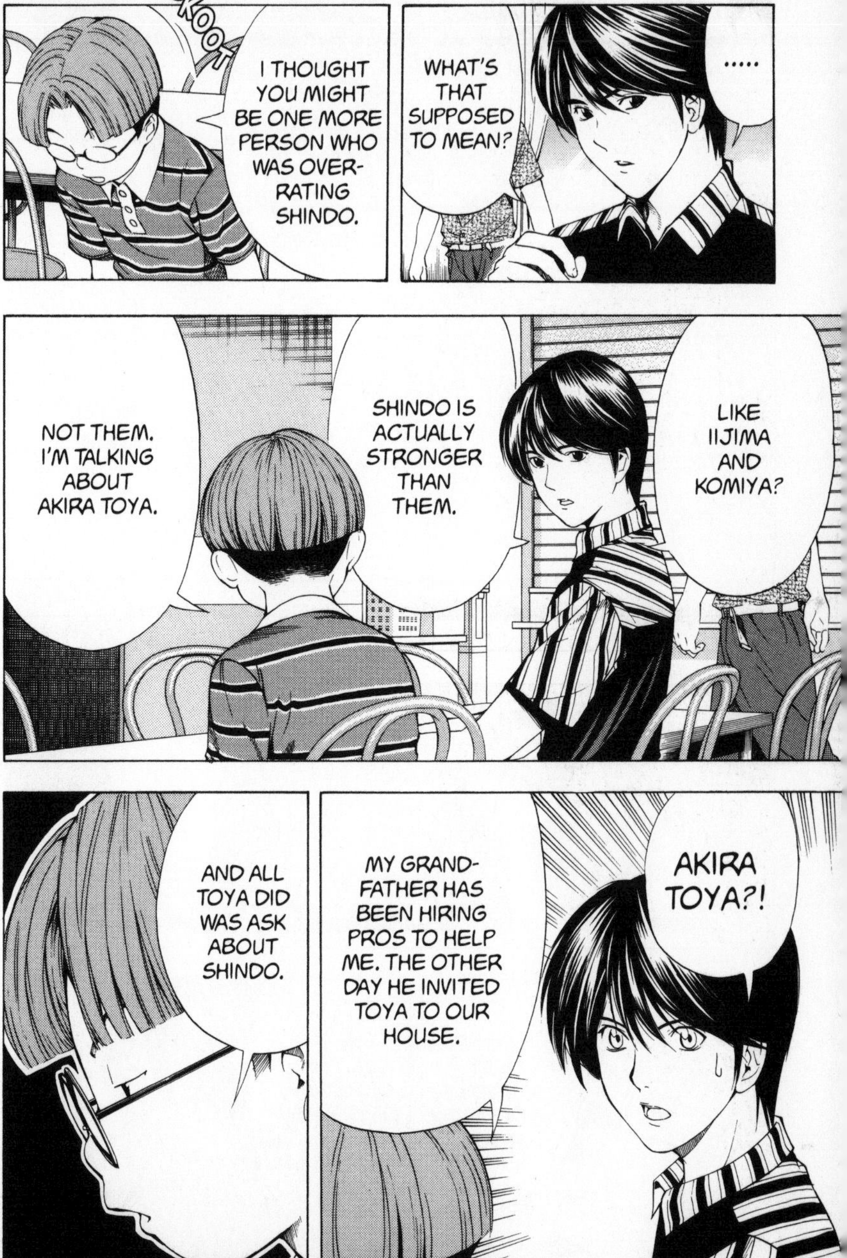
.....
WHAT'S THAT SUPPOSED TO MEAN?
SKOOT
I THOUGHT YOU MIGHT BE ONE MORE PERSON WHO WAS OVER-RATING SHINDO.
LIKE IIJIMA AND KOMIYA?
SHINDO IS ACTUALLY STRONGER THAN THEM.
NOT THEM. I'M TALKING ABOUT AKIRA TOYA.
AKIRA TOYA?!
MY GRAND-FATHER HAS BEEN HIRING PROS TO HELP ME. THE OTHER DAY HE INVITED TOYA TO OUR HOUSE.
AND ALL TOYA DID WAS ASK ABOUT SHINDO.

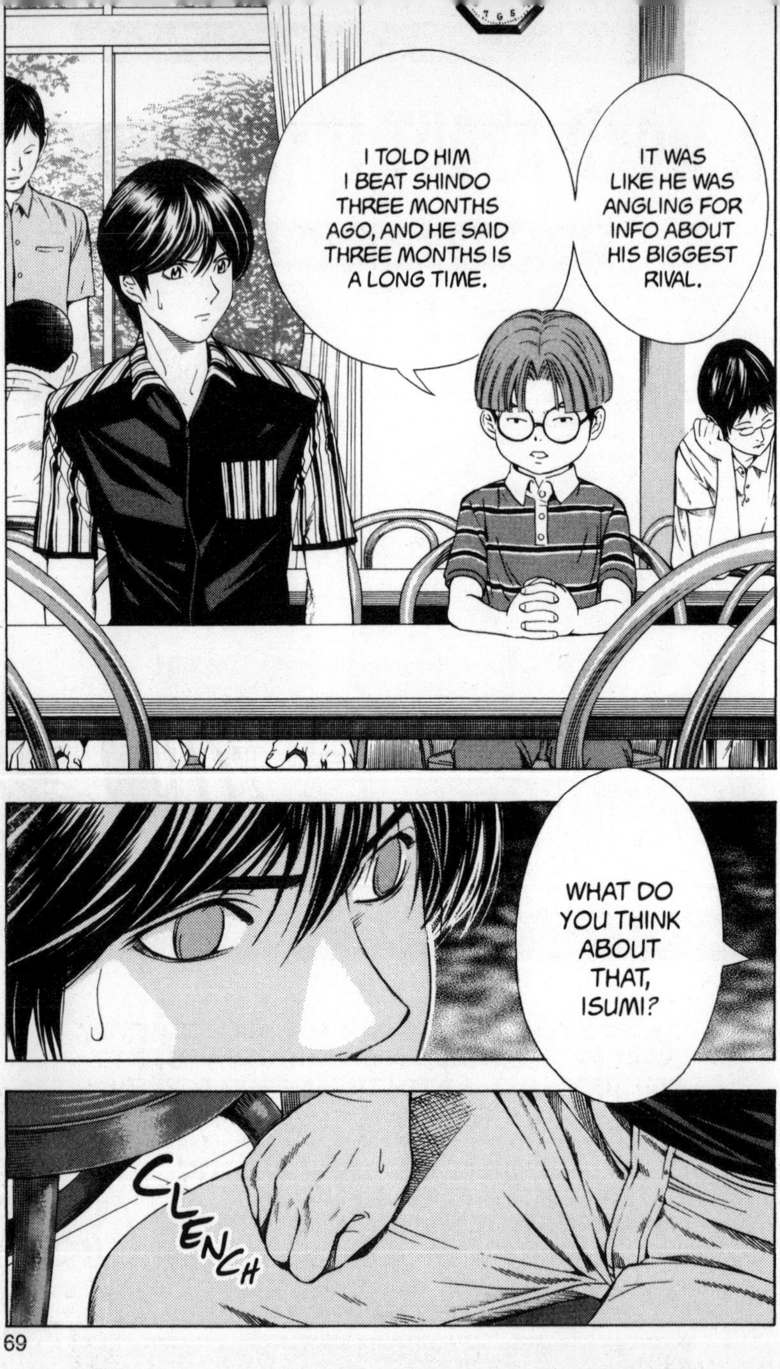
IT WAS LIKE HE WAS ANGLING FOR INFO ABOUT HIS BIGGEST RIVAL.
I TOLD HIM I BEAT SHINDO THREE MONTHS AGO, AND HE SAID THREE MONTHS IS A LONG TIME.
WHAT DO YOU THINK ABOUT THAT, ISUMI?
CLENCH

A WORD ABOUT HIKARU NO GO

JAPAN GO ASSOCIATION STUDY CENTER

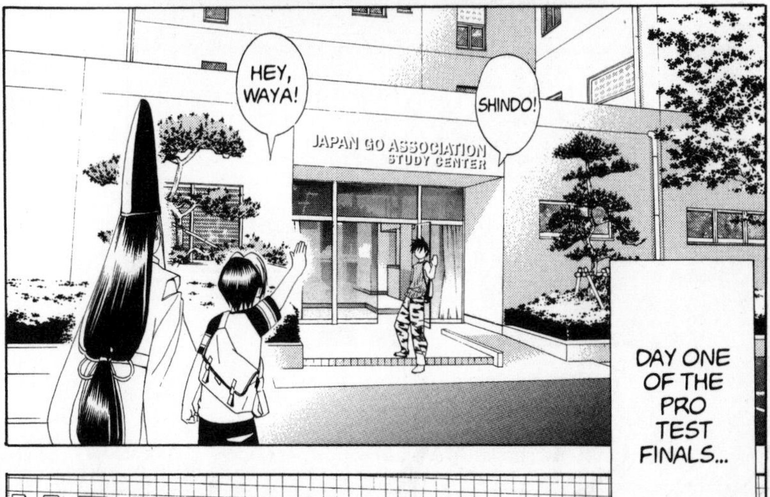
HEY, WAYA!
SHINDO!
JAPAN GO ASSOCIATION STUDY CENTER
DAY ONE OF THE PRO TEST FINALS...

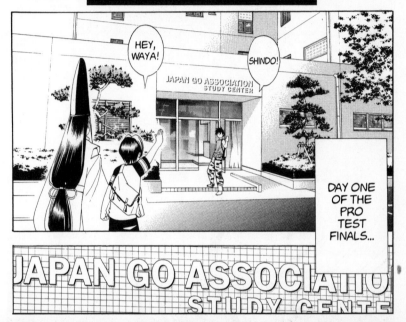

THE PRO TEST IS HELD IN A FORMER DORMITORY. INSEI FROM OUTSIDE THE TOKYO AREA USED TO STAY HERE, ALONG WITH THOSE FROM FOREIGN COUNTRIES.

SOMETIMES, INSEI WHO LIVED IN TOKYO WOULD SPEND THE NIGHT HERE ON WEEKENDS. MUST HAVE BEEN LOTS OF FUN!

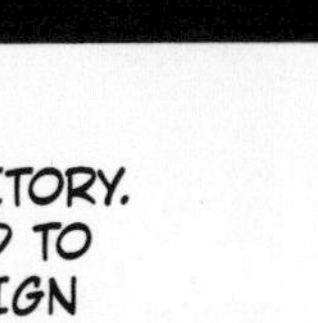

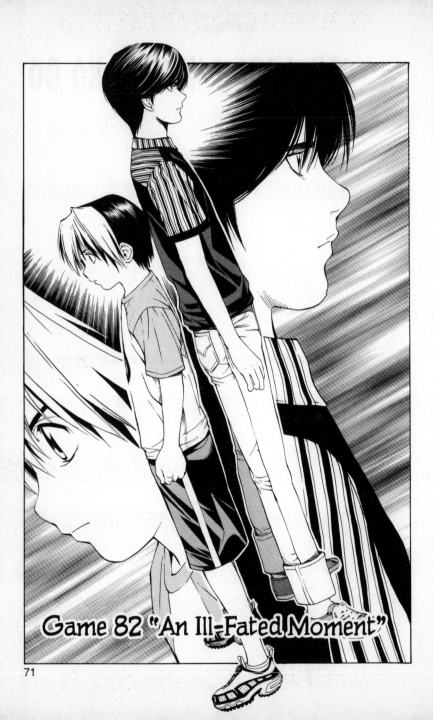

Game 82 "An Ill-Fated Moment"

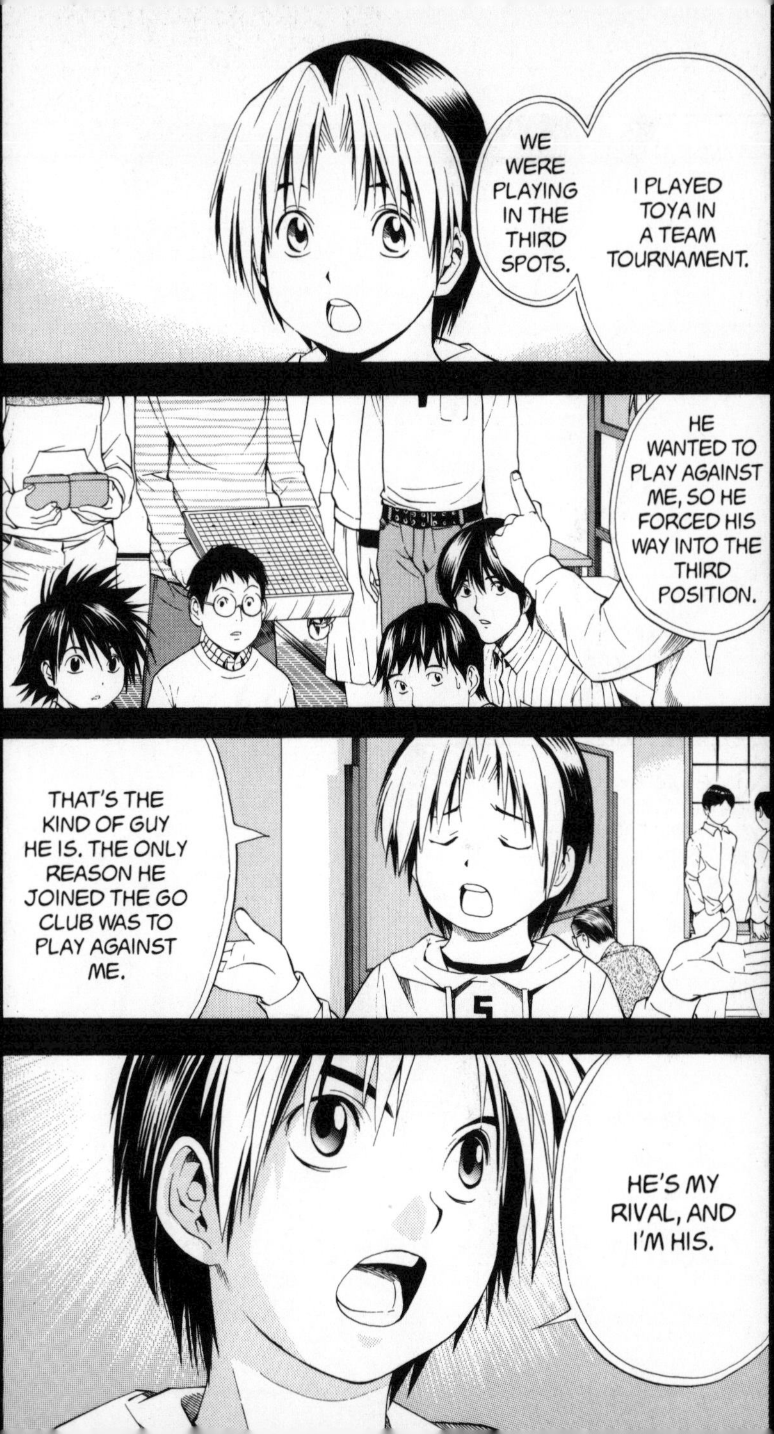
I PLAYED TOYA IN A TEAM TOURNAMENT.
WE WERE PLAYING IN THE THIRD SPOTS.
HE WANTED TO PLAY AGAINST ME, SO HE FORCED HIS WAY INTO THE THIRD POSITION.
THAT'S THE KIND OF GUY HE IS. THE ONLY REASON HE JOINED THE GO CLUB WAS TO PLAY AGAINST ME.
HE'S MY RIVAL, AND I'M HIS.

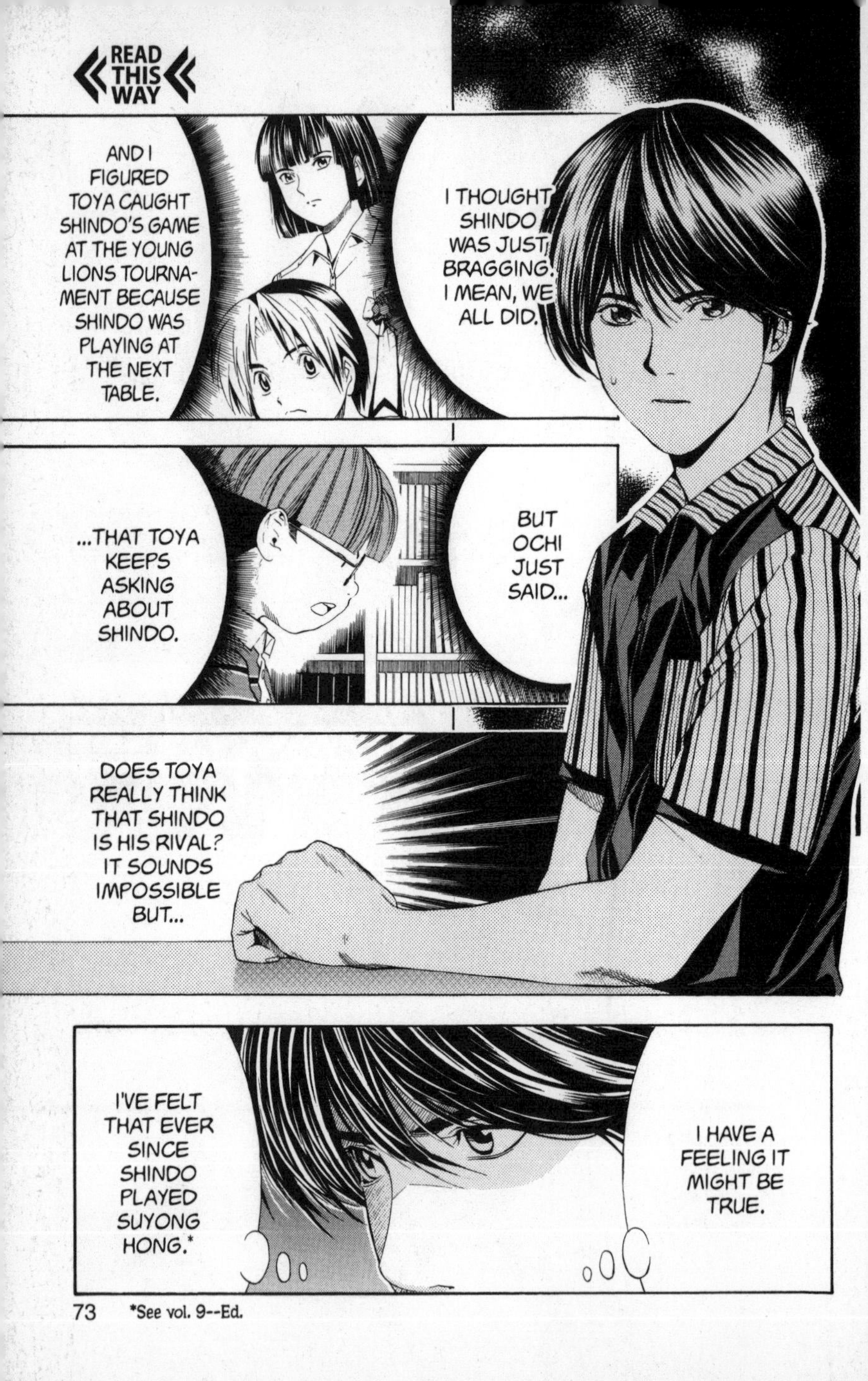
READ THIS WAY
I THOUGHT SHINDO WAS JUST BRAGGING. I MEAN, WE ALL DID.
AND I FIGURED TOYA CAUGHT SHINDO'S GAME AT THE YOUNG LIONS TOURNAMENT BECAUSE SHINDO WAS PLAYING AT THE NEXT TABLE.
BUT OCHI JUST SAID...
...THAT TOYA KEEPS ASKING ABOUT SHINDO.
DOES TOYA REALLY THINK THAT SHINDO IS HIS RIVAL? IT SOUNDS IMPOSSIBLE BUT...
I HAVE A FEELING IT MIGHT BE TRUE.
I'VE FELT THAT EVER SINCE SHINDO PLAYED SUYONG HONG.*

*See vol. 9--Ed.

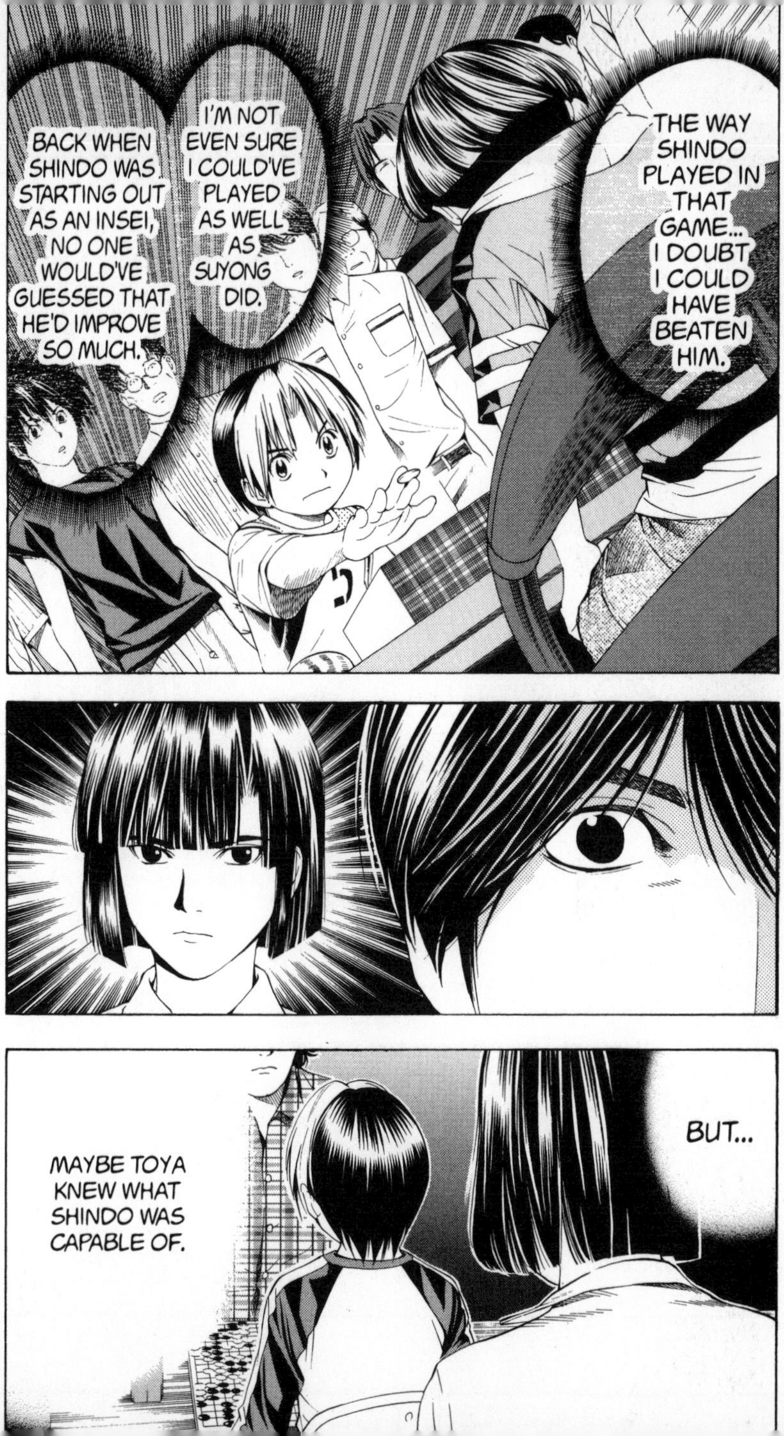
THE WAY SHINDO PLAYED IN THAT GAME... I DOUBT I COULD HAVE BEATEN HIM.
I'M NOT EVEN SURE I COULD'VE PLAYED AS WELL AS SUYONG DID.
BACK WHEN SHINDO WAS STARTING OUT AS AN INSEI, NO ONE WOULD'VE GUESSED THAT HE'D IMPROVE SO MUCH.
BUT...
MAYBE TOYA KNEW WHAT SHINDO WAS CAPABLE OF.

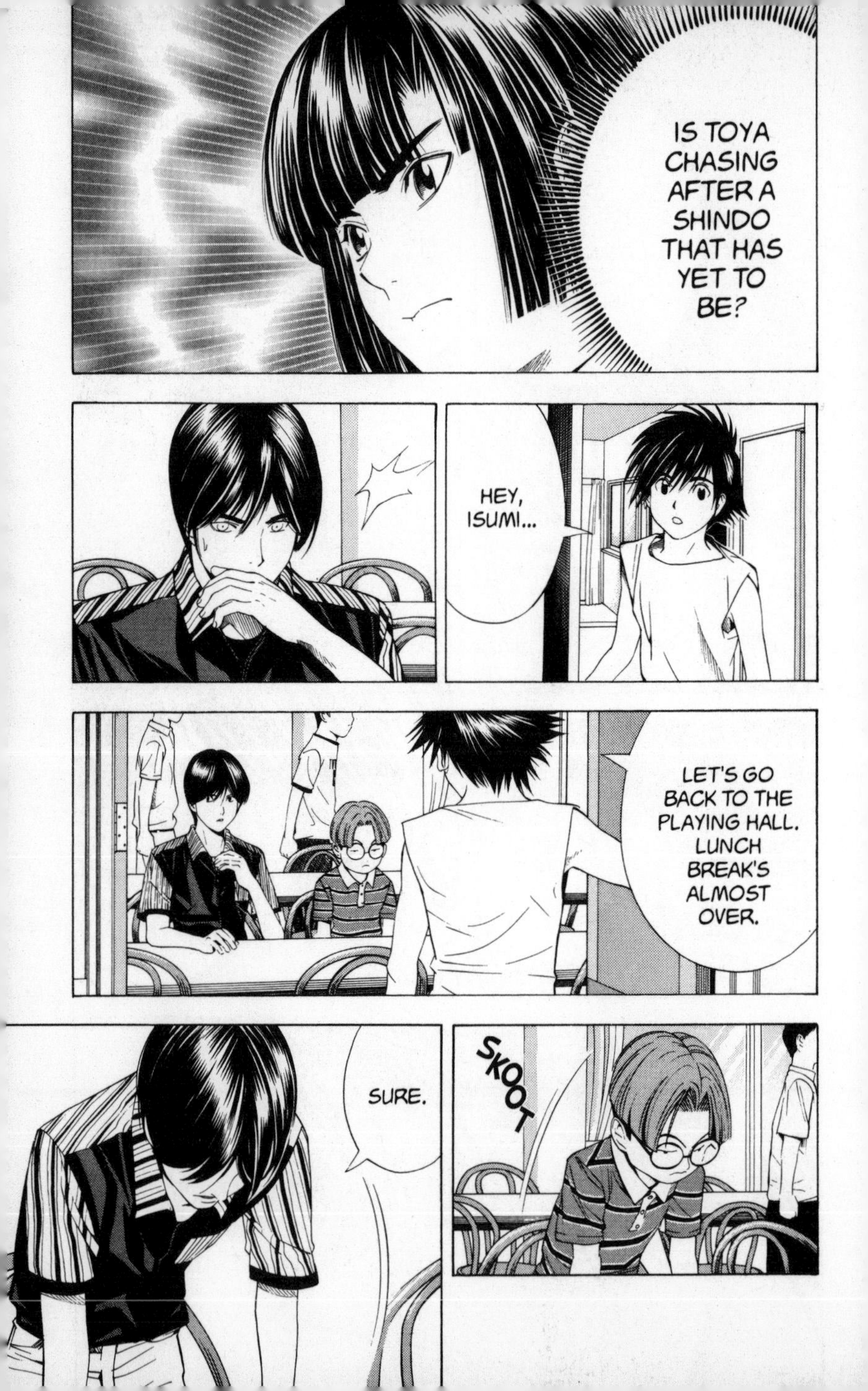
IS TOYA CHASING AFTER A SHINDO THAT HAS YET TO BE?
HEY, ISUMI...
LET'S GO BACK TO THE PLAYING HALL. LUNCH BREAK'S ALMOST OVER.
SKOOT
SURE.

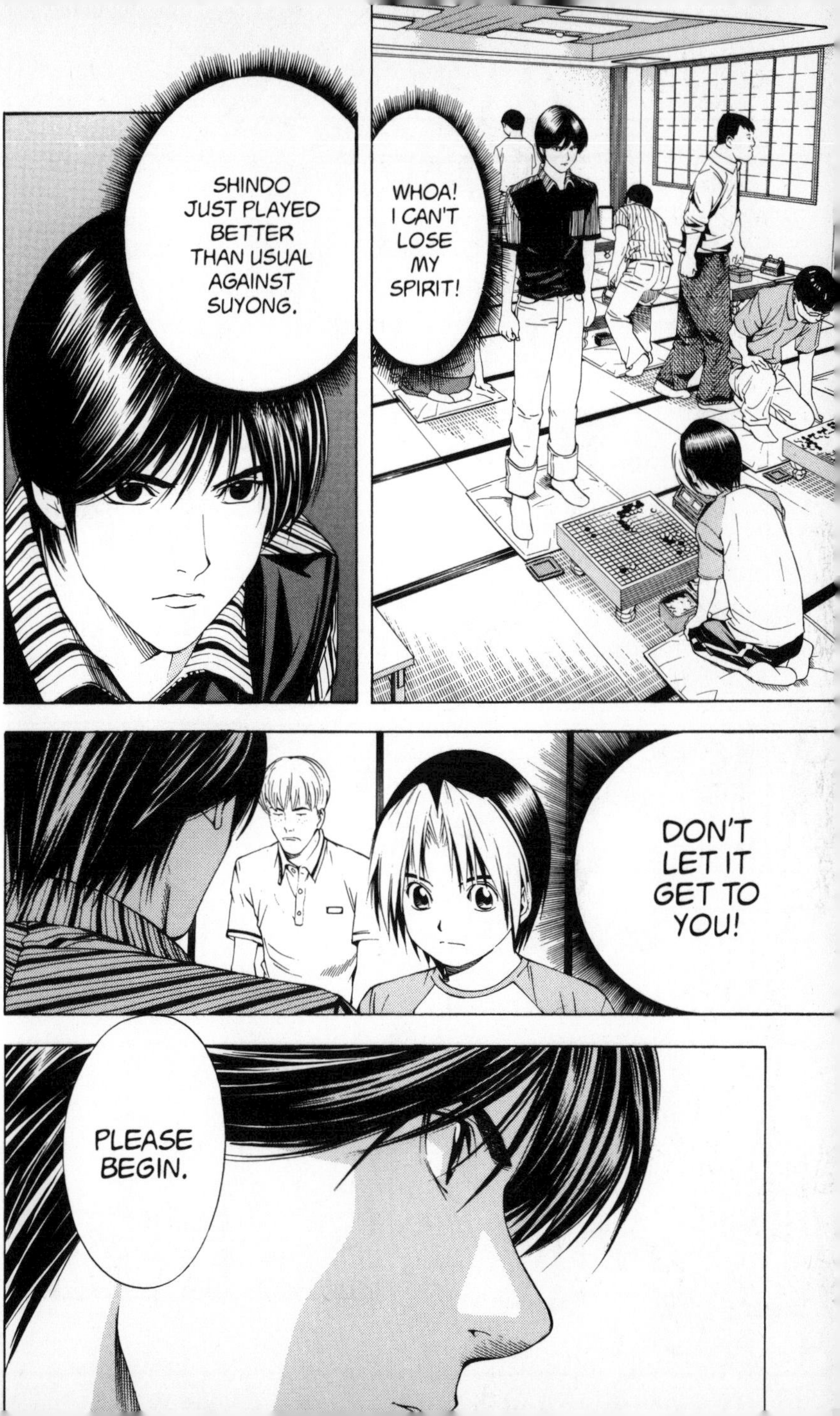
WHOA! I CAN'T LOSE MY SPIRIT!
SHINDO JUST PLAYED BETTER THAN USUAL AGAINST SUYONG.
DON'T LET IT GET TO YOU!
PLEASE BEGIN.

READ THIS WAY

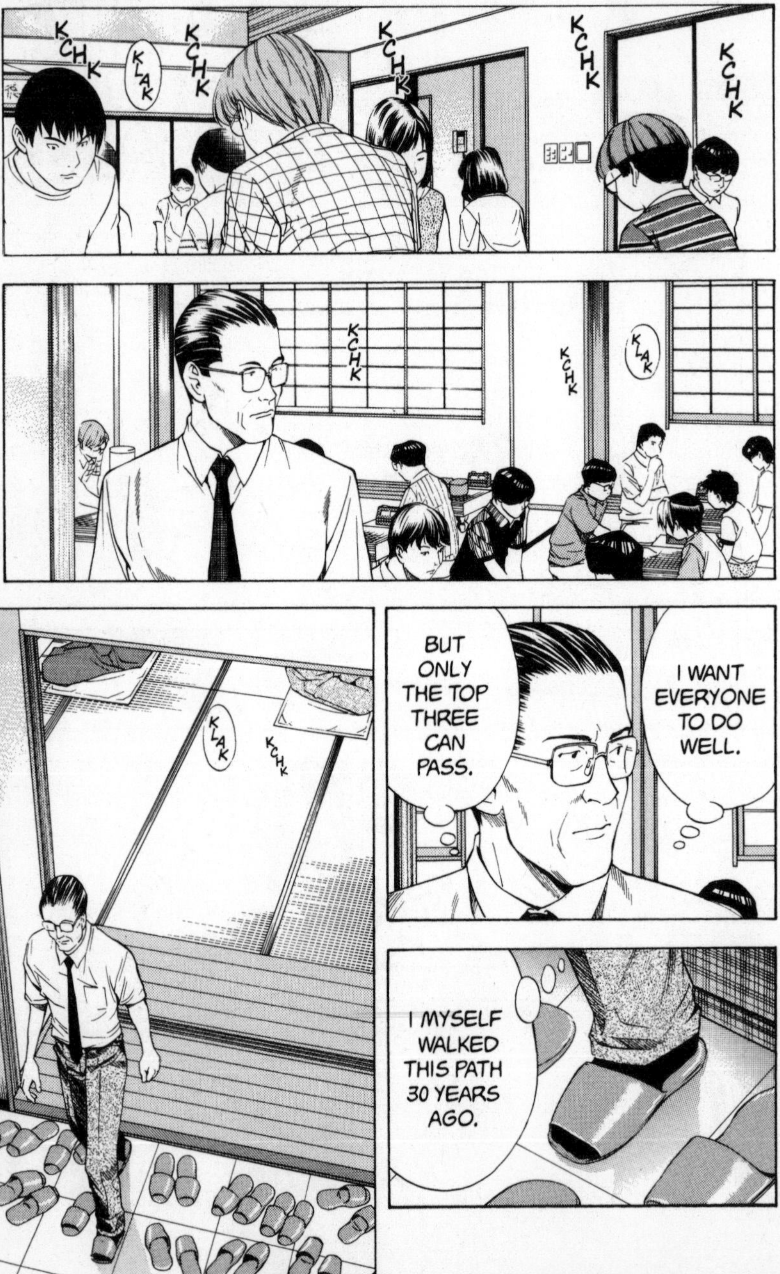
KCHK
KCHK
KCHK
KCHK
KLAK
KCHK
KLAK
KCHK
KCHK
I WANT EVERYONE TO DO WELL.
BUT ONLY THE TOP THREE CAN PASS.
I MYSELF WALKED THIS PATH 30 YEARS AGO.
KCHK
KLAK

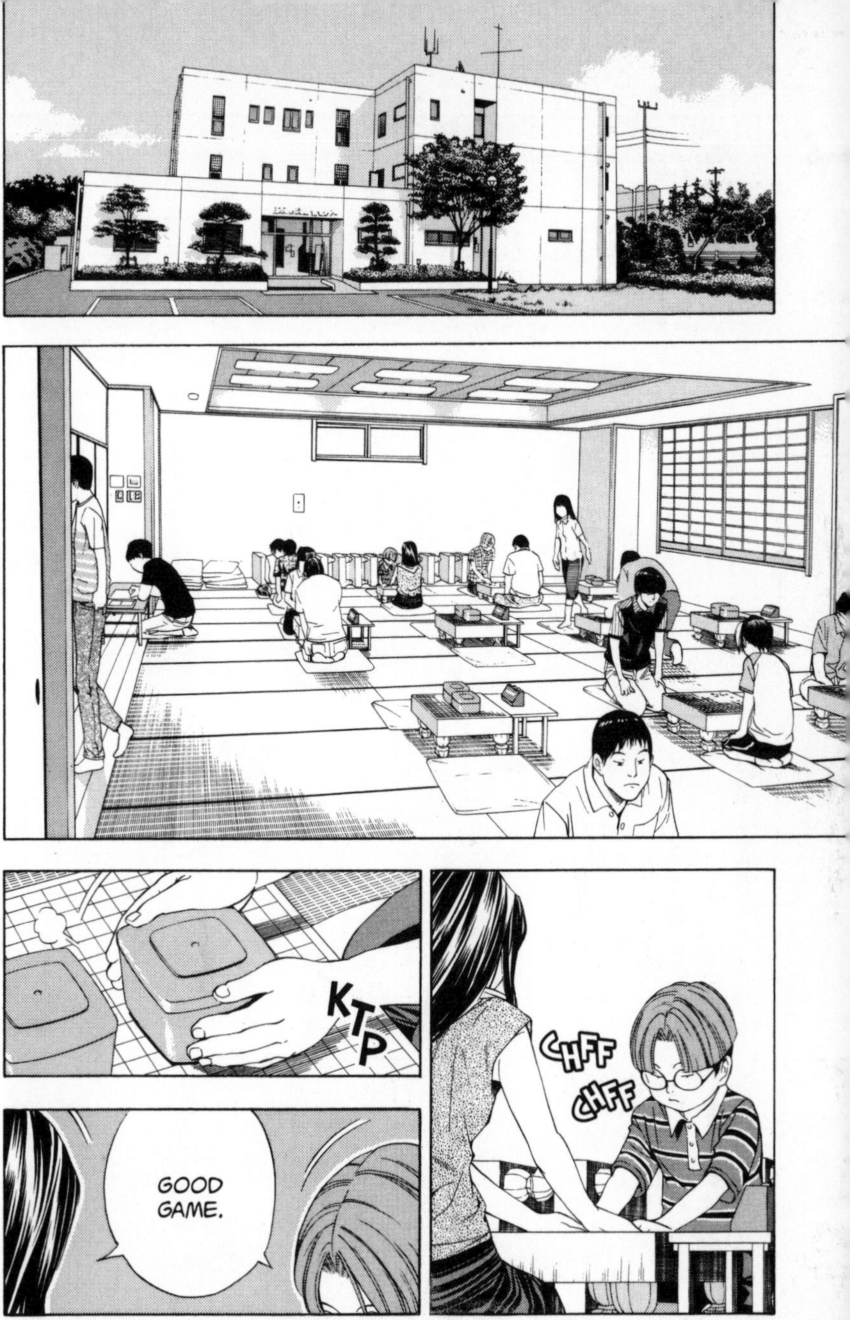
CHFF
CHFF
KTP
GOOD GAME.

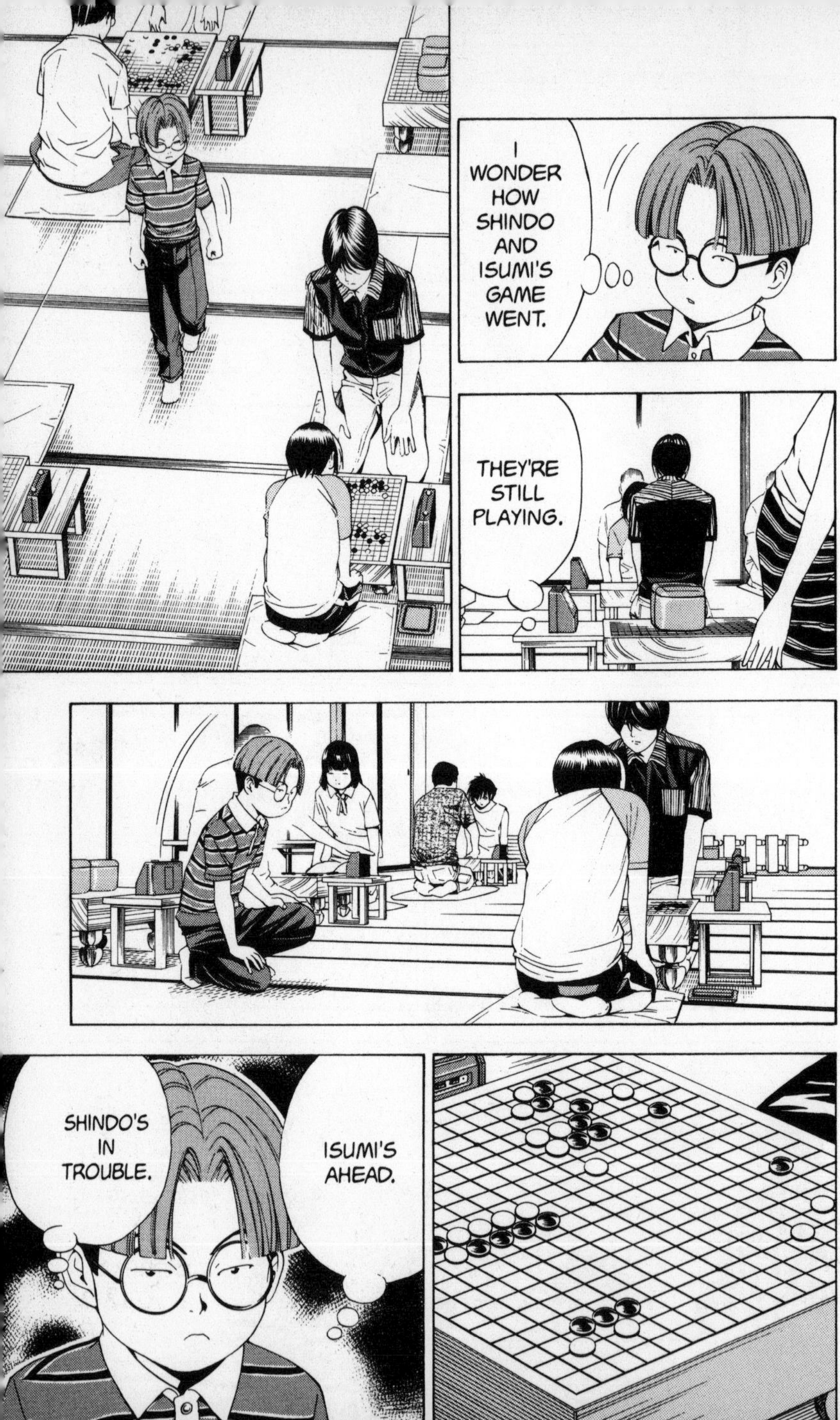
I WONDER HOW SHINDO AND ISUMI'S GAME WENT.
THEY'RE STILL PLAYING.
ISUMI'S AHEAD.
SHINDO'S IN TROUBLE.

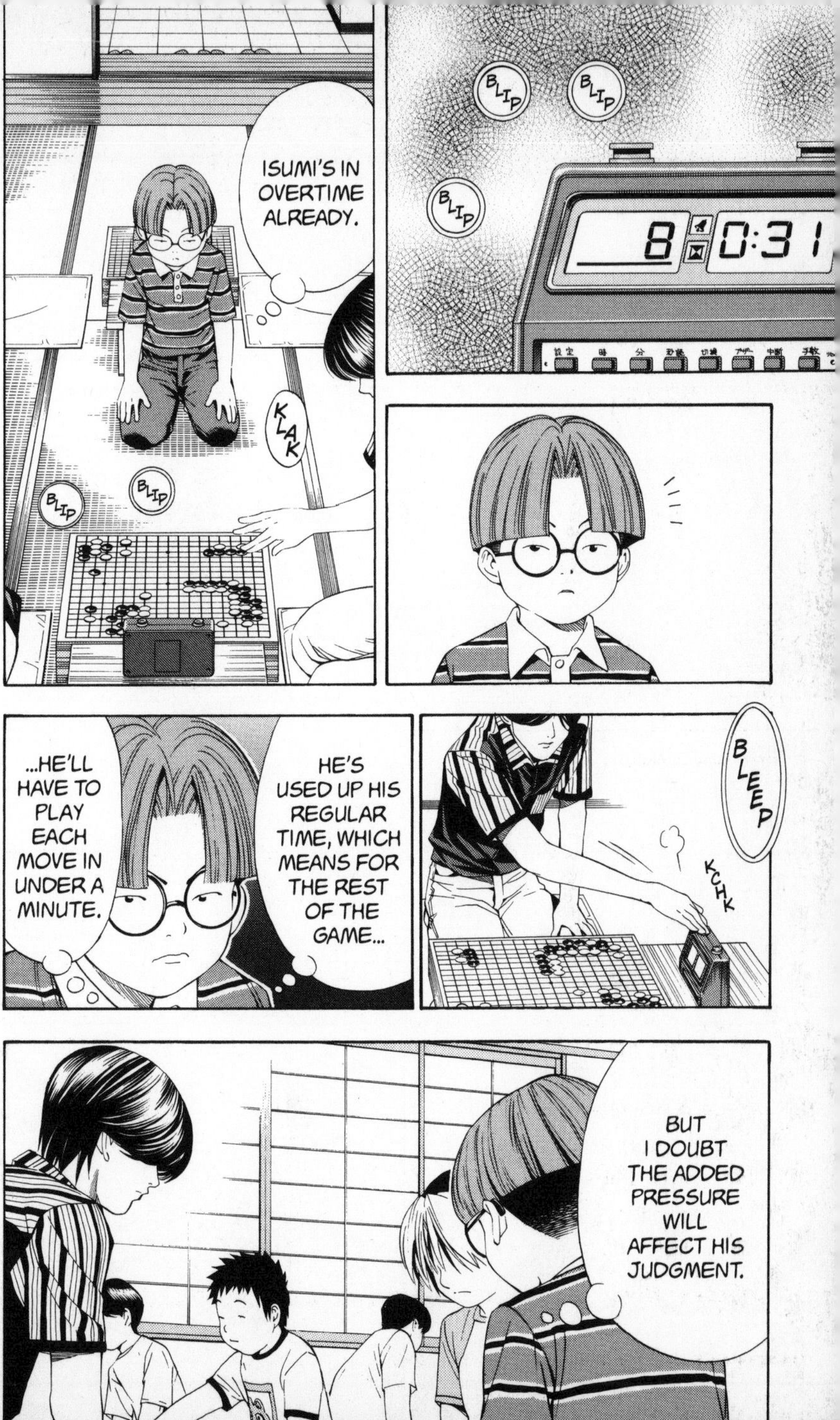
BLIP
BLIP
BLIP
8 0:31
ISUMI'S IN OVERTIME ALREADY.
KLAK
BLIP
BLIP
BLEEP
KCHK
HE'S USED UP HIS REGULAR TIME, WHICH MEANS FOR THE REST OF THE GAME...
...HE'LL HAVE TO PLAY EACH MOVE IN UNDER A MINUTE.
BUT I DOUBT THE ADDED PRESSURE WILL AFFECT HIS JUDGMENT.

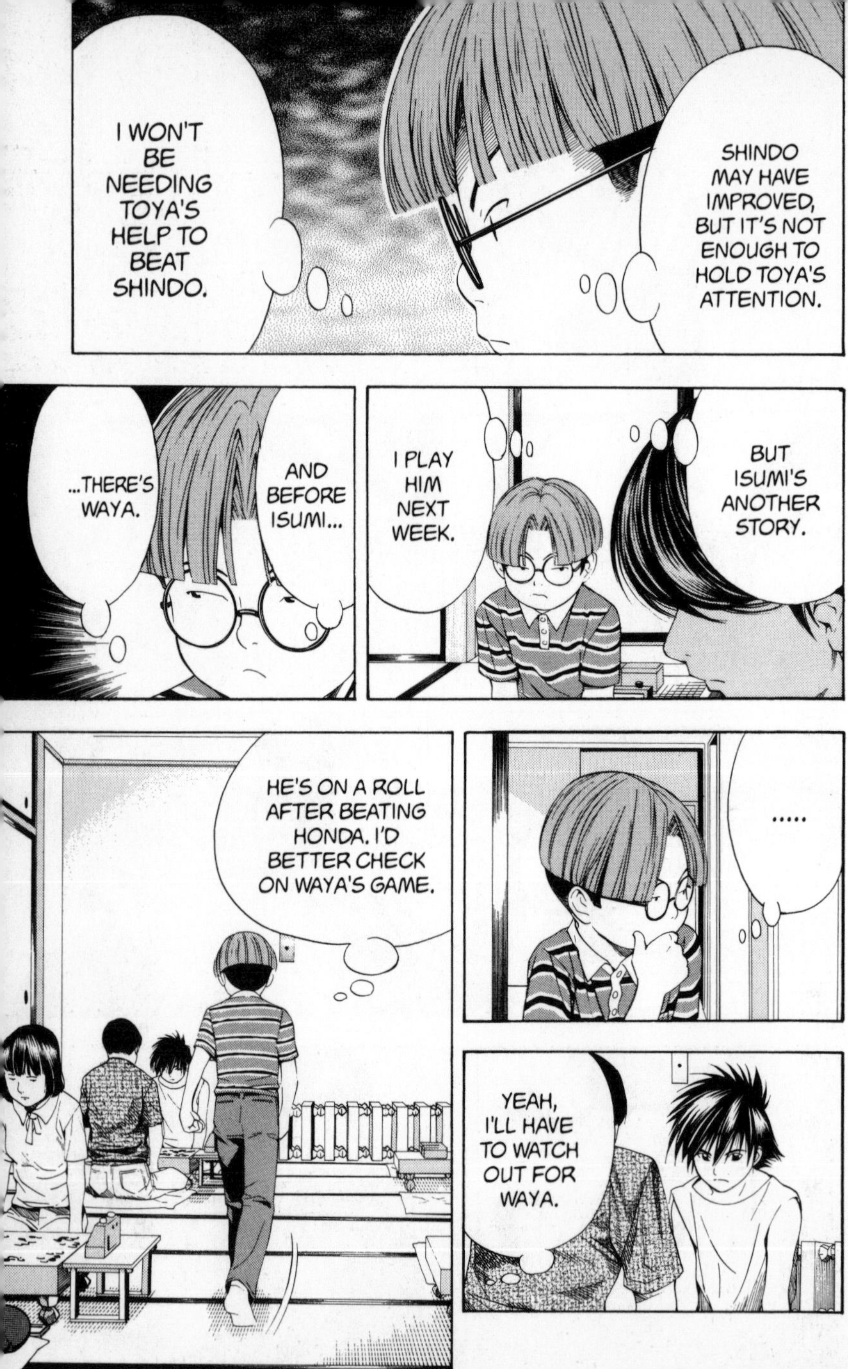
SHINDO MAY HAVE IMPROVED, BUT IT'S NOT ENOUGH TO HOLD TOYA'S ATTENTION.
I WON'T BE NEEDING TOYA'S HELP TO BEAT SHINDO.
BUT ISUMI'S ANOTHER STORY.
I PLAY HIM NEXT WEEK.
AND BEFORE ISUMI...
...THERE'S WAYA.
.....
YEAH, I'LL HAVE TO WATCH OUT FOR WAYA.
HE'S ON A ROLL AFTER BEATING HONDA. I'D BETTER CHECK ON WAYA'S GAME.

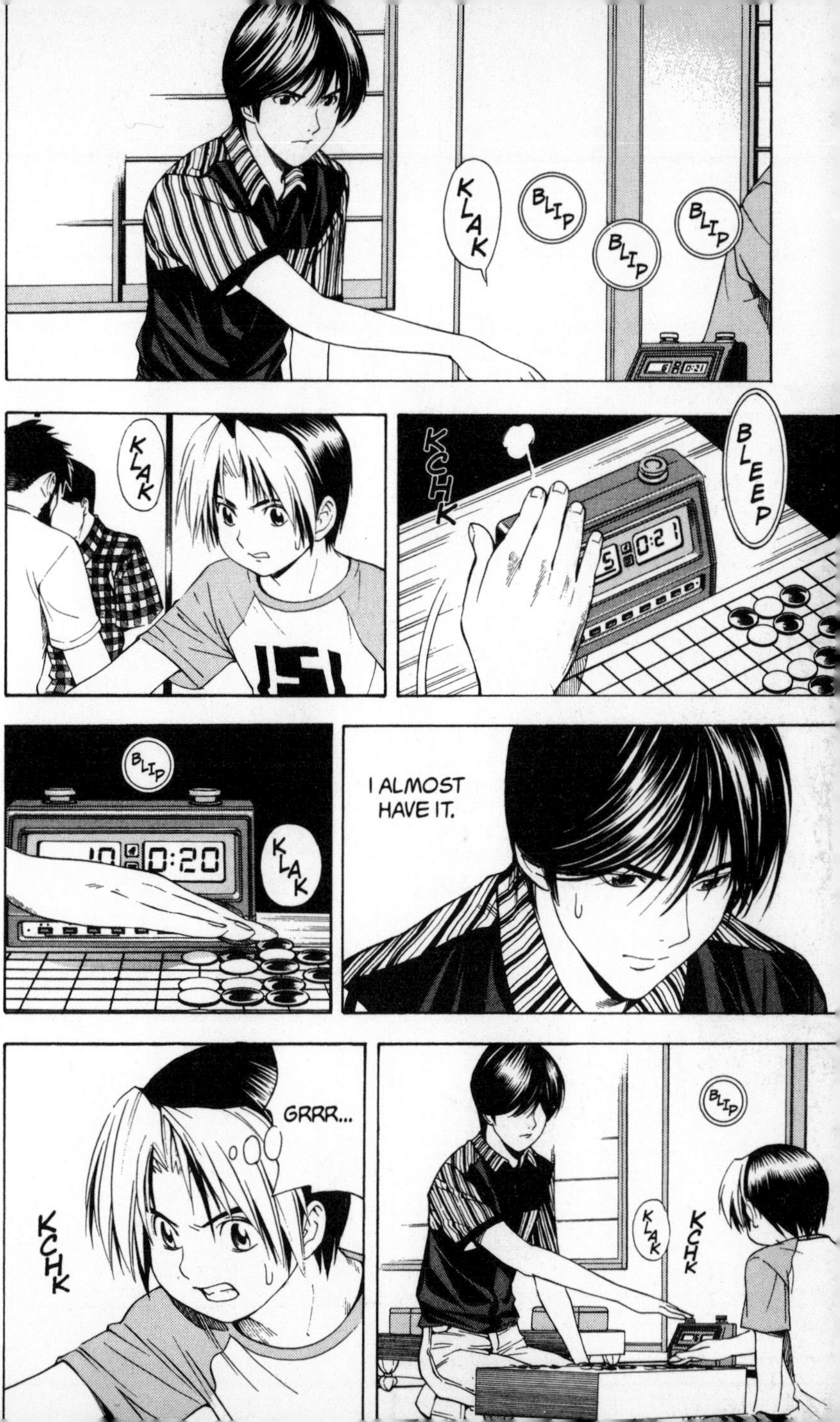
BLIP
BLIP
BLIP
KLAK
BLEEP
KCHK
KLAK
I ALMOST HAVE IT.
KLAK
BLIP
BLIP
KCHK
KLAK
GRRR...
KCHK

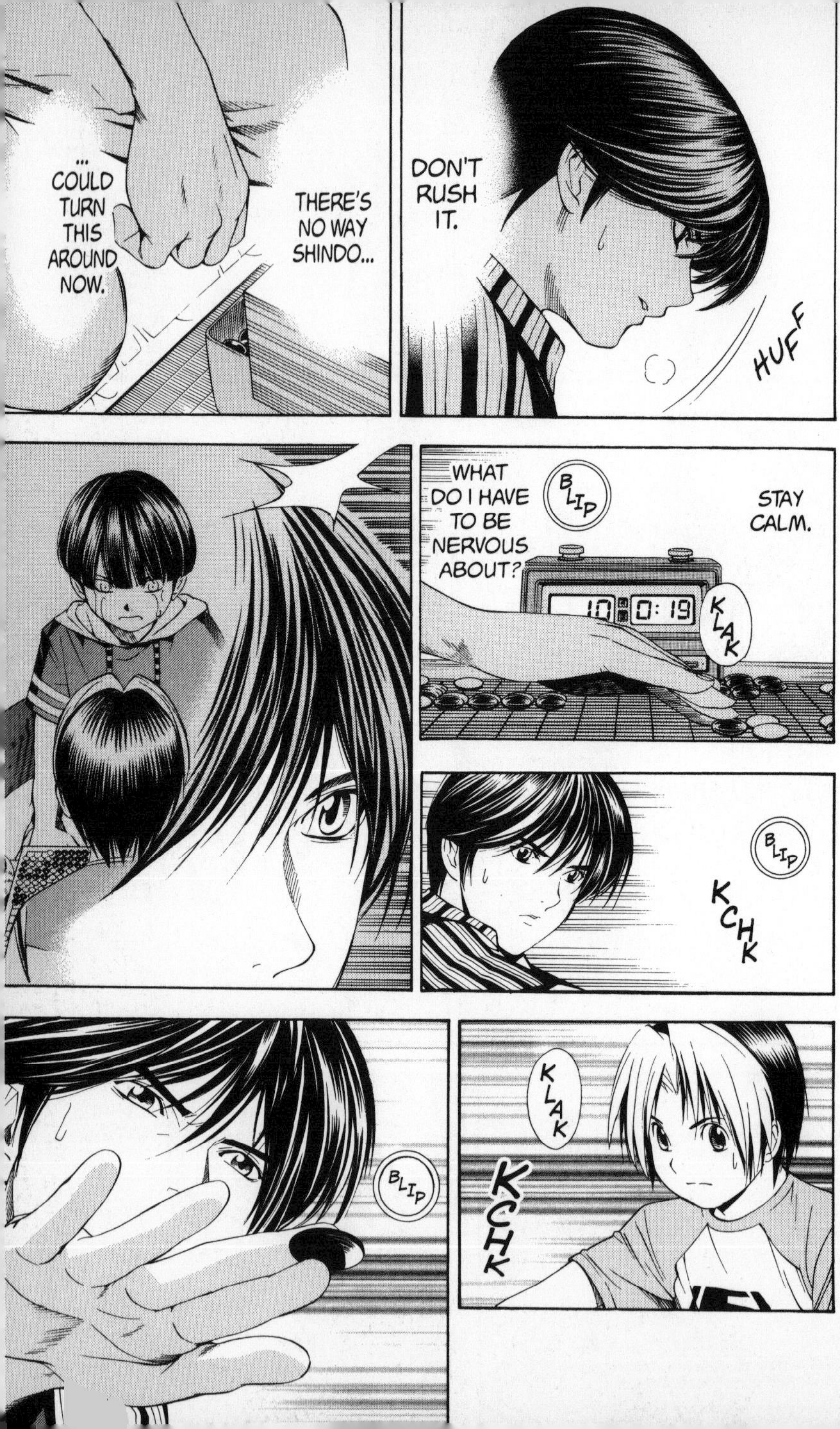
DON'T RUSH IT.
HUFF
THERE'S NO WAY SHINDO...
...COULD TURN THIS AROUND NOW.
STAY CALM.
BLIP
WHAT DO I HAVE TO BE NERVOUS ABOUT?
KLAK
BLIP
KCHK
KLAK
KCHK
BLIP

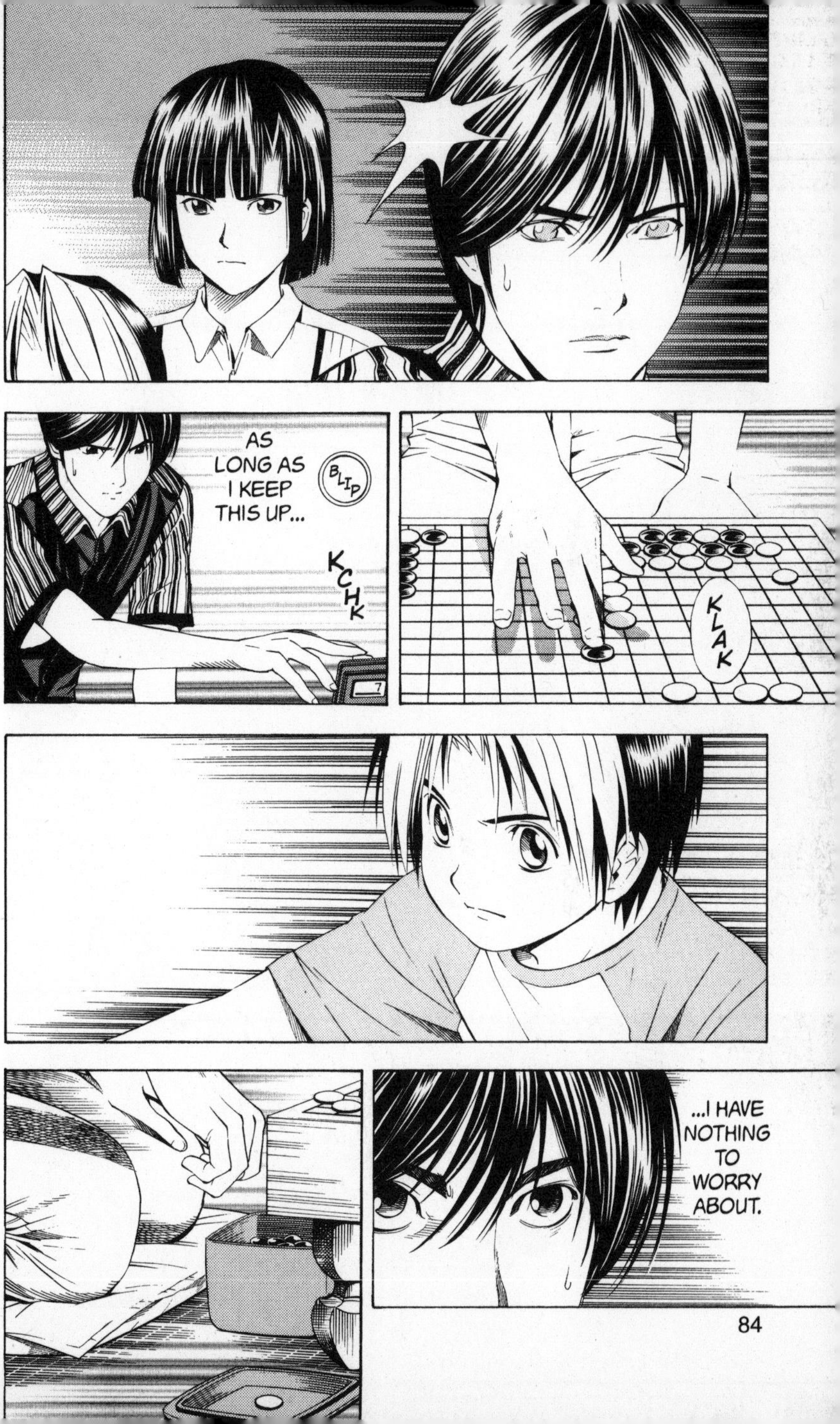
KLAK
AS LONG AS I KEEP THIS UP...
BLIP
KCHK
...I HAVE NOTHING TO WORRY ABOUT.

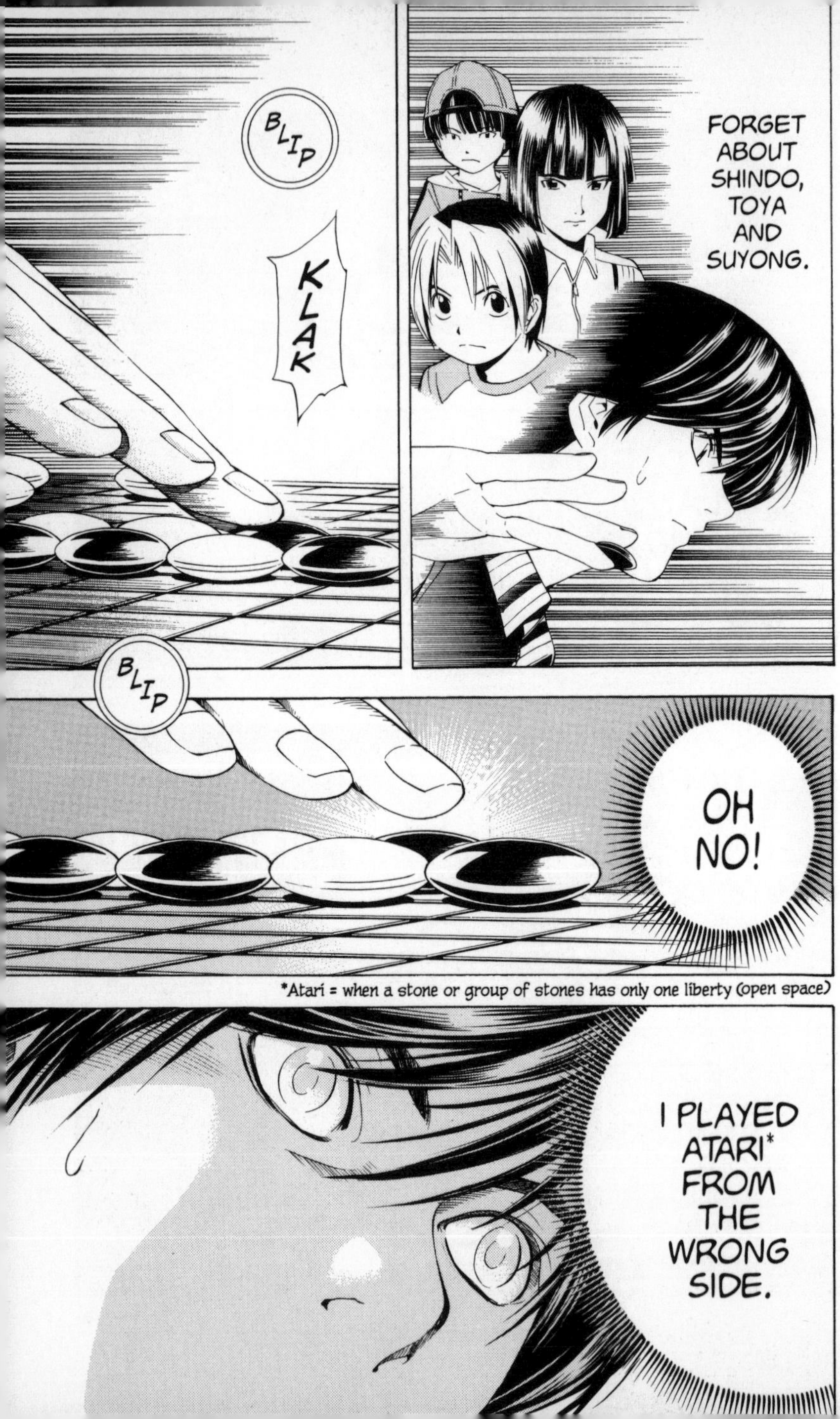
FORGET ABOUT SHINDO, TOYA AND SUYONG.
BLIP
KLAK
BLIP
OH NO!
I PLAYED ATARI* FROM THE WRONG SIDE.

*Atari = when a stone or group of stones has only one liberty (open space)

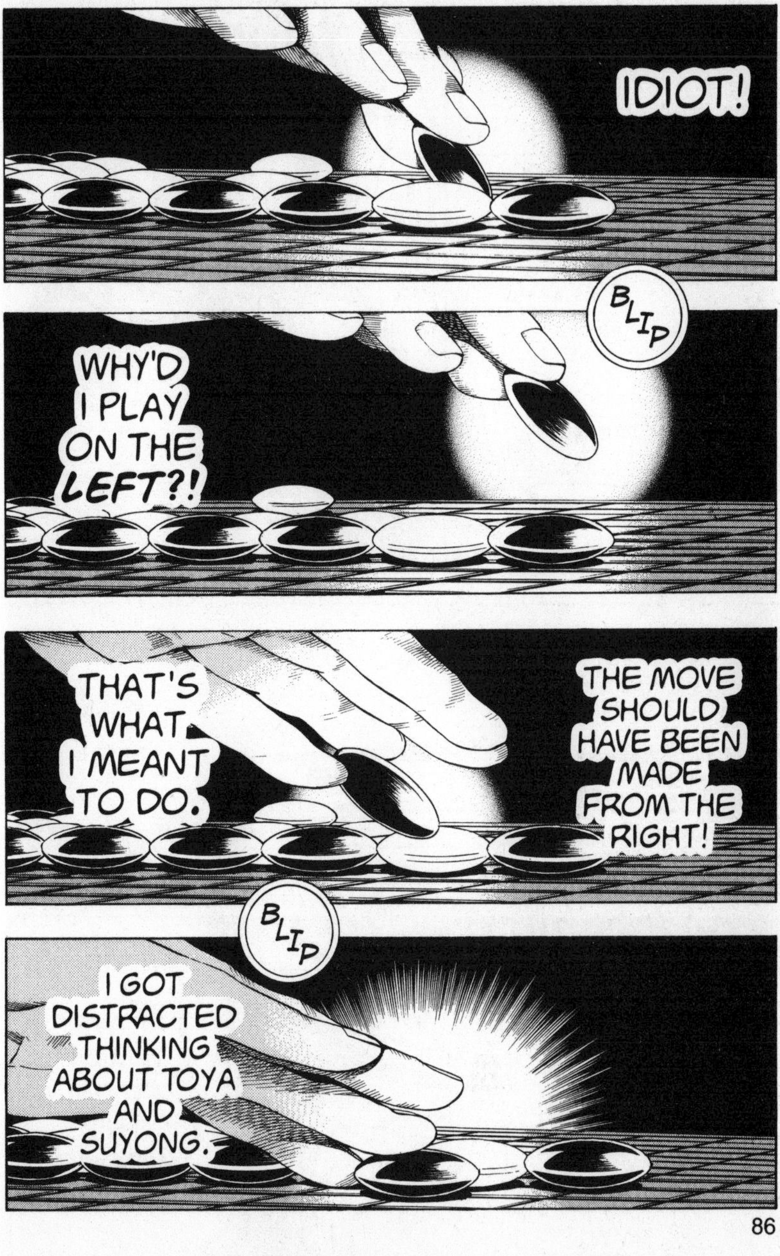
IDIOT!
BLIP
WHY'D I PLAY ON THE LEFT?!
THE MOVE SHOULD HAVE BEEN MADE FROM THE RIGHT!
THAT'S WHAT I MEANT TO DO.
BLIP
I GOT DISTRACTED THINKING ABOUT TOYA AND SUYONG.

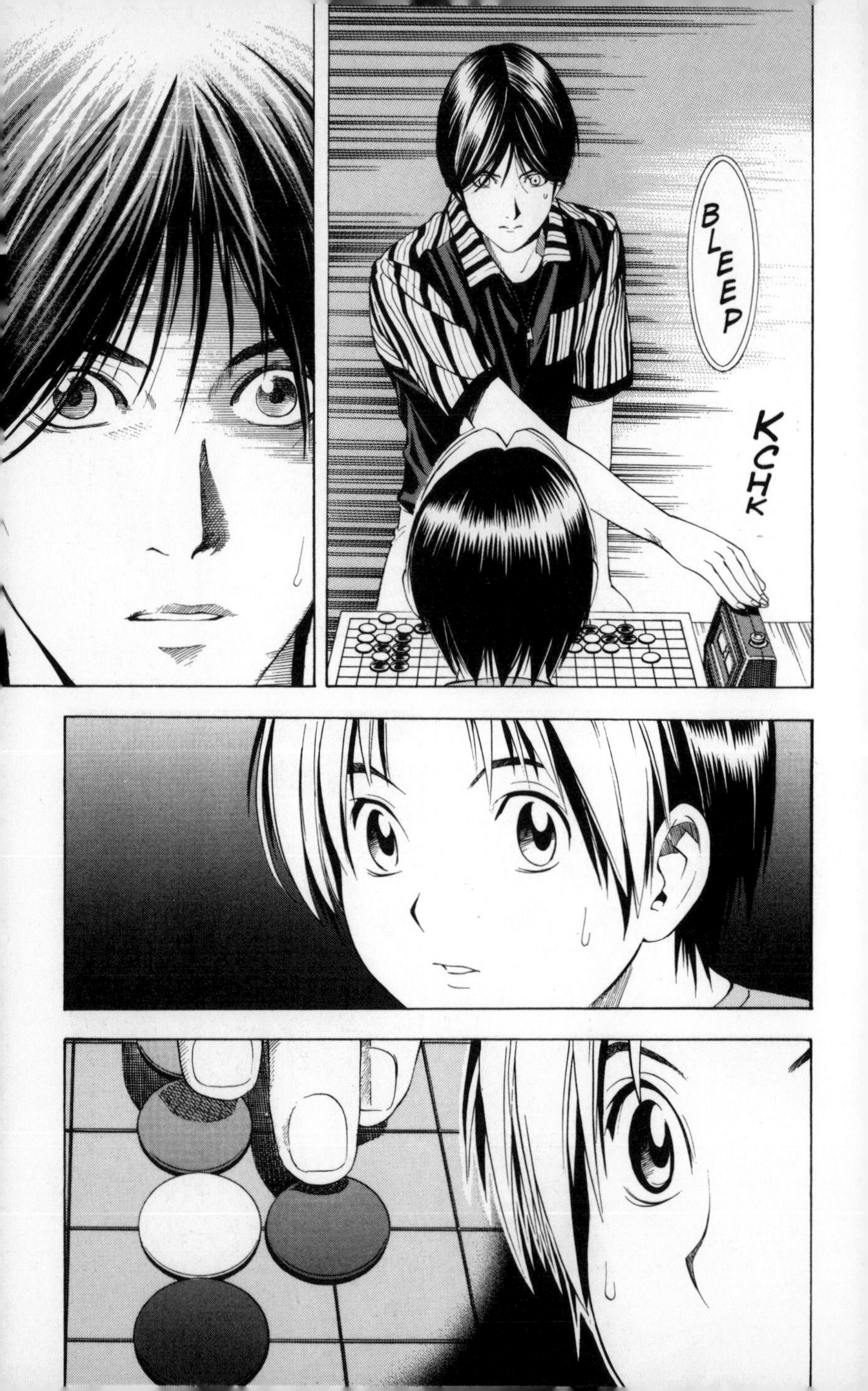
BLEEP
KCHK

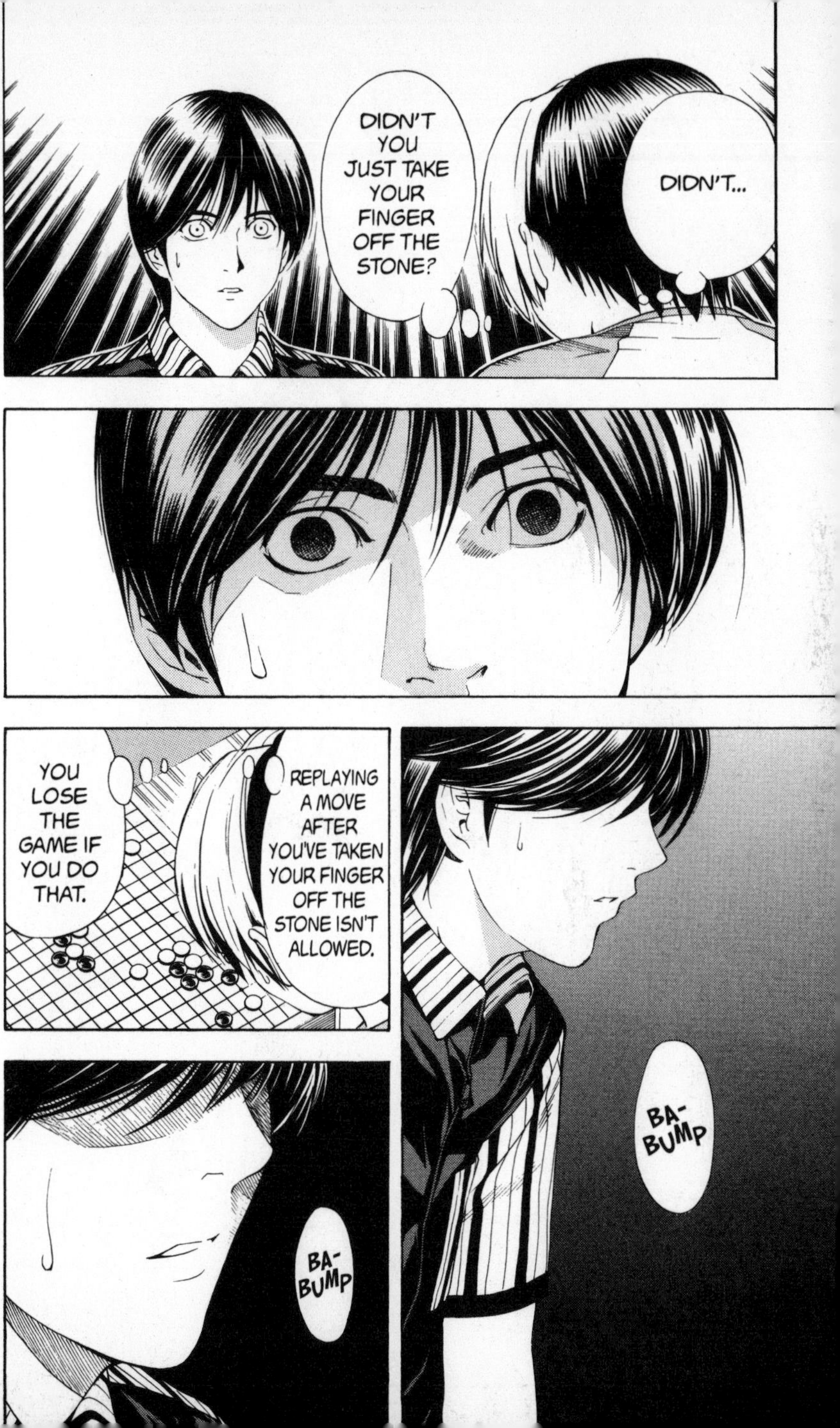
DIDN'T...
DIDN'T YOU JUST TAKE YOUR FINGER OFF THE STONE?
BA-BUMP
REPLAYING A MOVE AFTER YOU'VE TAKEN YOUR FINGER OFF THE STONE ISN'T ALLOWED.
YOU LOSE THE GAME IF YOU DO THAT.
BA-BUMP

READ THIS WAY

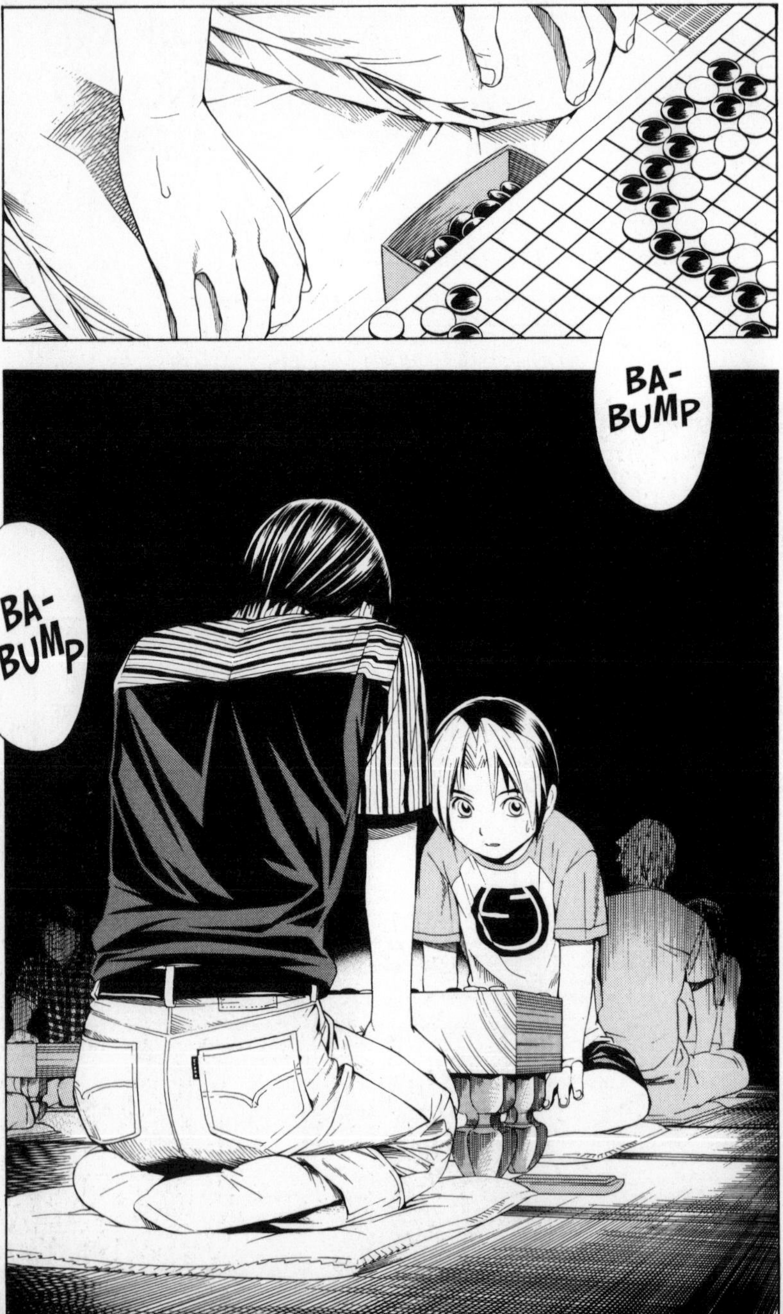
BA-BUMP
BA-BUMP

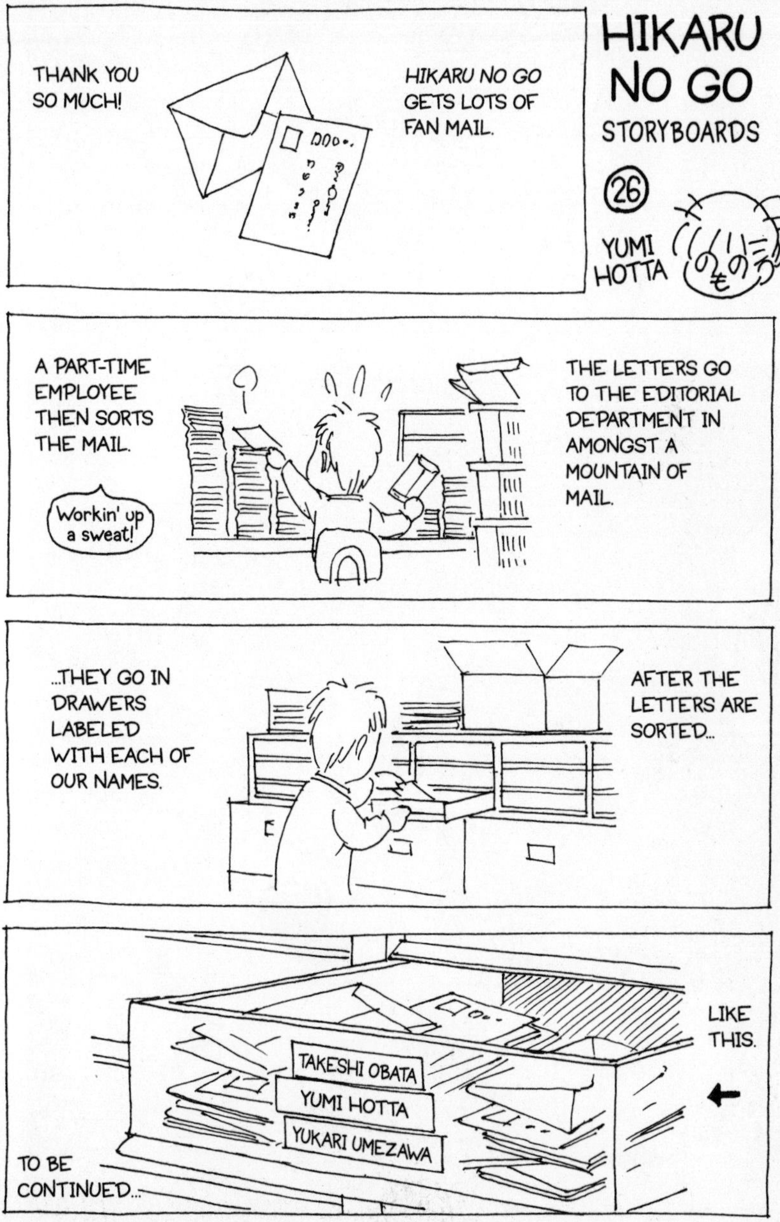
HIKARU NO GO STORYBOARDS
26
YUMI HOTTA
HIKARU NO GO GETS LOTS OF FAN MAIL.
THANK YOU SO MUCH!
THE LETTERS GO TO THE EDITORIAL DEPARTMENT IN AMONGST A MOUNTAIN OF MAIL.
A PART-TIME EMPLOYEE THEN SORTS THE MAIL.
Workin' up a sweat!
AFTER THE LETTERS ARE SORTED...
...THEY GO IN DRAWERS LABELED WITH EACH OF OUR NAMES.
LIKE THIS.
TAKESHI OBATA
YUMI HOTTA
YUKARI UMEZAWA
TO BE CONTINUED...

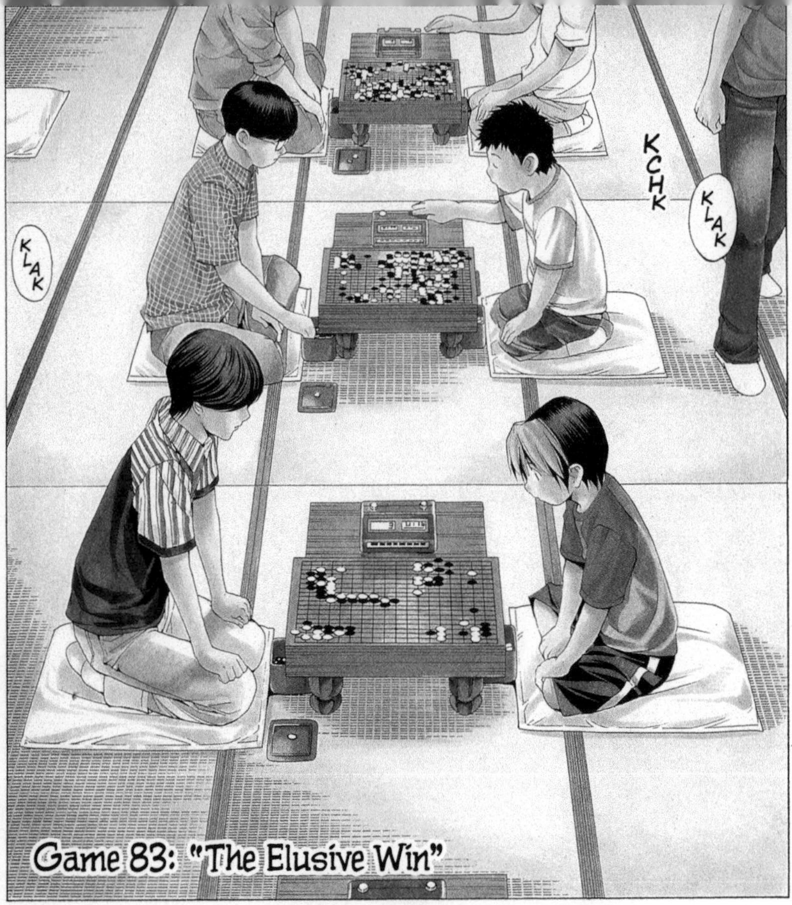
KLAK
KCHK
KLAK

Game 83: "The Elusive Win"

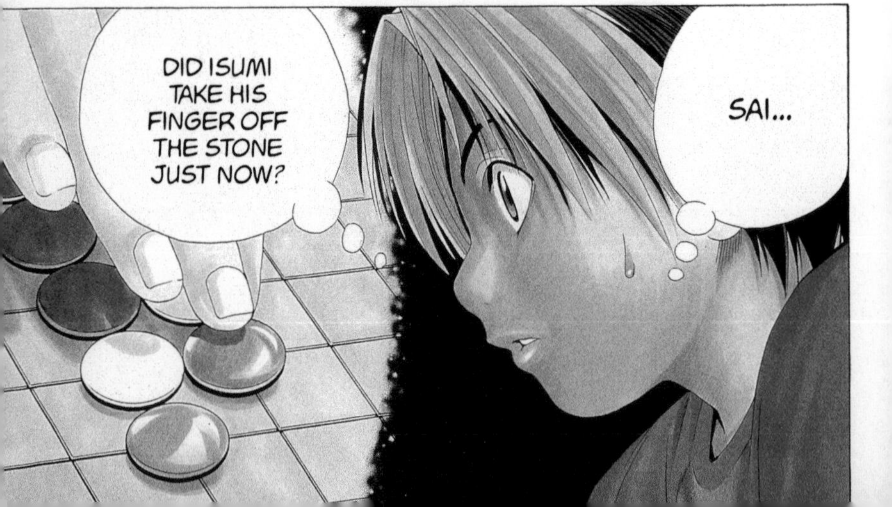
SAI...
DID ISUMI TAKE HIS FINGER OFF THE STONE JUST NOW?

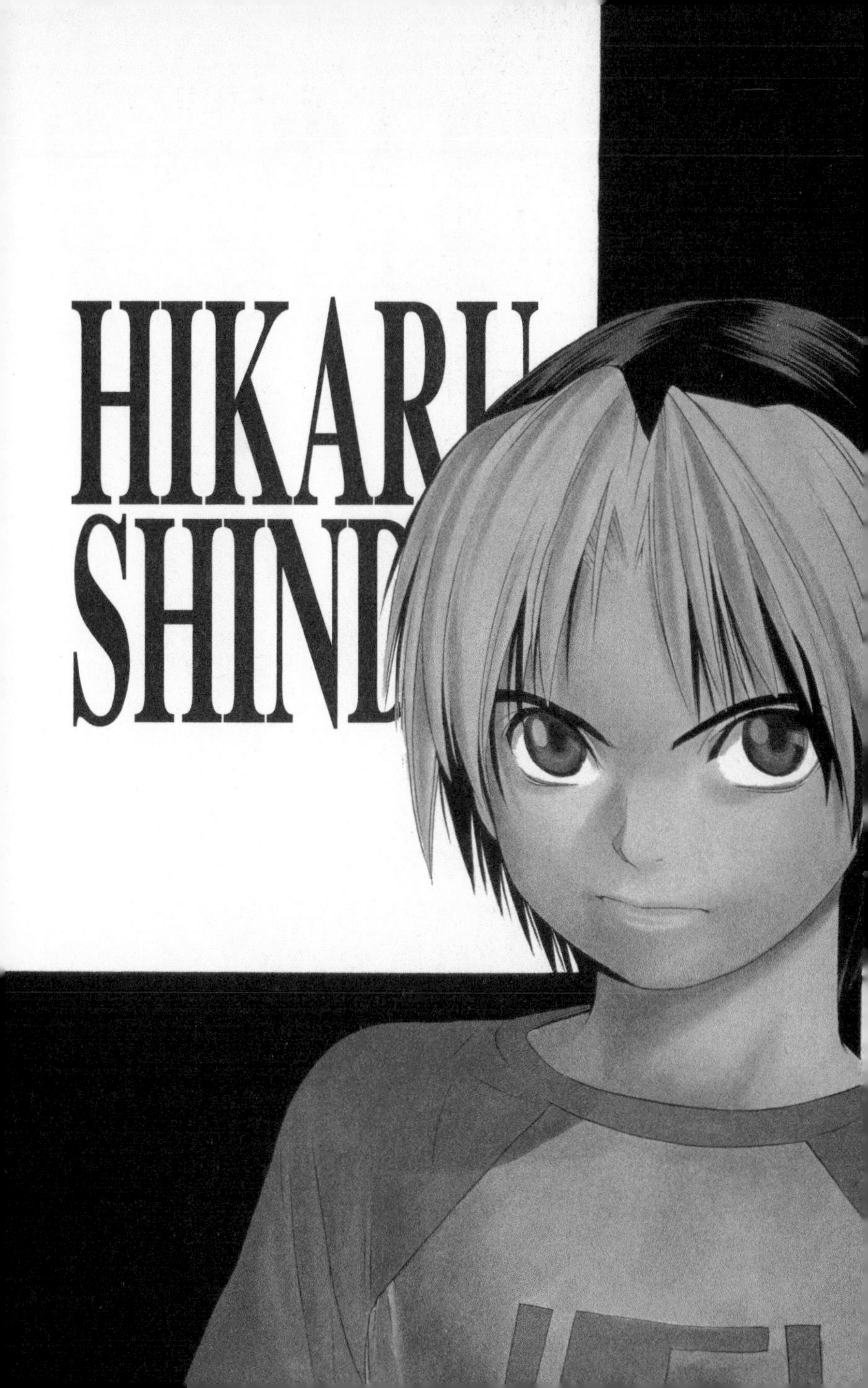
HIKAR
SHIND

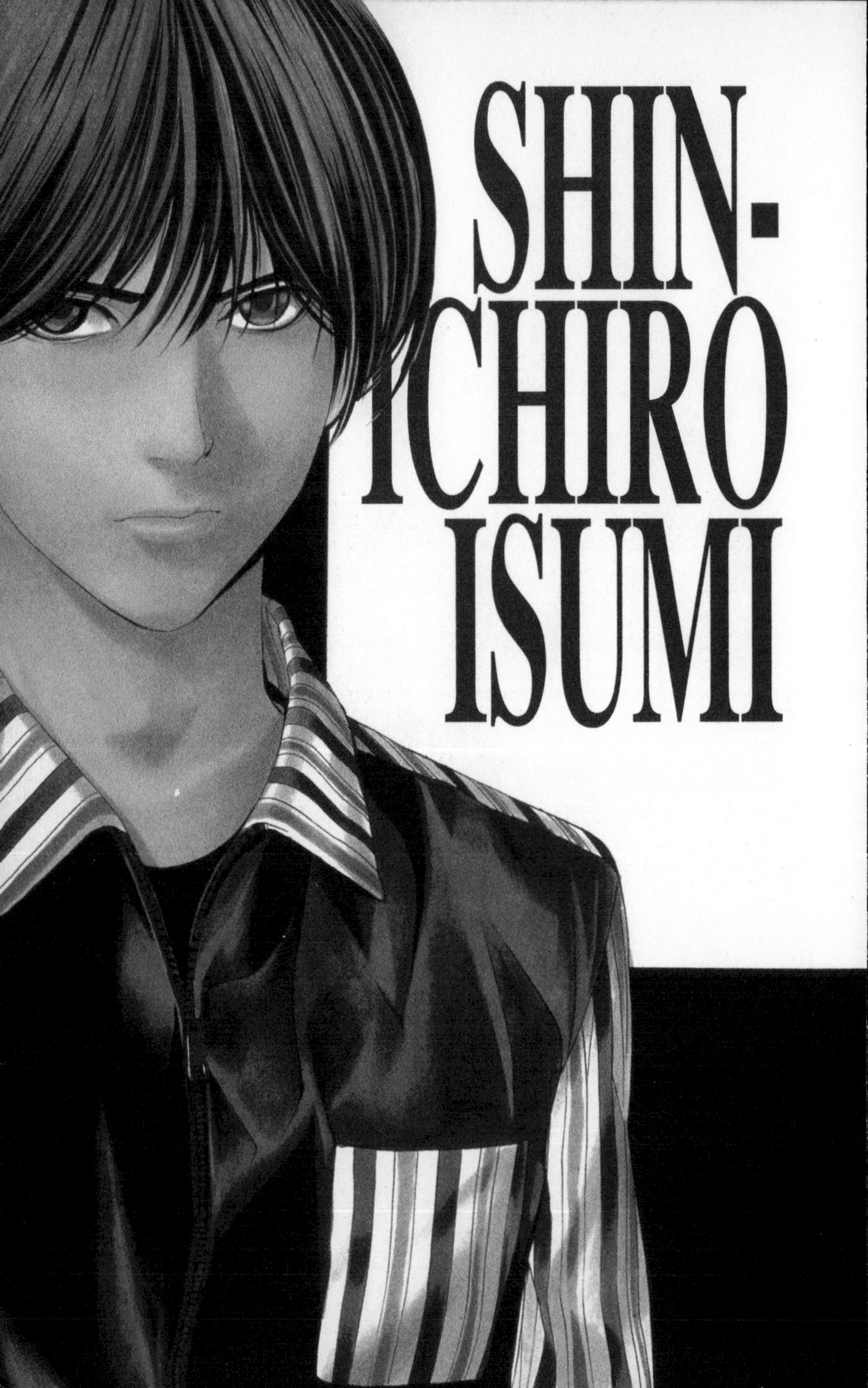
SHIN-
ICHIRO
ISUMI

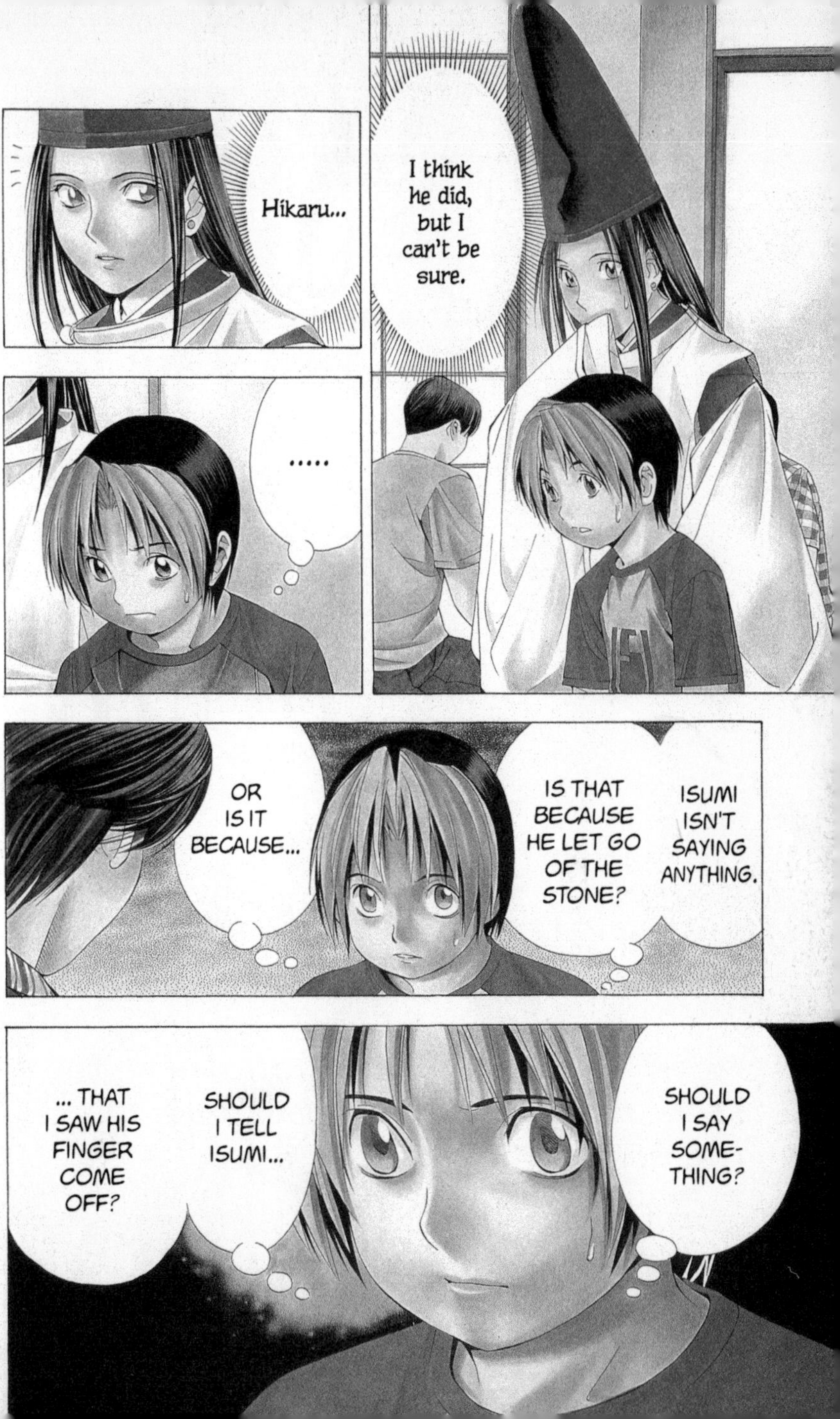
I think he did, but I can't be sure.
Hikaru...
.....
ISUMI ISN'T SAYING ANYTHING.
IS THAT BECAUSE HE LET GO OF THE STONE?
OR IS IT BECAUSE...
SHOULD I SAY SOME-THING?
SHOULD I TELL ISUMI...
... THAT I SAW HIS FINGER COME OFF?

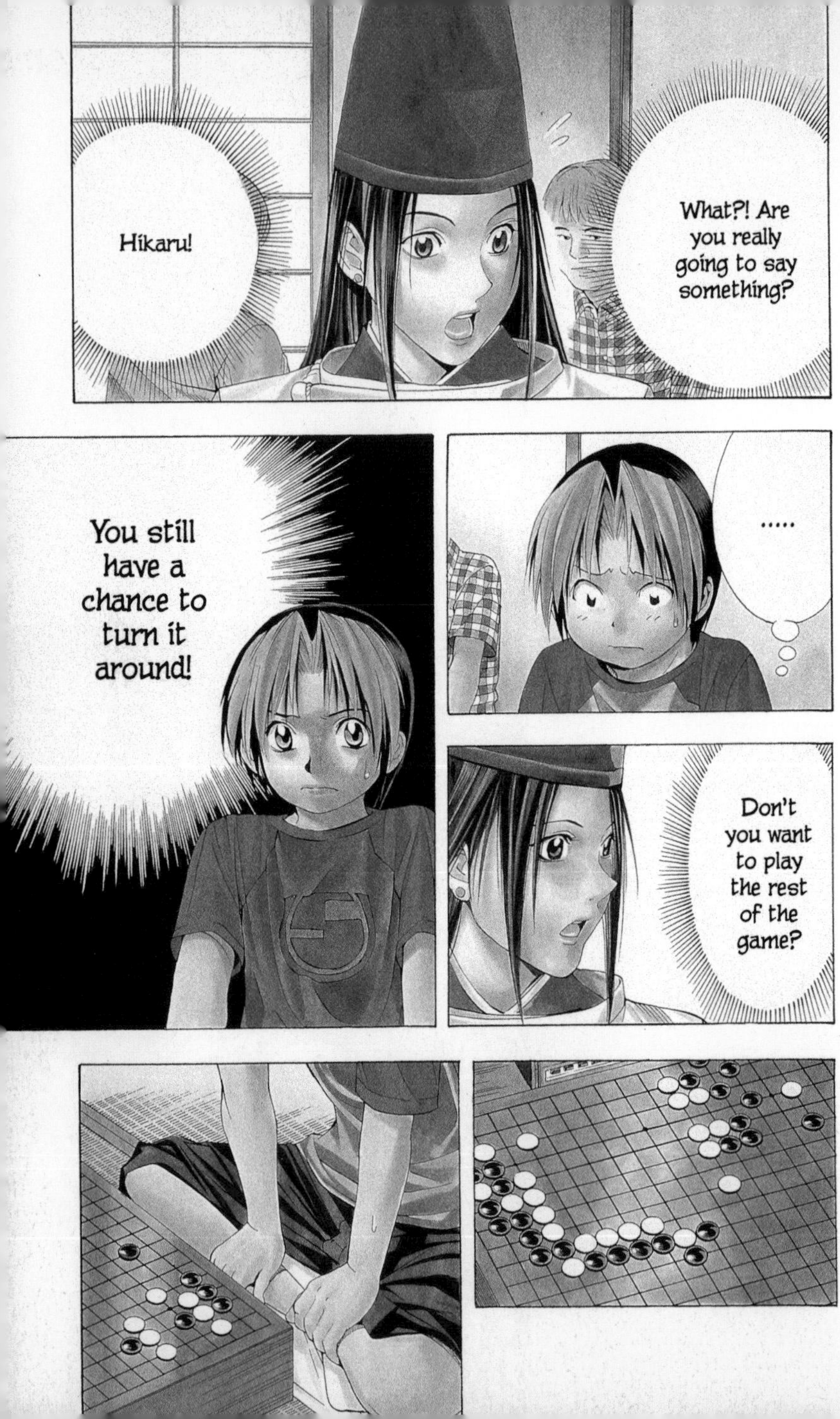
What?! Are you really going to say something?
Hikaru!
.....
Don't you want to play the rest of the game?
You still have a chance to turn it around!

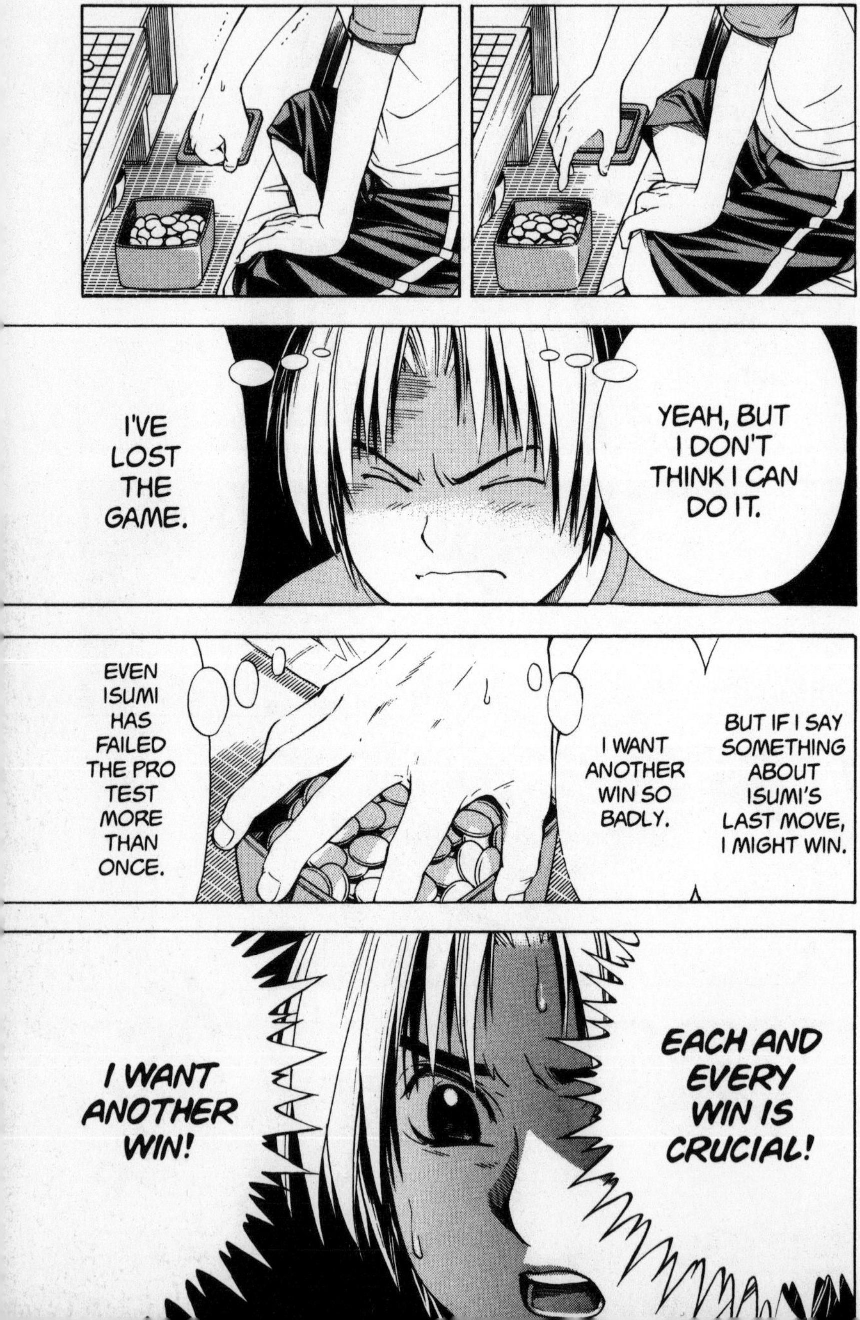
YEAH, BUT I DON'T THINK I CAN DO IT.
I'VE LOST THE GAME.
BUT IF I SAY SOMETHING ABOUT ISUMI'S LAST MOVE, I MIGHT WIN.
I WANT ANOTHER WIN SO BADLY.
EVEN ISUMI HAS FAILED THE PRO TEST MORE THAN ONCE.
EACH AND EVERY WIN IS CRUCIAL!
I WANT ANOTHER WIN!

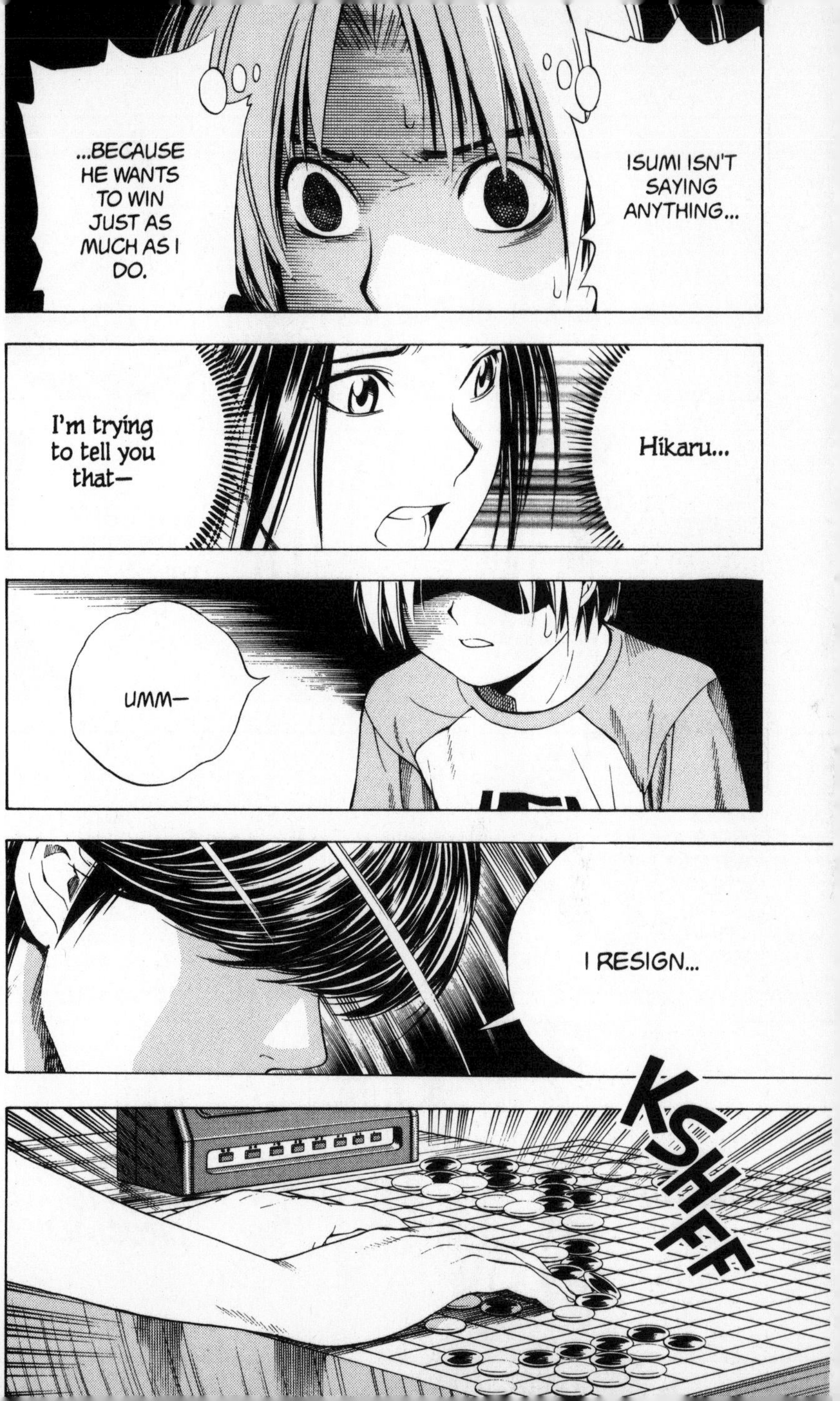
ISUMI ISN'T SAYING ANYTHING...
...BECAUSE HE WANTS TO WIN JUST AS MUCH AS I DO.
Hikaru...
I'm trying to tell you that—
UMM—
I RESIGN...
KSHFF

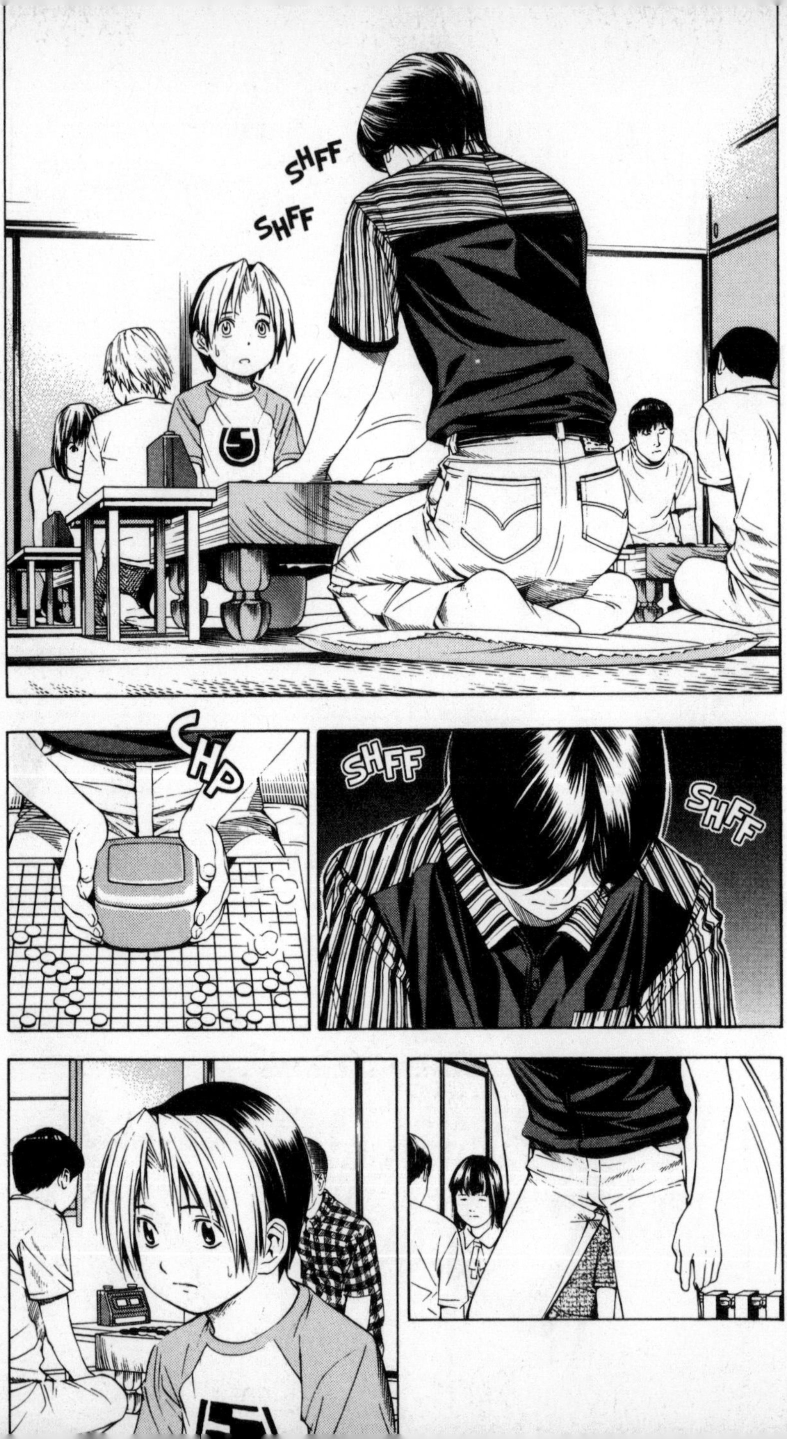
SHFF
SHFF
SHFF
SHFF
CHP

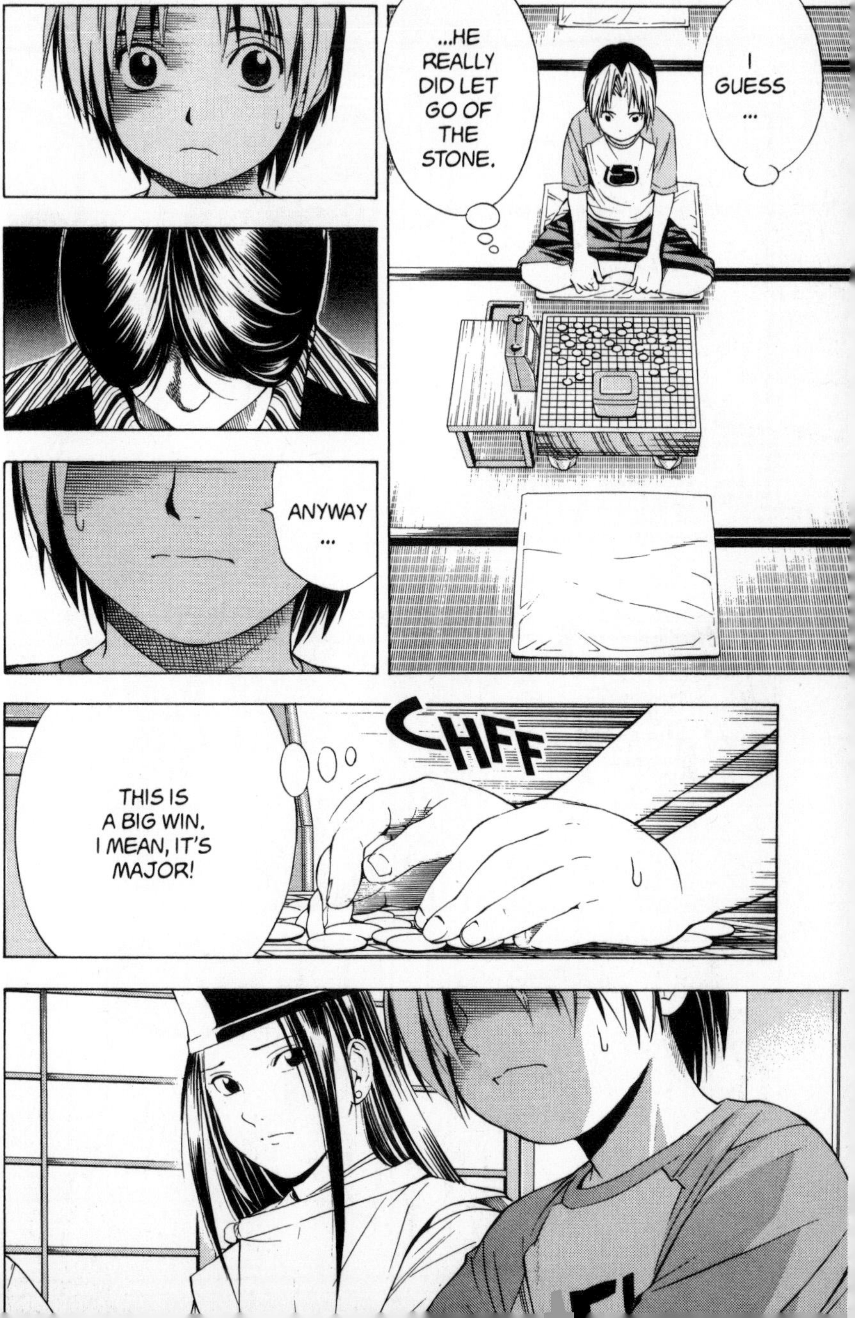
I GUESS ...
...HE REALLY DID LET GO OF THE STONE.
ANYWAY ...
CHFF
THIS IS A BIG WIN. I MEAN, IT'S MAJOR!

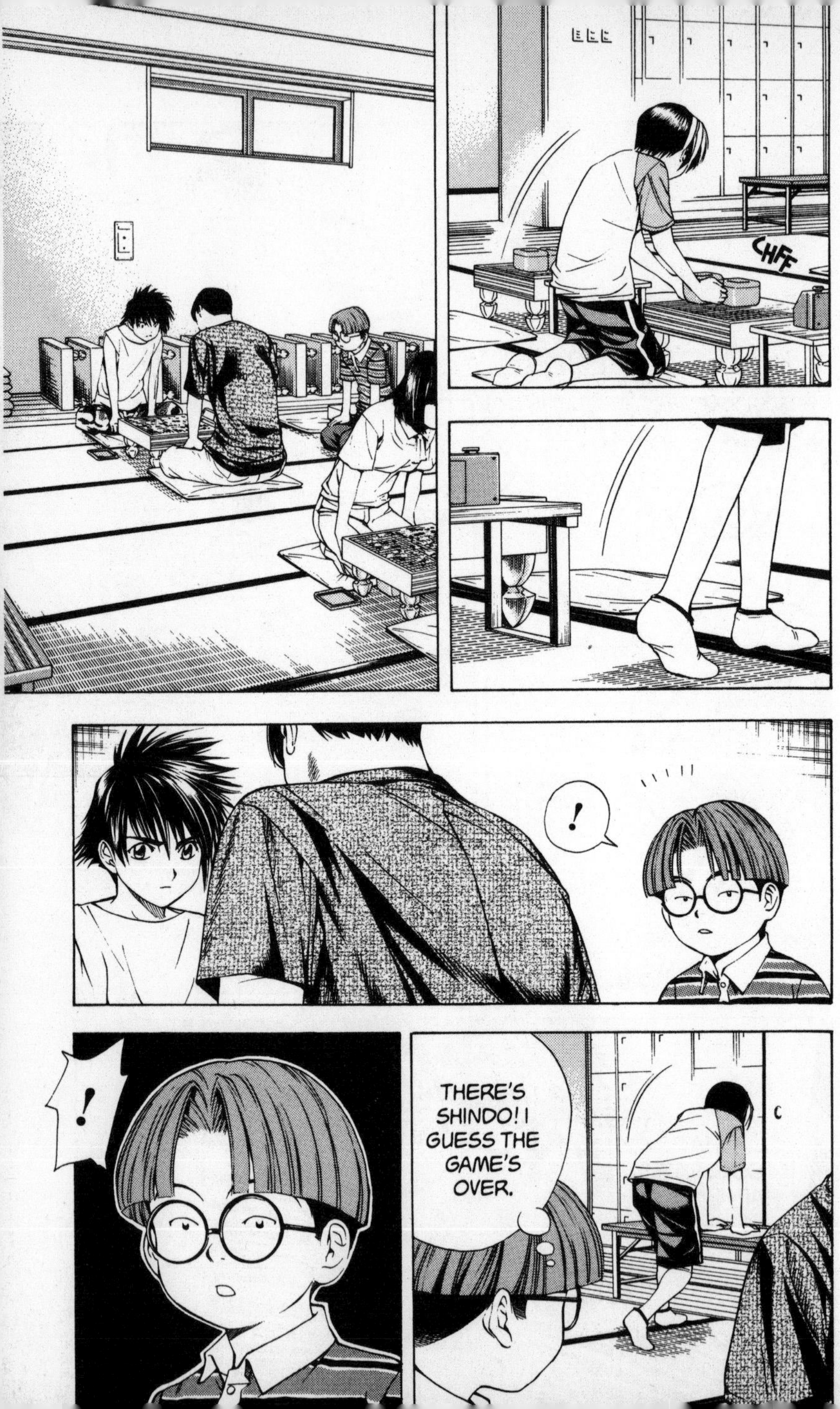
CHFF
!
!
THERE'S SHINDO! I GUESS THE GAME'S OVER.

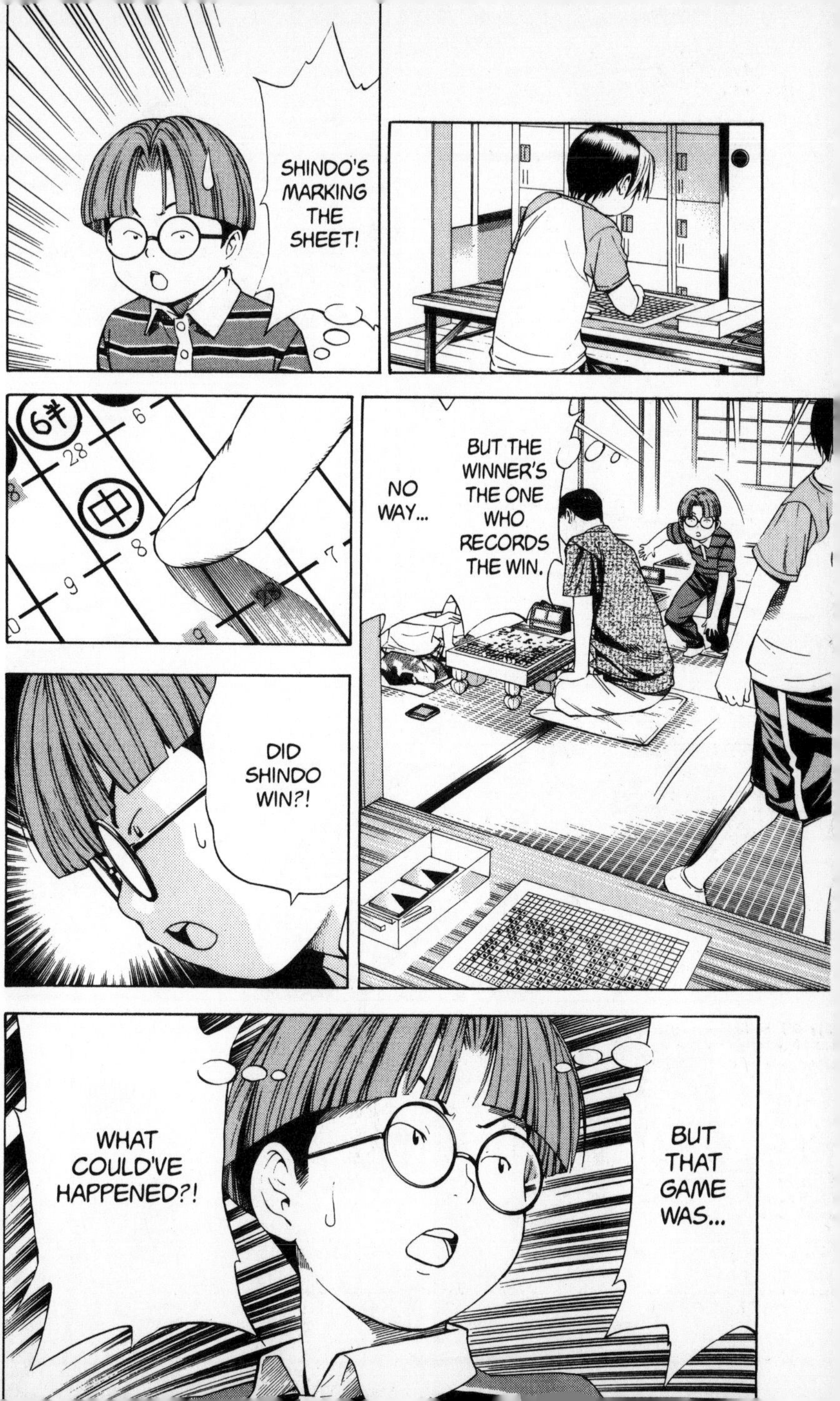
SHINDO'S MARKING THE SHEET!
BUT THE WINNER'S THE ONE WHO RECORDS THE WIN.
NO WAY...
DID SHINDO WIN?!
BUT THAT GAME WAS...
WHAT COULD'VE HAPPENED?!

READ THIS WAY

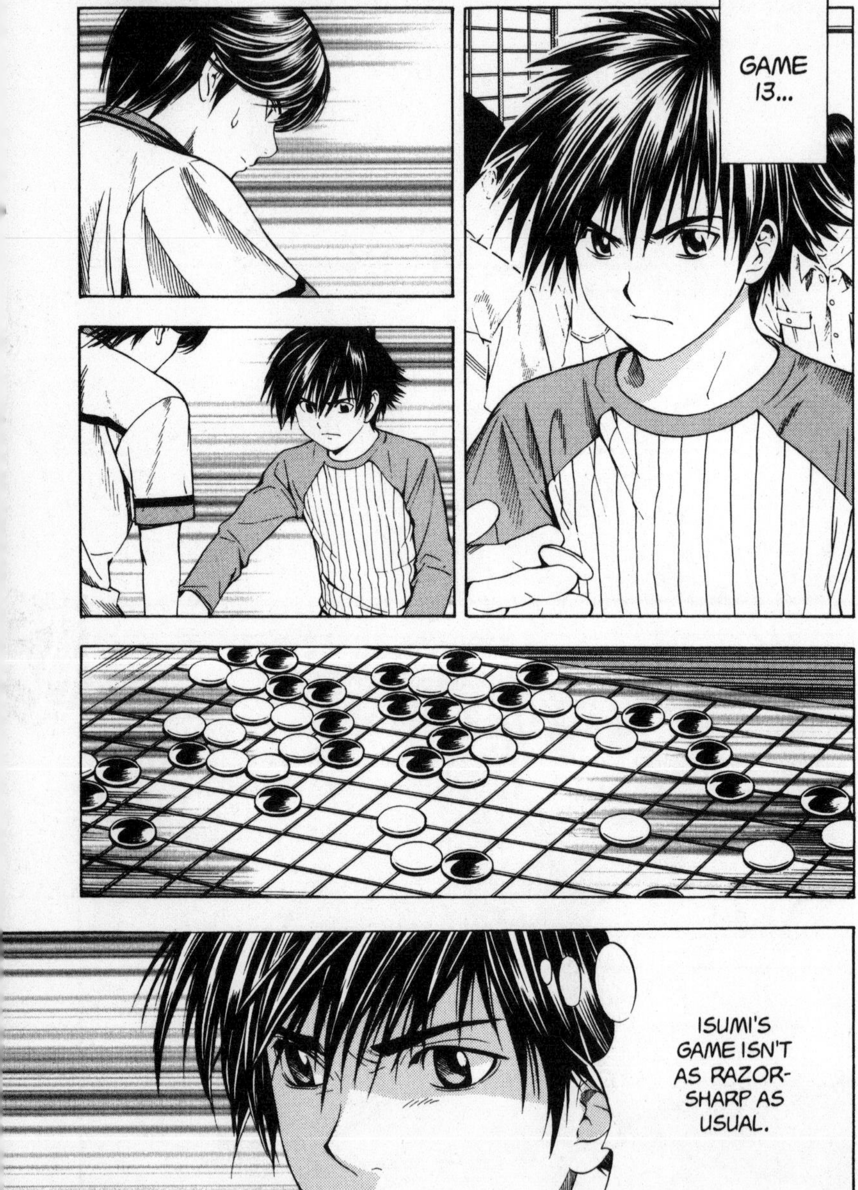
GAME 13...
ISUMI'S GAME ISN'T AS RAZOR-SHARP AS USUAL.

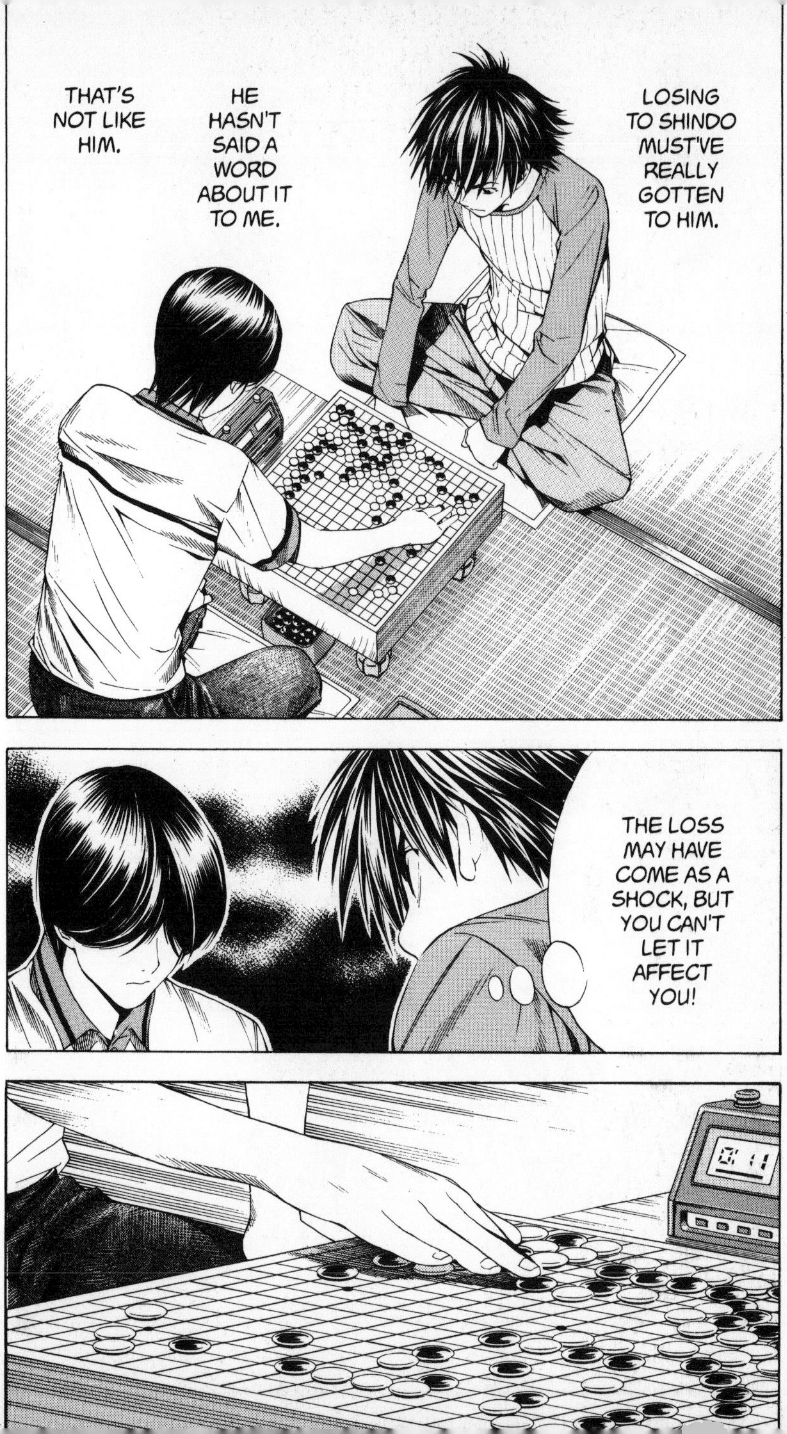
LOSING TO SHINDO MUST'VE REALLY GOTTEN TO HIM.
HE HASN'T SAID A WORD ABOUT IT TO ME.
THAT'S NOT LIKE HIM.
THE LOSS MAY HAVE COME AS A SHOCK, BUT YOU CAN'T LET IT AFFECT YOU!

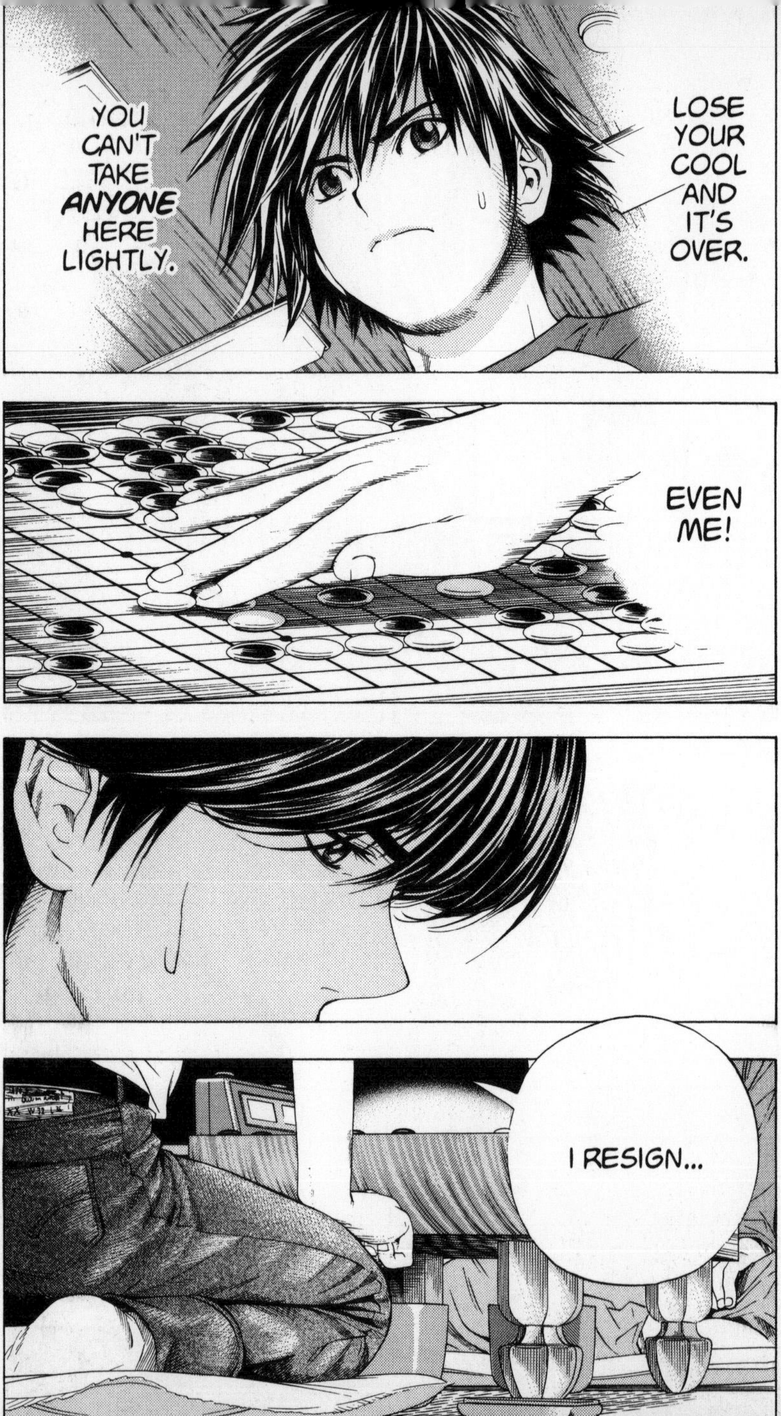
LOSE YOUR COOL AND IT'S OVER.
YOU CAN'T TAKE ANYONE HERE LIGHTLY.
EVEN ME!
I RESIGN...

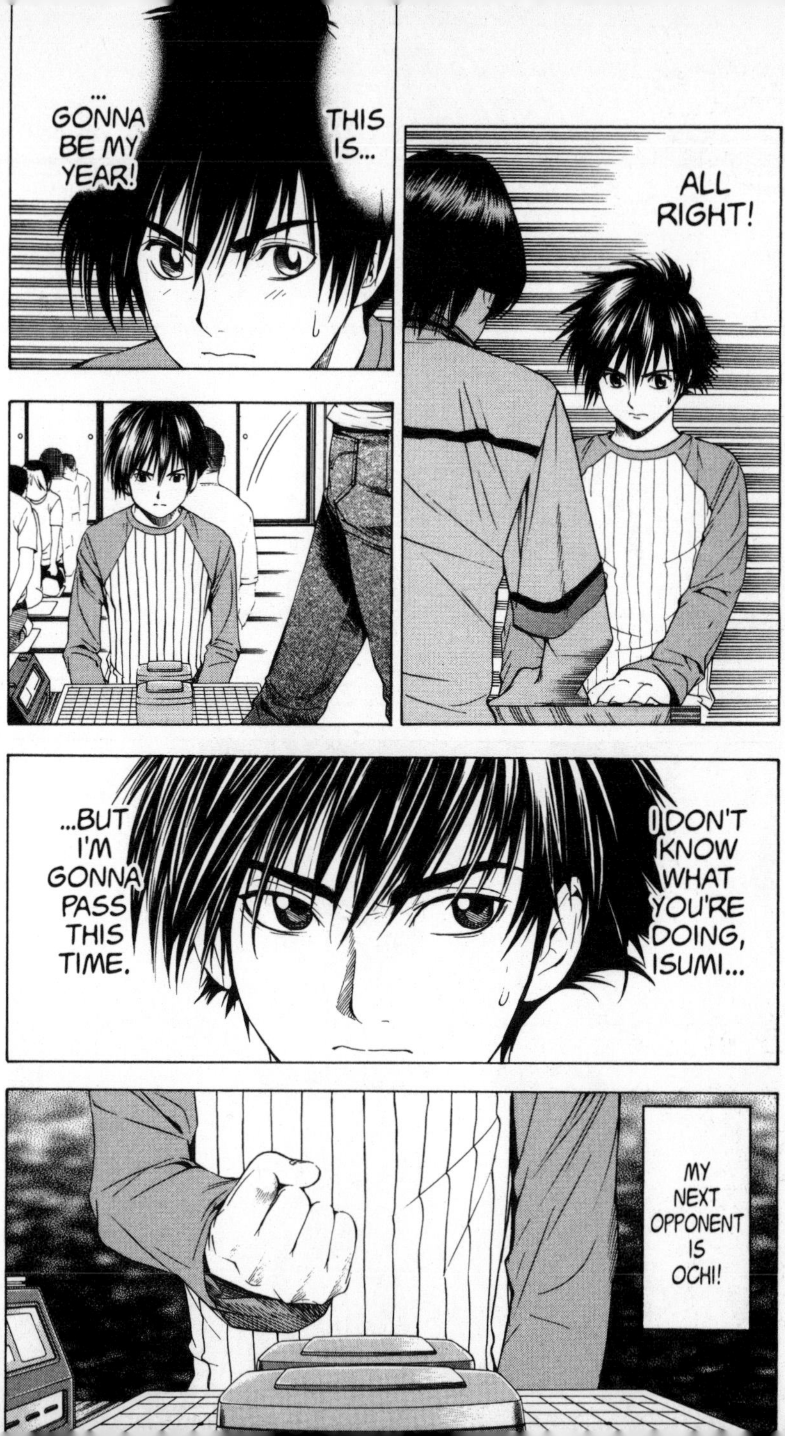
ALL RIGHT!
THIS IS...
... GONNA BE MY YEAR!
I DON'T KNOW WHAT YOU'RE DOING, ISUMI...
...BUT I'M GONNA PASS THIS TIME.
MY NEXT OPPONENT IS OCHI!

READ THIS WAY

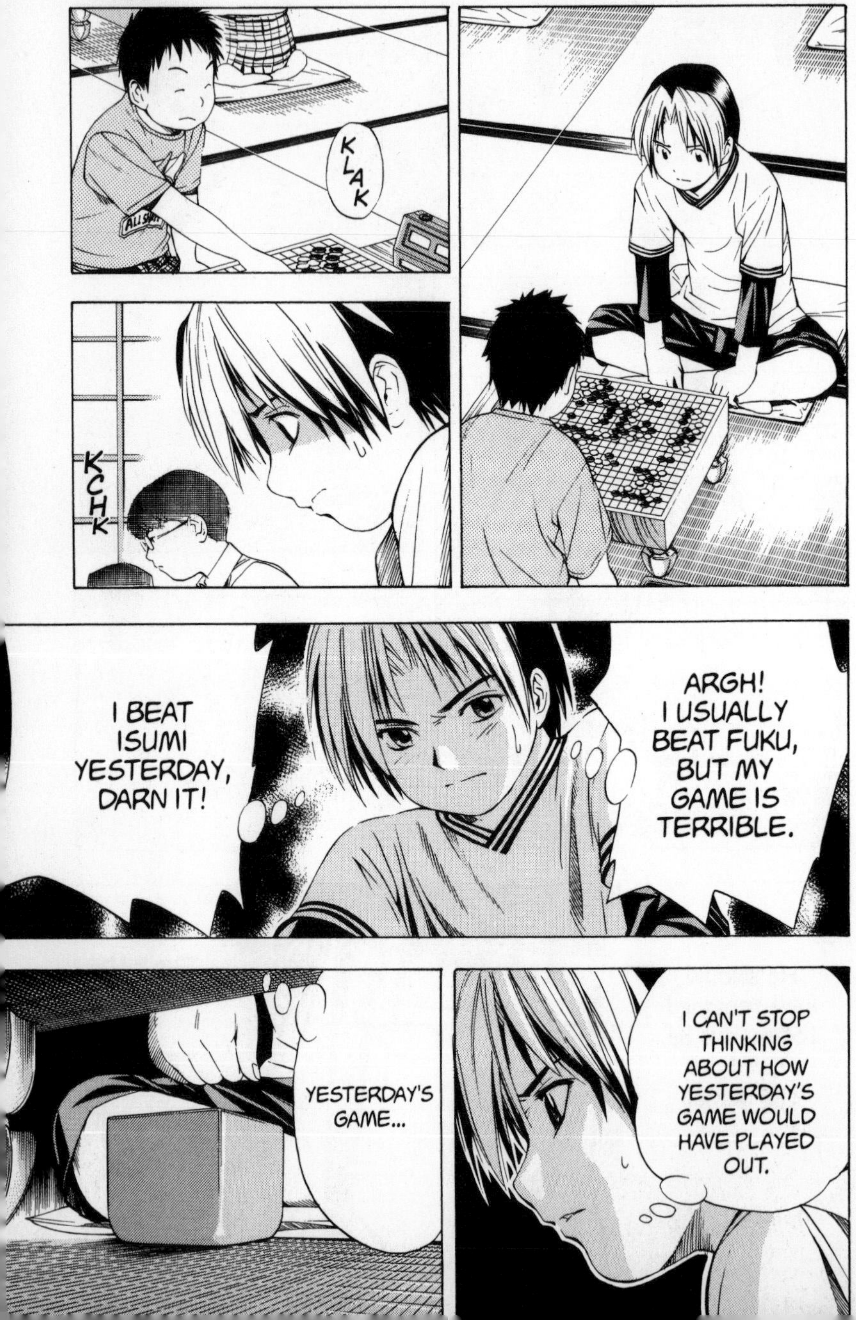
KLAK
KCHK
ARGH! I USUALLY BEAT FUKU, BUT MY GAME IS TERRIBLE.
I BEAT ISUMI YESTERDAY, DARN IT!
I CAN'T STOP THINKING ABOUT HOW YESTERDAY'S GAME WOULD HAVE PLAYED OUT.
YESTERDAY'S GAME...

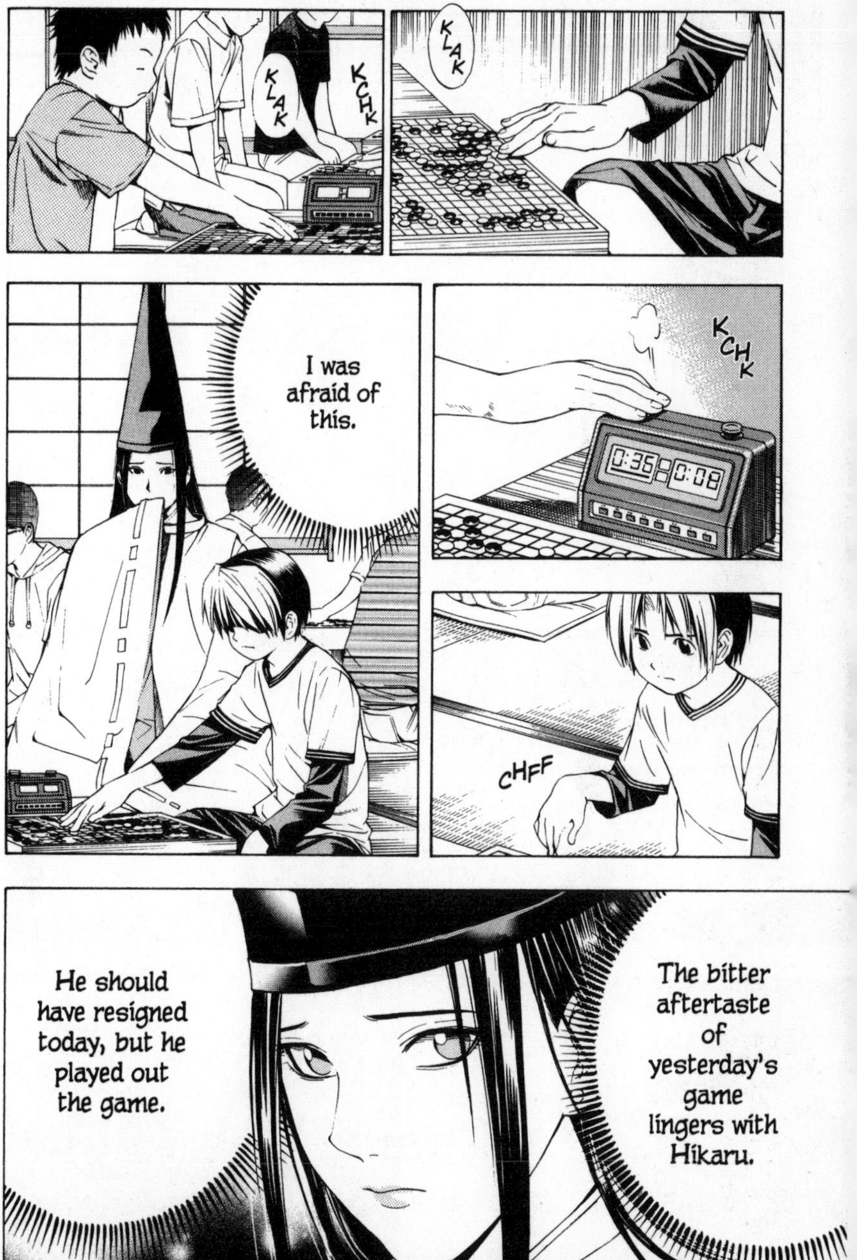
KLAK
KCHK
KLAK
KCHK
0:35 0:08
CHFF
I was afraid of this.
The bitter aftertaste of yesterday's game lingers with Hikaru.
He should have resigned today, but he played out the game.

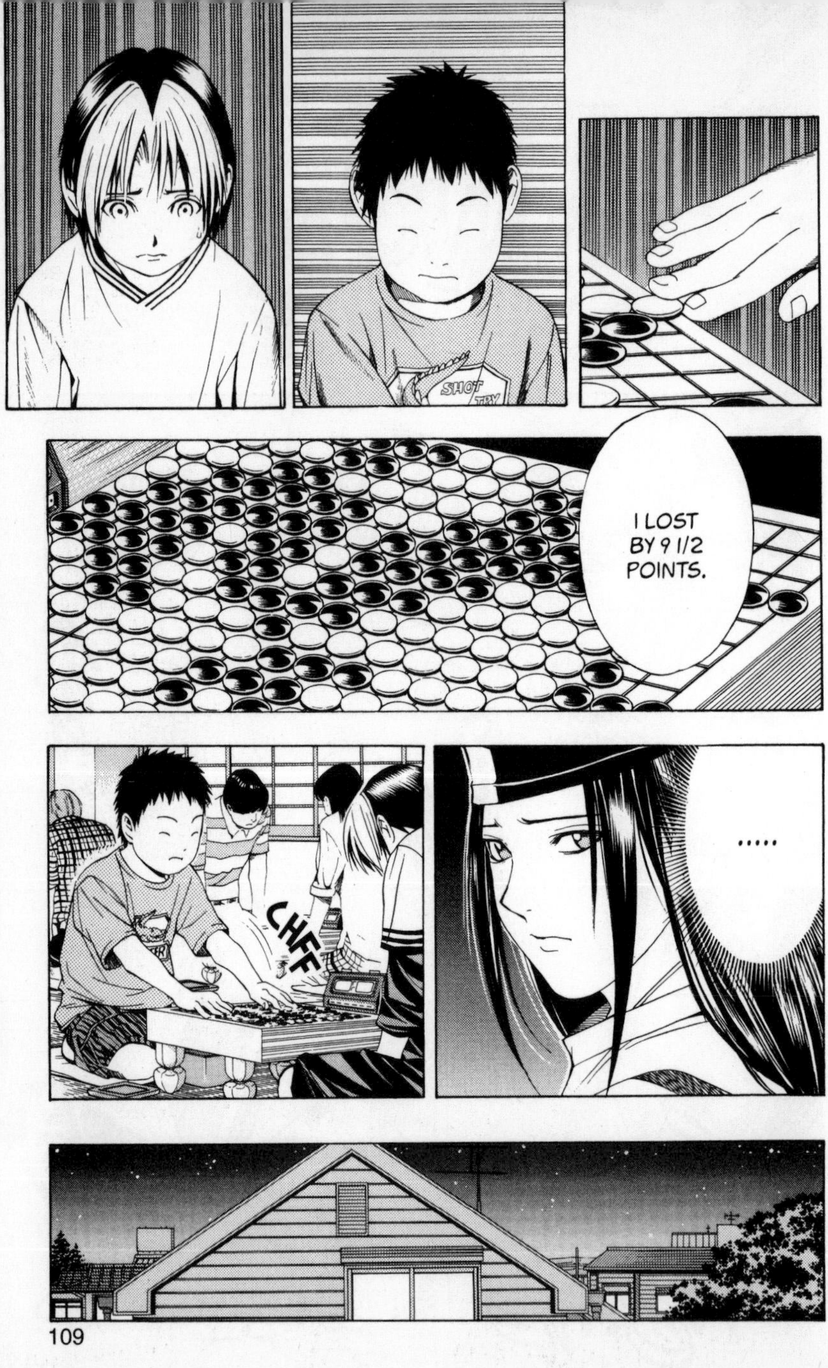
I LOST BY 9 1/2 POINTS.
.....
CHFF

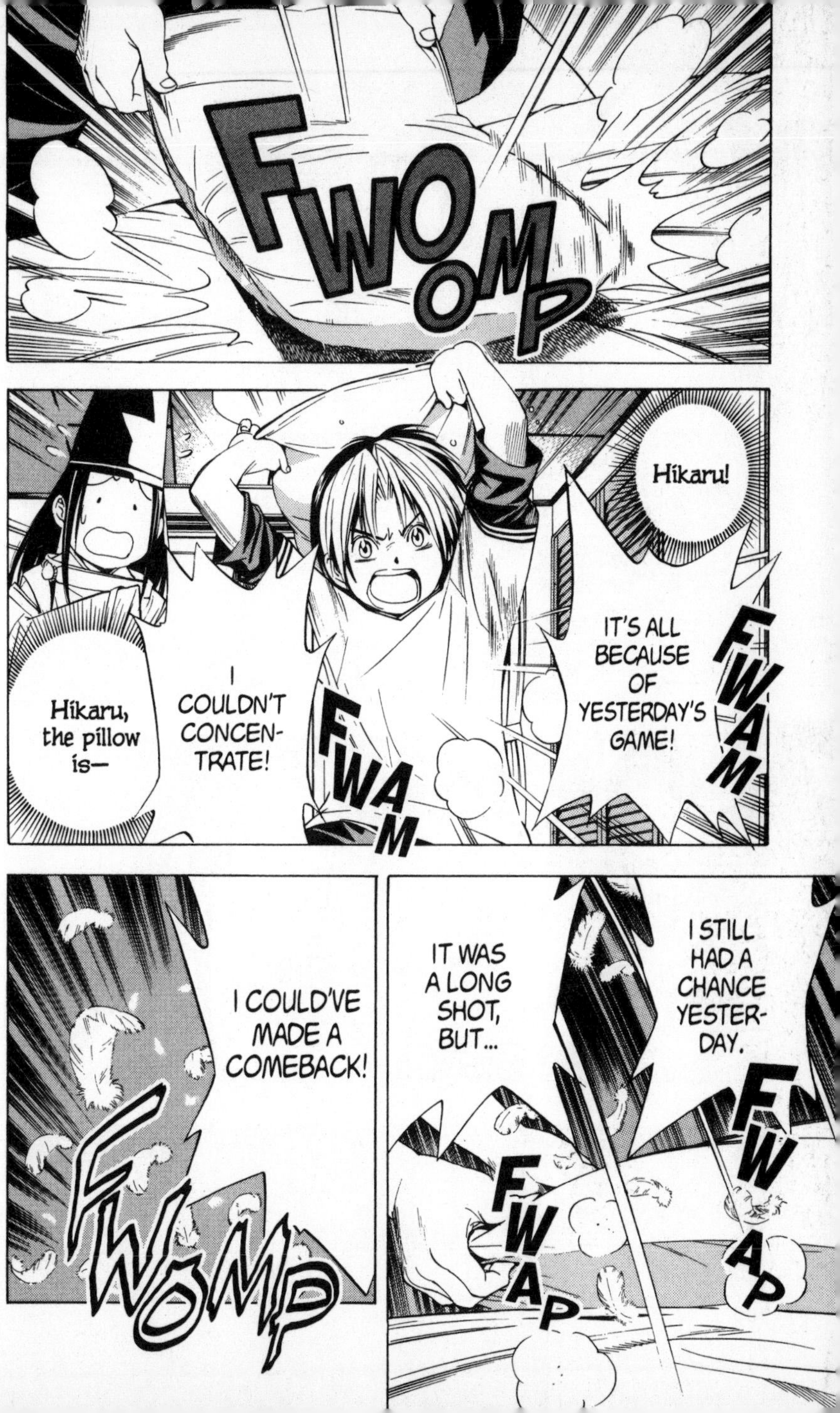
FWOOMP
Hikaru!
IT'S ALL BECAUSE OF YESTERDAY'S GAME!
FWAM
I COULDN'T CONCEN-TRATE!
FWAM-
Hikaru, the pillow is—
I STILL HAD A CHANCE YESTER-DAY.
FWAP
IT WAS A LONG SHOT, BUT...
FWAP
I COULD'VE MADE A COMEBACK!
FWOMP

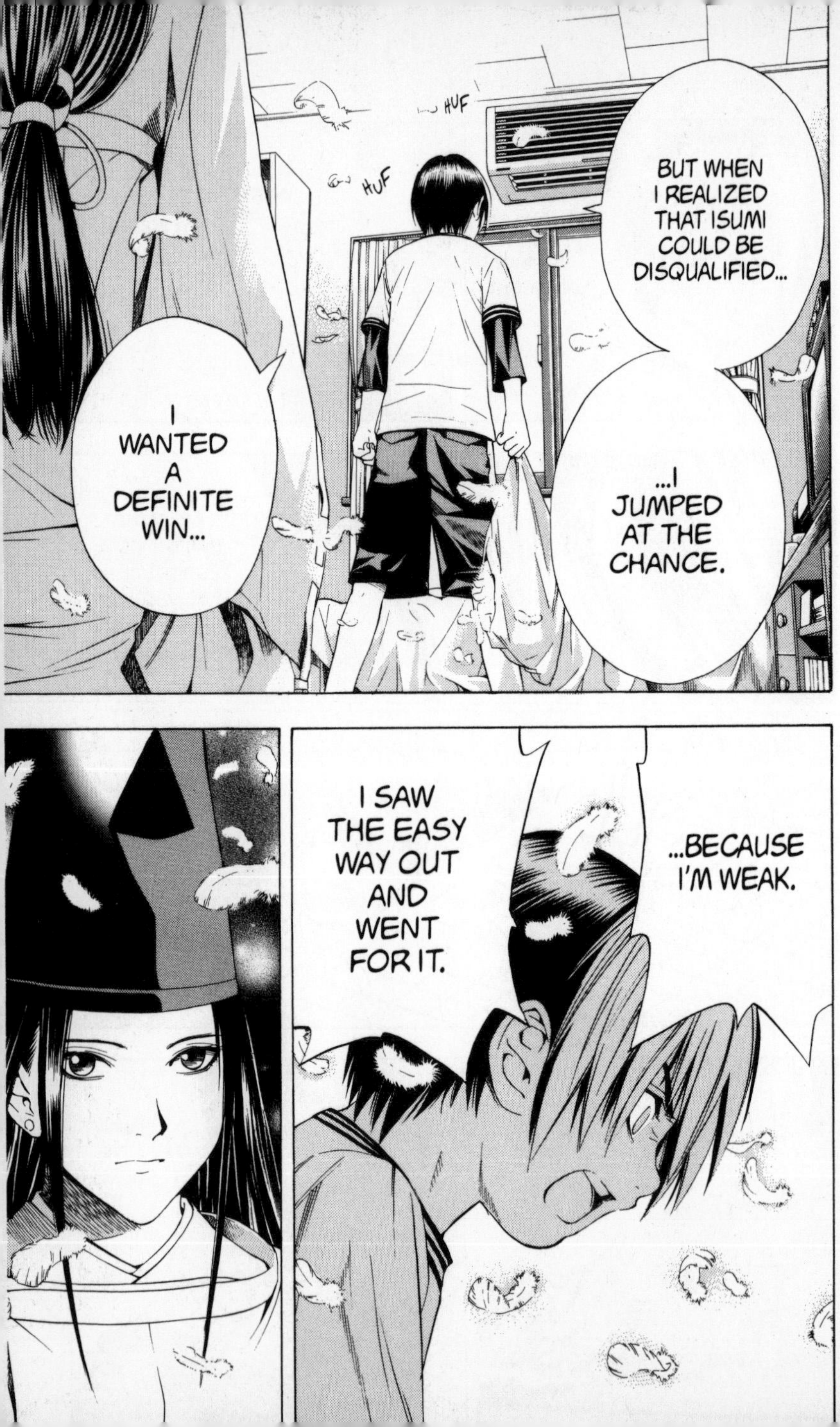
BUT WHEN I REALIZED THAT ISUMI COULD BE DISQUALIFIED...
...I JUMPED AT THE CHANCE.
HUF
HUF
I WANTED A DEFINITE WIN...
...BECAUSE I'M WEAK.
I SAW THE EASY WAY OUT AND WENT FOR IT.

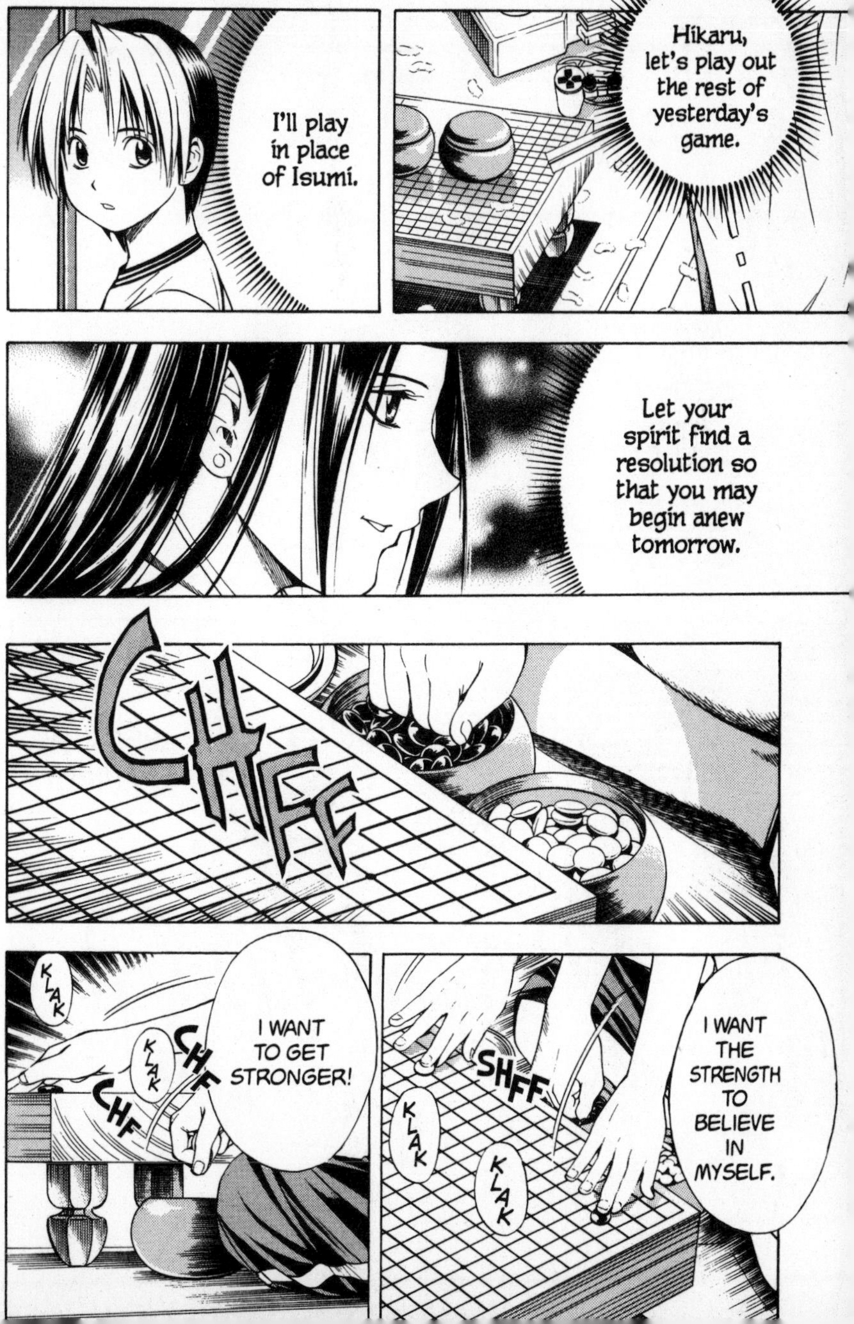
Hikaru, let's play out the rest of yesterday's game.
I'll play in place of Isumi.
Let your spirit find a resolution so that you may begin anew tomorrow.
CHFF
I WANT THE STRENGTH TO BELIEVE IN MYSELF.
SHFF
KLAK
KLAK
I WANT TO GET STRONGER!
CHF
CHF
KLAK
KLAK

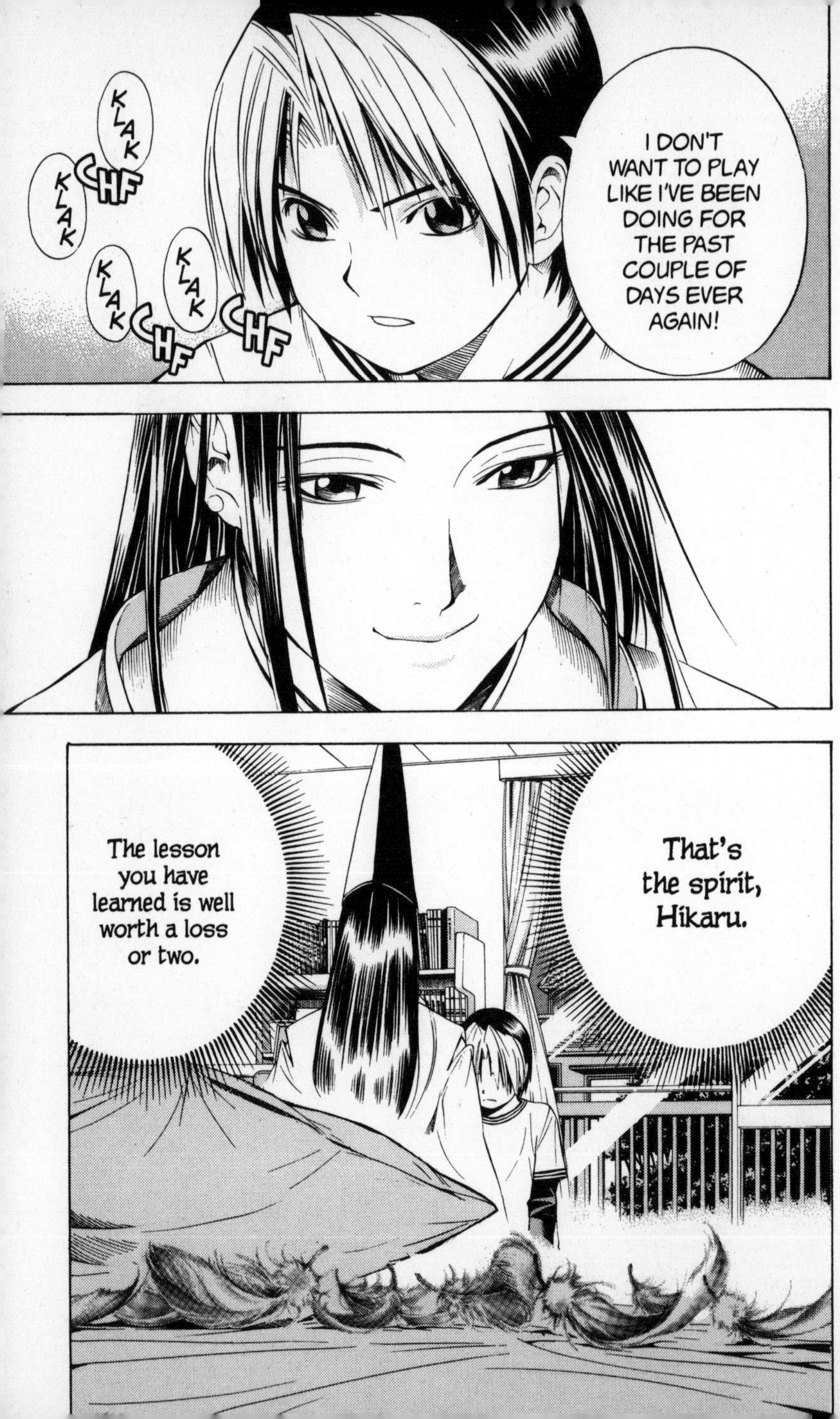
I DON'T WANT TO PLAY LIKE I'VE BEEN DOING FOR THE PAST COUPLE OF DAYS EVER AGAIN!
KLAK
CHF
KLAK
KLAK
CHF
KLAK
KLAK
CHF
That's the spirit, Hikaru.
The lesson you have learned is well worth a loss or two.

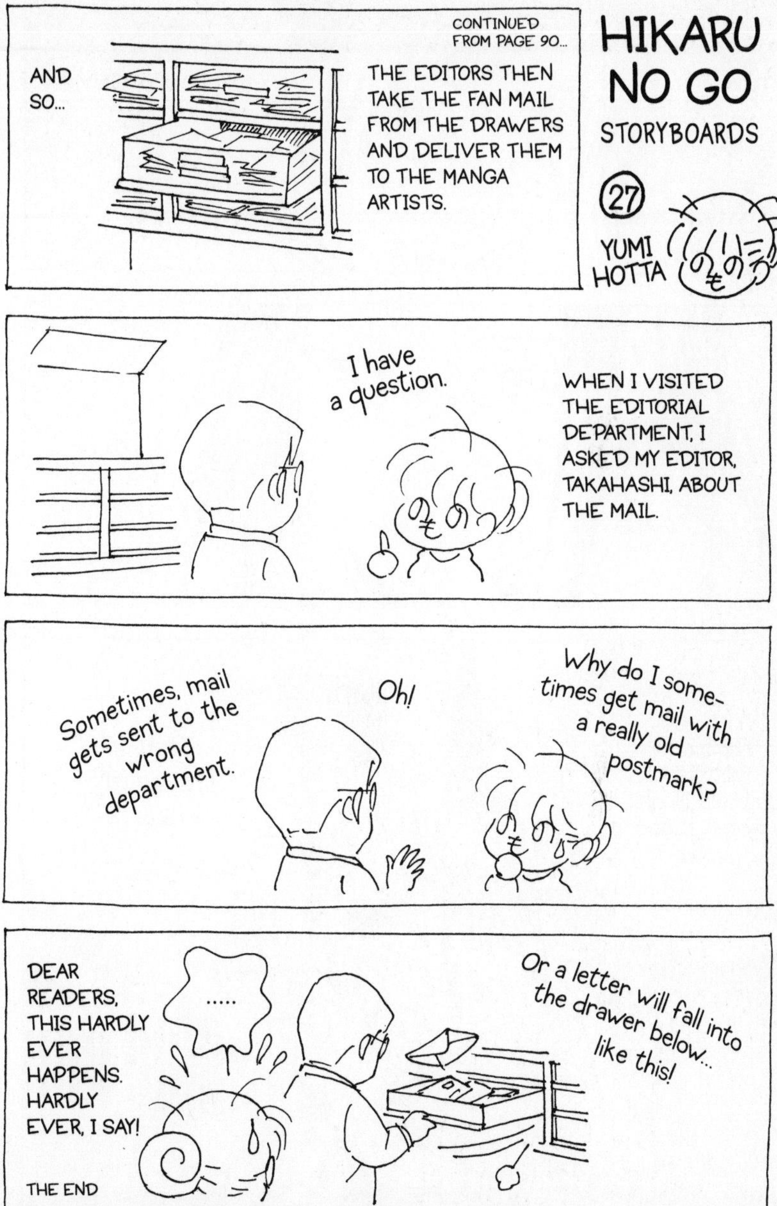
HIKARU NO GO
STORYBOARDS
27
YUMI HOTTA
CONTINUED FROM PAGE 90...
AND SO...
THE EDITORS THEN TAKE THE FAN MAIL FROM THE DRAWERS AND DELIVER THEM TO THE MANGA ARTISTS.
WHEN I VISITED THE EDITORIAL DEPARTMENT, I ASKED MY EDITOR, TAKAHASHI, ABOUT THE MAIL.
I have a question.
Why do I sometimes get mail with a really old postmark?
Oh!
Sometimes, mail gets sent to the wrong department.
Or a letter will fall into the drawer below... like this!
.....
DEAR READERS, THIS HARDLY EVER HAPPENS. HARDLY EVER, I SAY!
THE END

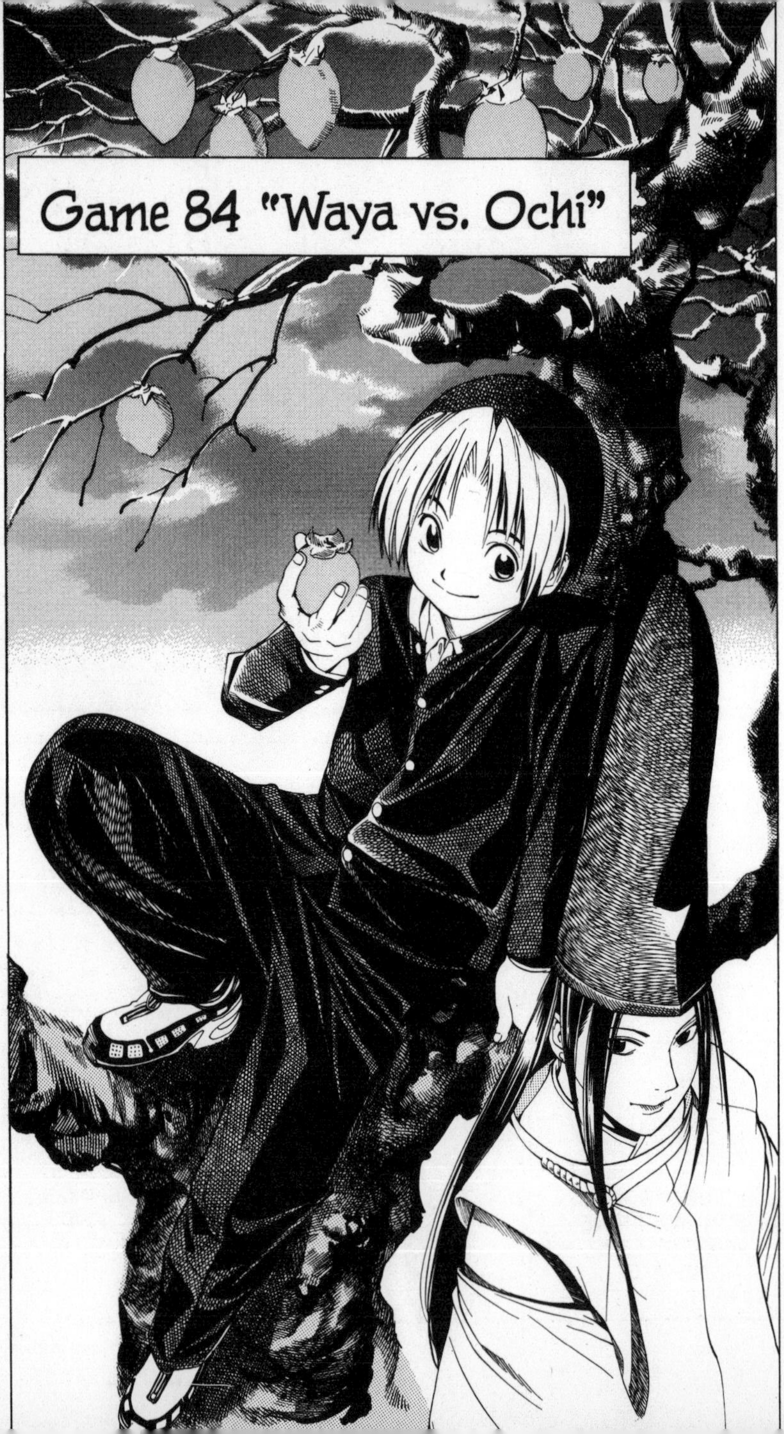
Game 84 "Waya vs. Ochi"

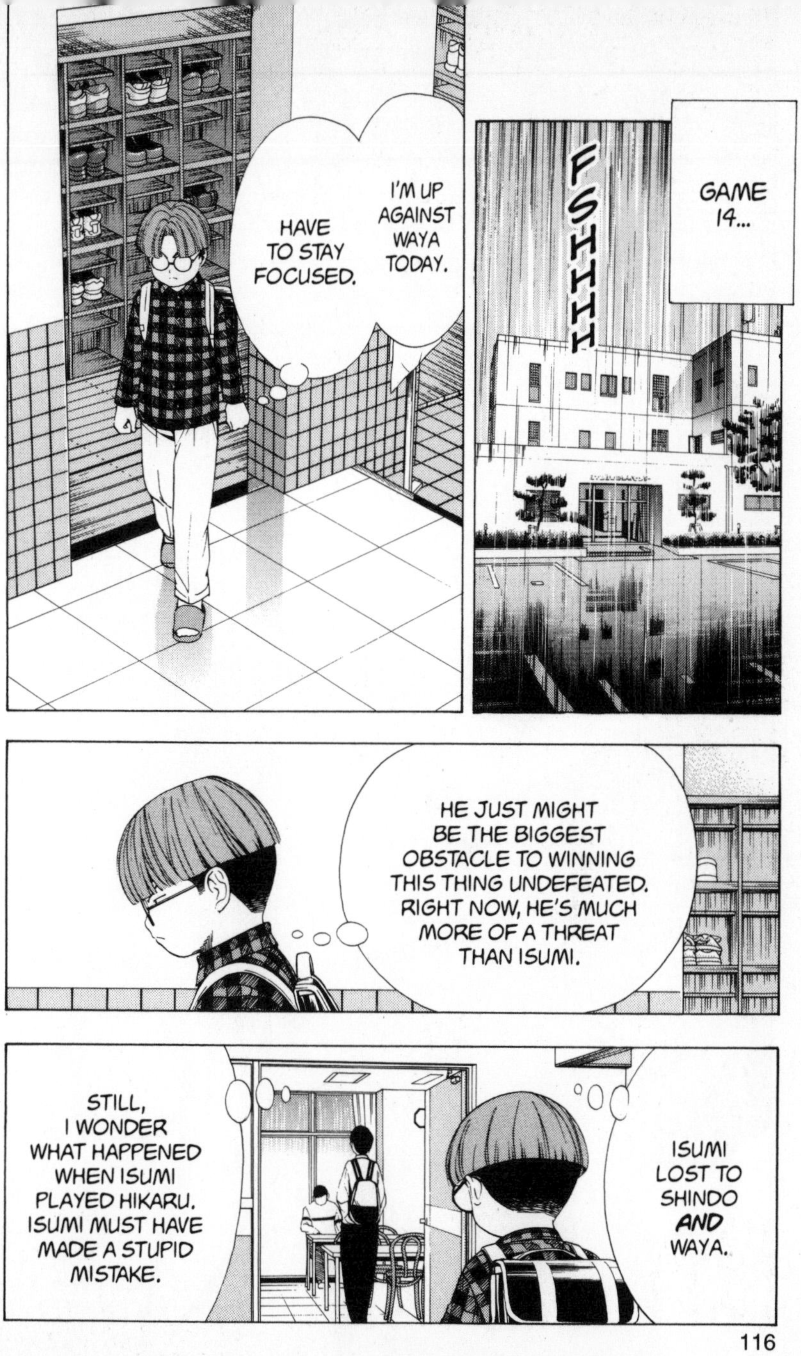
GAME 14...
FSHHHH
I'M UP AGAINST WAYA TODAY.
HAVE TO STAY FOCUSED.
HE JUST MIGHT BE THE BIGGEST OBSTACLE TO WINNING THIS THING UNDEFEATED. RIGHT NOW, HE'S MUCH MORE OF A THREAT THAN ISUMI.
ISUMI LOST TO SHINDO AND WAYA.
STILL, I WONDER WHAT HAPPENED WHEN ISUMI PLAYED HIKARU. ISUMI MUST HAVE MADE A STUPID MISTAKE.

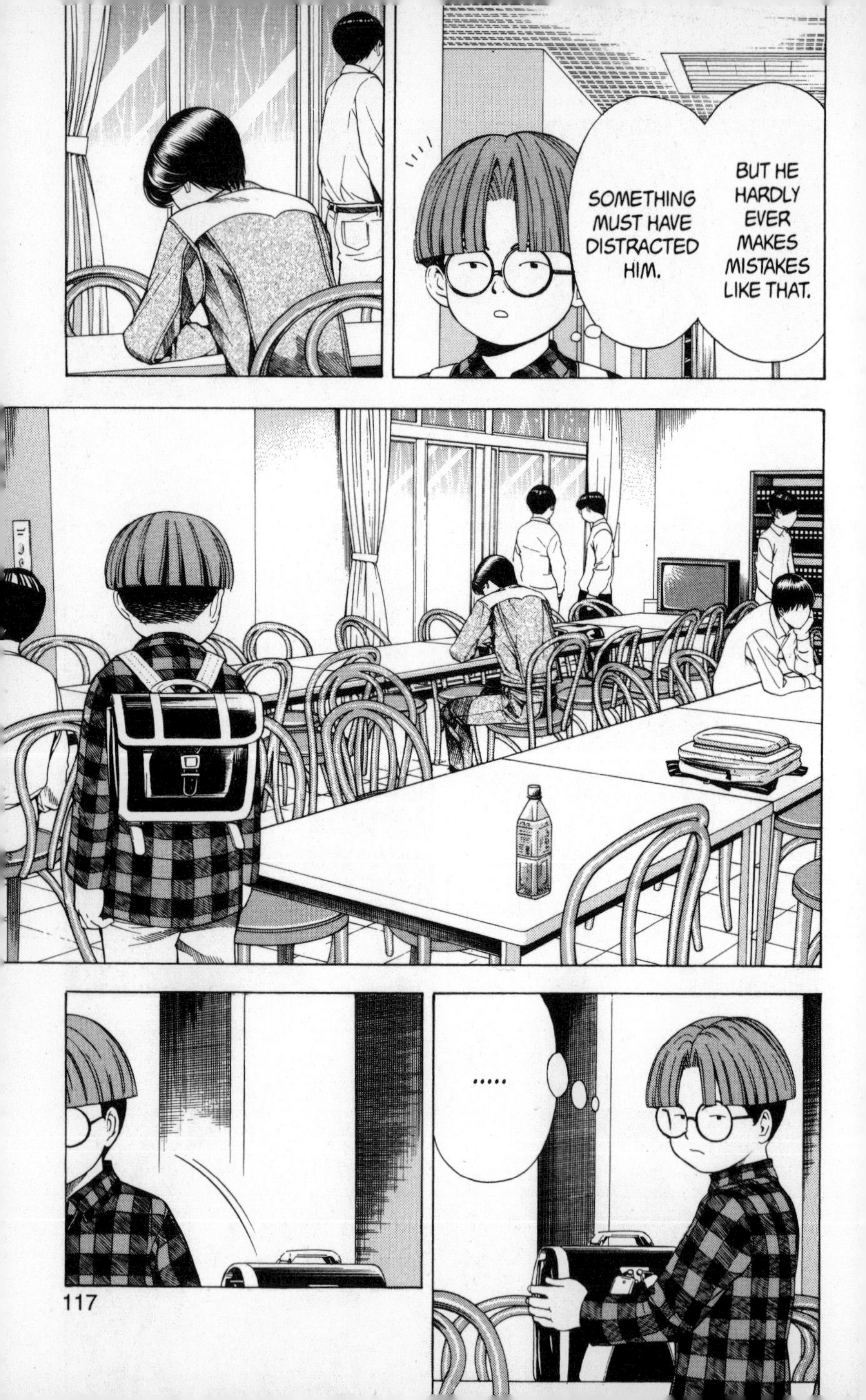
BUT HE HARDLY EVER MAKES MISTAKES LIKE THAT.
SOMETHING MUST HAVE DISTRACTED HIM.
.....

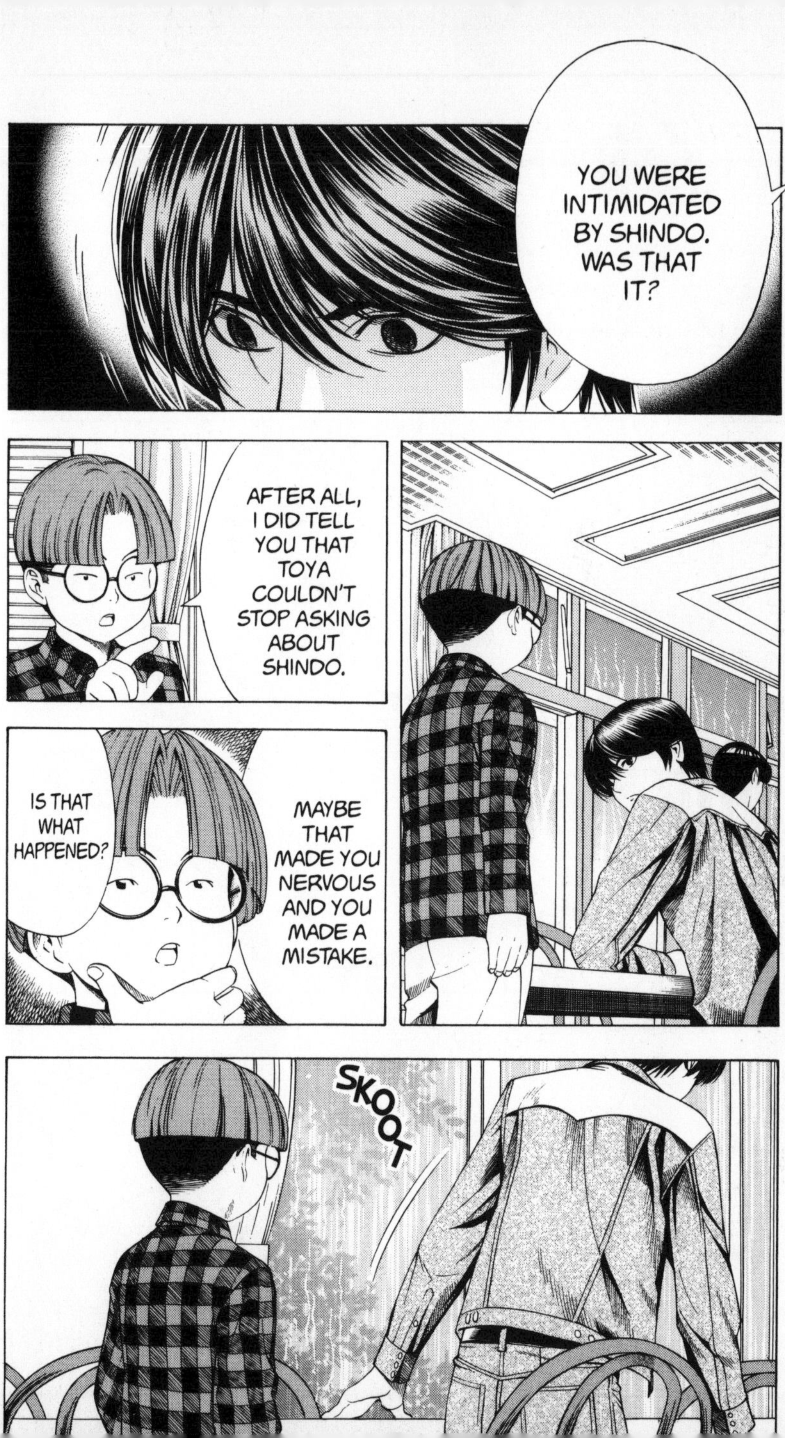
YOU WERE INTIMIDATED BY SHINDO. WAS THAT IT?
AFTER ALL, I DID TELL YOU THAT TOYA COULDN'T STOP ASKING ABOUT SHINDO.
MAYBE THAT MADE YOU NERVOUS AND YOU MADE A MISTAKE.
IS THAT WHAT HAPPENED?
SKOOT

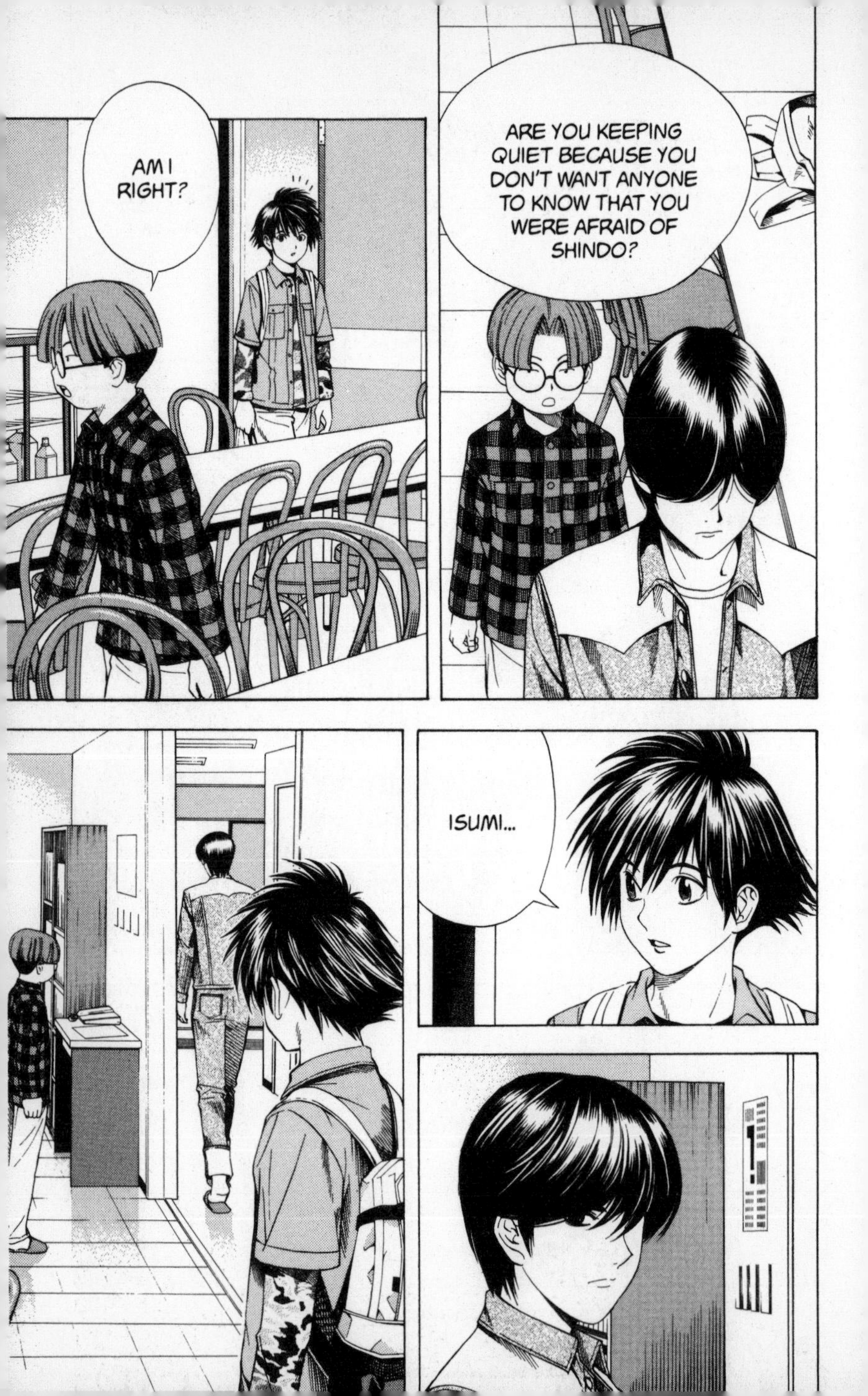
ARE YOU KEEPING QUIET BECAUSE YOU DON'T WANT ANYONE TO KNOW THAT YOU WERE AFRAID OF SHINDO?
AM I RIGHT?
ISUMI...

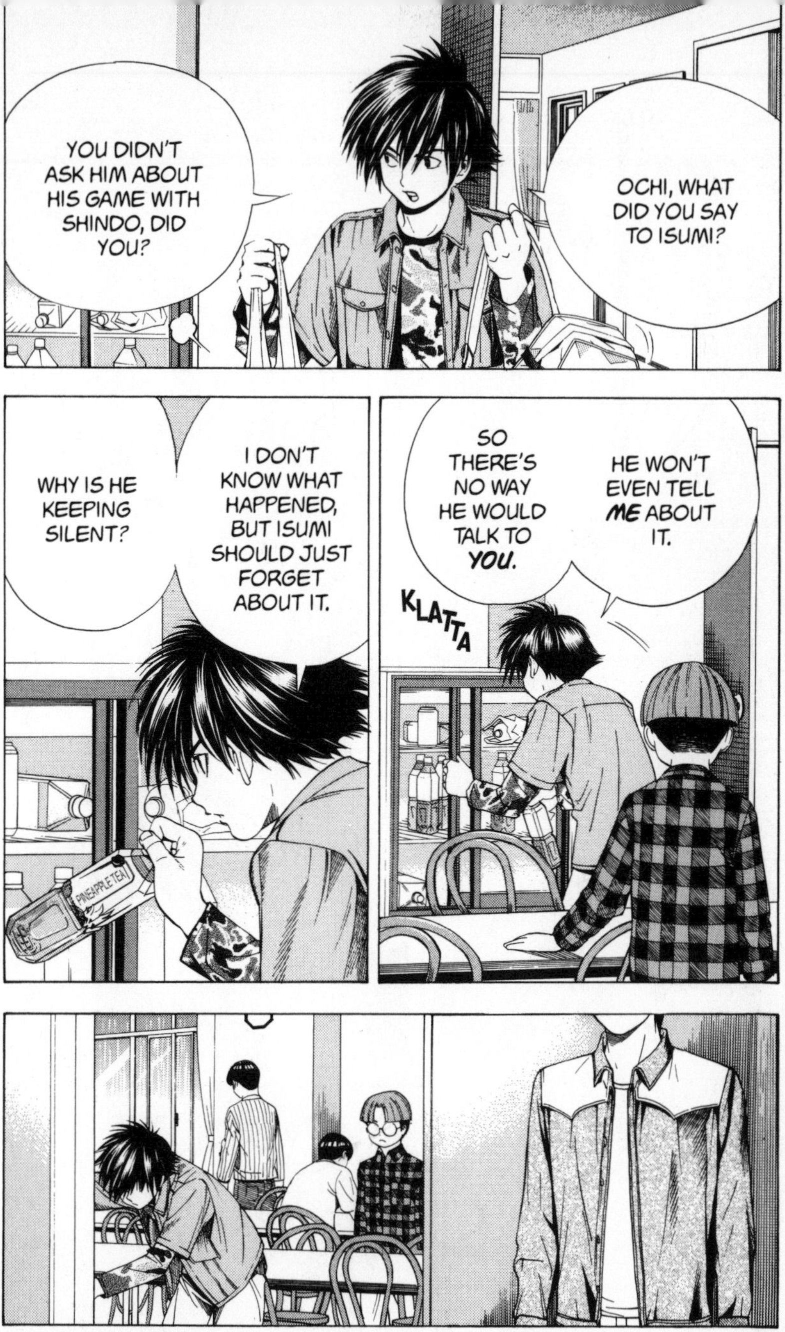
OCHI, WHAT DID YOU SAY TO ISUMI?
YOU DIDN'T ASK HIM ABOUT HIS GAME WITH SHINDO, DID YOU?
HE WON'T EVEN TELL *ME* ABOUT IT.
SO THERE'S NO WAY HE WOULD TALK TO *YOU*.
KLATTA
I DON'T KNOW WHAT HAPPENED, BUT ISUMI SHOULD JUST FORGET ABOUT IT.
WHY IS HE KEEPING SILENT?
PINEAPPLE TEA

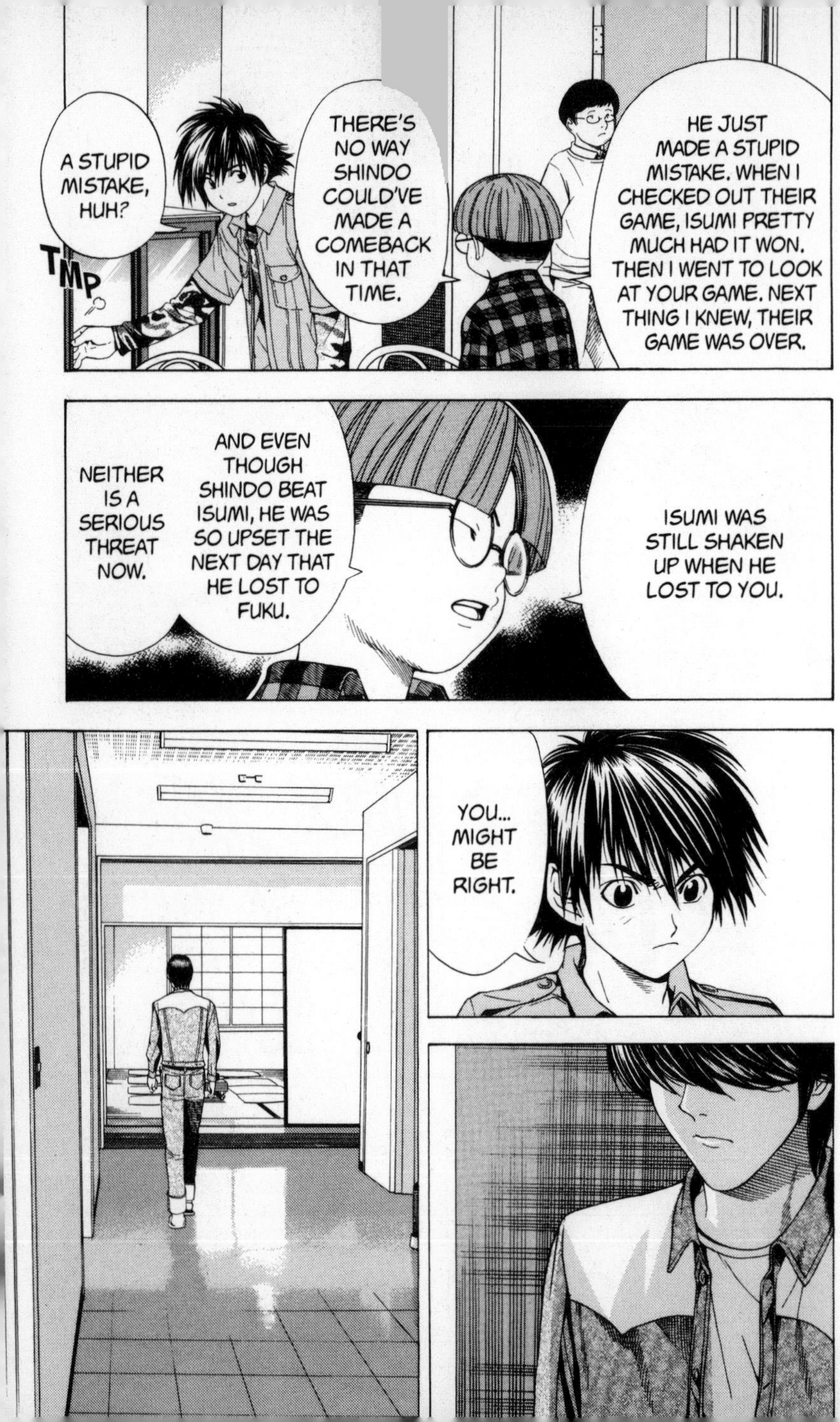
HE JUST MADE A STUPID MISTAKE. WHEN I CHECKED OUT THEIR GAME, ISUMI PRETTY MUCH HAD IT WON. THEN I WENT TO LOOK AT YOUR GAME. NEXT THING I KNEW, THEIR GAME WAS OVER.
THERE'S NO WAY SHINDO COULD'VE MADE A COMEBACK IN THAT TIME.
A STUPID MISTAKE, HUH?
TMP
ISUMI WAS STILL SHAKEN UP WHEN HE LOST TO YOU.
AND EVEN THOUGH SHINDO BEAT ISUMI, HE WAS SO UPSET THE NEXT DAY THAT HE LOST TO FUKU.
NEITHER IS A SERIOUS THREAT NOW.
YOU... MIGHT BE RIGHT.

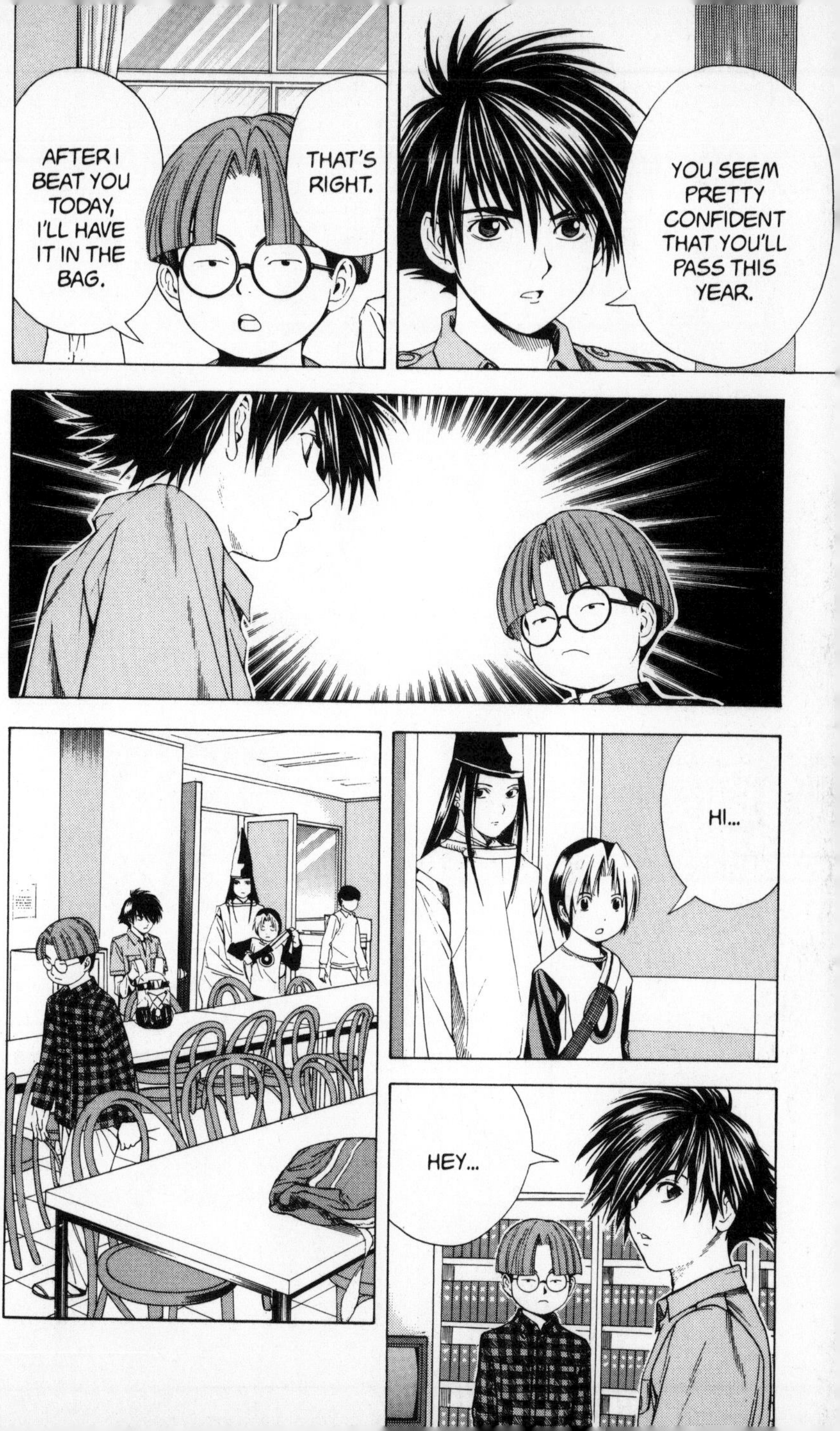
YOU SEEM PRETTY CONFIDENT THAT YOU'LL PASS THIS YEAR.
THAT'S RIGHT.
AFTER I BEAT YOU TODAY, I'LL HAVE IT IN THE BAG.
HI...
HEY...

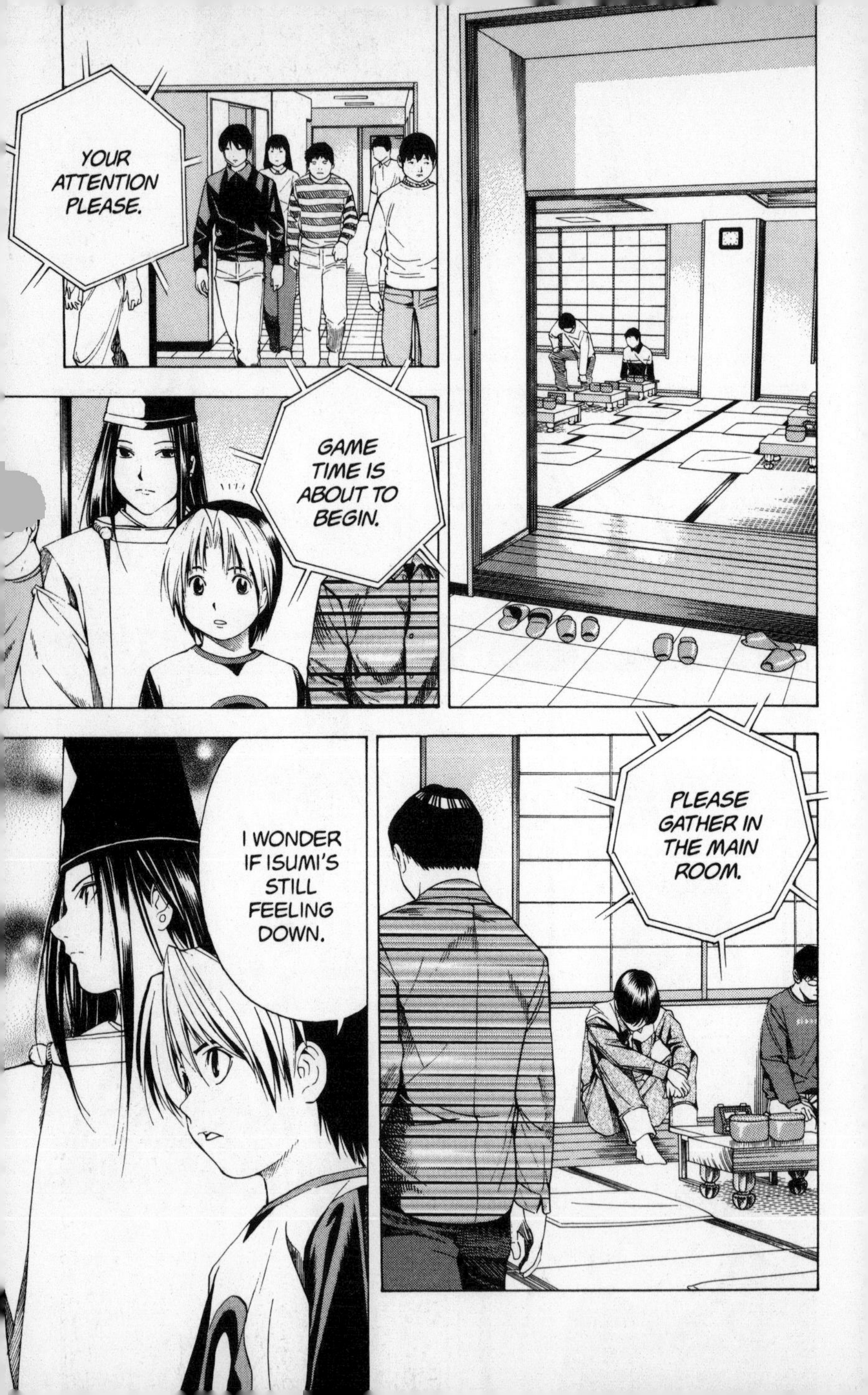
YOUR ATTENTION PLEASE.
GAME TIME IS ABOUT TO BEGIN.
PLEASE GATHER IN THE MAIN ROOM.
I WONDER IF ISUMI'S STILL FEELING DOWN.

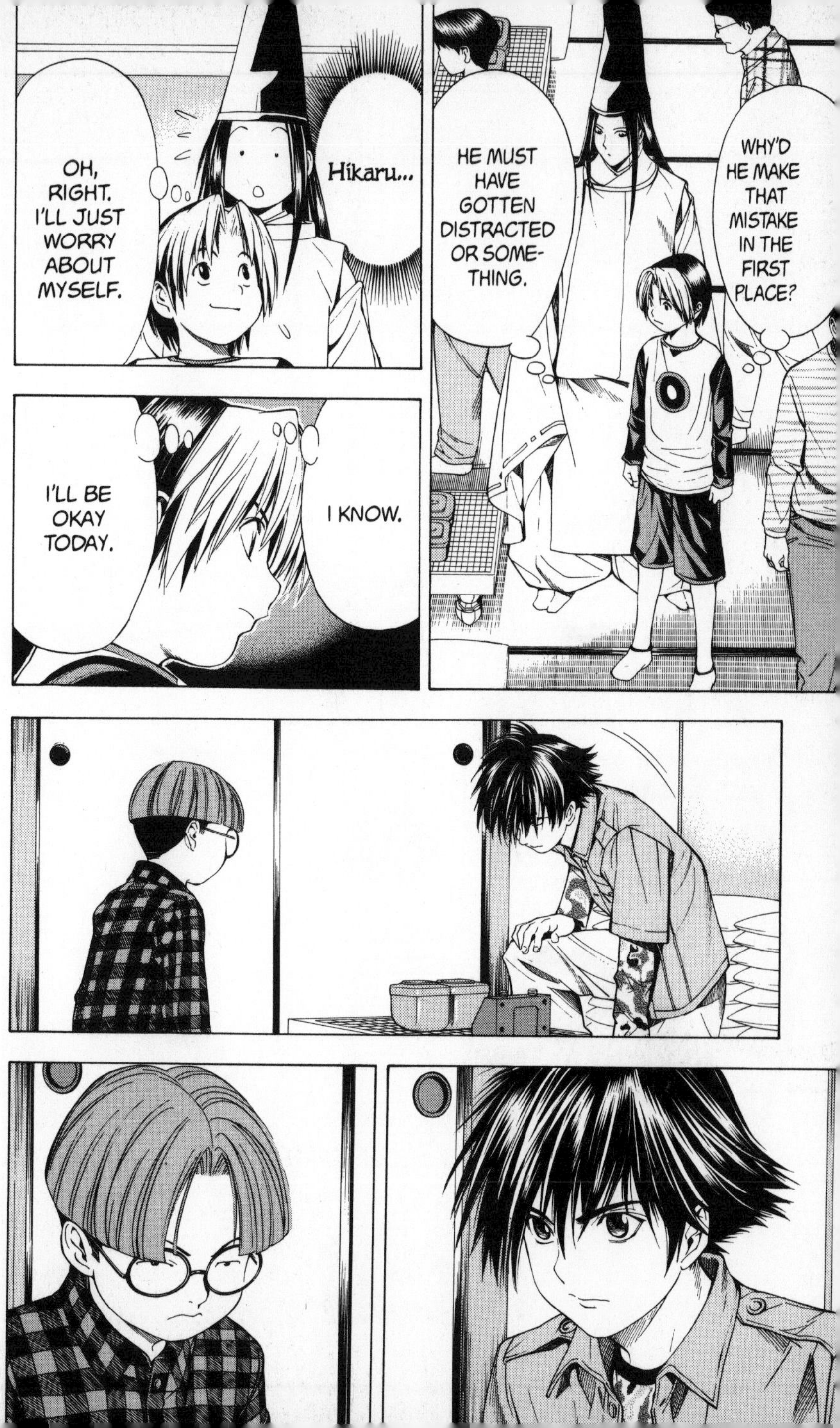
WHY'D HE MAKE THAT MISTAKE IN THE FIRST PLACE?
HE MUST HAVE GOTTEN DISTRACTED OR SOME-THING.
Hikaru...
OH, RIGHT. I'LL JUST WORRY ABOUT MYSELF.
I KNOW.
I'LL BE OKAY TODAY.

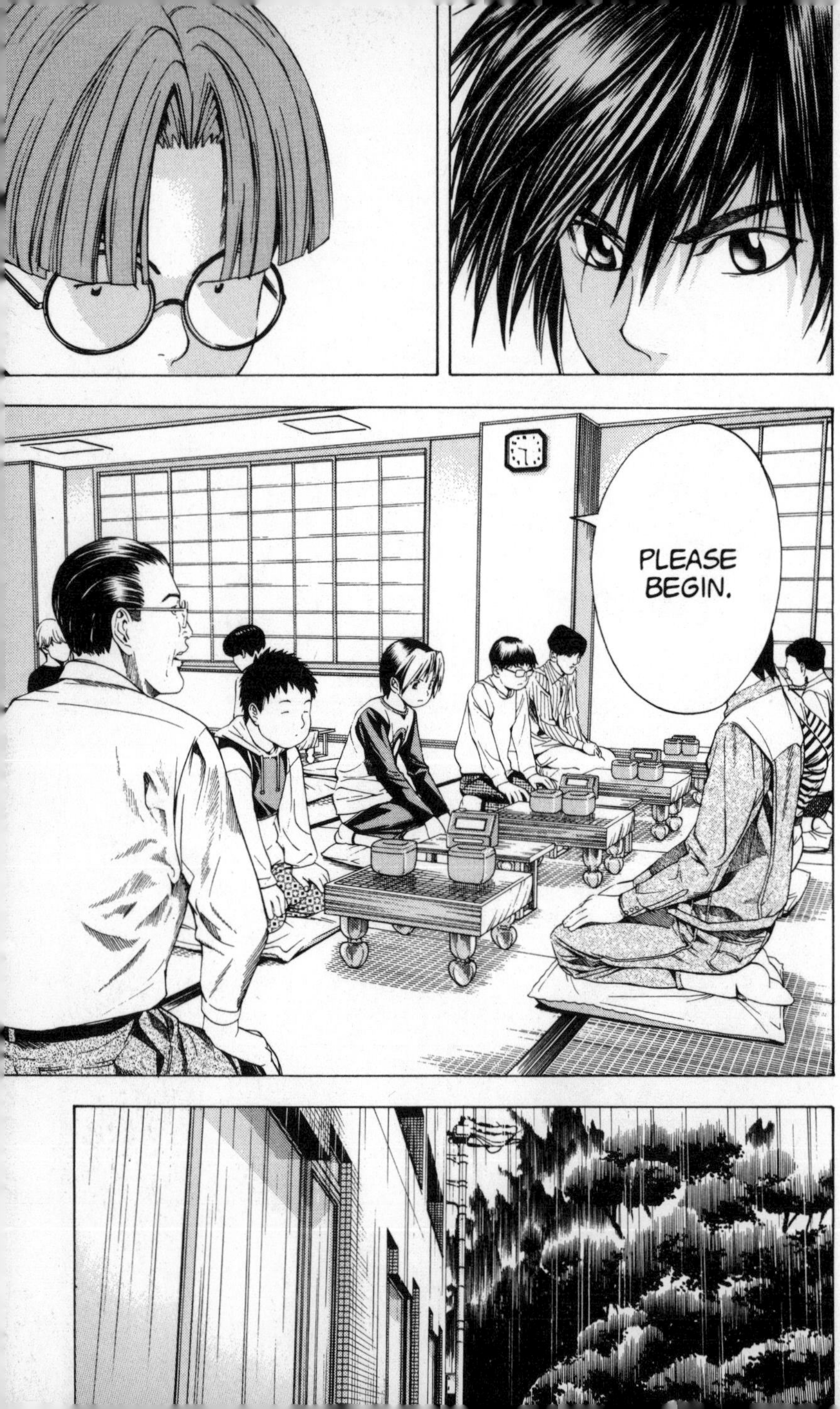
PLEASE BEGIN.

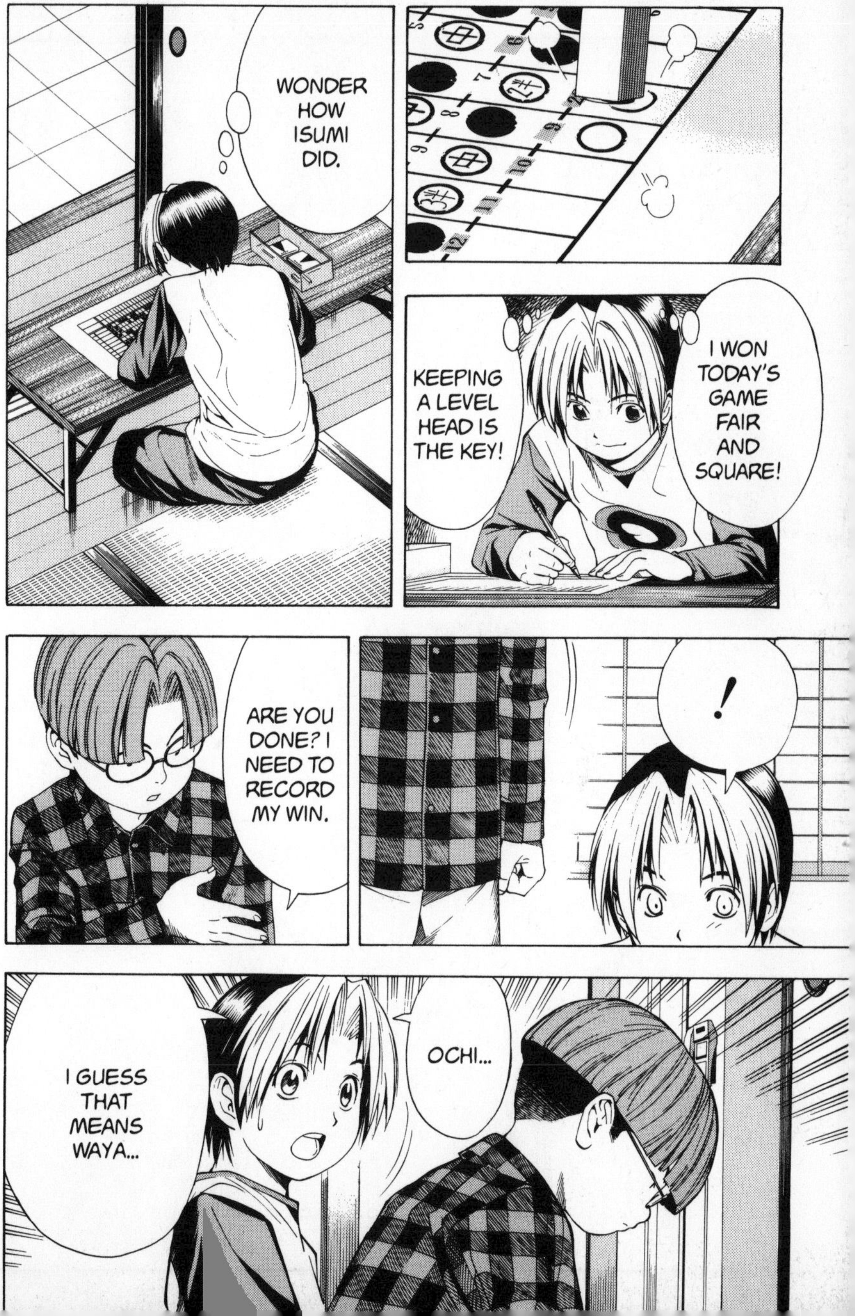
WONDER HOW ISUMI DID.
I WON TODAY'S GAME FAIR AND SQUARE!
KEEPING A LEVEL HEAD IS THE KEY!
!
ARE YOU DONE? I NEED TO RECORD MY WIN.
OCHI...
I GUESS THAT MEANS WAYA...

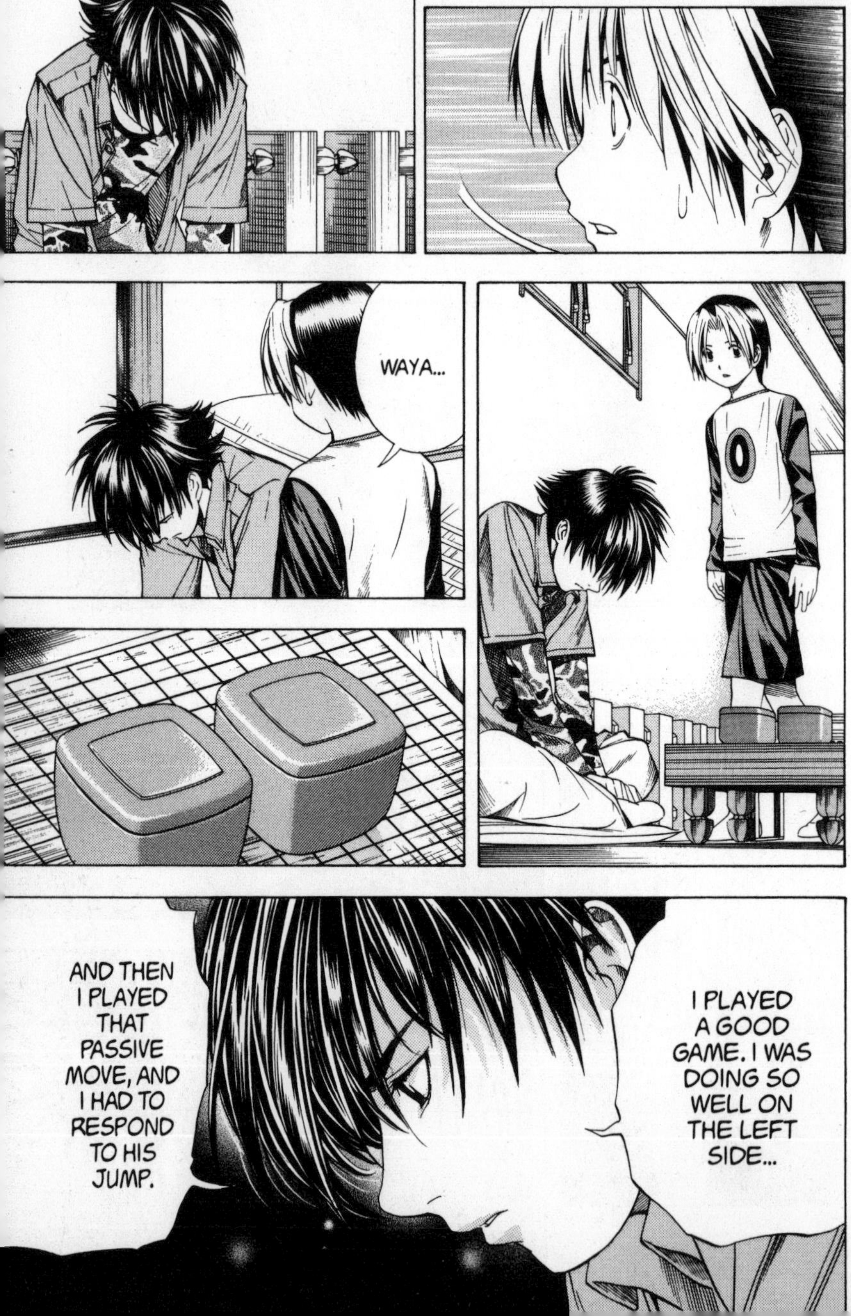
WAYA...
I PLAYED A GOOD GAME. I WAS DOING SO WELL ON THE LEFT SIDE...
AND THEN I PLAYED THAT PASSIVE MOVE, AND I HAD TO RESPOND TO HIS JUMP.

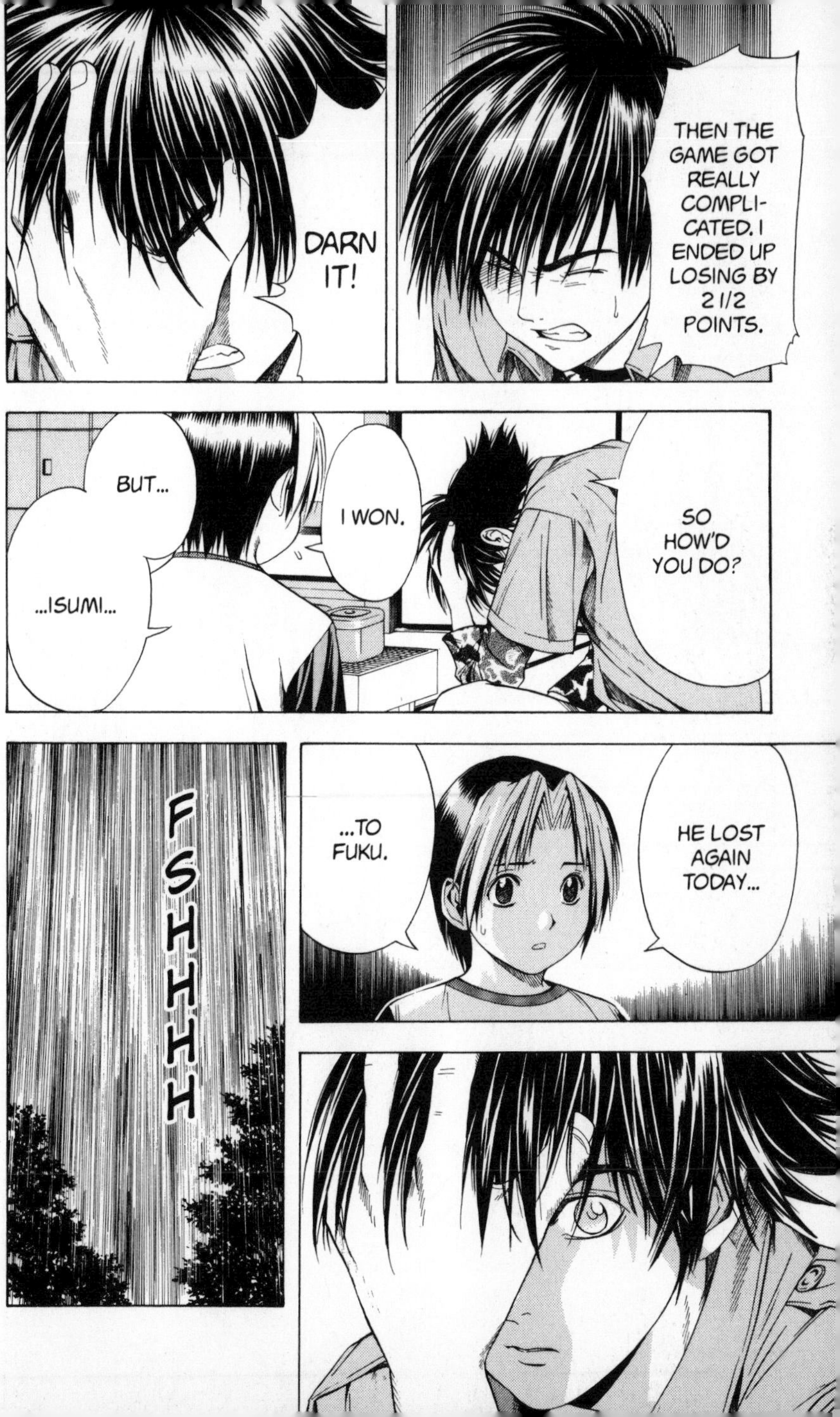
THEN THE GAME GOT REALLY COMPLI-CATED. I ENDED UP LOSING BY 2 1/2 POINTS.
DARN IT!
SO HOW'D YOU DO?
I WON.
BUT...
...ISUMI...
HE LOST AGAIN TODAY...
...TO FUKU.
FSHHHH

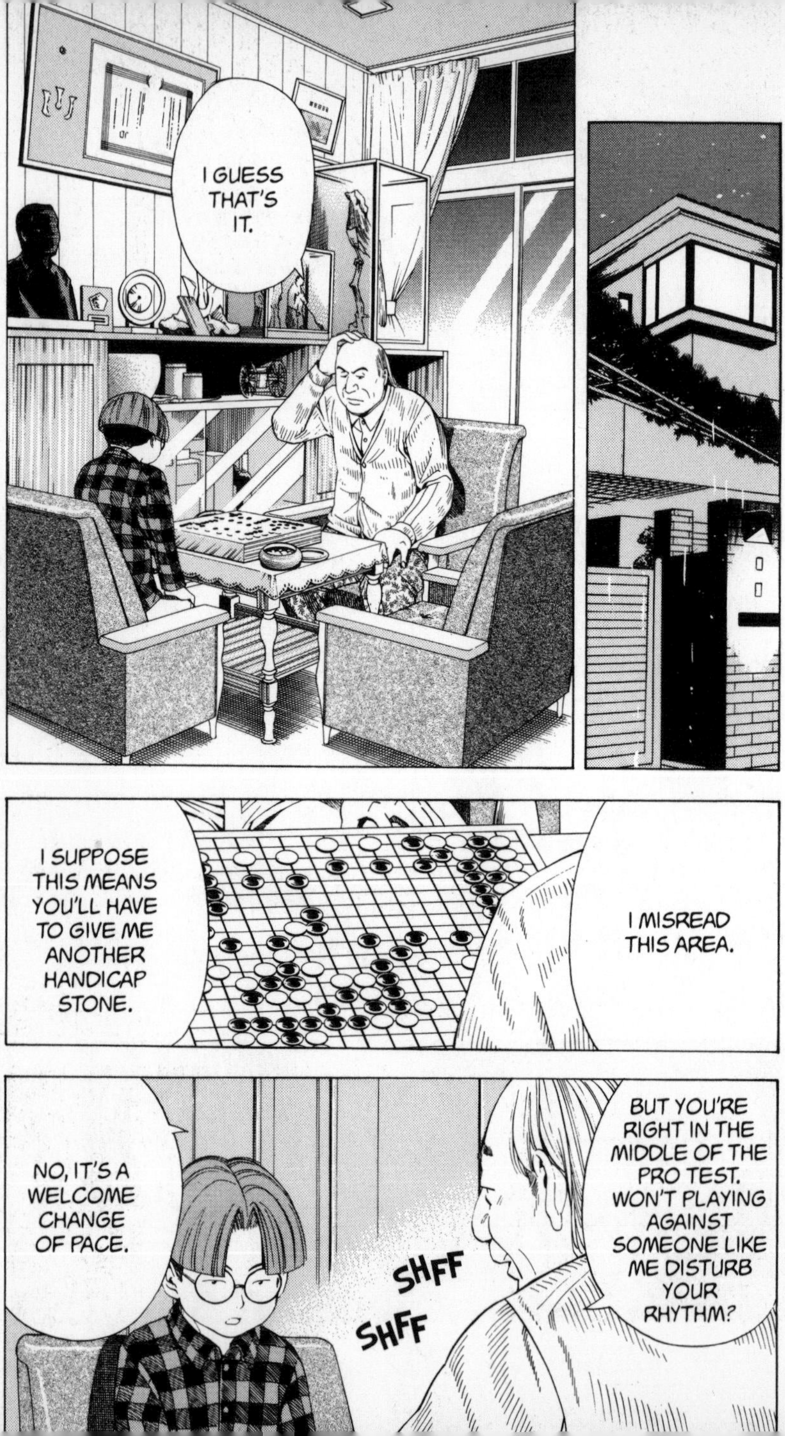
I GUESS THAT'S IT.
I MISREAD THIS AREA.
I SUPPOSE THIS MEANS YOU'LL HAVE TO GIVE ME ANOTHER HANDICAP STONE.
BUT YOU'RE RIGHT IN THE MIDDLE OF THE PRO TEST. WON'T PLAYING AGAINST SOMEONE LIKE ME DISTURB YOUR RHYTHM?
SHFF
SHFF
NO, IT'S A WELCOME CHANGE OF PACE.

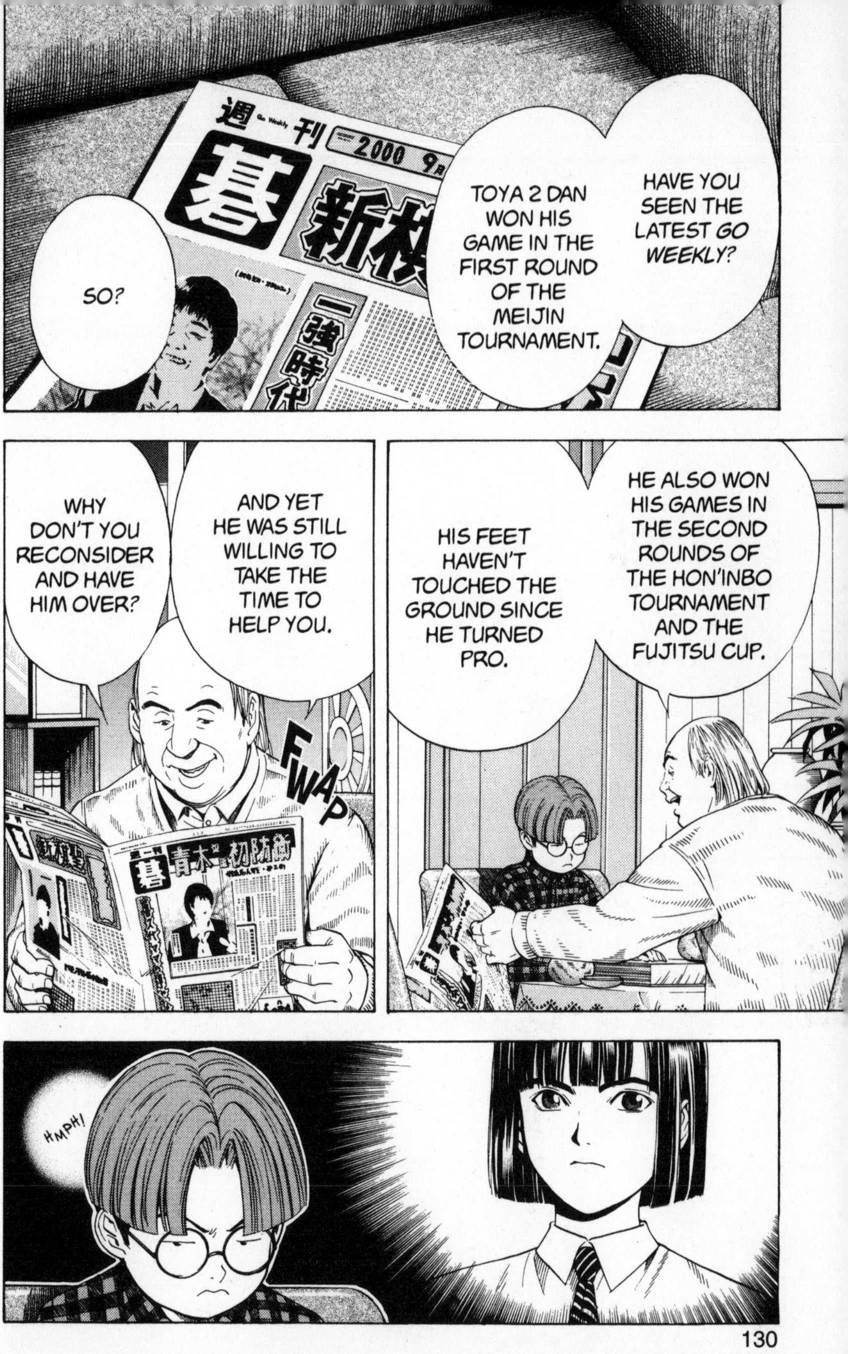
HAVE YOU SEEN THE LATEST GO WEEKLY?
TOYA 2 DAN WON HIS GAME IN THE FIRST ROUND OF THE MEIJIN TOURNAMENT.
SO?
HE ALSO WON HIS GAMES IN THE SECOND ROUNDS OF THE HON'INBO TOURNAMENT AND THE FUJITSU CUP.
HIS FEET HAVEN'T TOUCHED THE GROUND SINCE HE TURNED PRO.
AND YET HE WAS STILL WILLING TO TAKE THE TIME TO HELP YOU.
WHY DON'T YOU RECONSIDER AND HAVE HIM OVER?
FWAP
HMPH!

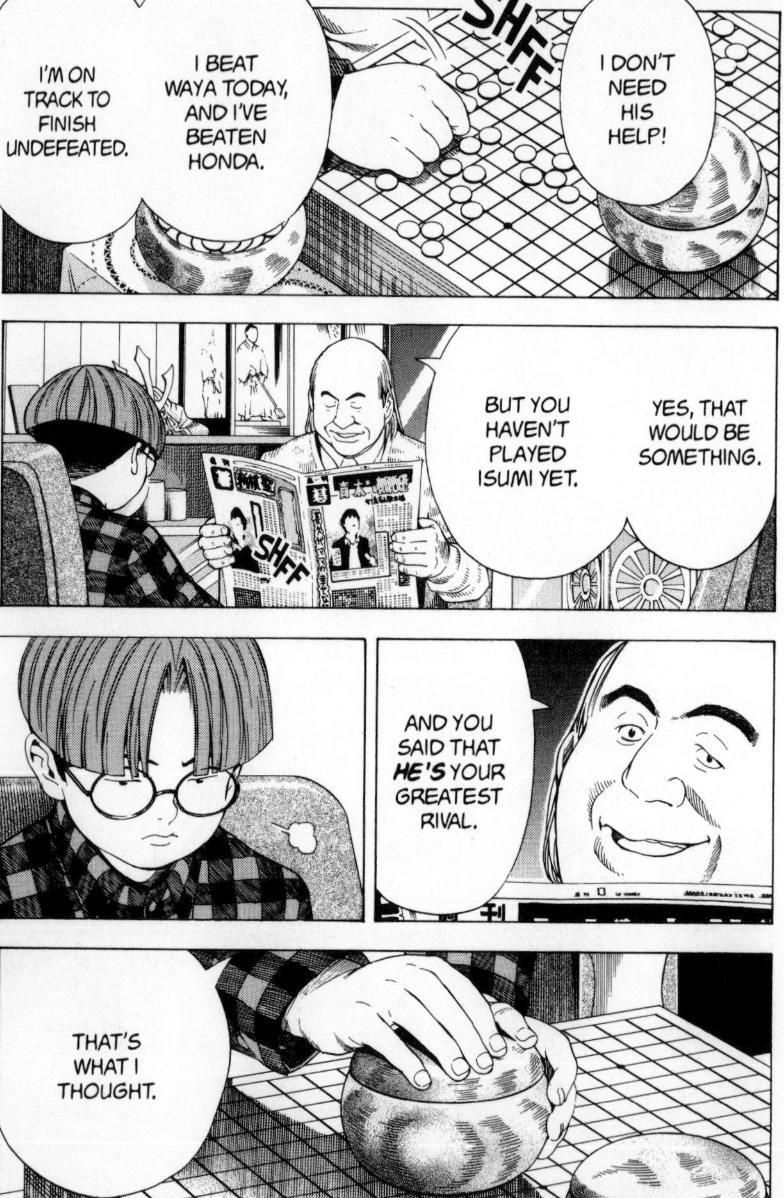
SHFF
I DON'T NEED HIS HELP!
I BEAT WAYA TODAY, AND I'VE BEATEN HONDA.
I'M ON TRACK TO FINISH UNDEFEATED.
YES, THAT WOULD BE SOMETHING.
BUT YOU HAVEN'T PLAYED ISUMI YET.
SHFF
AND YOU SAID THAT **HE'S** YOUR GREATEST RIVAL.
THAT'S WHAT I THOUGHT.

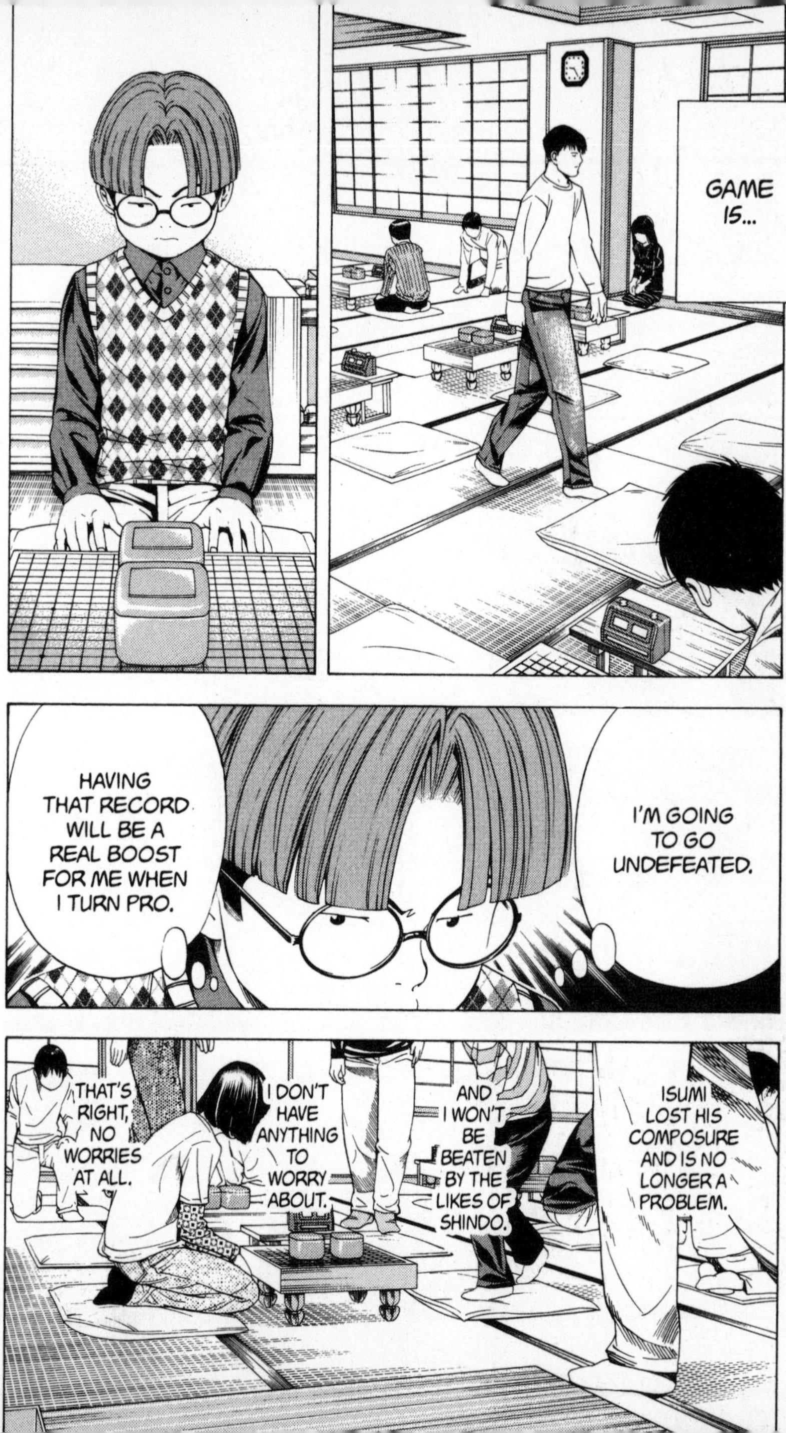
GAME IS...
I'M GOING TO GO UNDEFEATED.
HAVING THAT RECORD WILL BE A REAL BOOST FOR ME WHEN I TURN PRO.
ISUMI LOST HIS COMPOSURE AND IS NO LONGER A PROBLEM.
AND I WON'T BE BEATEN BY THE LIKES OF SHINDO.
I DON'T HAVE ANYTHING TO WORRY ABOUT.
THAT'S RIGHT, NO WORRIES AT ALL.

READ THIS WAY

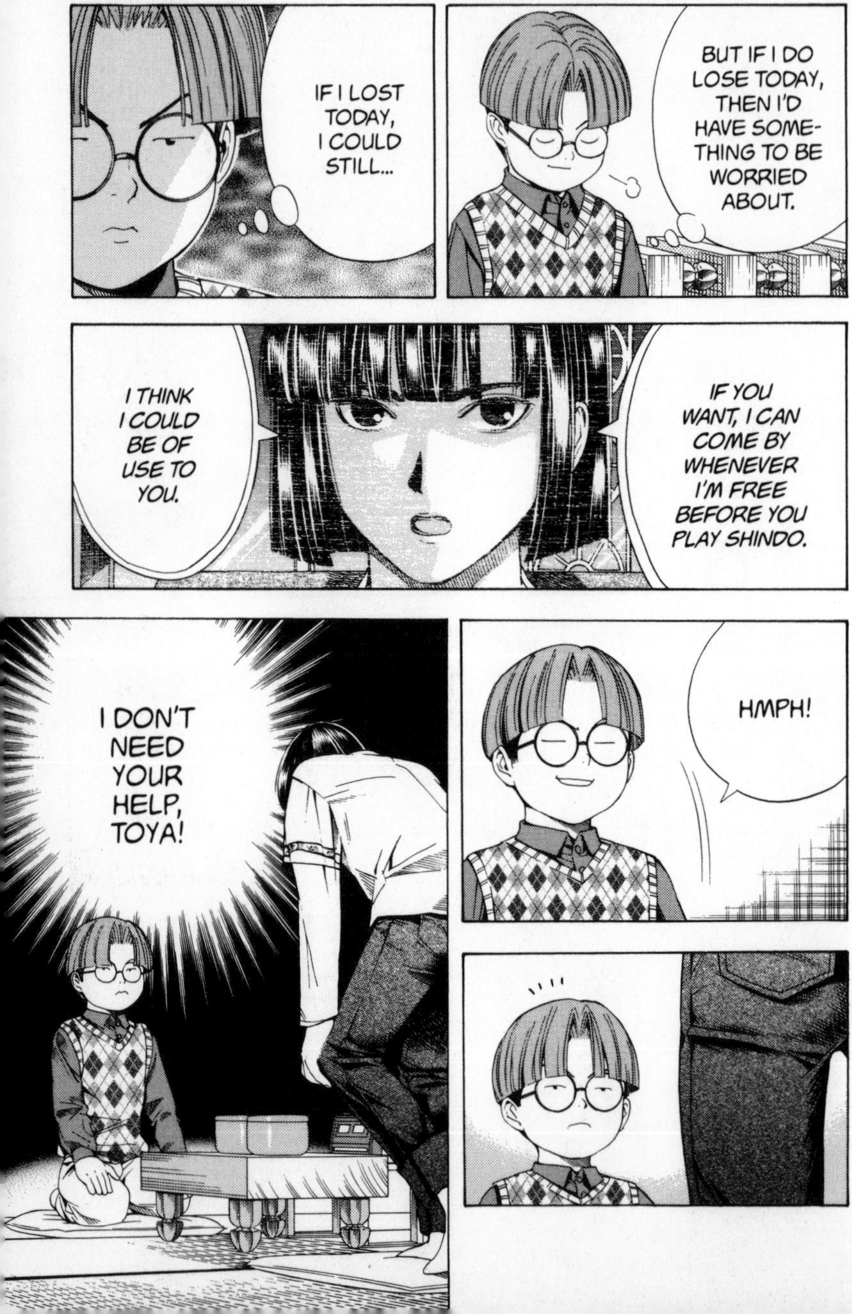
BUT IF I DO LOSE TODAY, THEN I'D HAVE SOME-THING TO BE WORRIED ABOUT.
IF I LOST TODAY, I COULD STILL...
IF YOU WANT, I CAN COME BY WHENEVER I'M FREE BEFORE YOU PLAY SHINDO.
I THINK I COULD BE OF USE TO YOU.
HMPH!
I DON'T NEED YOUR HELP, TOYA!

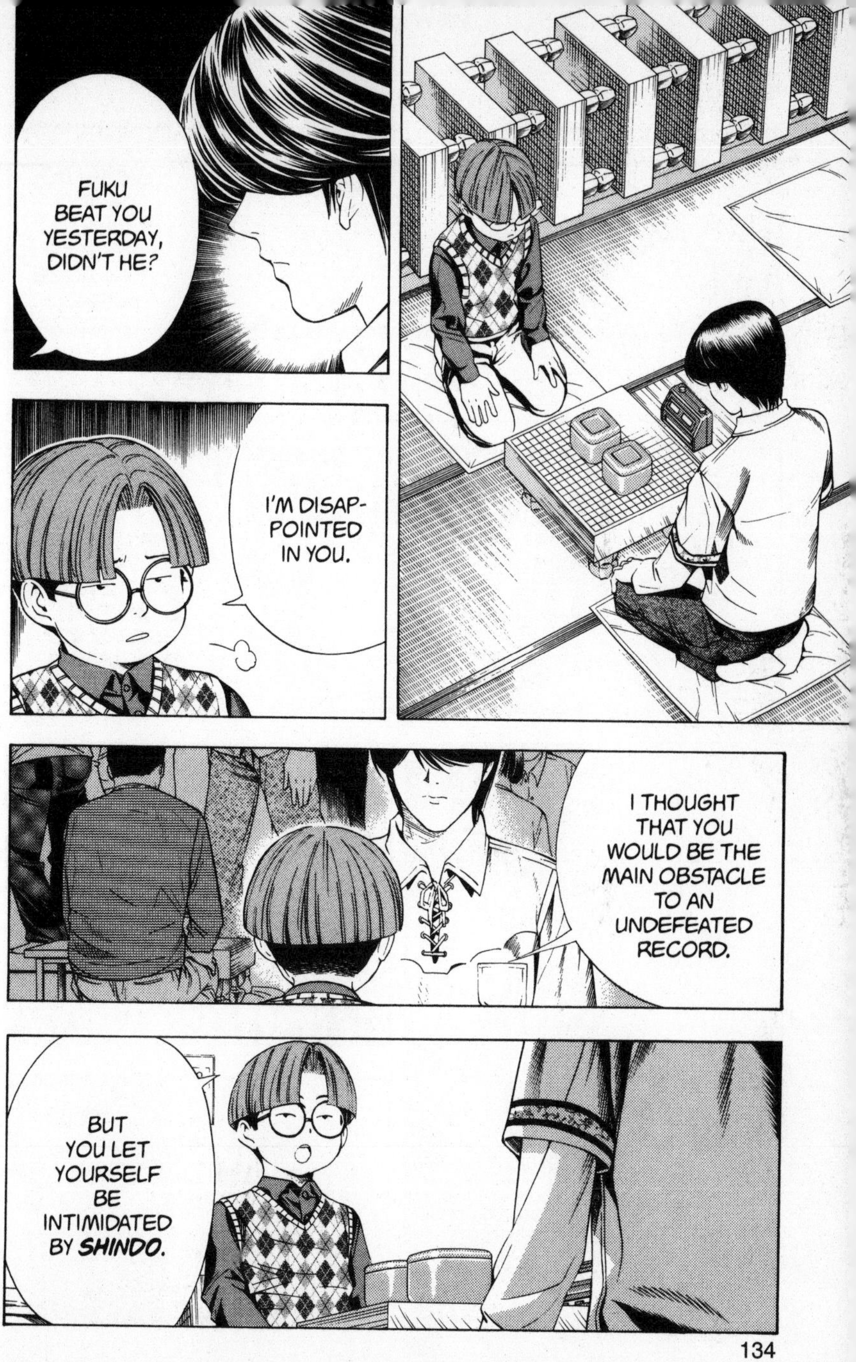
FUKU BEAT YOU YESTERDAY, DIDN'T HE?
I'M DISAP-POINTED IN YOU.
I THOUGHT THAT YOU WOULD BE THE MAIN OBSTACLE TO AN UNDEFEATED RECORD.
BUT YOU LET YOURSELF BE INTIMIDATED BY *SHINDO*.

READ THIS WAY

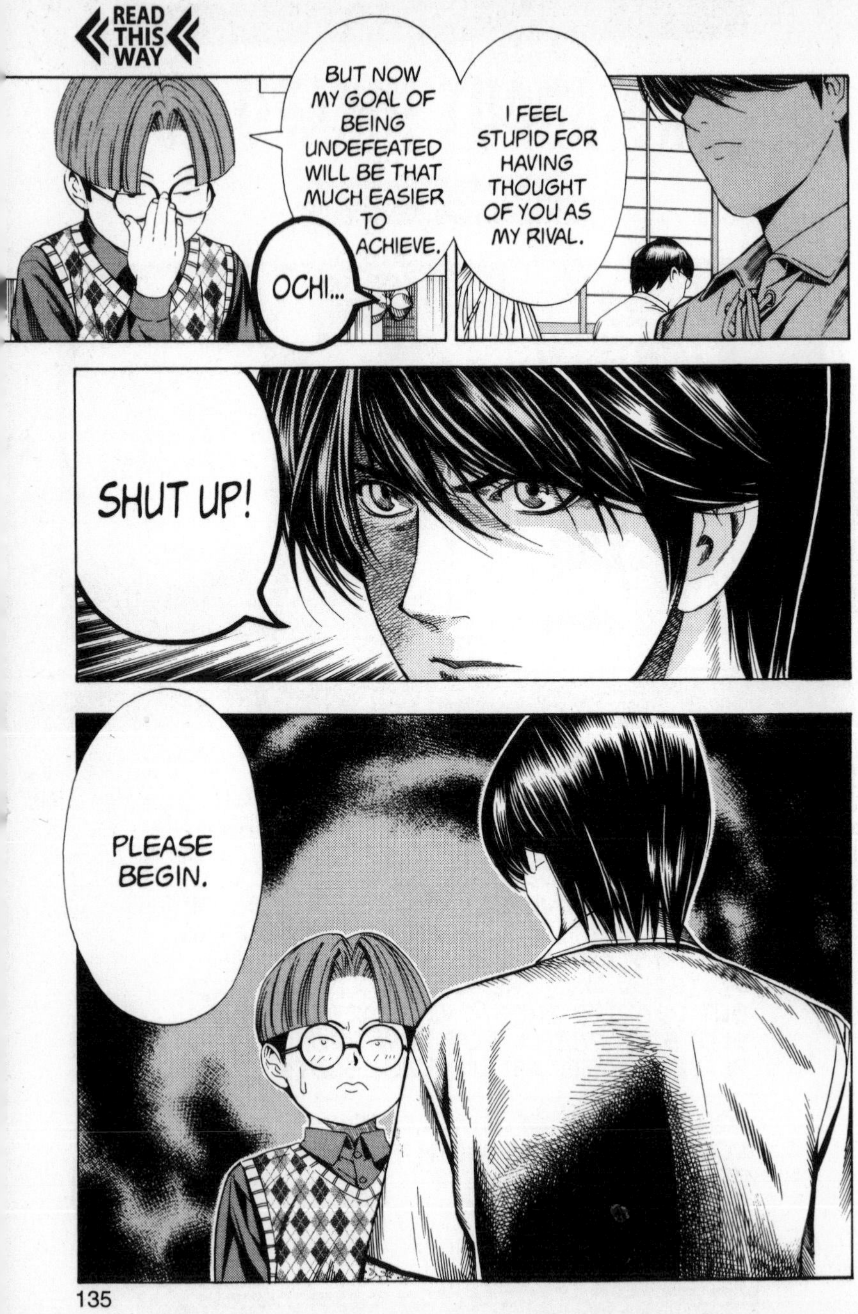
I FEEL STUPID FOR HAVING THOUGHT OF YOU AS MY RIVAL.
BUT NOW MY GOAL OF BEING UNDEFEATED WILL BE THAT MUCH EASIER TO ACHIEVE.
OCHI...
SHUT UP!
PLEASE BEGIN.

A WORD ABOUT HIKARU NO GO

THE PRO TEST

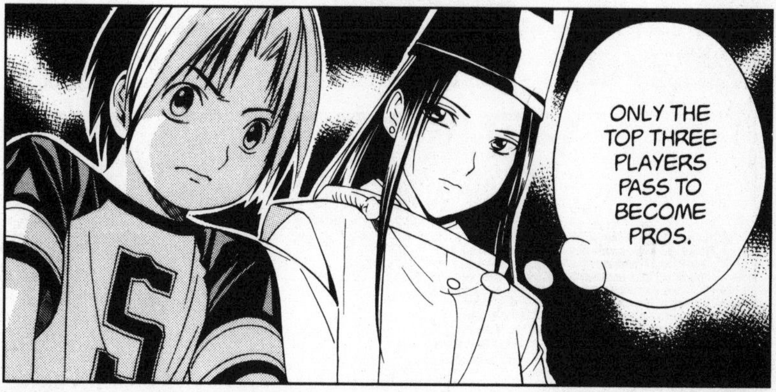
ONLY THE TOP THREE PLAYERS PASS TO BECOME PROS.

THE PRO TEST FOR THE GENERAL BRANCH

BESIDES THE GENERAL BRANCH IN TOKYO, THERE ARE SEVERAL OTHER BRANCHES OF GO ASSOCIATIONS, SUCH AS THE CENTRAL AND WESTERN BRANCHES, THE WOMEN'S DIVISION, AND THE KANSAI KI-IN BRANCH. BUT DESPITE THIS, THERE AREN'T MANY SLOTS ALLOCATED FOR NEW PROFESSIONAL PLAYERS–ONLY ABOUT FOUR SLOTS IN TOTAL.

FOR THE SAKE OF SIMPLICITY, *HIKARU NO GO* DEALS ONLY WITH THE GENERAL BRANCH.

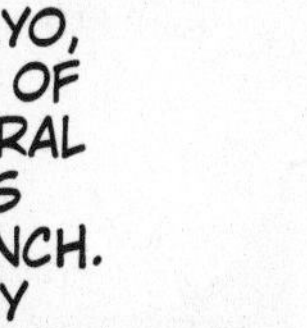

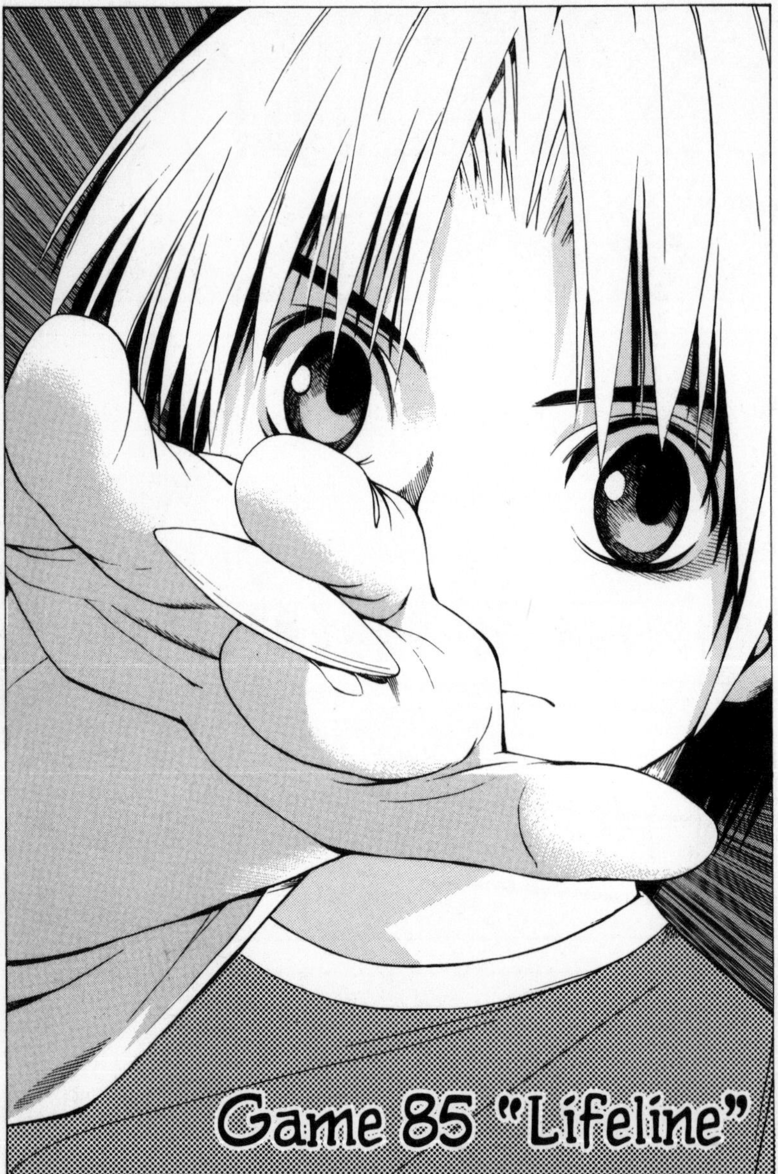
Game 85 "Lifeline"

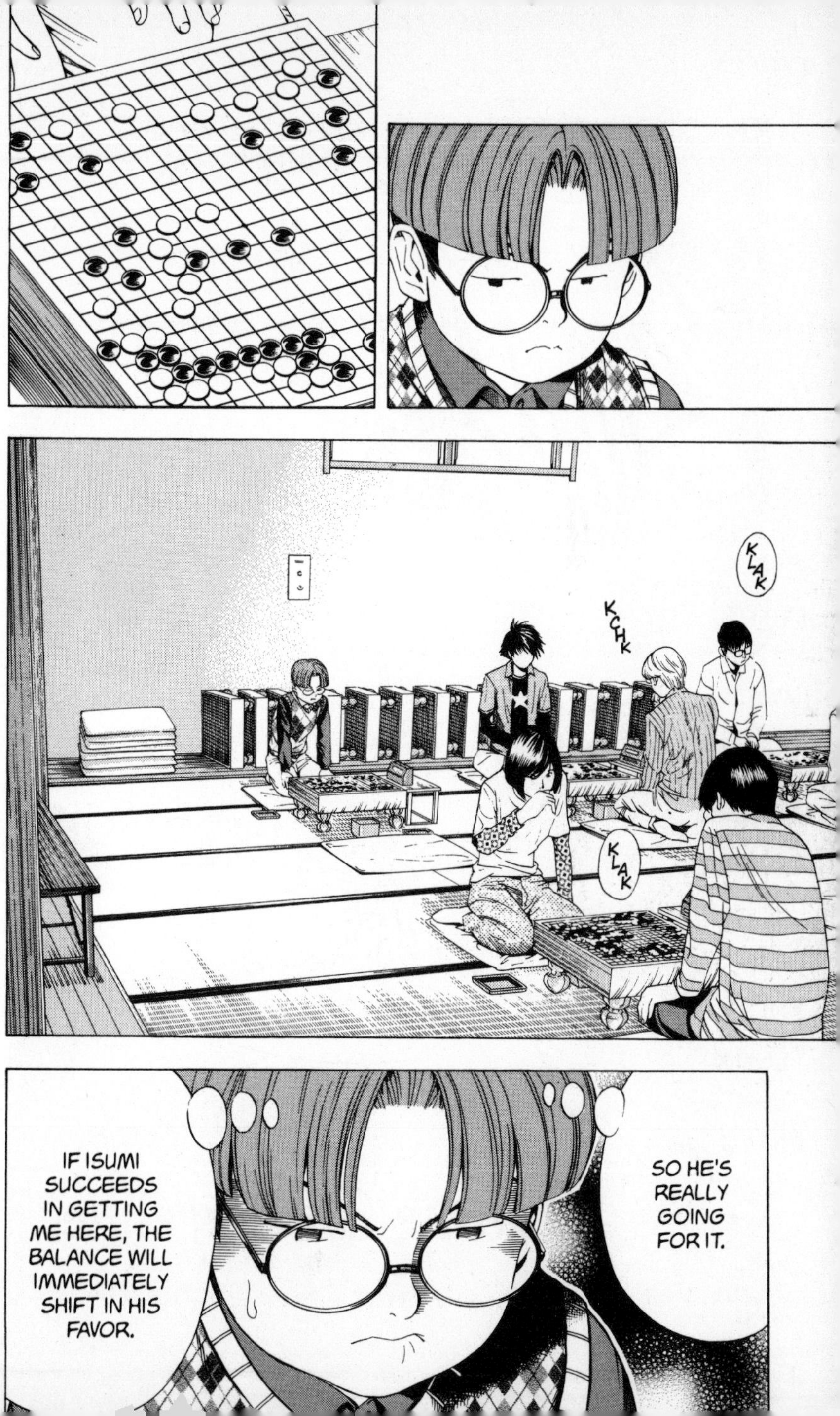
KLAK
KCHK
KLAK
SO HE'S REALLY GOING FOR IT.
IF ISUMI SUCCEEDS IN GETTING ME HERE, THE BALANCE WILL IMMEDIATELY SHIFT IN HIS FAVOR.

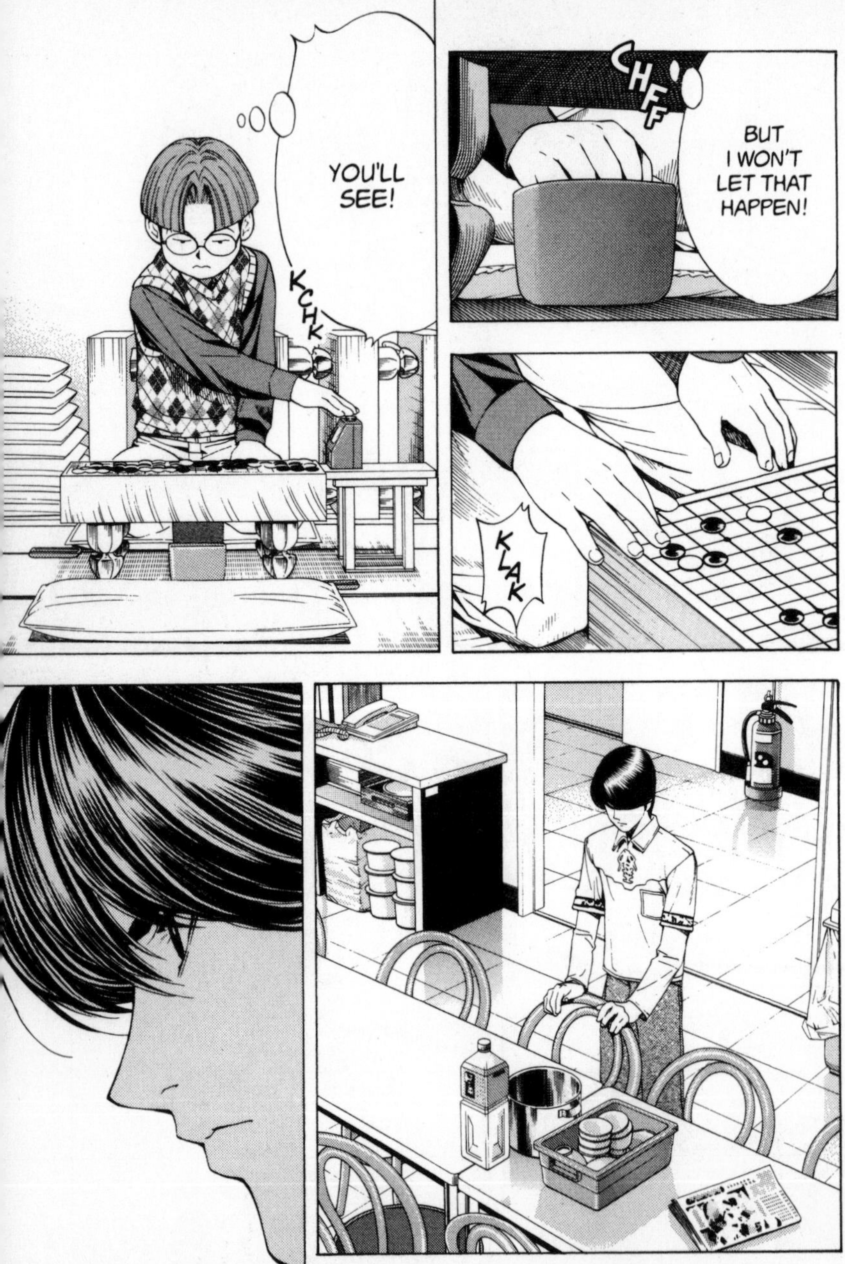
CHFF
BUT I WON'T LET THAT HAPPEN!
KLAK
YOU'LL SEE!
KCHK

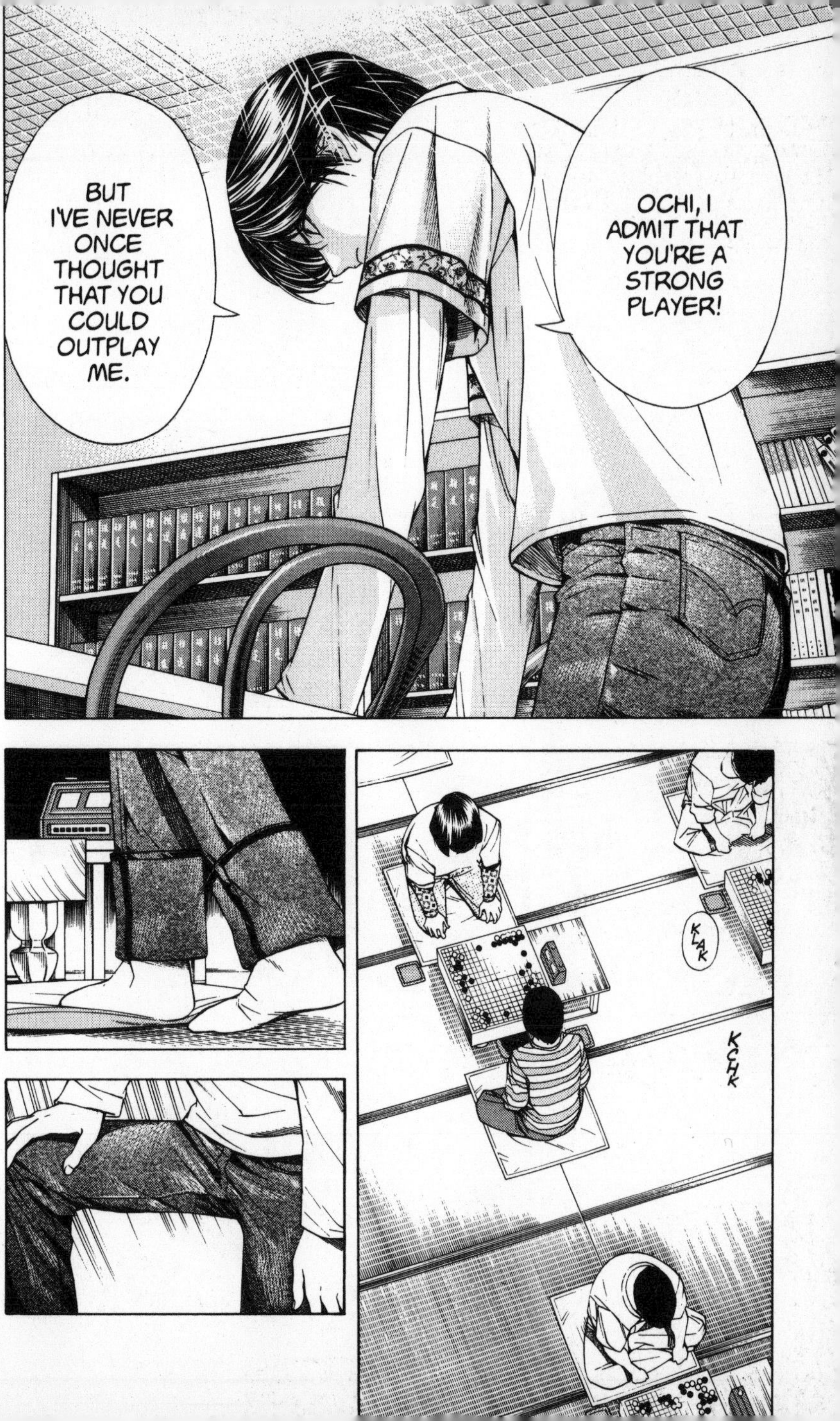
OCHI, I ADMIT THAT YOU'RE A STRONG PLAYER!
BUT I'VE NEVER ONCE THOUGHT THAT YOU COULD OUTPLAY ME.
KLAK
KCHK

READ THIS WAY

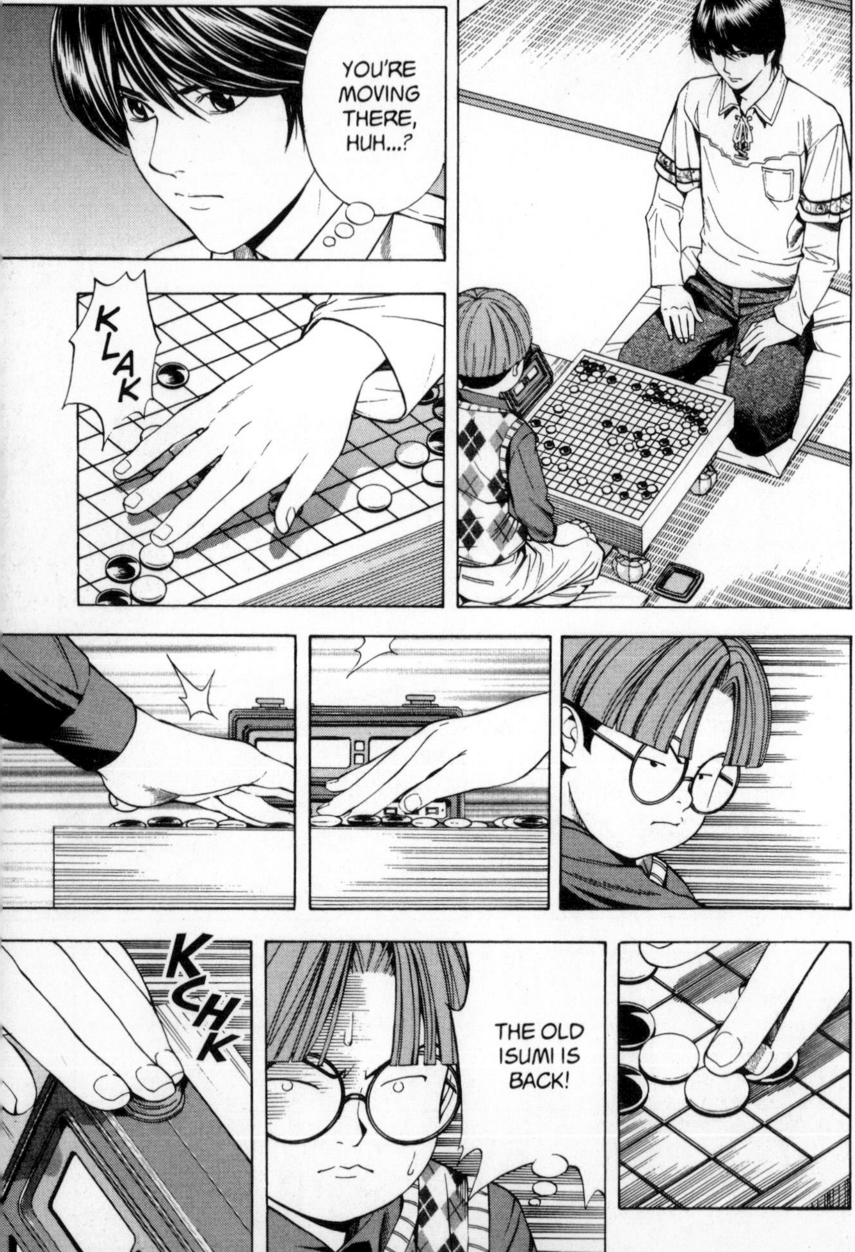
YOU'RE MOVING THERE, HUH...?
KLAK
THE OLD ISUMI IS BACK!
KCHK

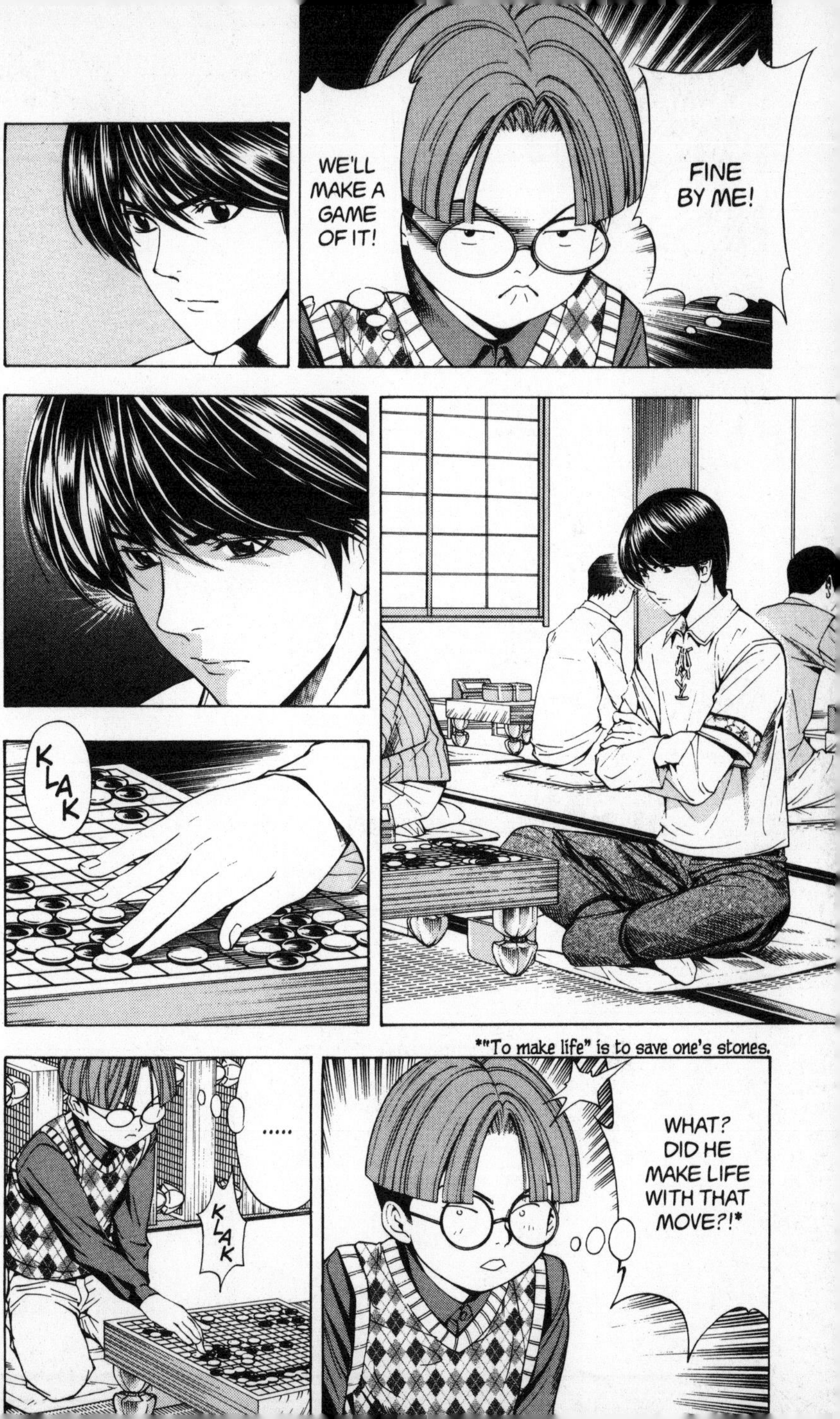
FINE BY ME!
WE'LL MAKE A GAME OF IT!
KLAK
*"To make life" is to save one's stones.
WHAT? DID HE MAKE LIFE WITH THAT MOVE?!*
.....
KLAK

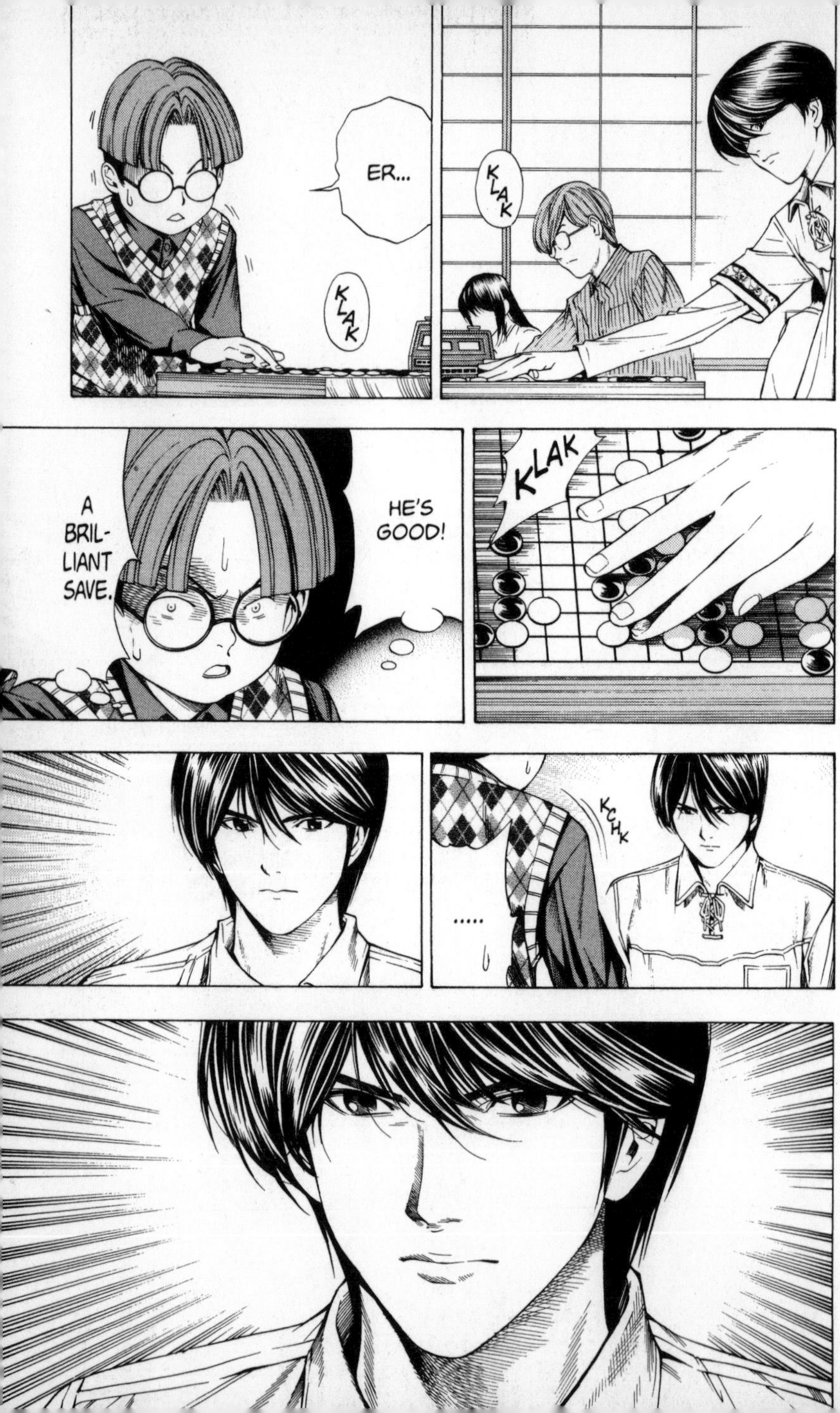
KLAK
ER...
KLAK
KLAK
HE'S GOOD!
A BRIL-LIANT SAVE.
KCHK
.....

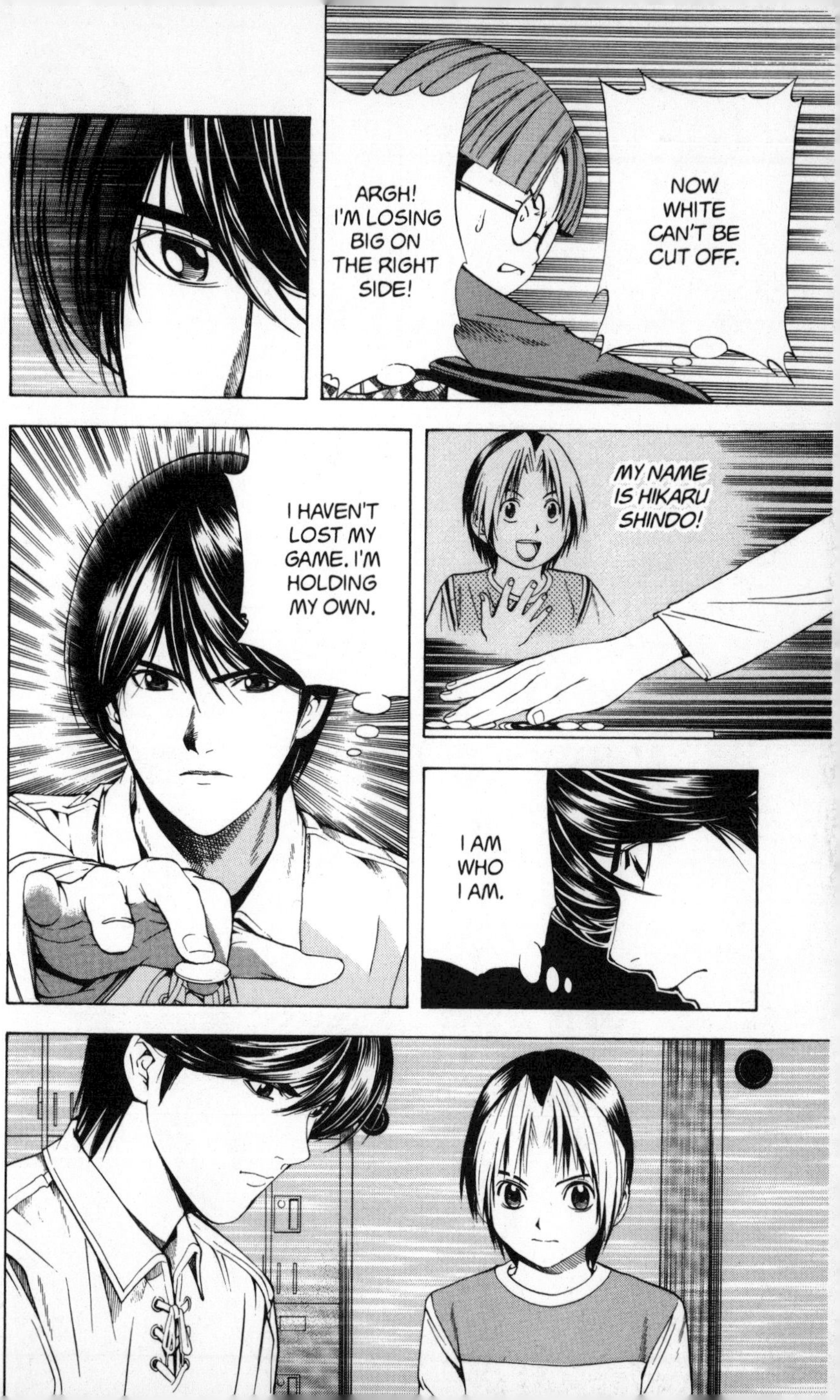
NOW WHITE CAN'T BE CUT OFF.
ARGH! I'M LOSING BIG ON THE RIGHT SIDE!
MY NAME IS HIKARU SHINDO!
I AM WHO I AM.
I HAVEN'T LOST MY GAME. I'M HOLDING MY OWN.

READ THIS WAY

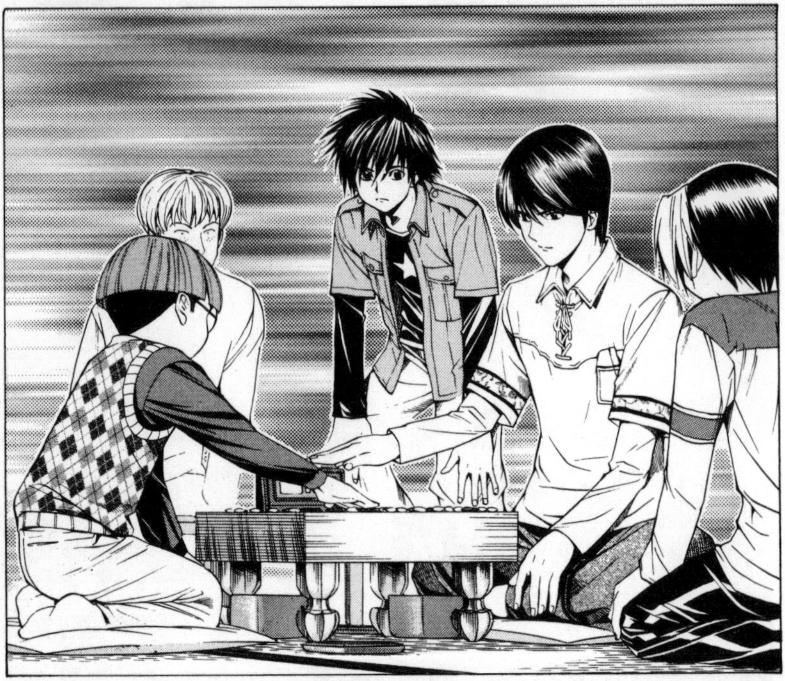

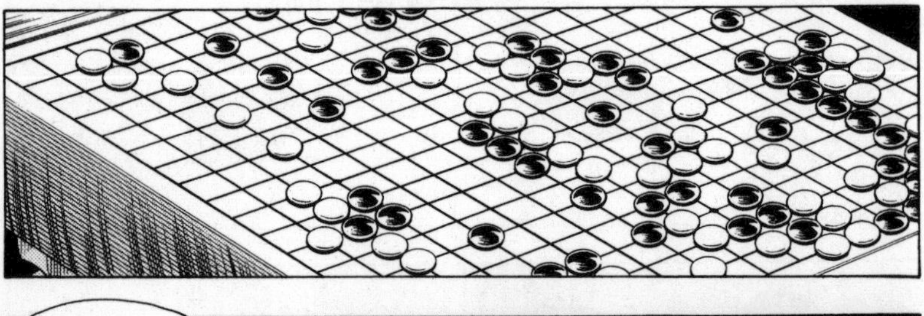

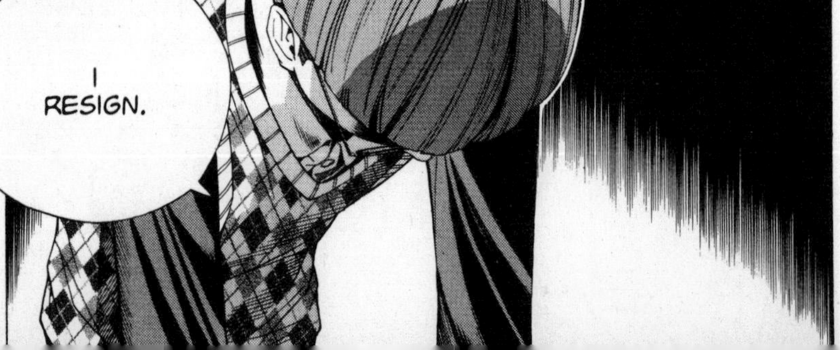
I RESIGN.

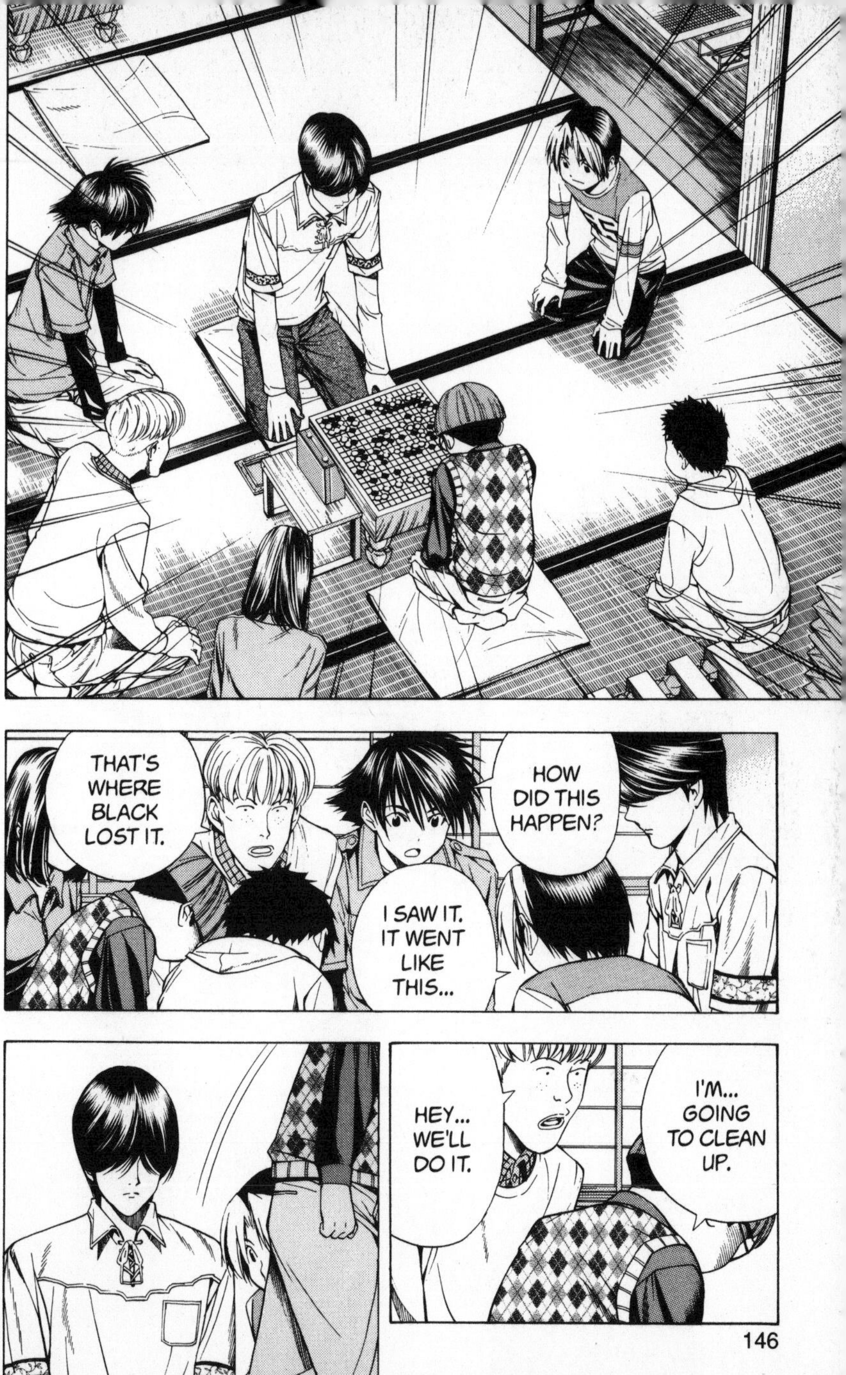
HOW DID THIS HAPPEN?
THAT'S WHERE BLACK LOST IT.
I SAW IT. IT WENT LIKE THIS...
I'M... GOING TO CLEAN UP.
HEY... WE'LL DO IT.

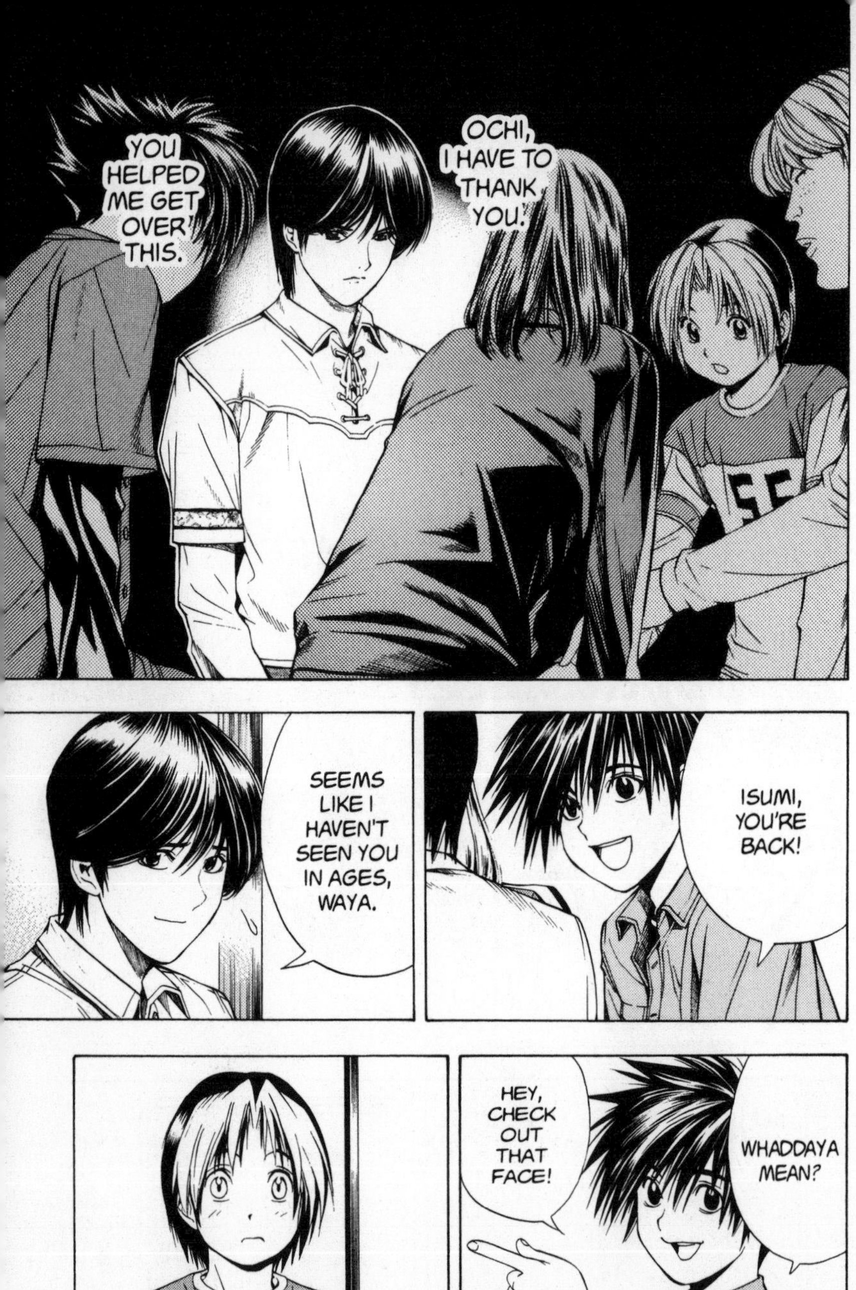
OCHI, I HAVE TO THANK YOU.
YOU HELPED ME GET OVER THIS.
ISUMI, YOU'RE BACK!
SEEMS LIKE I HAVEN'T SEEN YOU IN AGES, WAYA.
WHADDAYA MEAN?
HEY, CHECK OUT THAT FACE!

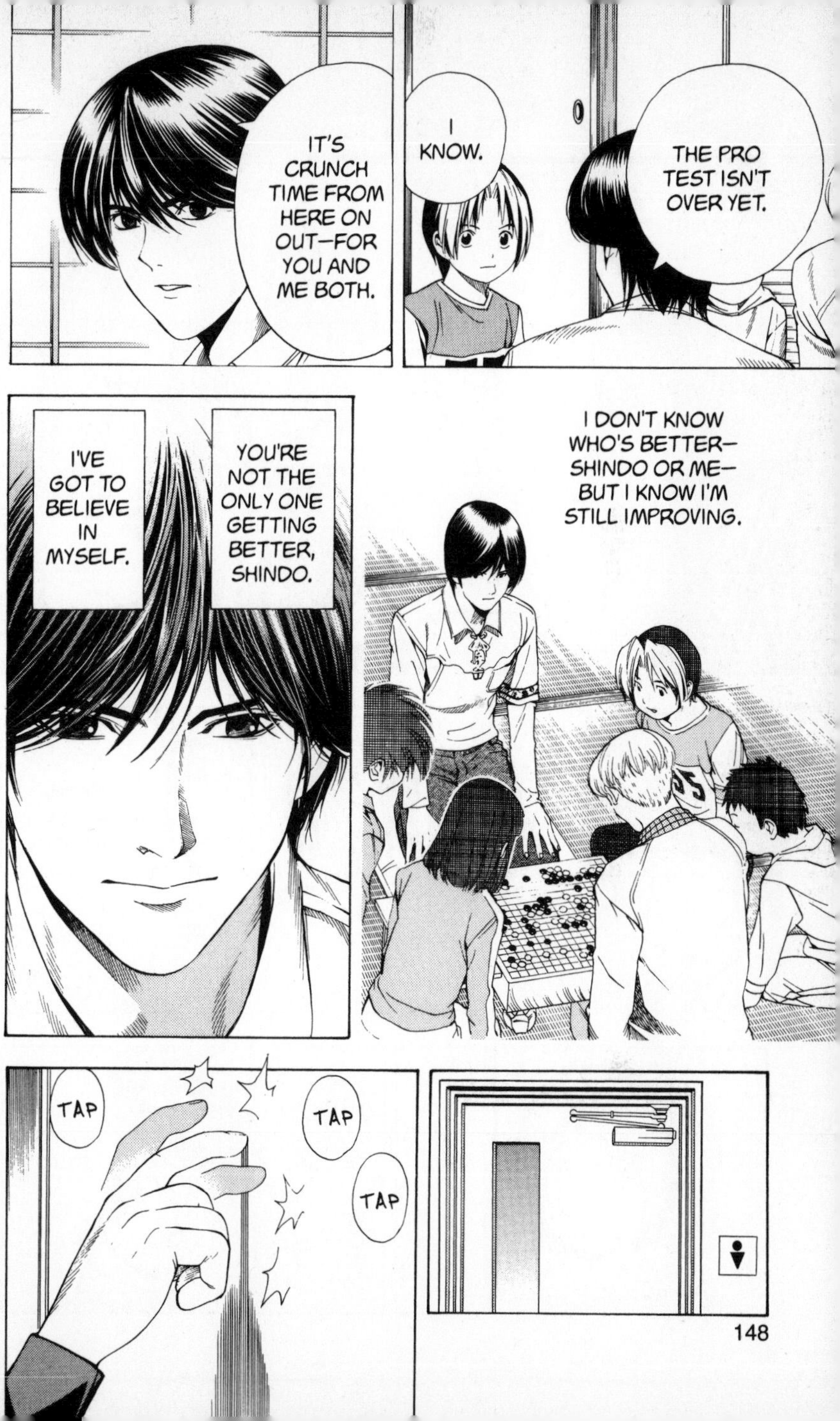
THE PRO TEST ISN'T OVER YET.
I KNOW.
IT'S CRUNCH TIME FROM HERE ON OUT—FOR YOU AND ME BOTH.
I DON'T KNOW WHO'S BETTER—SHINDO OR ME—BUT I KNOW I'M STILL IMPROVING.
YOU'RE NOT THE ONLY ONE GETTING BETTER, SHINDO.
I'VE GOT TO BELIEVE IN MYSELF.
TAP
TAP
TAP

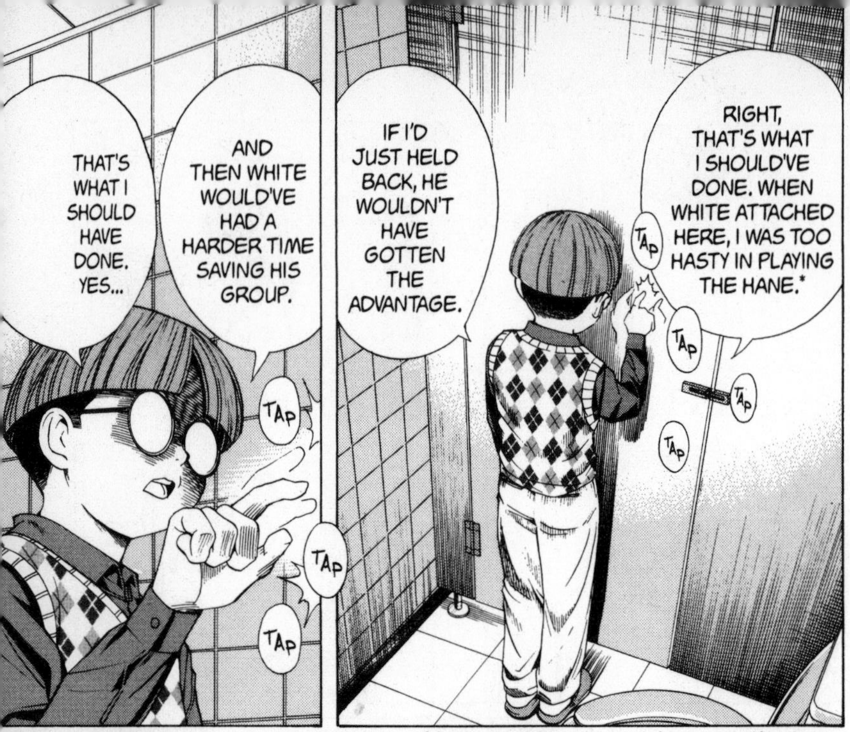
RIGHT, THAT'S WHAT I SHOULD'VE DONE. WHEN WHITE ATTACHED HERE, I WAS TOO HASTY IN PLAYING THE HANE.*
TAP
TAP
TAP
TAP
IF I'D JUST HELD BACK, HE WOULDN'T HAVE GOTTEN THE ADVANTAGE.
AND THEN WHITE WOULD'VE HAD A HARDER TIME SAVING HIS GROUP.
THAT'S WHAT I SHOULD HAVE DONE. YES...
TAP
TAP
TAP

*A move used to block one's opponent's stones

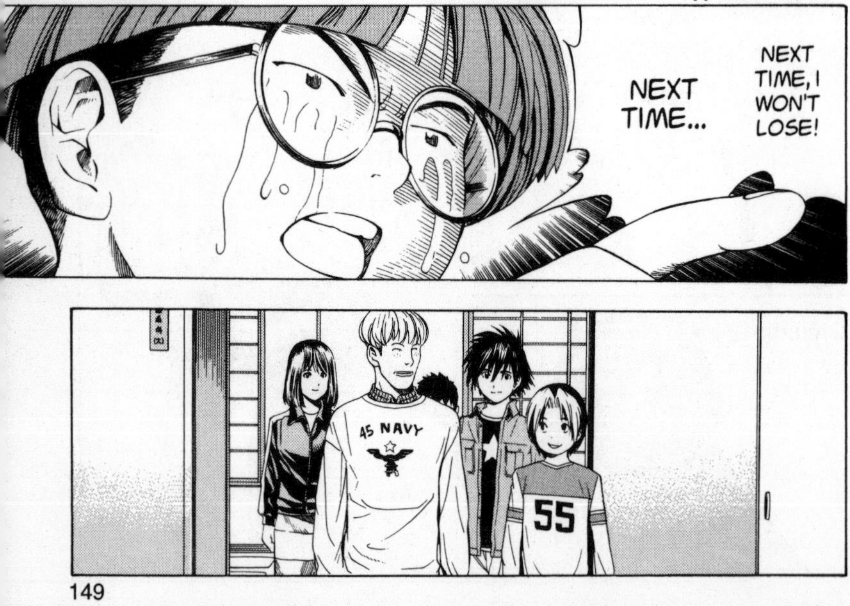
NEXT TIME, I WON'T LOSE!
NEXT TIME...
45 NAVY
55

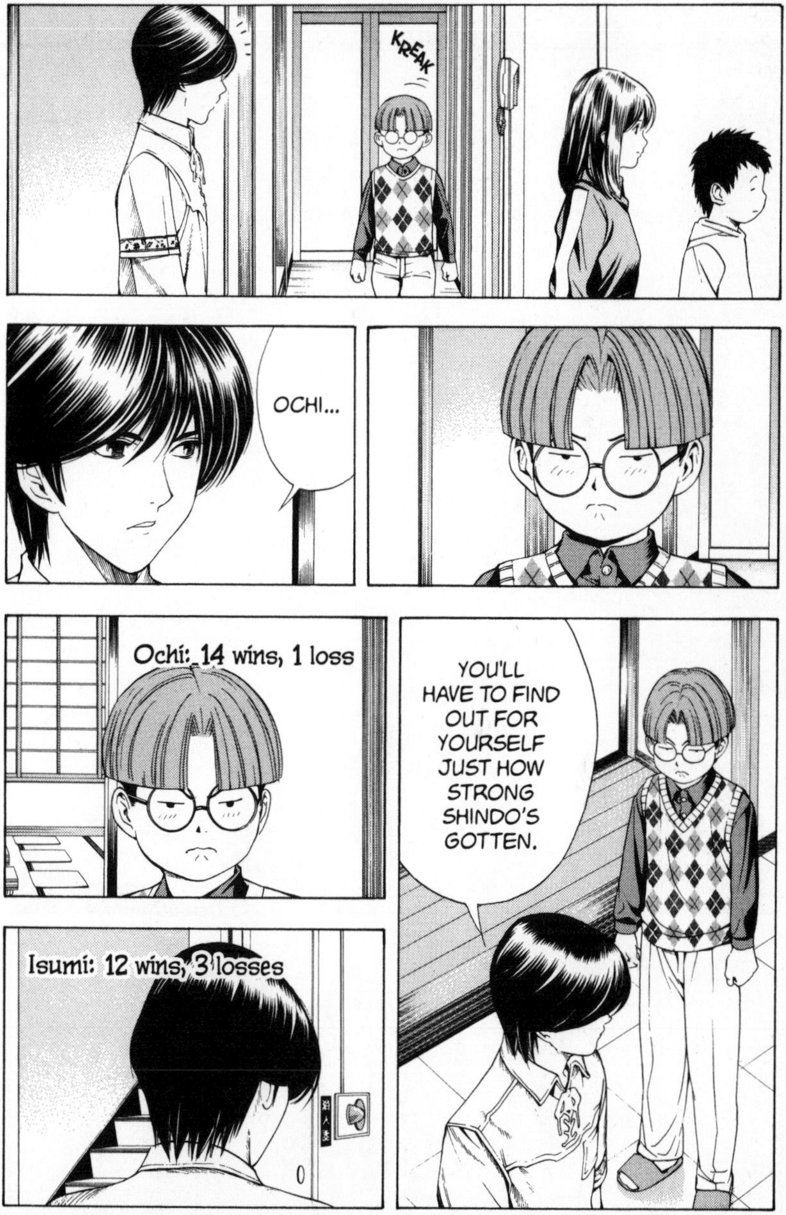
KREAK
OCHI...
YOU'LL HAVE TO FIND OUT FOR YOURSELF JUST HOW STRONG SHINDO'S GOTTEN.
Ochi: 14 wins, 1 loss
Isumi: 12 wins, 3 losses

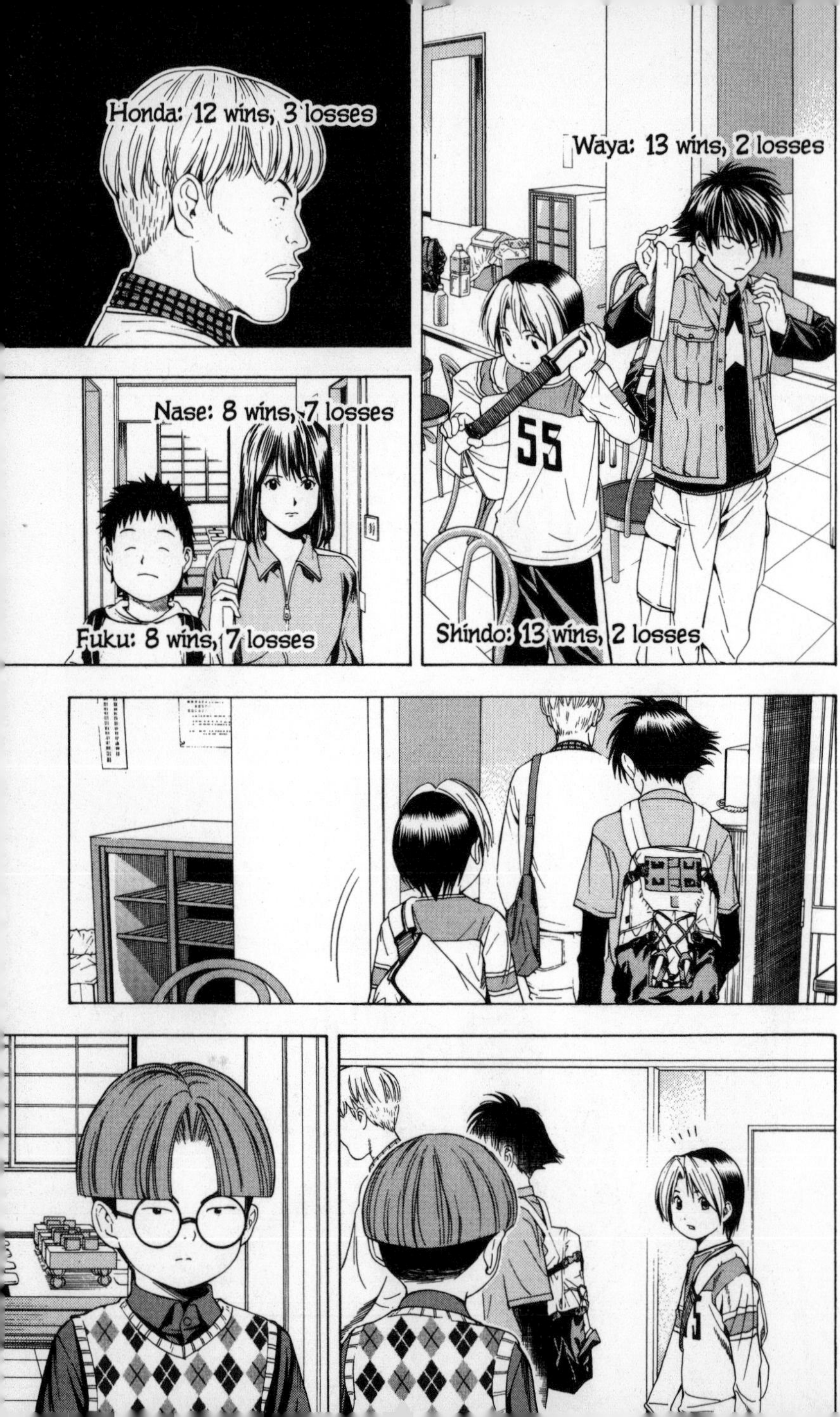
Waya: 13 wins, 2 losses
Shindo: 13 wins, 2 losses
Honda: 12 wins, 3 losses
Nase: 8 wins, 7 losses
Fuku: 8 wins, 7 losses

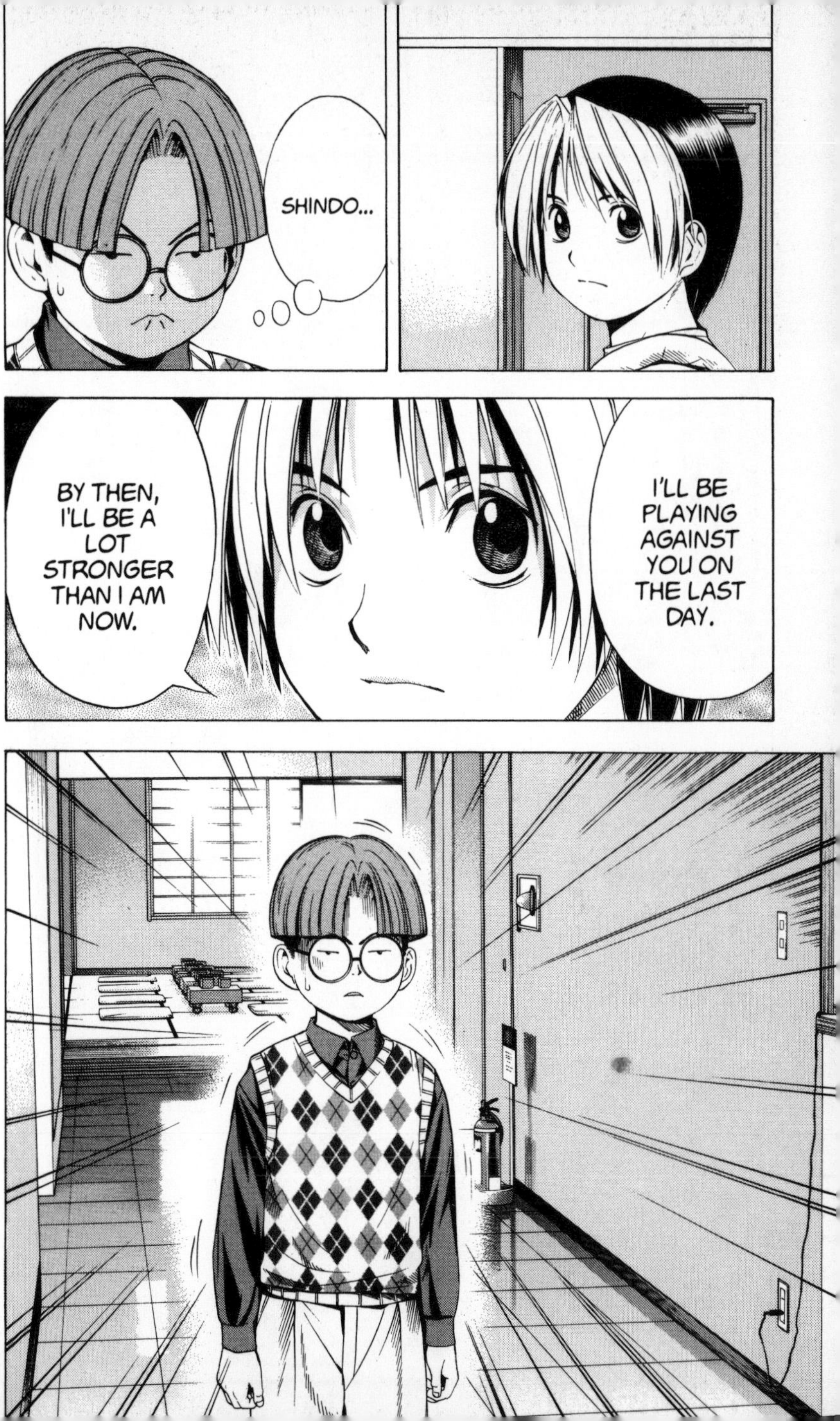
SHINDO...
I'LL BE PLAYING AGAINST YOU ON THE LAST DAY.
BY THEN, I'LL BE A LOT STRONGER THAN I AM NOW.

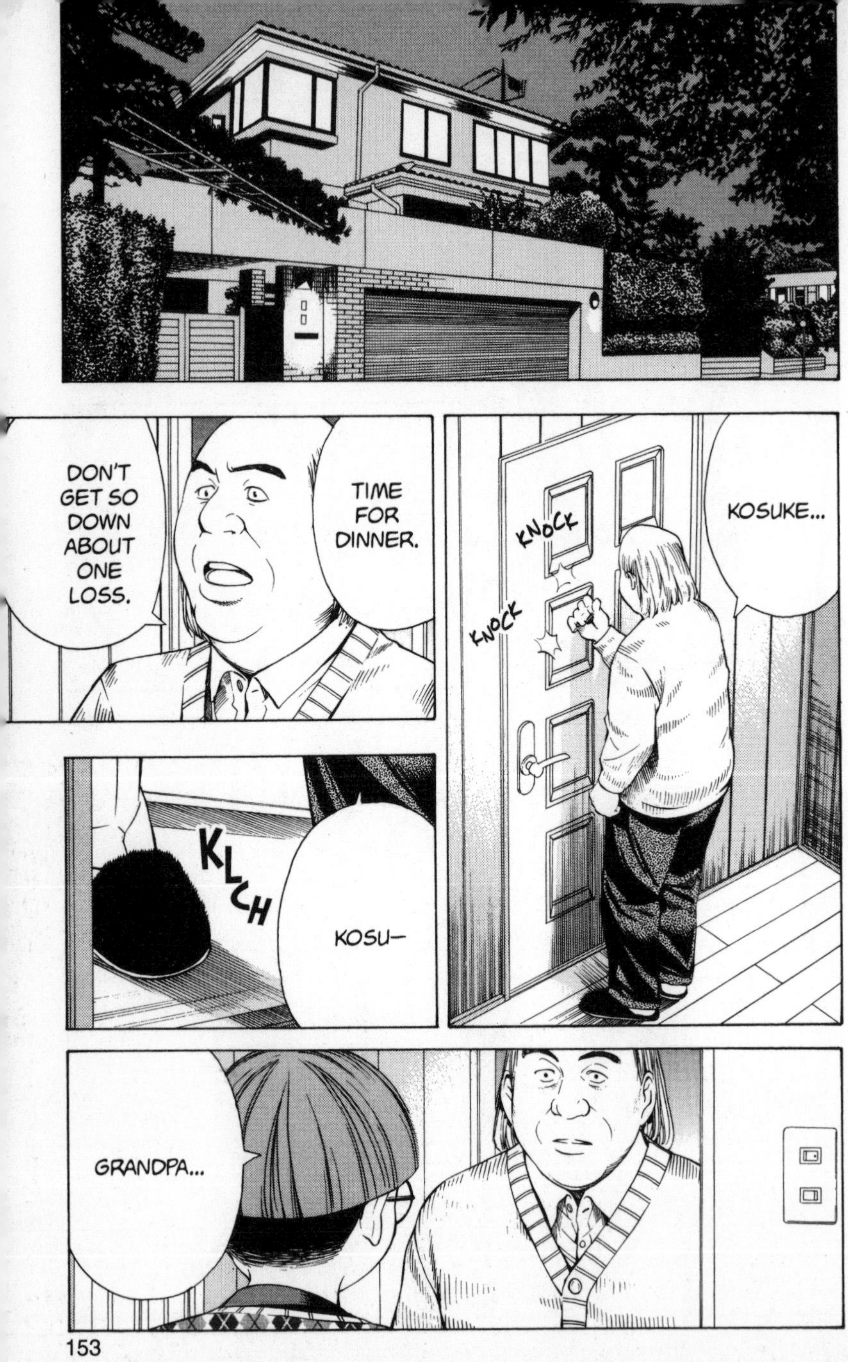

KOSUKE...
KNOCK
KNOCK
TIME FOR DINNER.
DON'T GET SO DOWN ABOUT ONE LOSS.
KLCH
KOSU—
GRANDPA...

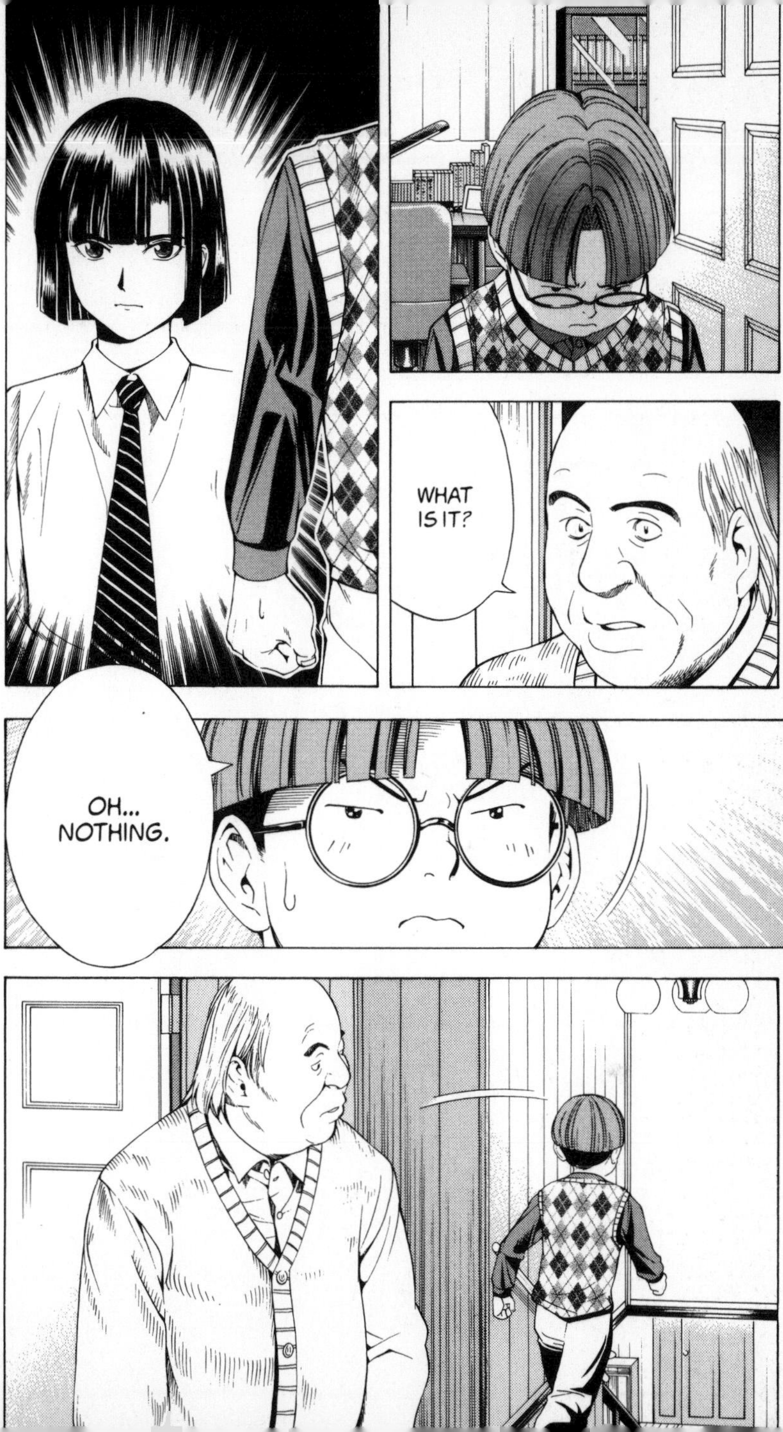
WHAT IS IT?
OH... NOTHING.

READ THIS WAY

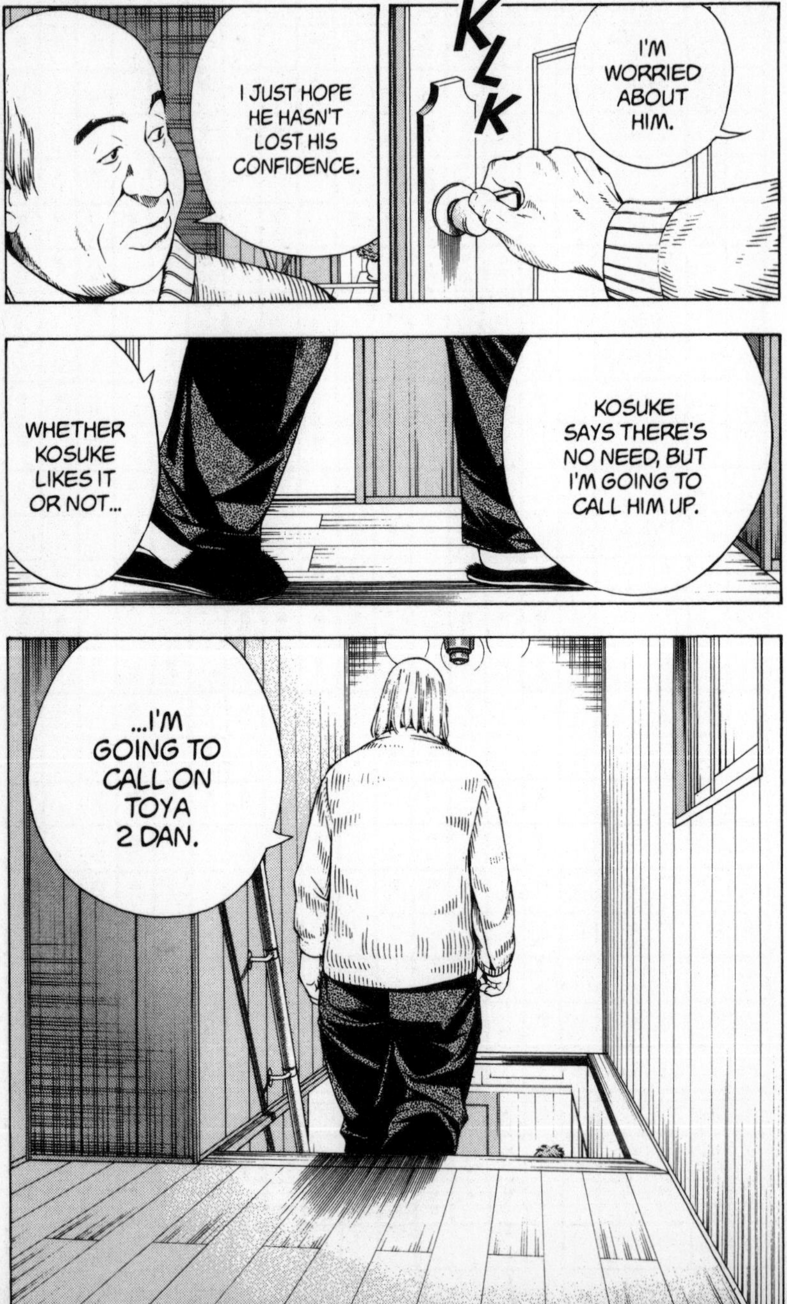
I'M WORRIED ABOUT HIM.
KLK
I JUST HOPE HE HASN'T LOST HIS CONFIDENCE.
KOSUKE SAYS THERE'S NO NEED, BUT I'M GOING TO CALL HIM UP.
WHETHER KOSUKE LIKES IT OR NOT...
...I'M GOING TO CALL ON TOYA 2 DAN.

PRO TEST STANDINGS FOR GAMES 1-15

ENTRY NO.		NAME	AGE	1 8/27	2 8/29	3 9/2	4 9/3	5 9/5	6 9/9	7 9/10	8 9/12	9 9/16	10 9/17	11 9/19	12 9/23	13 9/24	14 9/26	15 9/30
1	outside	Kazuhiko Hino	24	●2	●3	●4	●5	●6	●7	●8	●9	●10	●11	●12	○13	●14	●15	●16
2	outside	Toshiro Tsubaki	29	○1	●28	●3	○4	○5	●6	●7	○8	○9	●10	○11	○12	○13	○14	○15
3	insei	Eiji Komiya	16	○27	●1	●2	●28	○4	○5	●6	●7	●8	●9	○10	○11	●12	●13	○14
4	insei	Takashi Nakamura	14	●26	○27	●1	●2	●3	●28	●5	●6	○7	●8	○9	○10	○11	●12	○13
5	outside	Hiroshi Oshima	20	○25	●26	○27	●1	●2	●3	●4	●28	○6	●7	○8	○9	○10	○11	●12
6	insei	Nobuyuki Takakura	15	●24	○25	○26	○27	●1	○2	●3	●4	●5	●28	●7	○8	○9	●10	●11
7	insei	Hikaru Shindo	13	○23	○24	○25	○26	○27	○1	○2	●3	○4	●5	○6	○28	●8	○9	○10
8	insei	Yuta Fukui	12	●22	●23	○24	●25	●26	○27	●1	○2	●3	●4	●5	●6	○7	○28	○9
9	insei	Jun Kaneda	17	○21	●22	○23	●24	●25	●26	○27	●1	●2	○3	●4	○5	●6	●7	●8
10	outside	Koji Tachiyama	22	○20	●21	●22	○23	●24	●25	●26	○27	●1	○2	●3	●4	●5	●6	●7
11	insei	Asumi Nase	16	○19	●20	●21	●22	●23	●24	●25	●26	○27	●1	○2	●3	○4	●5	○6
12	insei	Toshinori Honda	17	○18	○19	○20	●21	●22	○23	●24	●25	○26	●27	●1	○2	●3	●4	○5
13	outside	Yasutoshi Sugishita	20	●17	○18	●19	○20	●21	●22	●23	●24	○25	●26	○27	●1	●2	●3	●4
14	insei	Shogo Nozaki	16	●16	●17	●18	●19	○20	●21	●22	●23	●24	●25	○26	○27	○1	●2	●3
15	outside	Kazunari Ishikawa	23	●28	●16	●17	●18	○19	○20	●21	●22	○23	●24	○25	●26	●27	○1	●2
16	outside	Kyohei Katagiri	25	○14	○15	●28	○17	●18	●19	●20	●21	●22	○23	●24	○25	●26	○27	○1
17	insei	Toshiki Adachi	16	○13	○14	○15	●16	●28	○18	●19	●20	○21	●22	○23	●24	●25	●26	○27
18	insei	Tatsuya Hayashi	14	●12	●13	●14	○15	○16	○17	●28	○19	●20	●21	●22	●23	●24	○25	●26
19	insei	Mai Sasaki	16	●11	●12	○13	●14	○15	●16	○17	●18	●28	●20	○21	●22	●23	○24	●25
20	outside	Masahiro Hatanaka	27	●10	○11	●12	●13	●14	○15	●16	○17	●18	○19	●28	○21	●22	●23	●24
21	insei	Yoshitaka Waya	15	○9	○10	○11	○12	○13	○14	○15	○16	○17	○18	○19	○20	●28	●22	○23
22	insei	Kosuke Ochi	12	●8	○9	●10	●11	○12	●13	○14	○15	○16	○17	○18	○19	○20	○21	●28
23	insei	Ryo Iijima	17	●7	○8	●9	○10	○11	●12	○13	○14	●15	●16	○17	●18	○19	●20	●21
24	outside	Saki Miura	20	○6	●7	●8	●9	○10	●11	●12	●13	○14	●15	●16	○17	○18	●19	○20
25	insei	Naoto Isobe	16	○5	○6	●7	○8	○9	○10	●11	○12	●13	○14	○15	○16	●17	○18	○19
26	outside	Yuriko Kitahara	22	○4	●5	●6	●7	●8	○9	○10	●11	●12	●13	●14	●15	●16	●17	●18
27	insei	Mitsuru Sawai	16	●3	●4	●5	●6	●7	●8	●9	○10	●11	●12	●13	●14	○15	●16	●17
28	insei	Shinichiro Isumi	18	○15	○2	○16	○3	○17	○4	○18	○5	○19	○6	○20	●7	●21	●8	○22

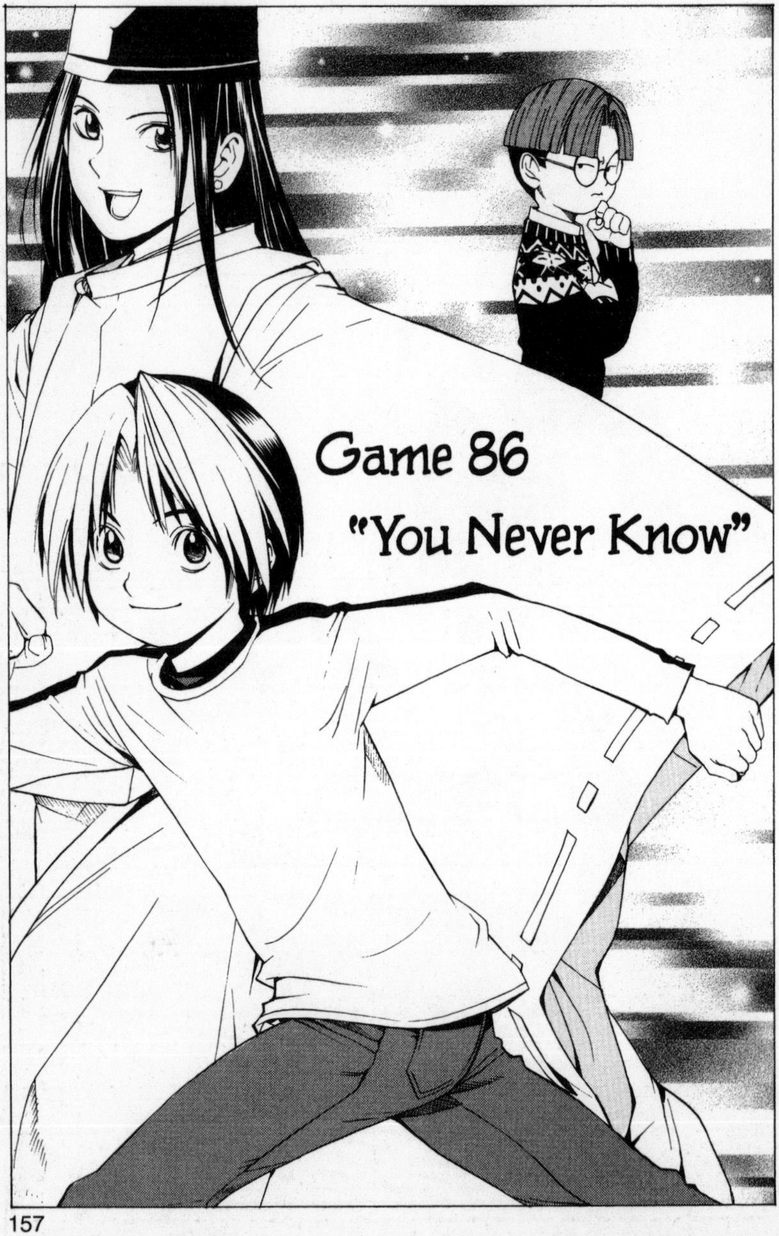
Game 86
"You Never Know"

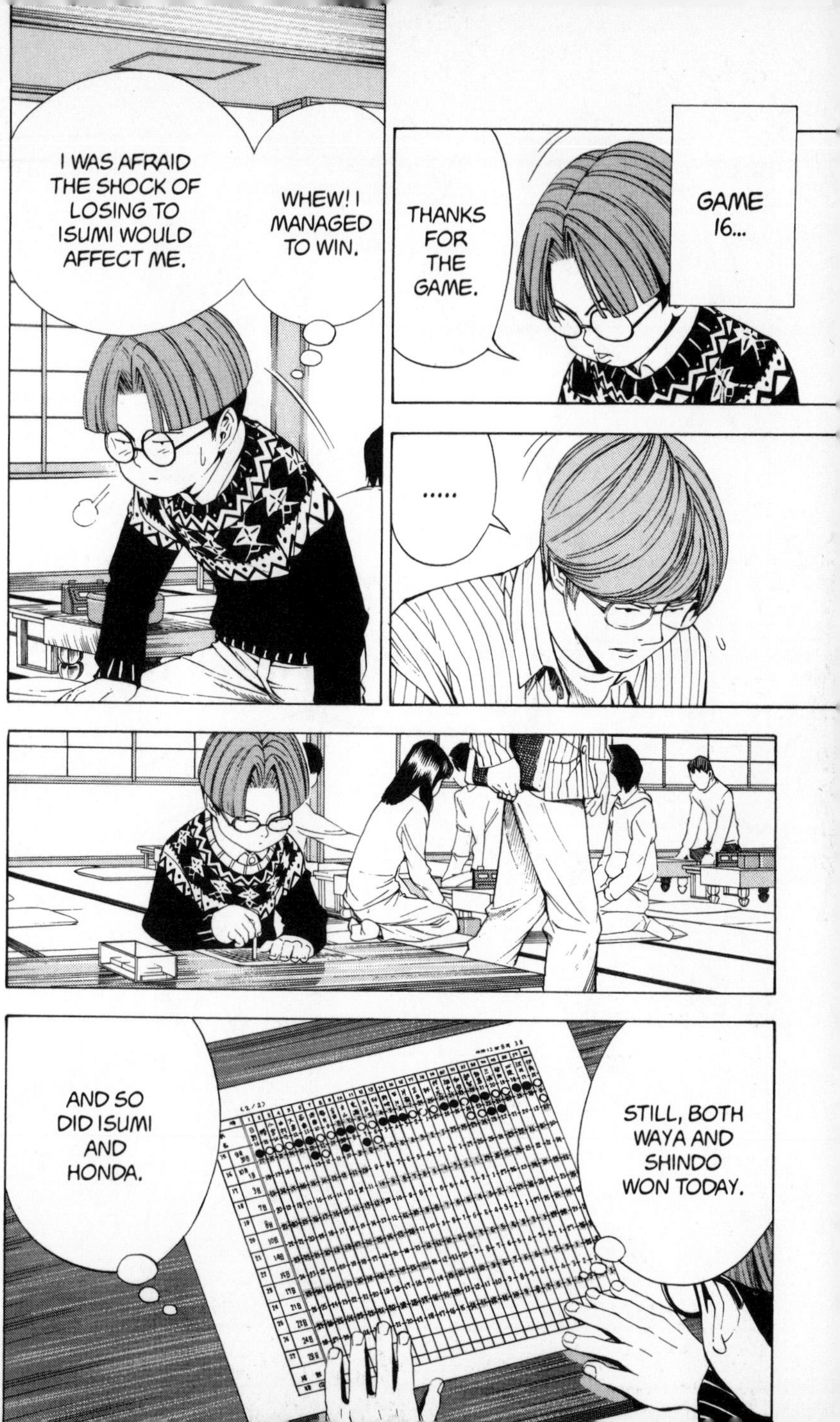
GAME 16...
THANKS FOR THE GAME.
.....
WHEW! I MANAGED TO WIN.
I WAS AFRAID THE SHOCK OF LOSING TO ISUMI WOULD AFFECT ME.
STILL, BOTH WAYA AND SHINDO WON TODAY.
AND SO DID ISUMI AND HONDA.

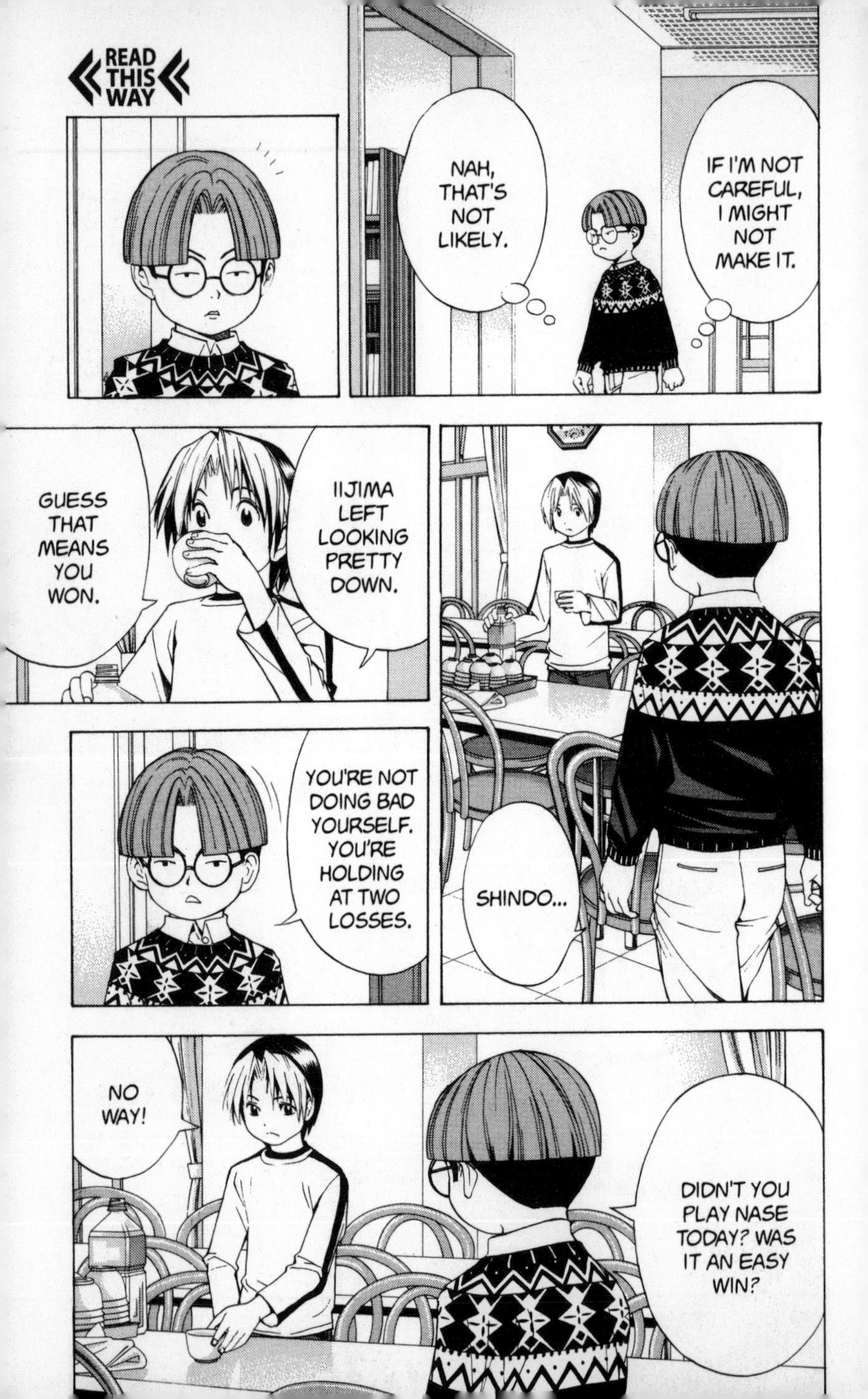
READ THIS WAY
IF I'M NOT CAREFUL, I MIGHT NOT MAKE IT.
NAH, THAT'S NOT LIKELY.
SHINDO...
IIJIMA LEFT LOOKING PRETTY DOWN.
GUESS THAT MEANS YOU WON.
YOU'RE NOT DOING BAD YOURSELF. YOU'RE HOLDING AT TWO LOSSES.
DIDN'T YOU PLAY NASE TODAY? WAS IT AN EASY WIN?
NO WAY!

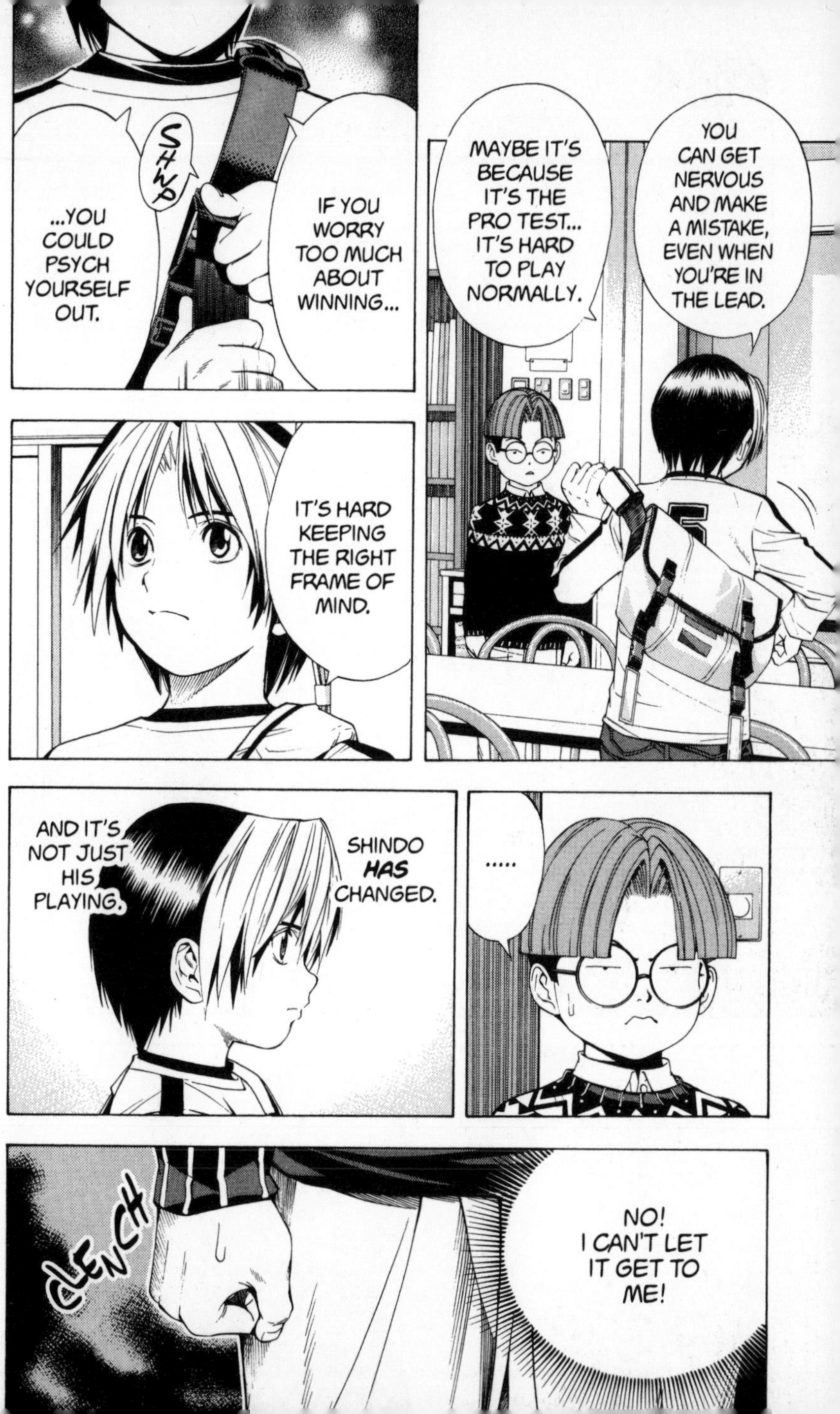
YOU CAN GET NERVOUS AND MAKE A MISTAKE, EVEN WHEN YOU'RE IN THE LEAD.
MAYBE IT'S BECAUSE IT'S THE PRO TEST... IT'S HARD TO PLAY NORMALLY.
SHWP
IF YOU WORRY TOO MUCH ABOUT WINNING...
...YOU COULD PSYCH YOURSELF OUT.
IT'S HARD KEEPING THE RIGHT FRAME OF MIND.
.....
SHINDO **HAS** CHANGED.
AND IT'S NOT JUST HIS PLAYING.
NO! I CAN'T LET IT GET TO ME!
CLENCH

READ THIS WAY

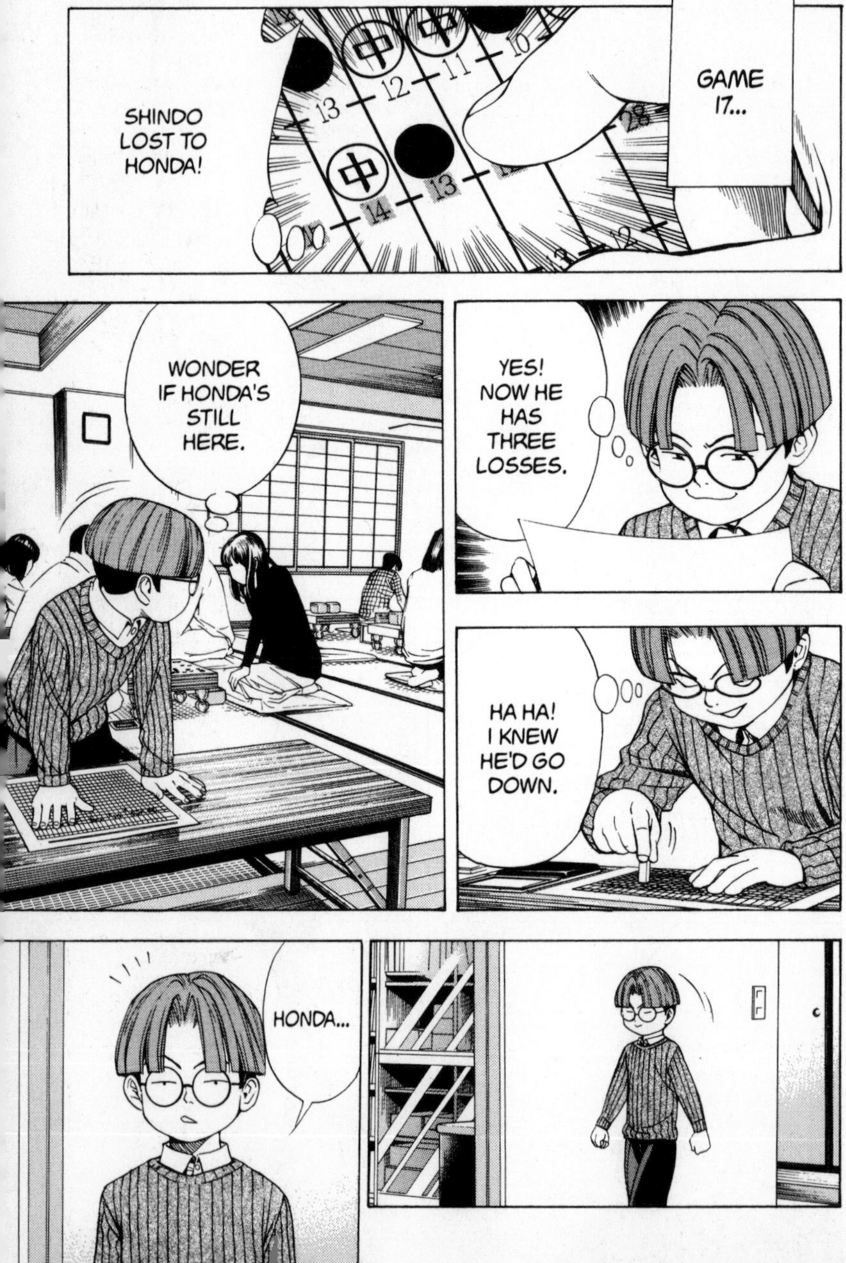
GAME 17...
SHINDO LOST TO HONDA!
YES! NOW HE HAS THREE LOSSES.
HA HA! I KNEW HE'D GO DOWN.
WONDER IF HONDA'S STILL HERE.
HONDA...

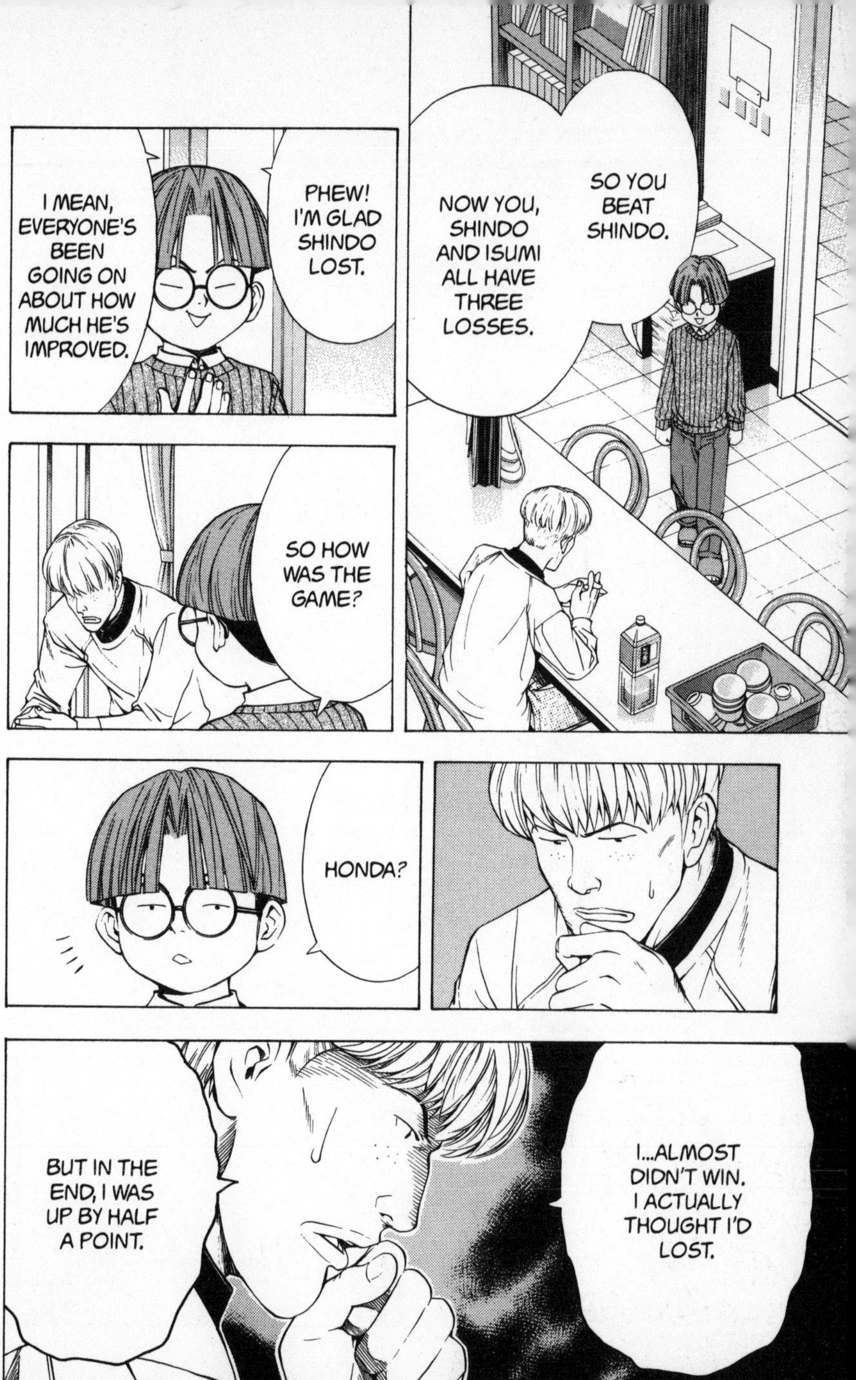
SO YOU BEAT SHINDO.
NOW YOU, SHINDO AND ISUMI ALL HAVE THREE LOSSES.
PHEW! I'M GLAD SHINDO LOST.
I MEAN, EVERYONE'S BEEN GOING ON ABOUT HOW MUCH HE'S IMPROVED.
SO HOW WAS THE GAME?
HONDA?
I...ALMOST DIDN'T WIN. I ACTUALLY THOUGHT I'D LOST.
BUT IN THE END, I WAS UP BY HALF A POINT.

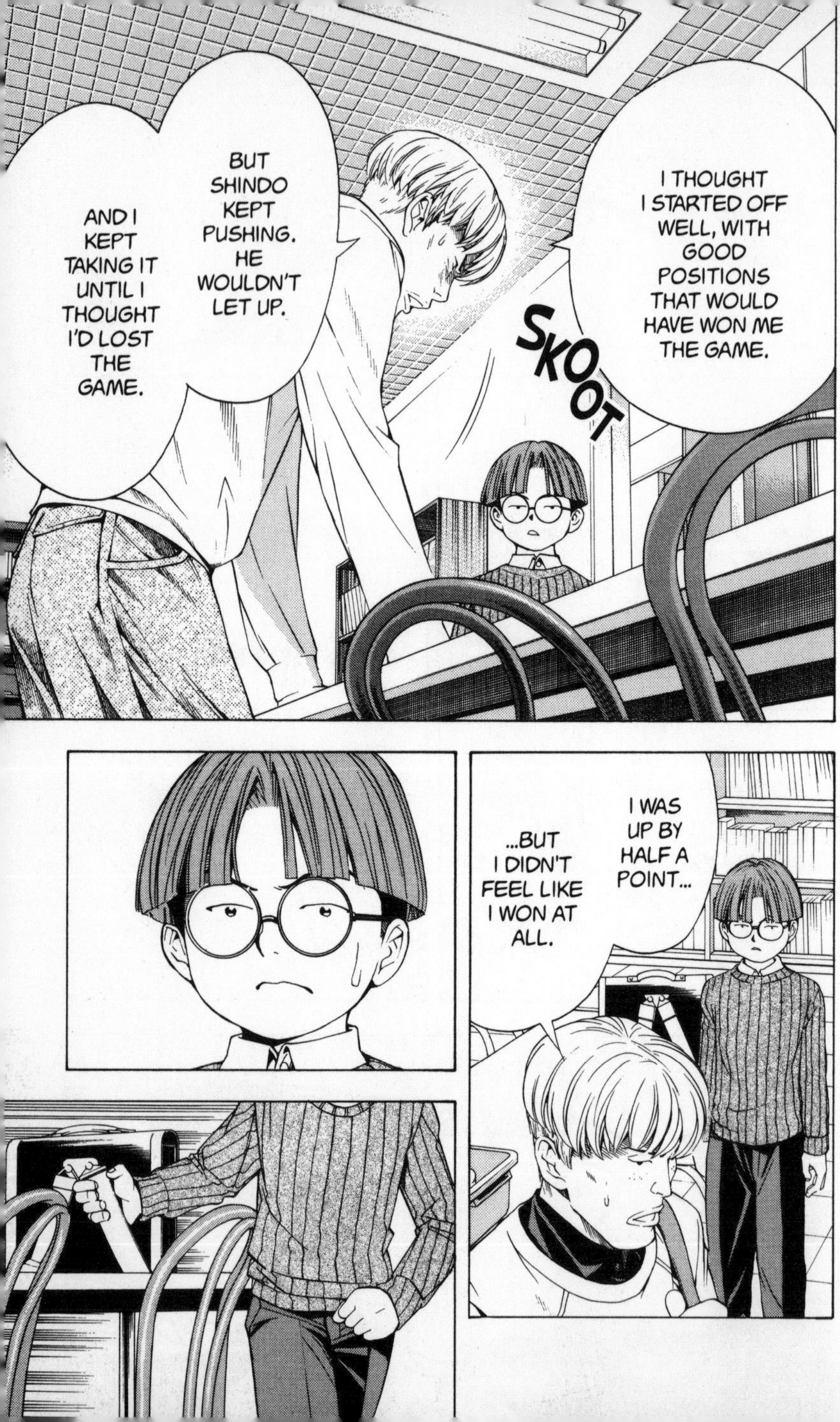
I THOUGHT I STARTED OFF WELL, WITH GOOD POSITIONS THAT WOULD HAVE WON ME THE GAME.
SKOOT
BUT SHINDO KEPT PUSHING. HE WOULDN'T LET UP.
AND I KEPT TAKING IT UNTIL I THOUGHT I'D LOST THE GAME.
I WAS UP BY HALF A POINT...
...BUT I DIDN'T FEEL LIKE I WON AT ALL.

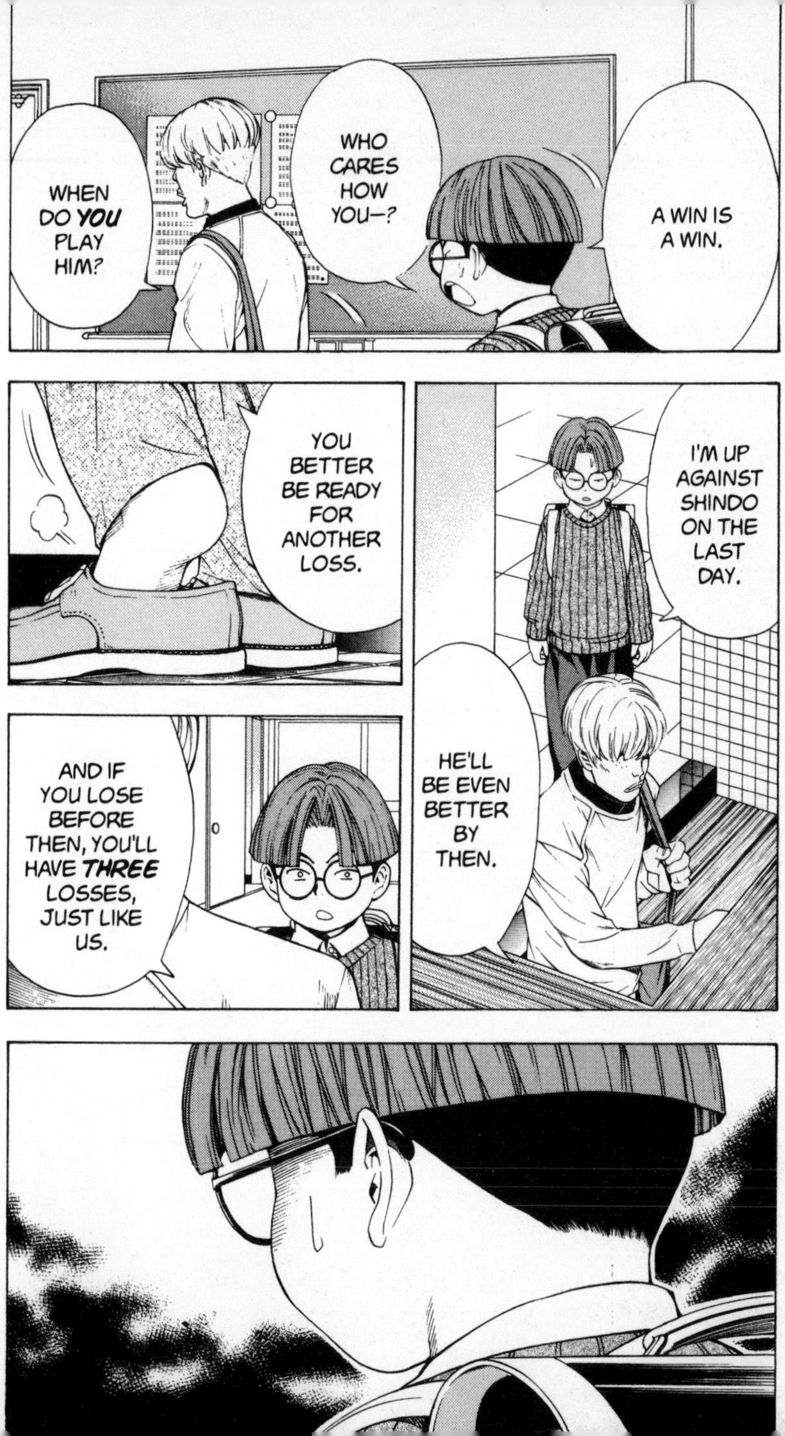
A WIN IS A WIN.
WHO CARES HOW YOU—?
WHEN DO *YOU* PLAY HIM?
I'M UP AGAINST SHINDO ON THE LAST DAY.
HE'LL BE EVEN BETTER BY THEN.
YOU BETTER BE READY FOR ANOTHER LOSS.
AND IF YOU LOSE BEFORE THEN, YOU'LL HAVE *THREE* LOSSES, JUST LIKE US.

READ THIS WAY

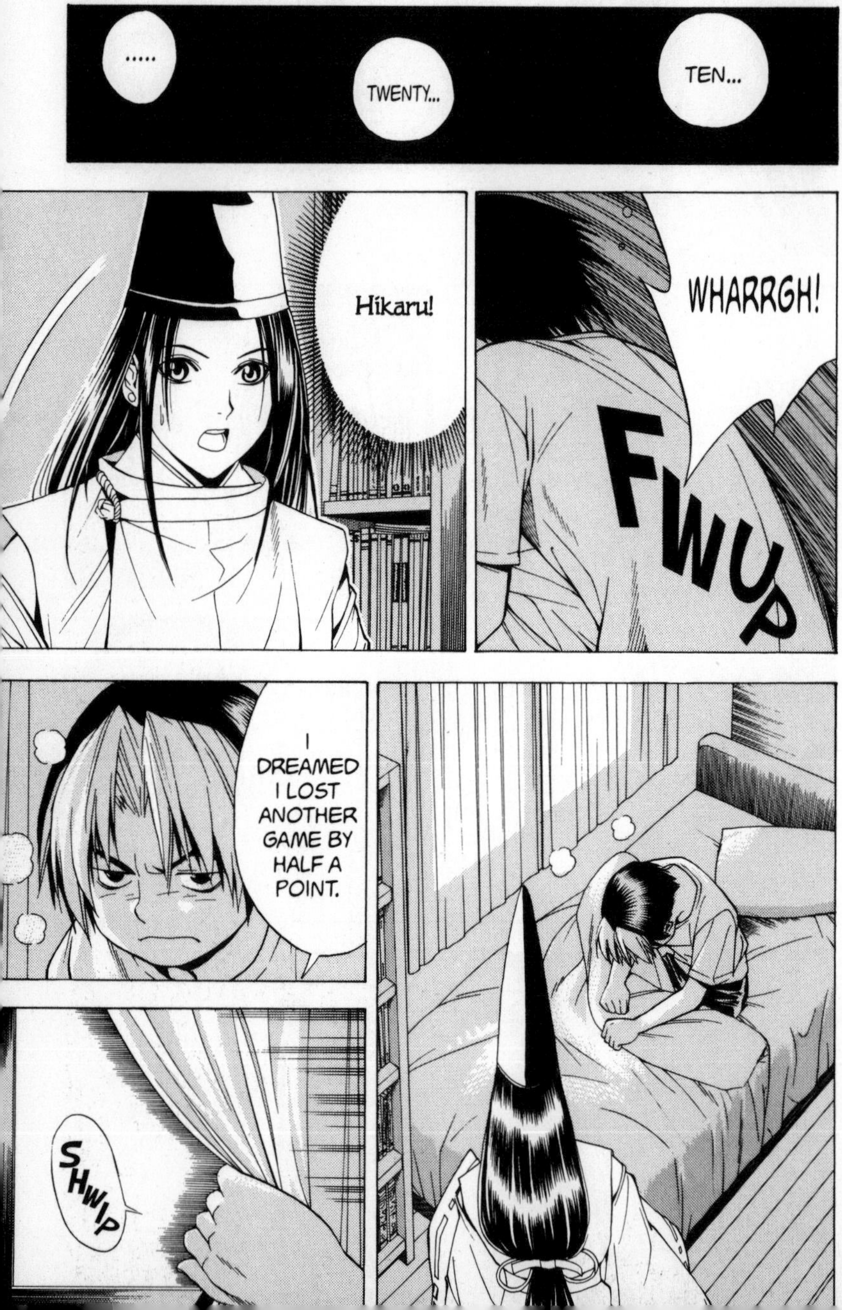
TEN...
TWENTY...
......
WHARRGH!
FWUP
Hikaru!
I DREAMED I LOST ANOTHER GAME BY HALF A POINT.
SHWIP

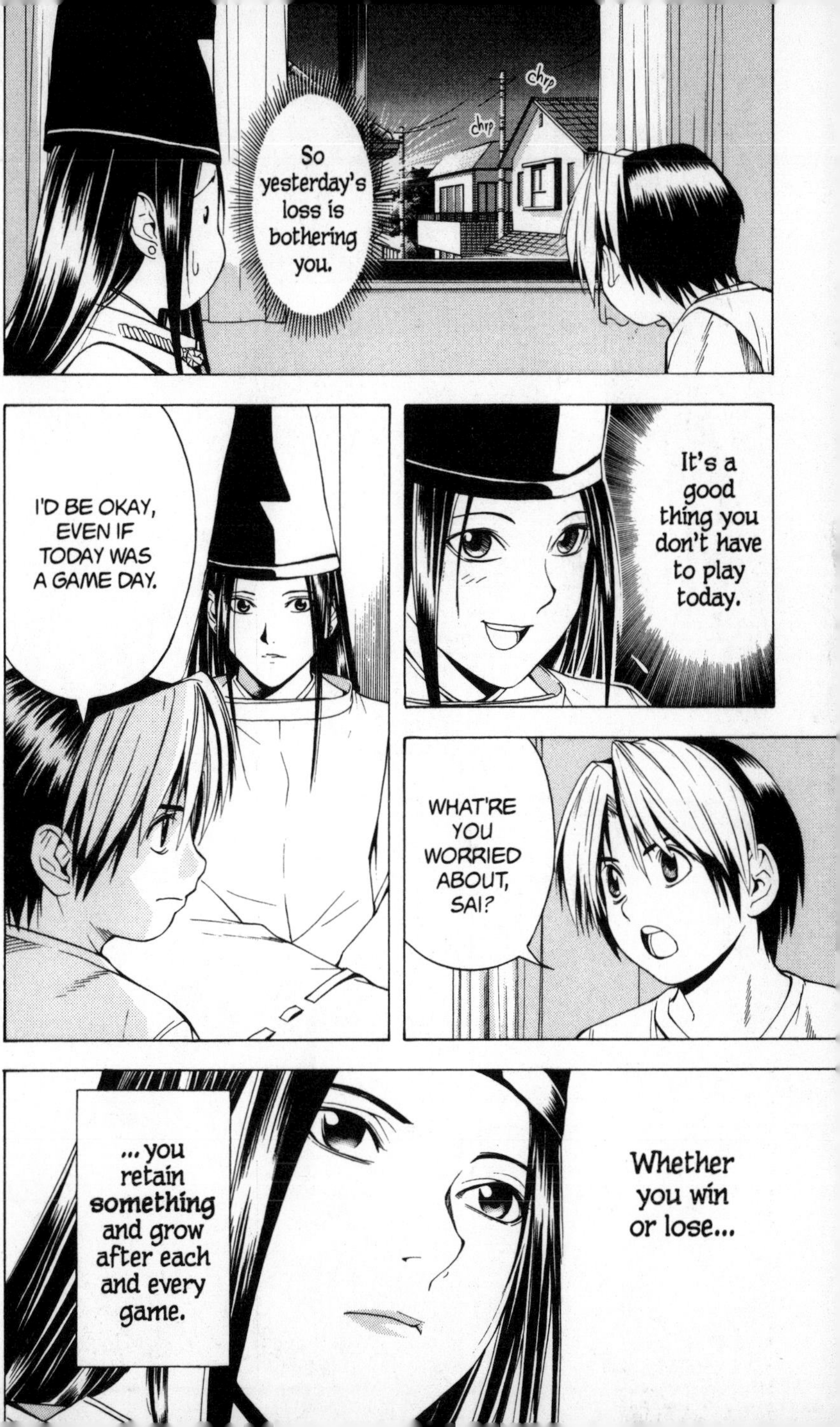
chrp
chrp
So yesterday's loss is bothering you.
It's a good thing you don't have to play today.
WHAT'RE YOU WORRIED ABOUT, SAI?
I'D BE OKAY, EVEN IF TODAY WAS A GAME DAY.
Whether you win or lose...
...you retain something and grow after each and every game.

READ THIS WAY

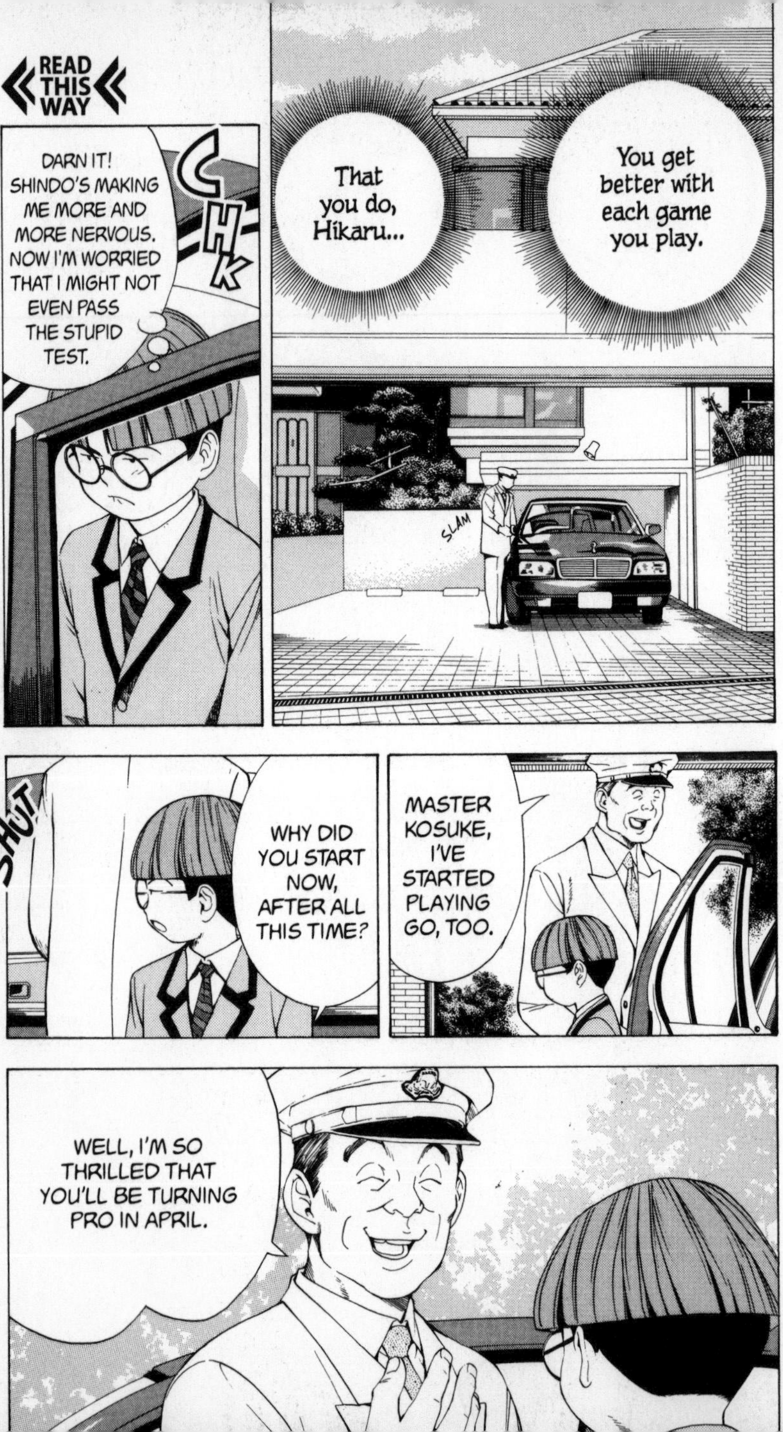
You get better with each game you play.
That you do, Hikaru...
SLAM
CHK
DARN IT! SHINDO'S MAKING ME MORE AND MORE NERVOUS. NOW I'M WORRIED THAT I MIGHT NOT EVEN PASS THE STUPID TEST.
MASTER KOSUKE, I'VE STARTED PLAYING GO, TOO.
WHY DID YOU START NOW, AFTER ALL THIS TIME?
SHUT
WELL, I'M SO THRILLED THAT YOU'LL BE TURNING PRO IN APRIL.

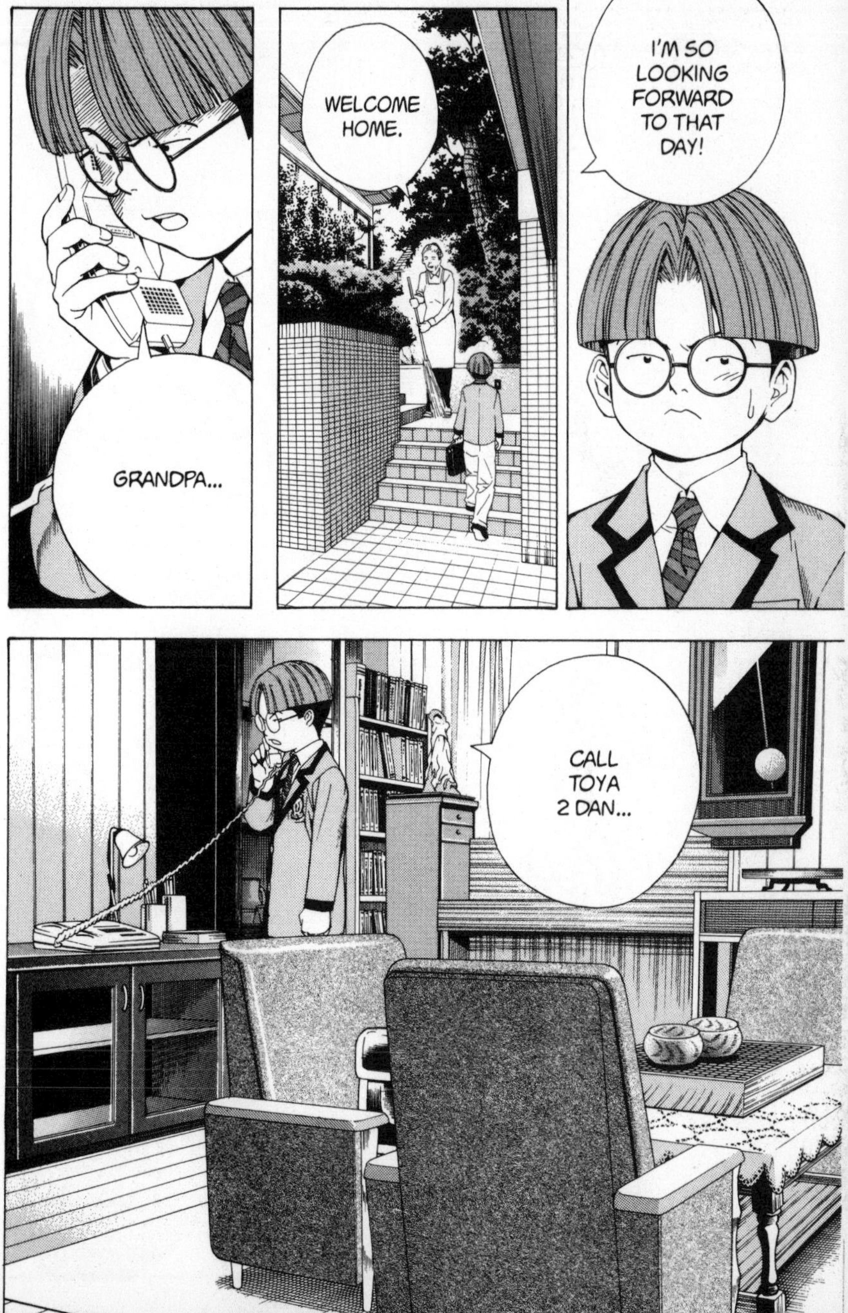
I'M SO LOOKING FORWARD TO THAT DAY!
WELCOME HOME.
GRANDPA...
CALL TOYA 2 DAN...

READ THIS WAY

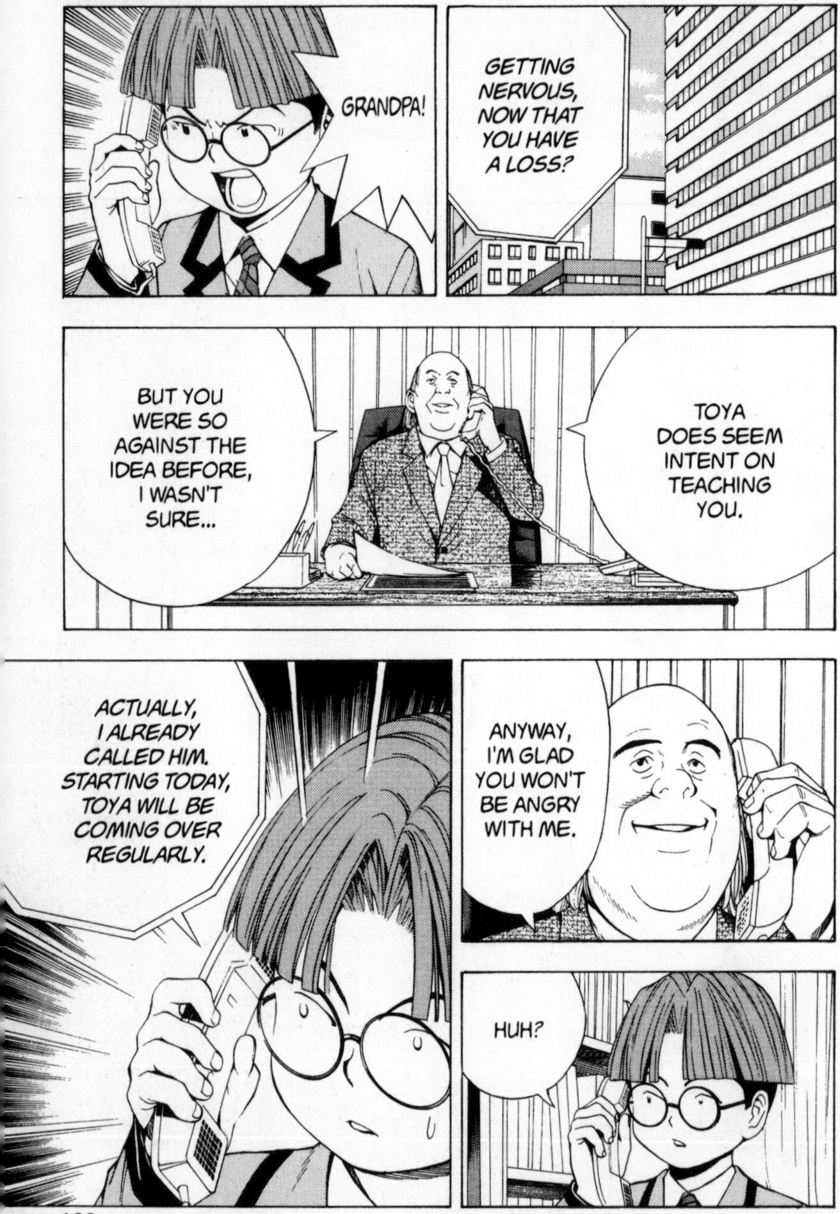

GETTING NERVOUS, NOW THAT YOU HAVE A LOSS?
GRANDPA!
TOYA DOES SEEM INTENT ON TEACHING YOU.
BUT YOU WERE SO AGAINST THE IDEA BEFORE, I WASN'T SURE...
ANYWAY, I'M GLAD YOU WON'T BE ANGRY WITH ME.
HUH?
ACTUALLY, I ALREADY CALLED HIM. STARTING TODAY, TOYA WILL BE COMING OVER REGULARLY.

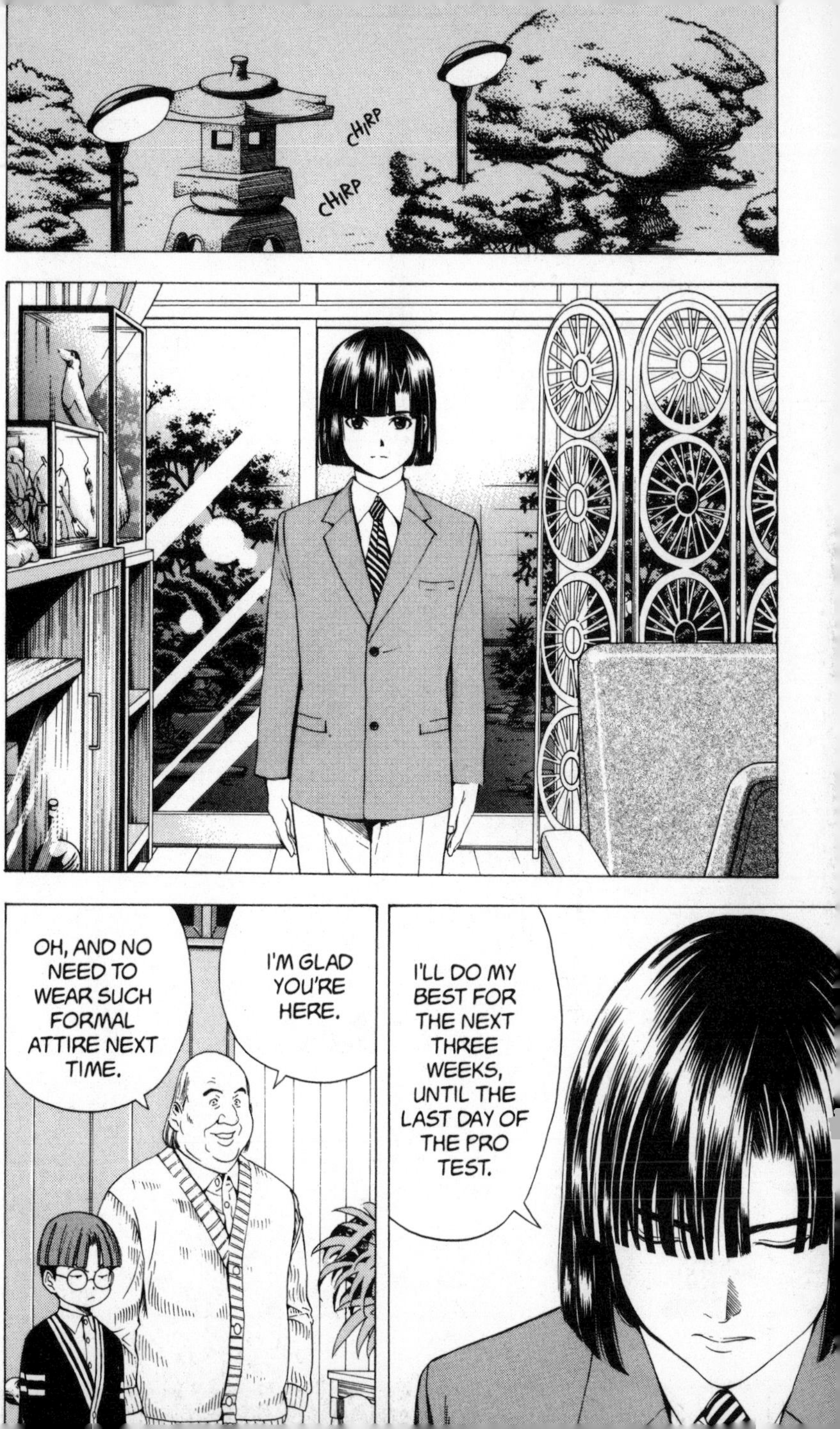

CHIRP
CHIRP
I'LL DO MY BEST FOR THE NEXT THREE WEEKS, UNTIL THE LAST DAY OF THE PRO TEST.
I'M GLAD YOU'RE HERE.
OH, AND NO NEED TO WEAR SUCH FORMAL ATTIRE NEXT TIME.

READ THIS WAY

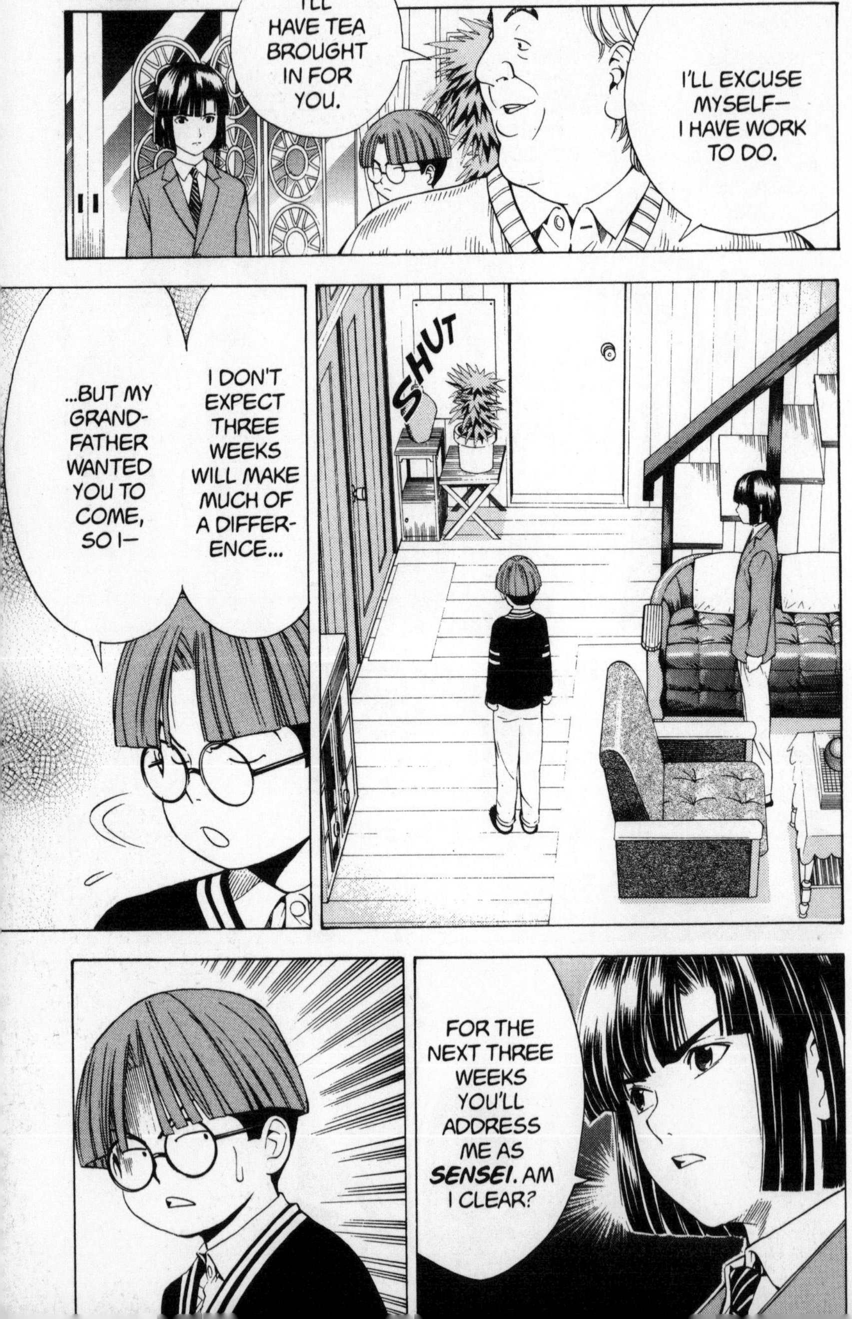
I'LL EXCUSE MYSELF— I HAVE WORK TO DO.
I'LL HAVE TEA BROUGHT IN FOR YOU.
SHUT
I DON'T EXPECT THREE WEEKS WILL MAKE MUCH OF A DIFFERENCE...
...BUT MY GRANDFATHER WANTED YOU TO COME, SO I—
FOR THE NEXT THREE WEEKS YOU'LL ADDRESS ME AS **SENSEI**. AM I CLEAR?

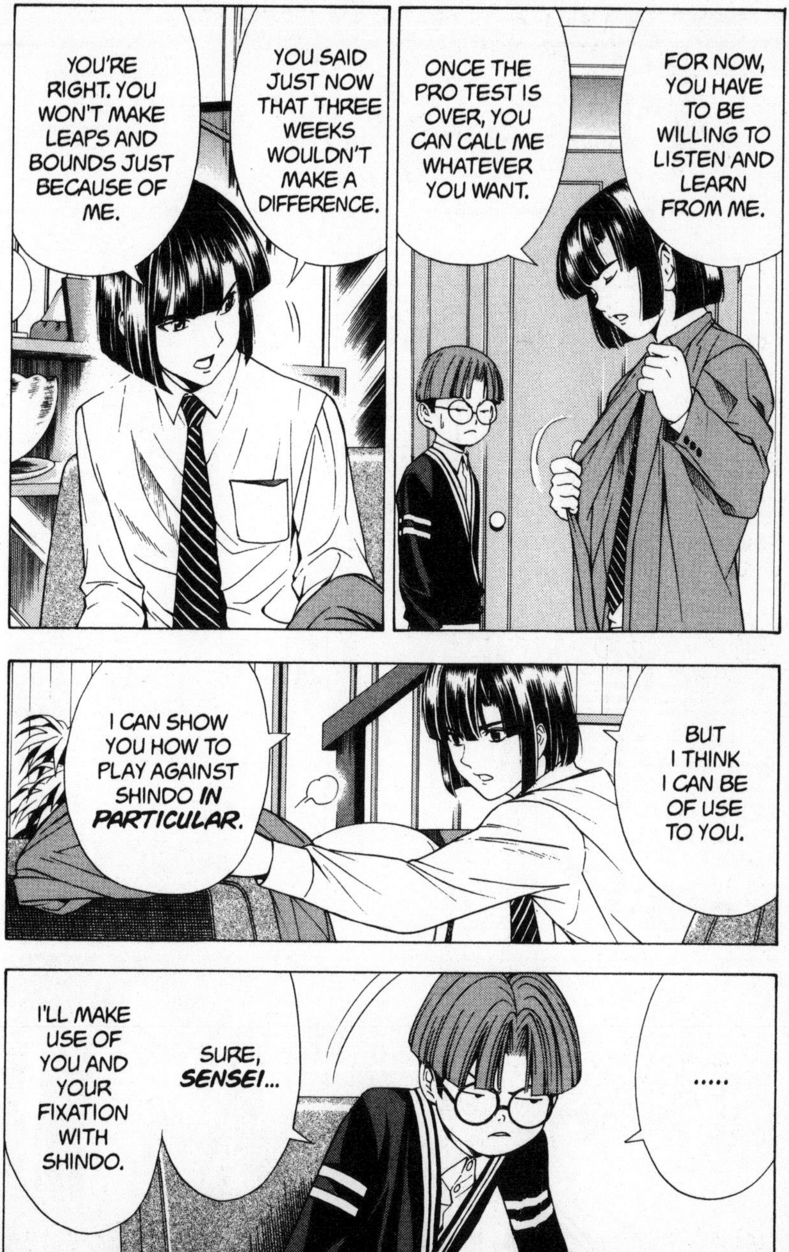
FOR NOW, YOU HAVE TO BE WILLING TO LISTEN AND LEARN FROM ME.
ONCE THE PRO TEST IS OVER, YOU CAN CALL ME WHATEVER YOU WANT.
YOU SAID JUST NOW THAT THREE WEEKS WOULDN'T MAKE A DIFFERENCE.
YOU'RE RIGHT. YOU WON'T MAKE LEAPS AND BOUNDS JUST BECAUSE OF ME.
BUT I THINK I CAN BE OF USE TO YOU.
I CAN SHOW YOU HOW TO PLAY AGAINST SHINDO ***IN PARTICULAR***.
.....
SURE, ***SENSEI***...
I'LL MAKE USE OF YOU AND YOUR FIXATION WITH SHINDO.

READ THIS WAY

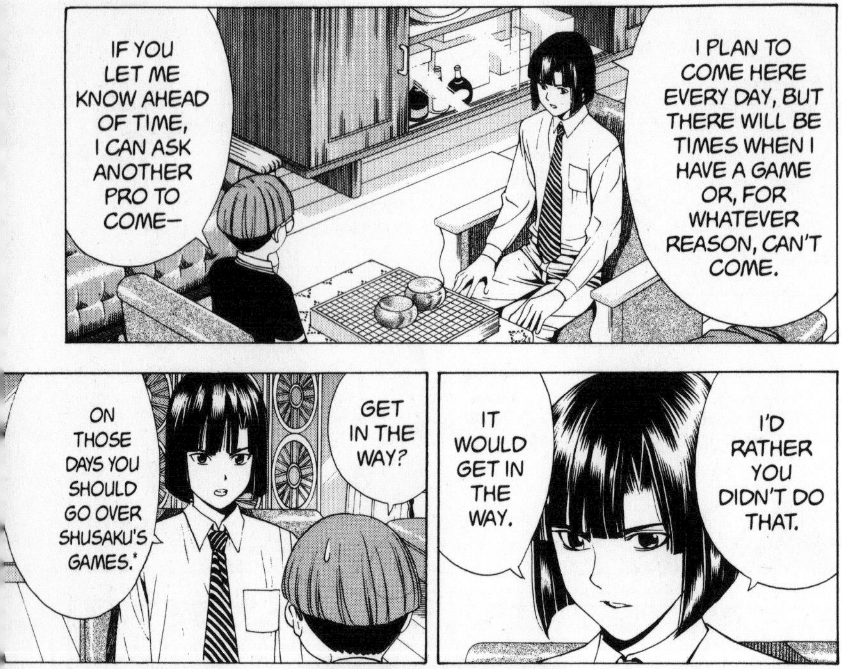
I PLAN TO COME HERE EVERY DAY, BUT THERE WILL BE TIMES WHEN I HAVE A GAME OR, FOR WHATEVER REASON, CAN'T COME.
IF YOU LET ME KNOW AHEAD OF TIME, I CAN ASK ANOTHER PRO TO COME—
I'D RATHER YOU DIDN'T DO THAT.
IT WOULD GET IN THE WAY.
GET IN THE WAY?
ON THOSE DAYS YOU SHOULD GO OVER SHUSAKU'S GAMES.*

*Hon'inbo Shusaku was a great Go player of the 19th century.

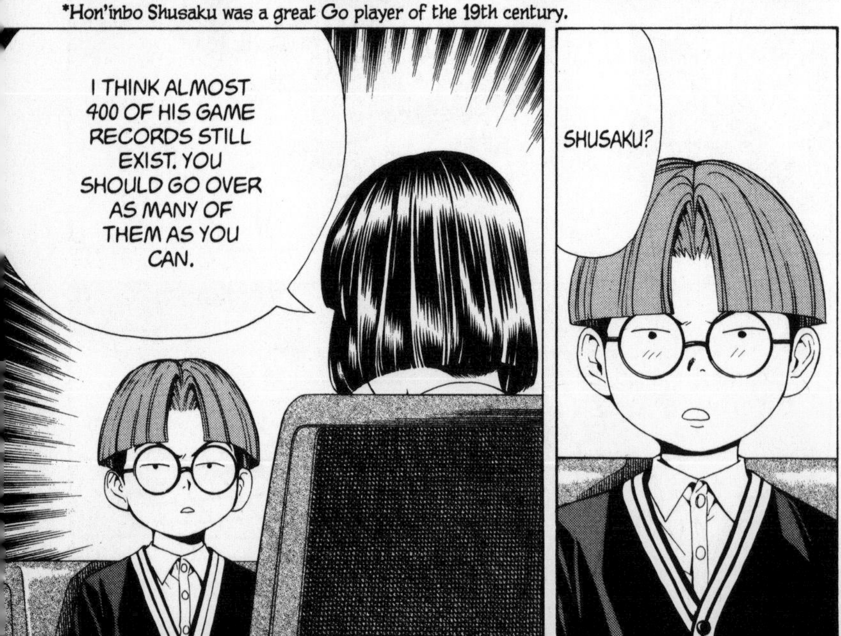
SHUSAKU?
I THINK ALMOST 400 OF HIS GAME RECORDS STILL EXIST. YOU SHOULD GO OVER AS MANY OF THEM AS YOU CAN.

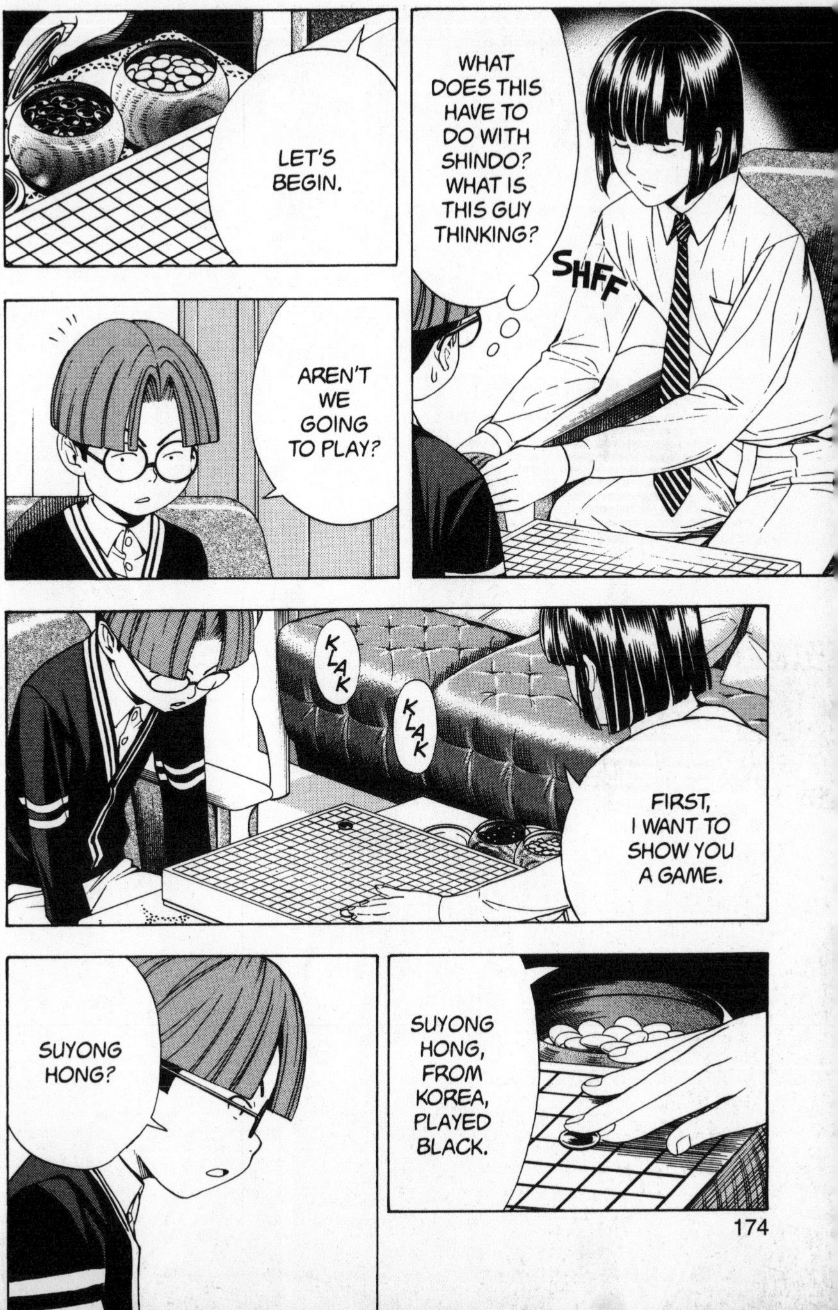
WHAT DOES THIS HAVE TO DO WITH SHINDO? WHAT IS THIS GUY THINKING?
SHFF
LET'S BEGIN.
AREN'T WE GOING TO PLAY?
KLAK
KLAK
FIRST, I WANT TO SHOW YOU A GAME.
SUYONG HONG, FROM KOREA, PLAYED BLACK.
SUYONG HONG?

READ THIS WAY

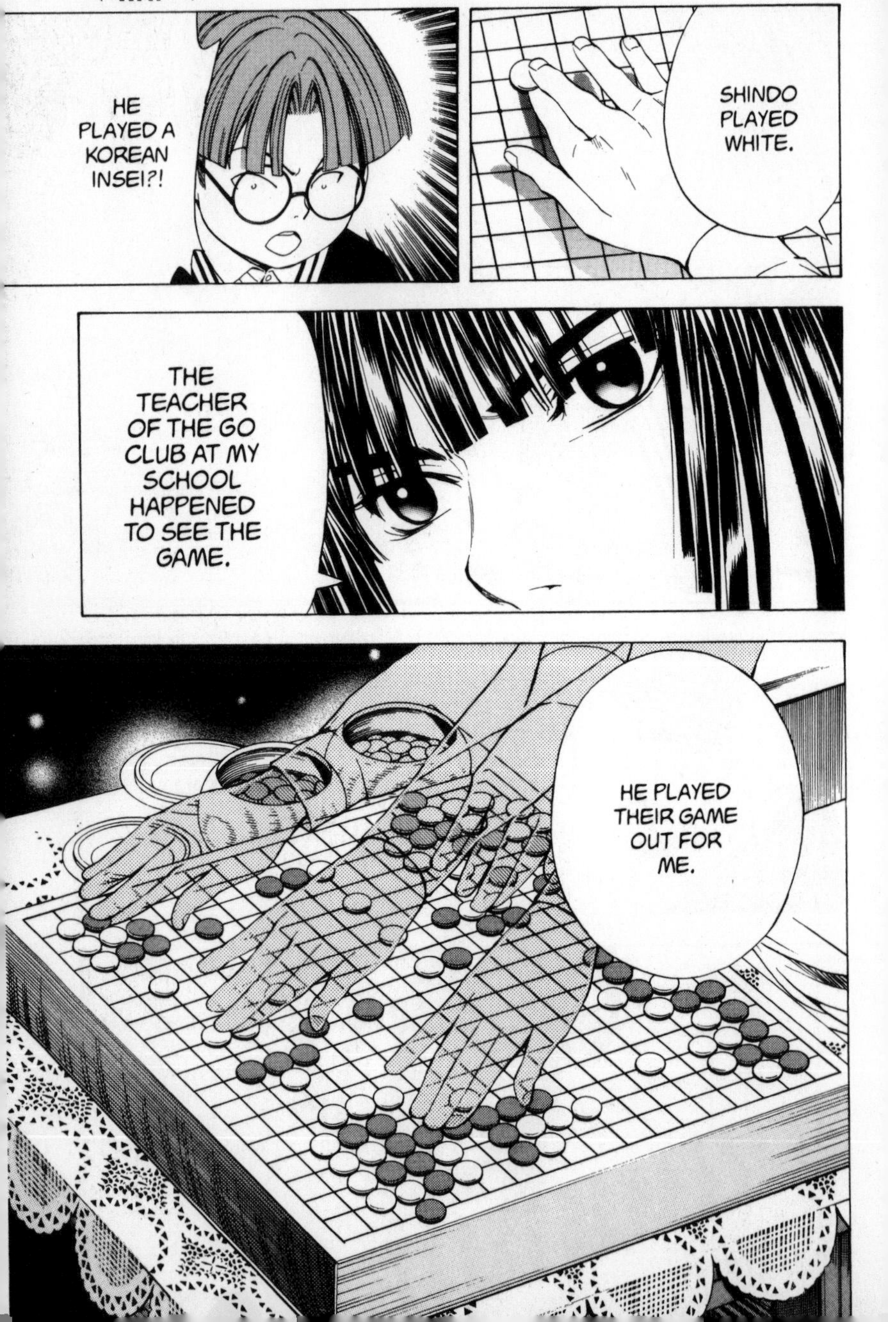
SHINDO PLAYED WHITE.
HE PLAYED A KOREAN INSEI?!
THE TEACHER OF THE GO CLUB AT MY SCHOOL HAPPENED TO SEE THE GAME.
HE PLAYED THEIR GAME OUT FOR ME.

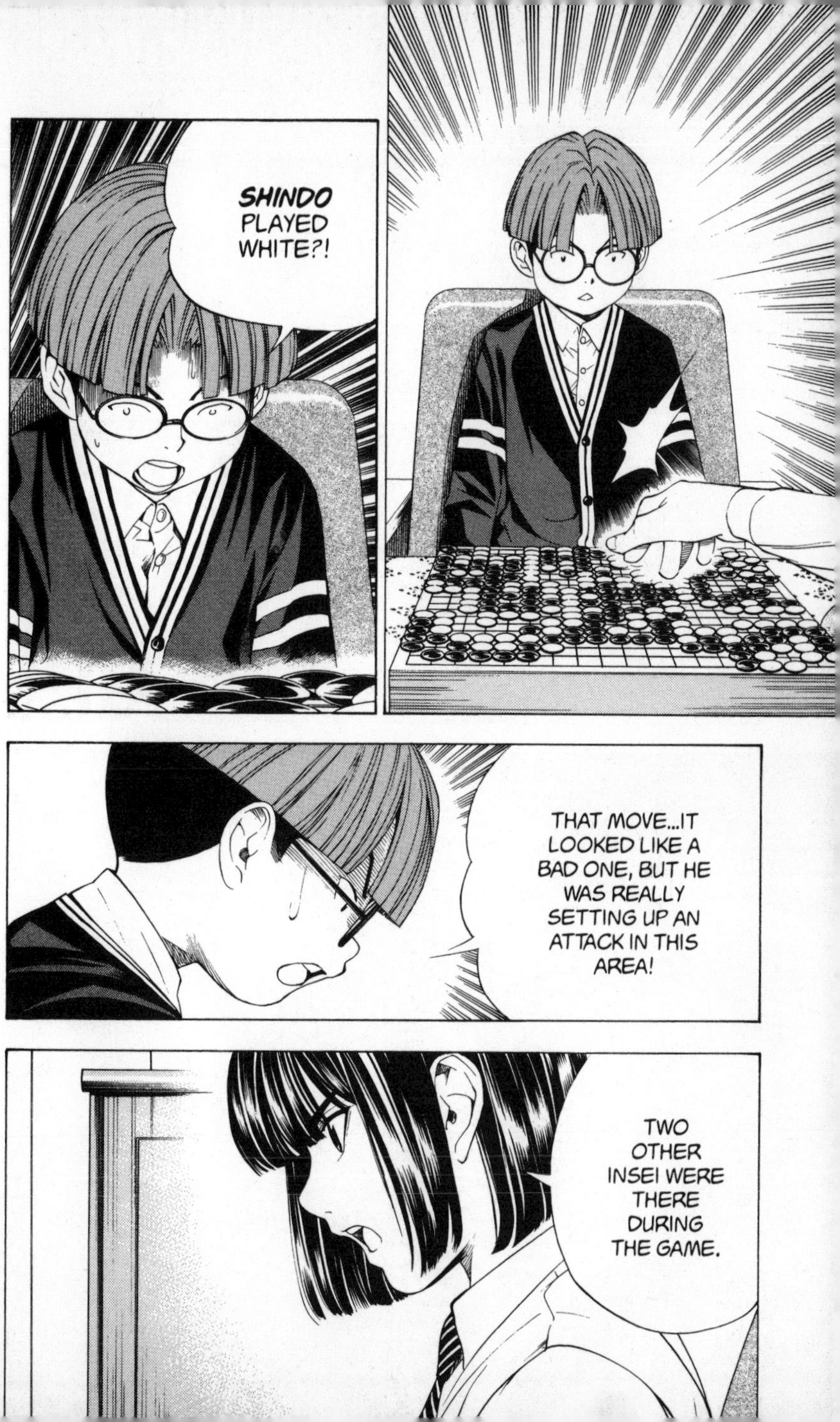

SHINDO PLAYED WHITE?!
THAT MOVE...IT LOOKED LIKE A BAD ONE, BUT HE WAS REALLY SETTING UP AN ATTACK IN THIS AREA!
TWO OTHER INSEI WERE THERE DURING THE GAME.

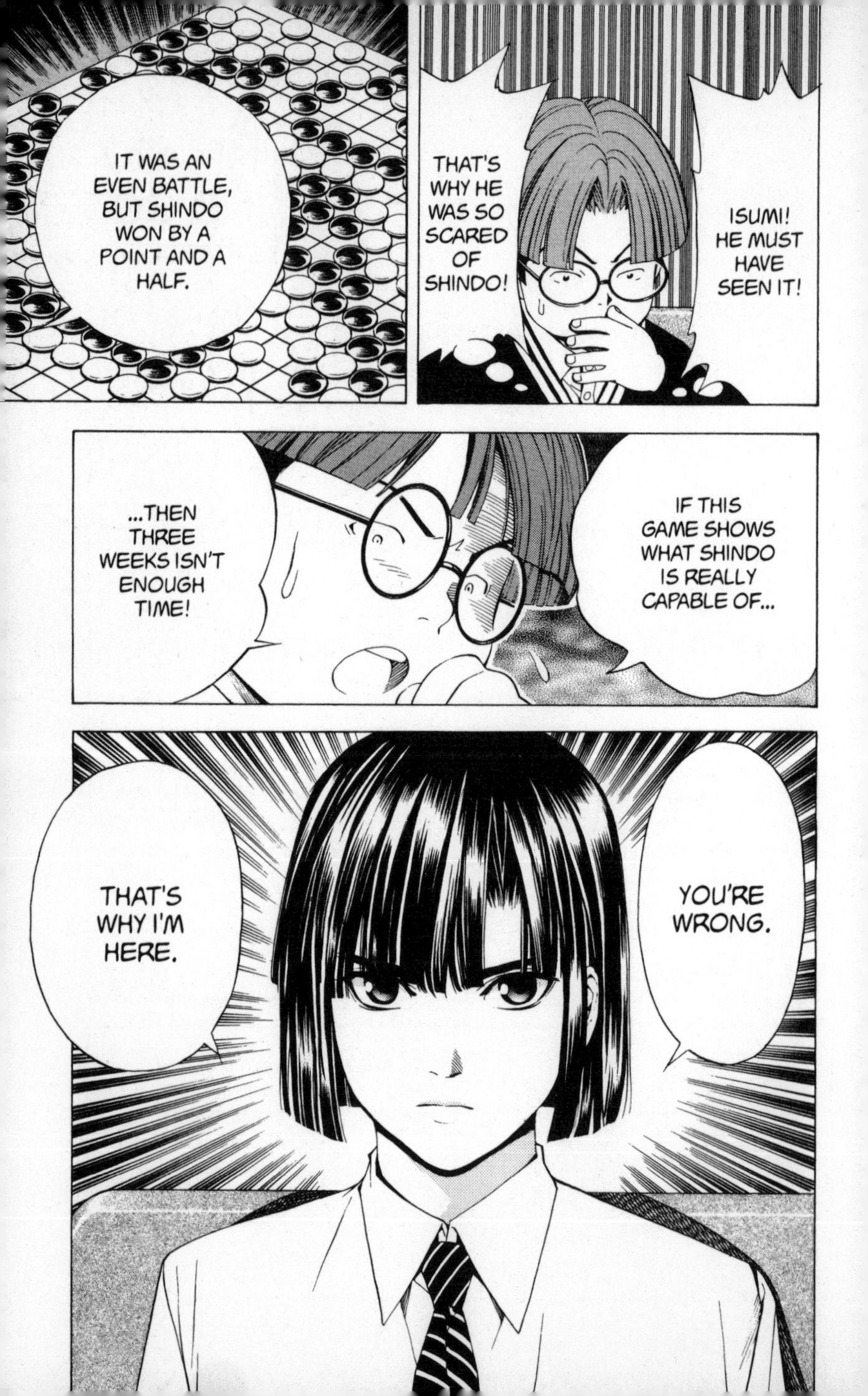
ISUMI! HE MUST HAVE SEEN IT!
THAT'S WHY HE WAS SO SCARED OF SHINDO!
IT WAS AN EVEN BATTLE, BUT SHINDO WON BY A POINT AND A HALF.
IF THIS GAME SHOWS WHAT SHINDO IS REALLY CAPABLE OF...
...THEN THREE WEEKS ISN'T ENOUGH TIME!
YOU'RE WRONG.
THAT'S WHY I'M HERE.

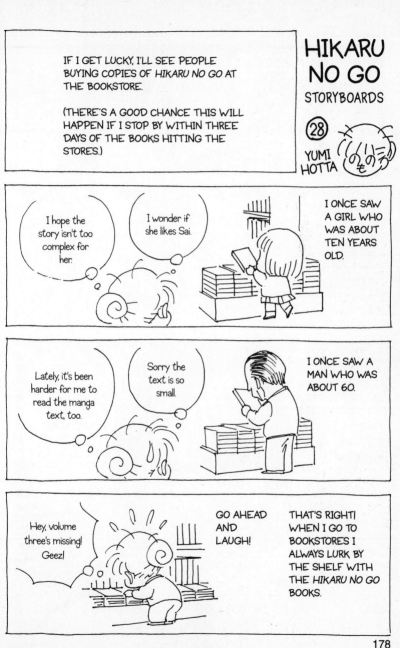

HIKARU NO GO

STORYBOARDS

(28)

YUMI HOTTA

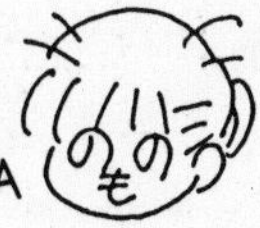

IF I GET LUCKY, I'LL SEE PEOPLE BUYING COPIES OF *HIKARU NO GO* AT THE BOOKSTORE.

(THERE'S A GOOD CHANCE THIS WILL HAPPEN IF I STOP BY WITHIN THREE DAYS OF THE BOOKS HITTING THE STORES.)

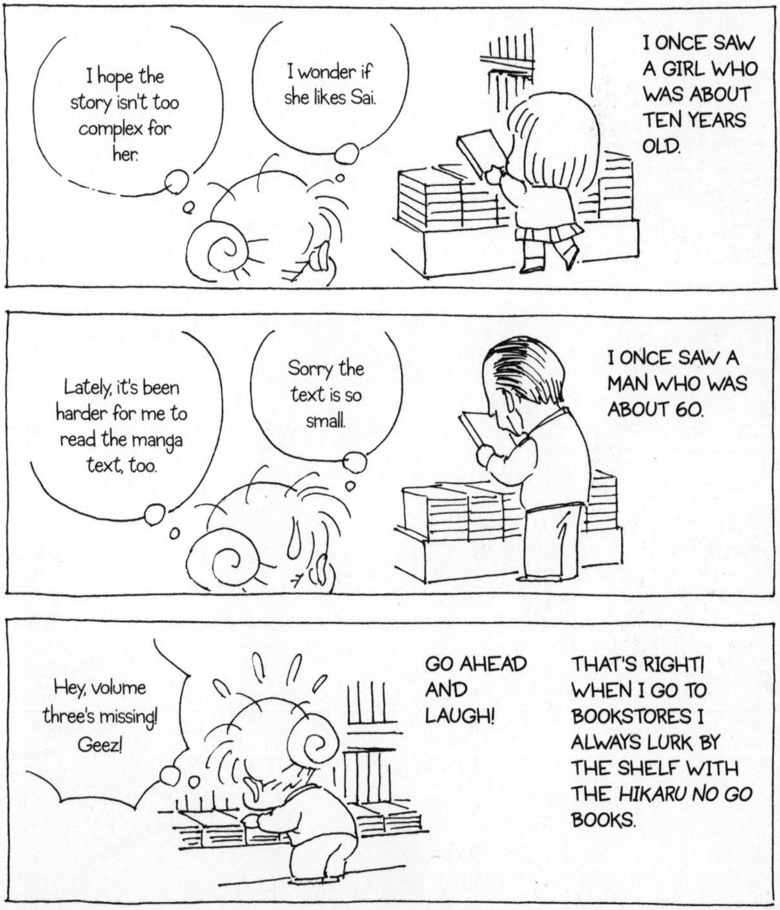

I ONCE SAW A GIRL WHO WAS ABOUT TEN YEARS OLD.
I wonder if she likes Sai.
I hope the story isn't too complex for her.
I ONCE SAW A MAN WHO WAS ABOUT 60.
Sorry the text is so small.
Lately, it's been harder for me to read the manga text, too.
THAT'S RIGHT! WHEN I GO TO BOOKSTORES I ALWAYS LURK BY THE SHELF WITH THE *HIKARU NO GO* BOOKS.
GO AHEAD AND LAUGH!
Hey, volume three's missing! Geez!

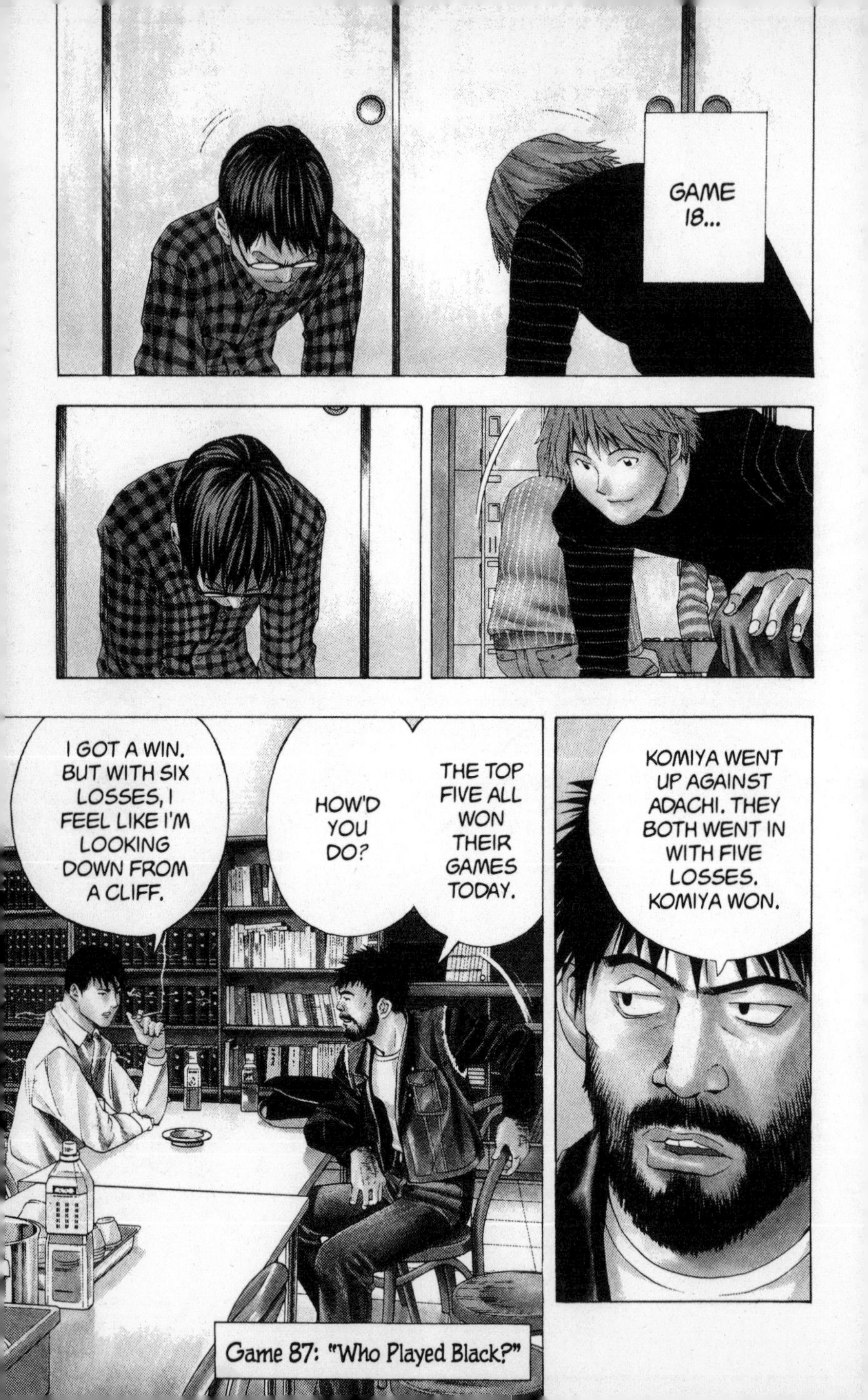
GAME 18...
KOMIYA WENT UP AGAINST ADACHI. THEY BOTH WENT IN WITH FIVE LOSSES. KOMIYA WON.
THE TOP FIVE ALL WON THEIR GAMES TODAY.
HOW'D YOU DO?
I GOT A WIN. BUT WITH SIX LOSSES, I FEEL LIKE I'M LOOKING DOWN FROM A CLIFF.
Game 87: "Who Played Black?"

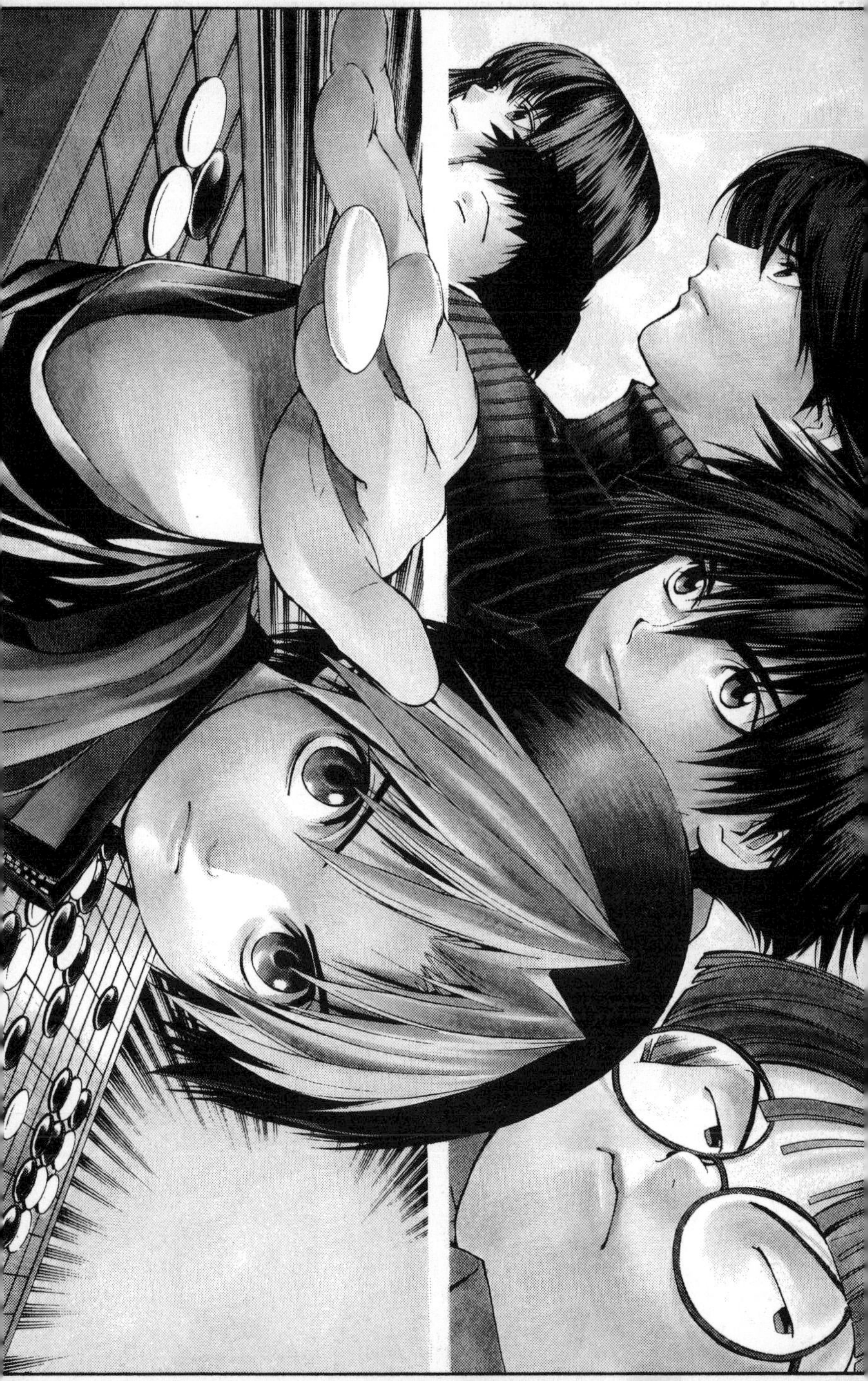

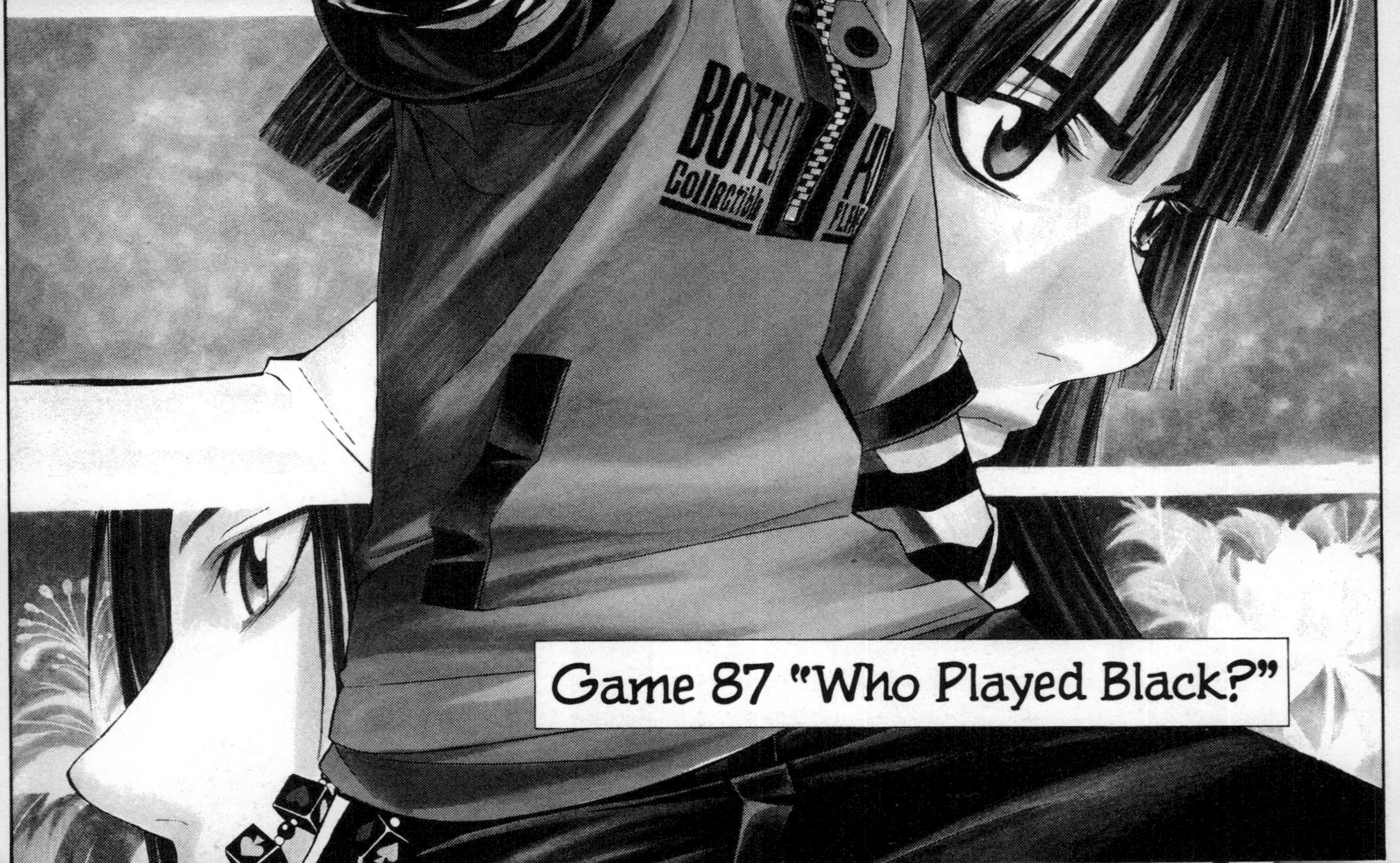
Game 87 "Who Played Black?"

HIKARU 5 SHINDO

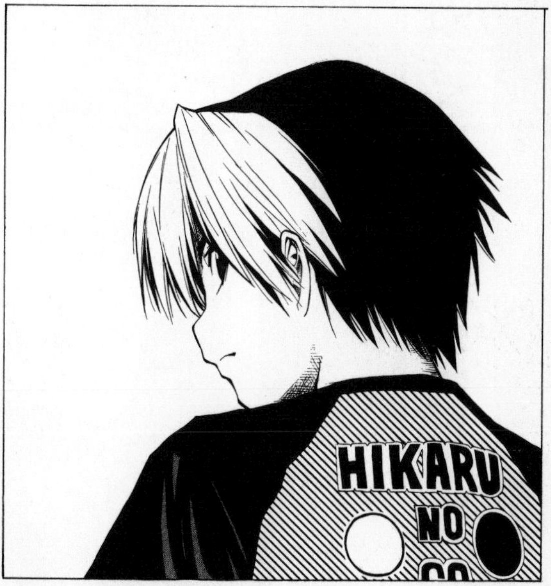
HIKARU
NO

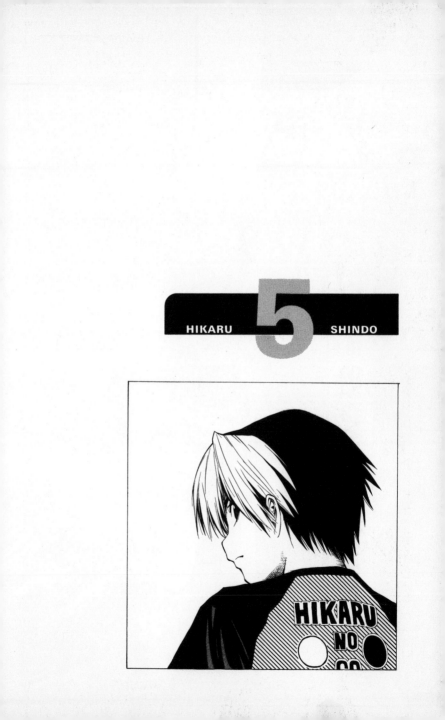

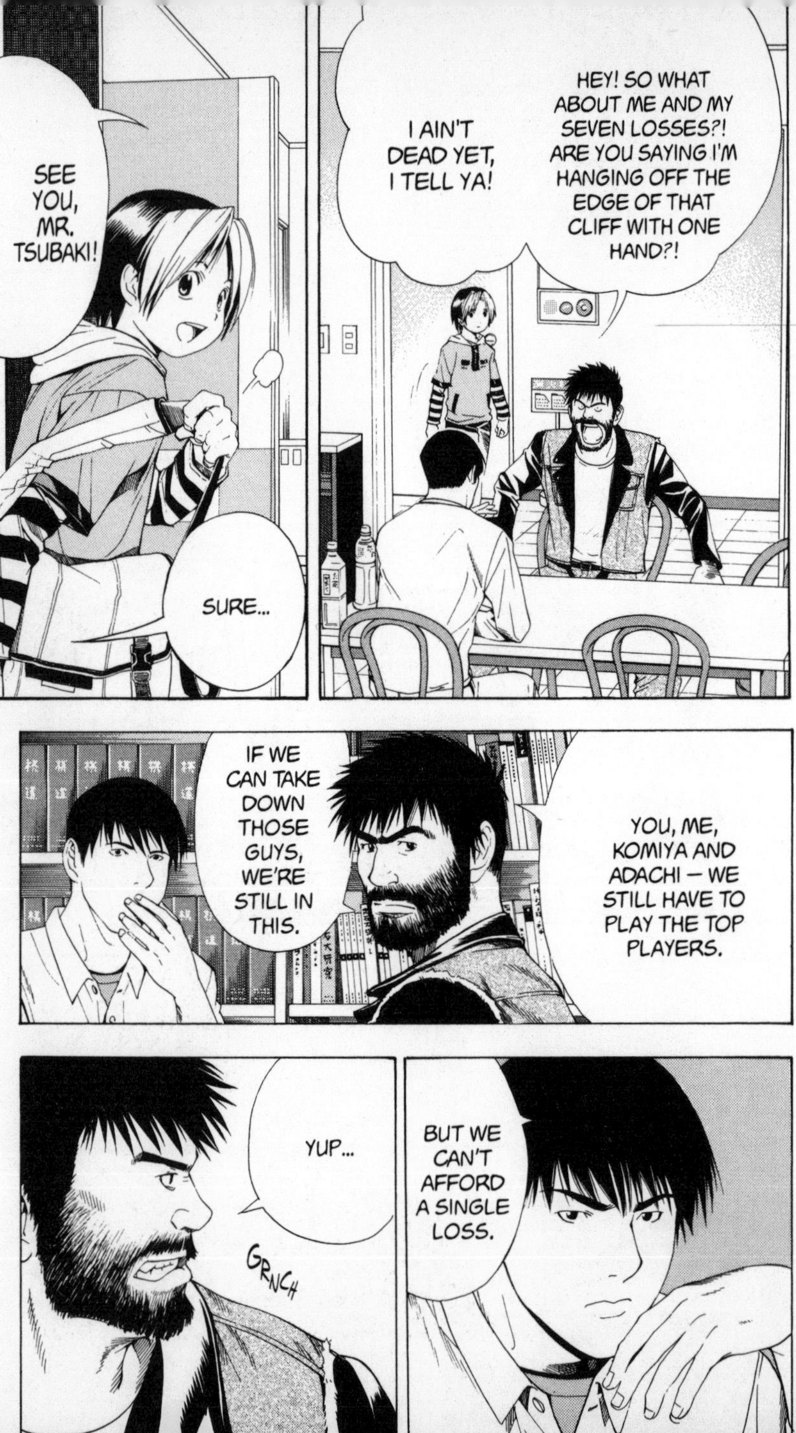
HEY! SO WHAT ABOUT ME AND MY SEVEN LOSSES?! ARE YOU SAYING I'M HANGING OFF THE EDGE OF THAT CLIFF WITH ONE HAND?!
I AIN'T DEAD YET, I TELL YA!
SEE YOU, MR. TSUBAKI!
SURE...
YOU, ME, KOMIYA AND ADACHI — WE STILL HAVE TO PLAY THE TOP PLAYERS.
IF WE CAN TAKE DOWN THOSE GUYS, WE'RE STILL IN THIS.
BUT WE CAN'T AFFORD A SINGLE LOSS.
YUP...
GRNCH

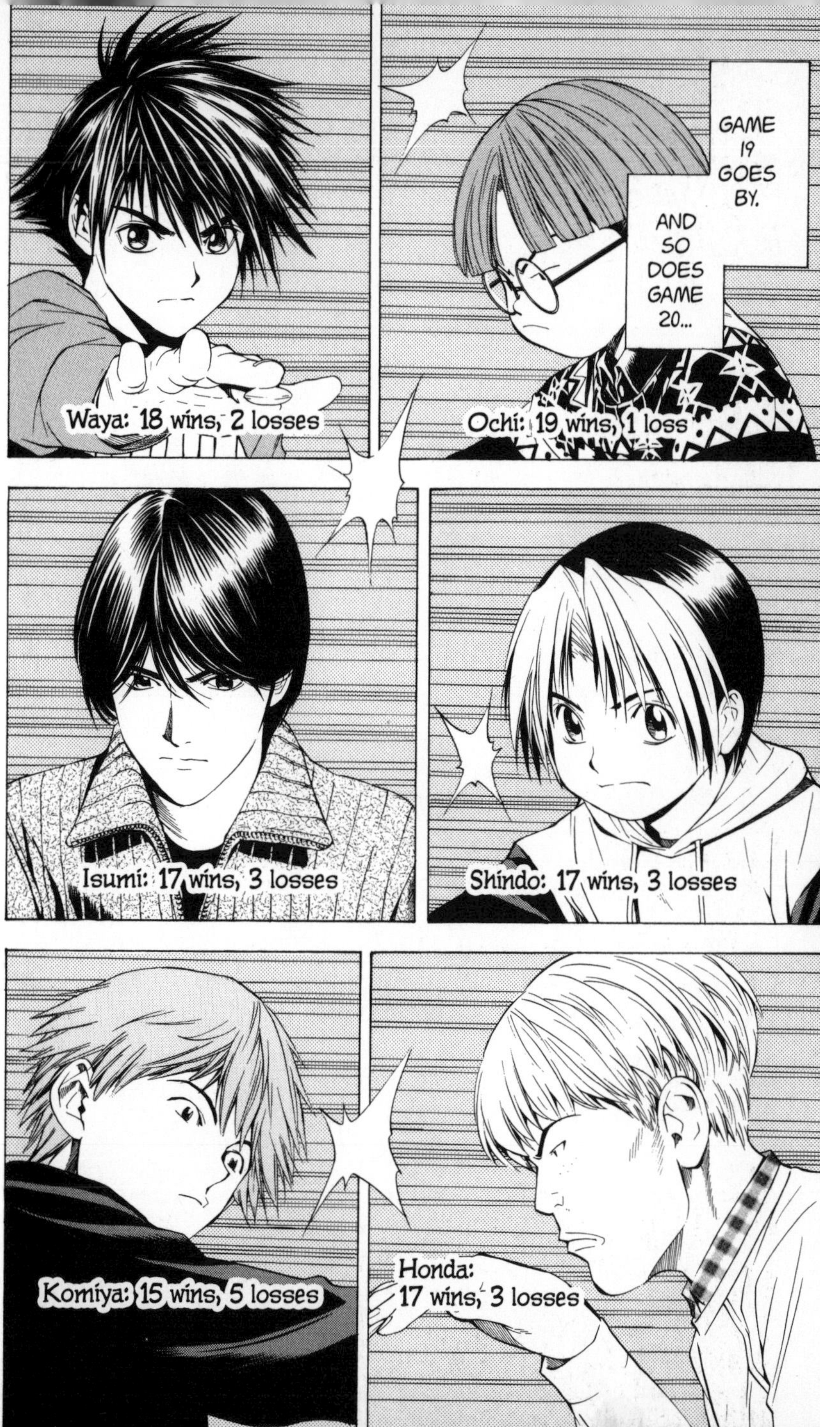
GAME 19 GOES BY.
AND SO DOES GAME 20...
Ochi: 19 wins, 1 loss
Waya: 18 wins, 2 losses
Shindo: 17 wins, 3 losses
Isumi: 17 wins, 3 losses
Honda: 17 wins, 3 losses
Komiya: 15 wins, 5 losses

READ THIS WAY

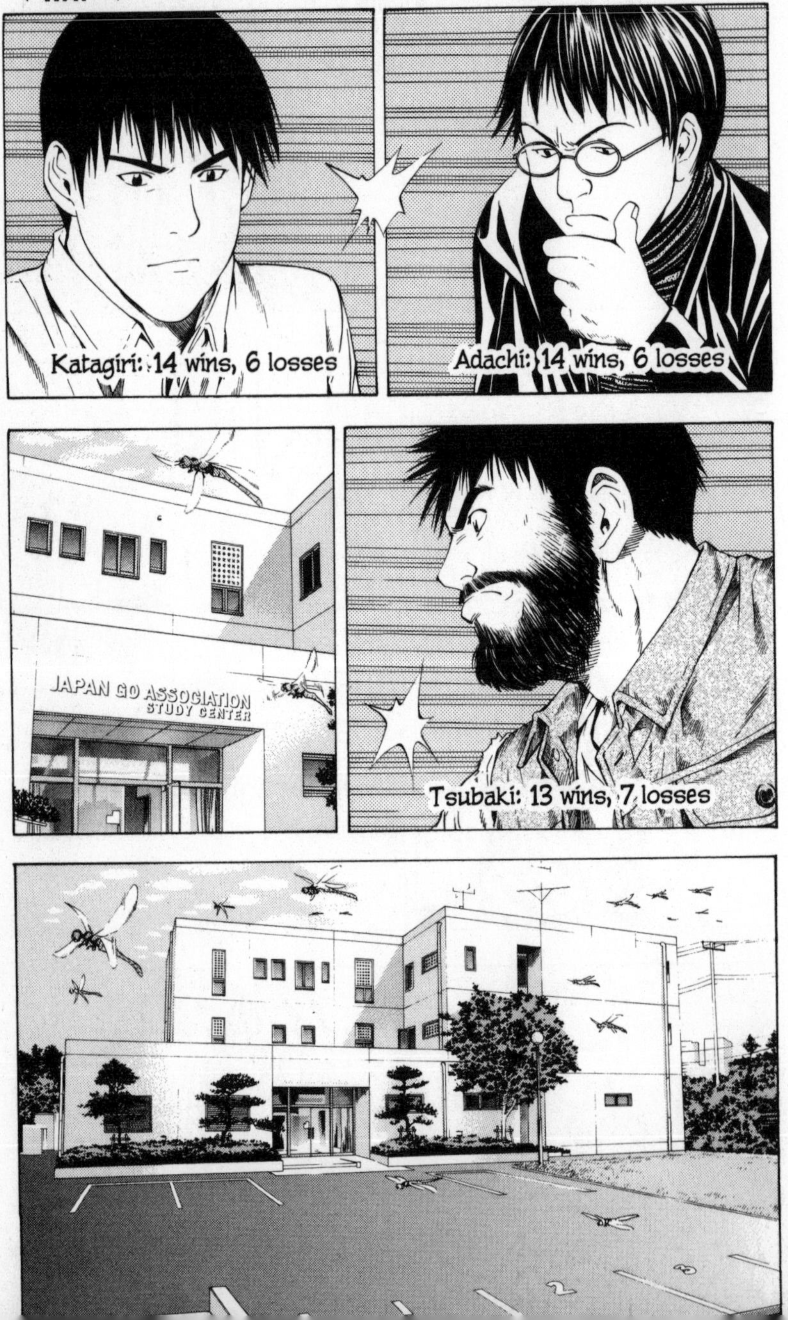
Adachi: 14 wins, 6 losses
Katagiri: 14 wins, 6 losses
Tsubaki: 13 wins, 7 losses
JAPAN GO ASSOCIATION
STUDY CENTER

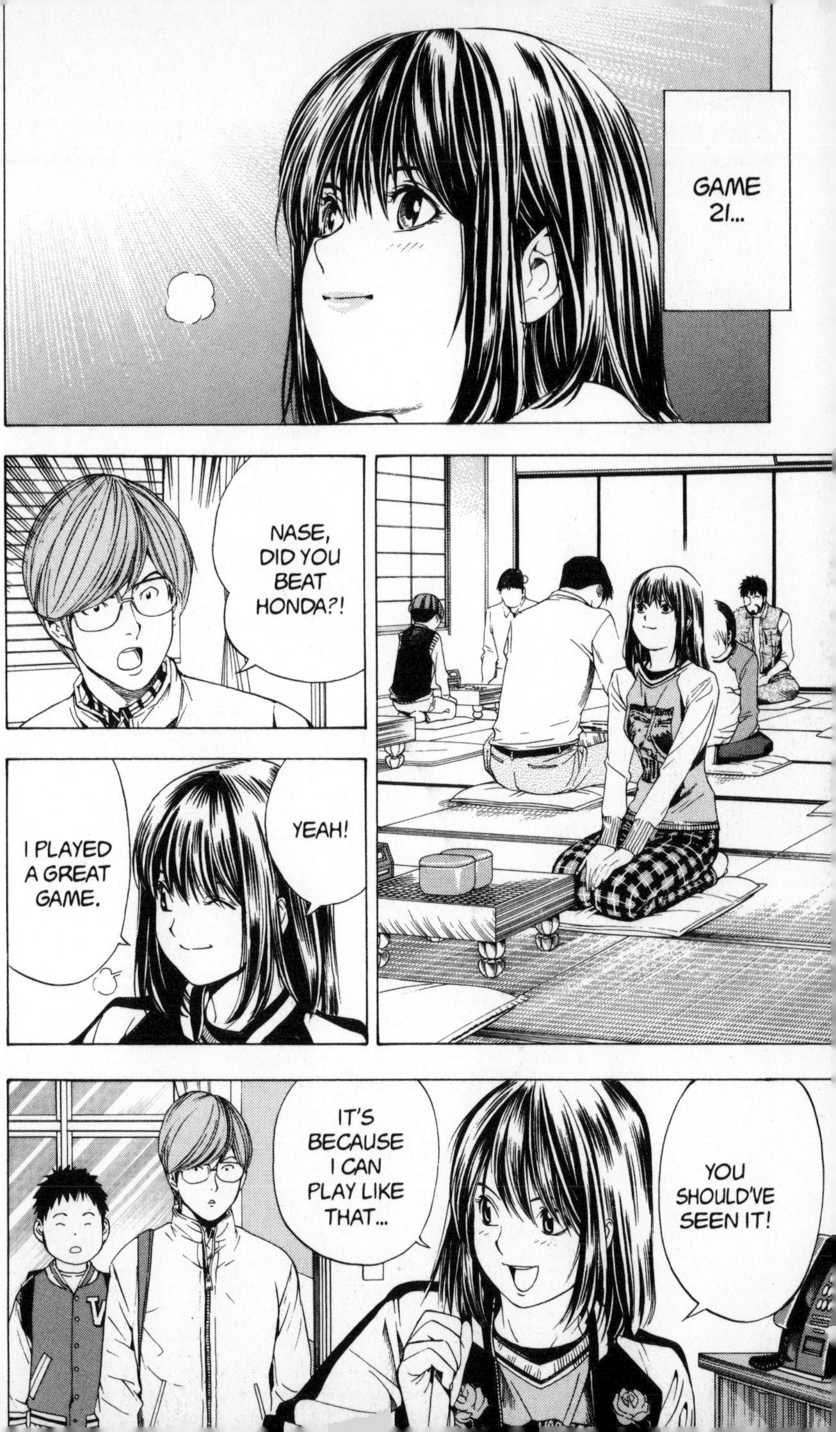
GAME 21...
NASE, DID YOU BEAT HONDA?!
YEAH!
I PLAYED A GREAT GAME.
YOU SHOULD'VE SEEN IT!
IT'S BECAUSE I CAN PLAY LIKE THAT...

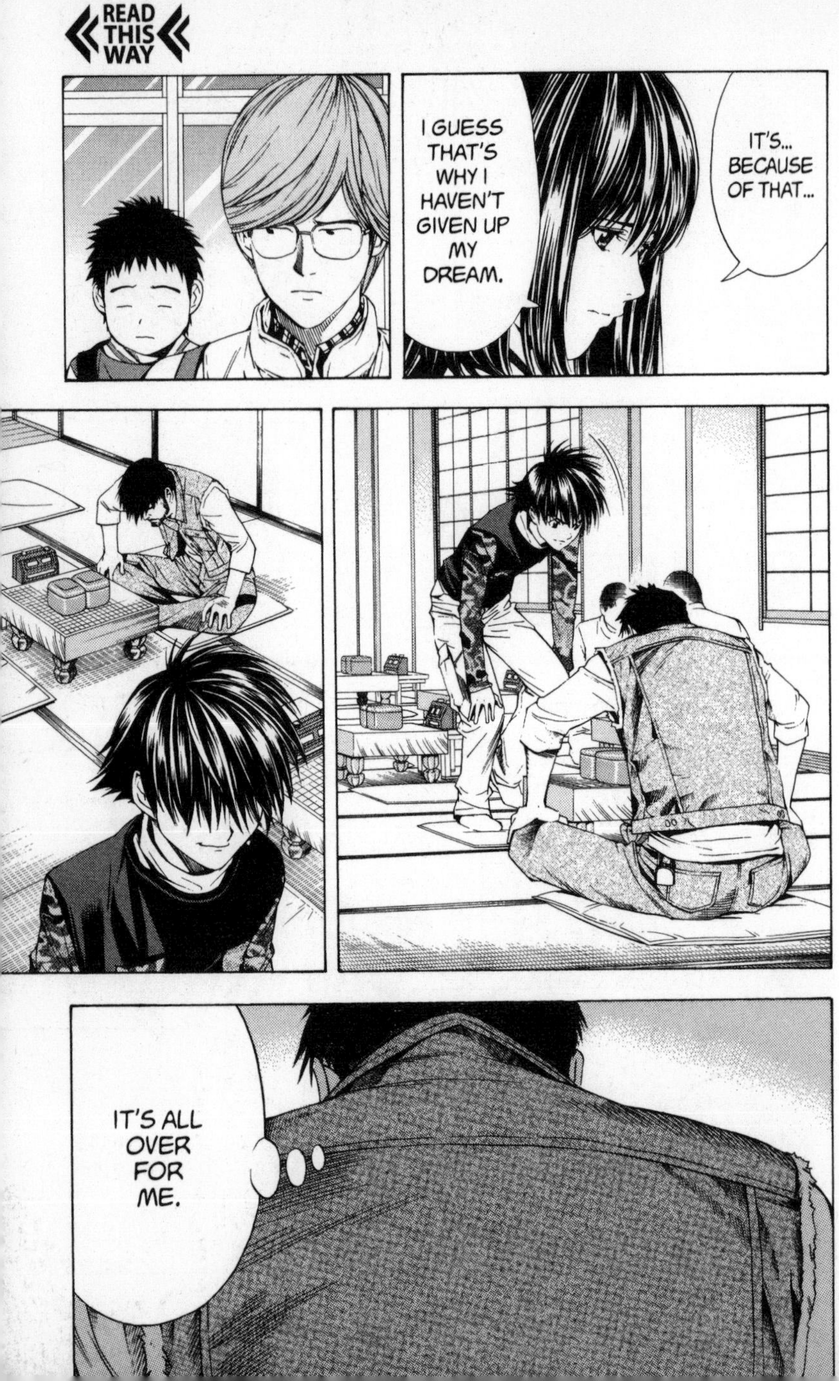
READ THIS WAY
IT'S... BECAUSE OF THAT...
I GUESS THAT'S WHY I HAVEN'T GIVEN UP MY DREAM.
IT'S ALL OVER FOR ME.

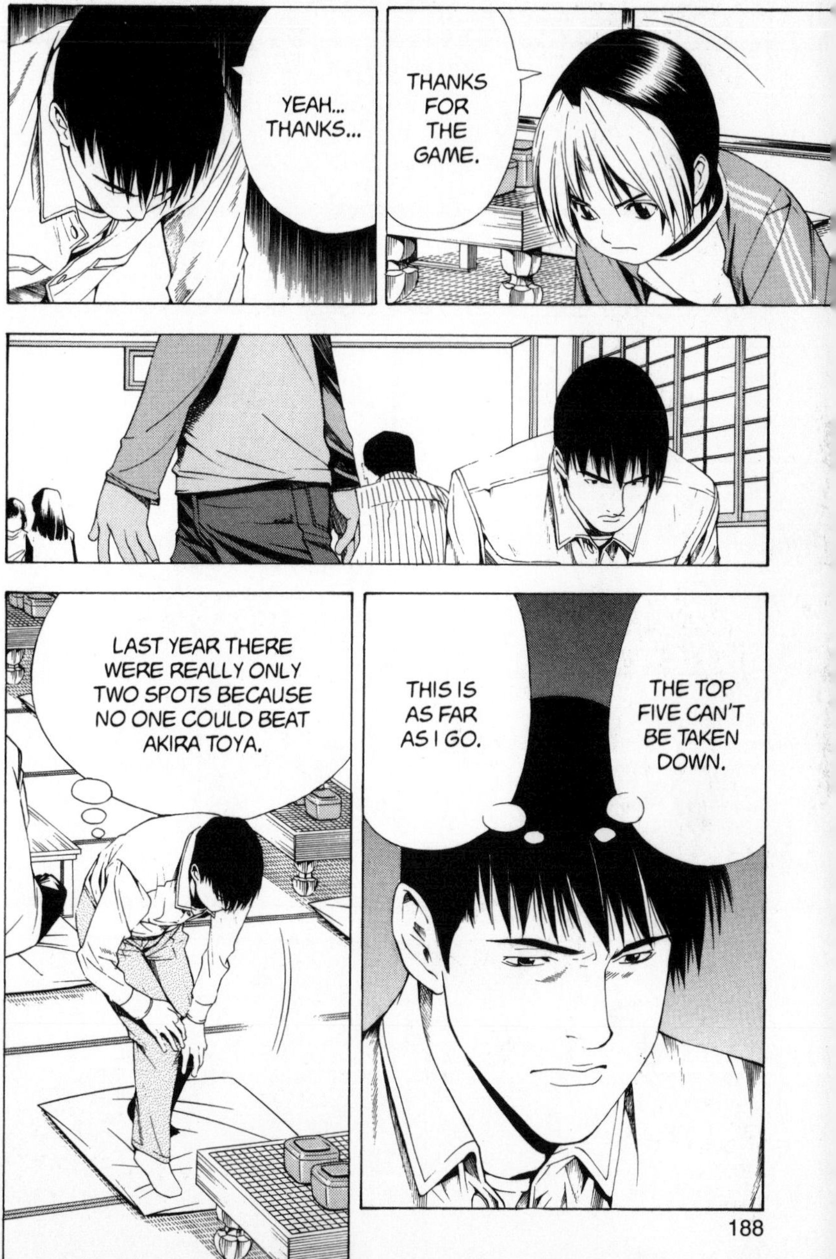
THANKS FOR THE GAME.
YEAH... THANKS...
THE TOP FIVE CAN'T BE TAKEN DOWN.
THIS IS AS FAR AS I GO.
LAST YEAR THERE WERE REALLY ONLY TWO SPOTS BECAUSE NO ONE COULD BEAT AKIRA TOYA.

READ THIS WAY

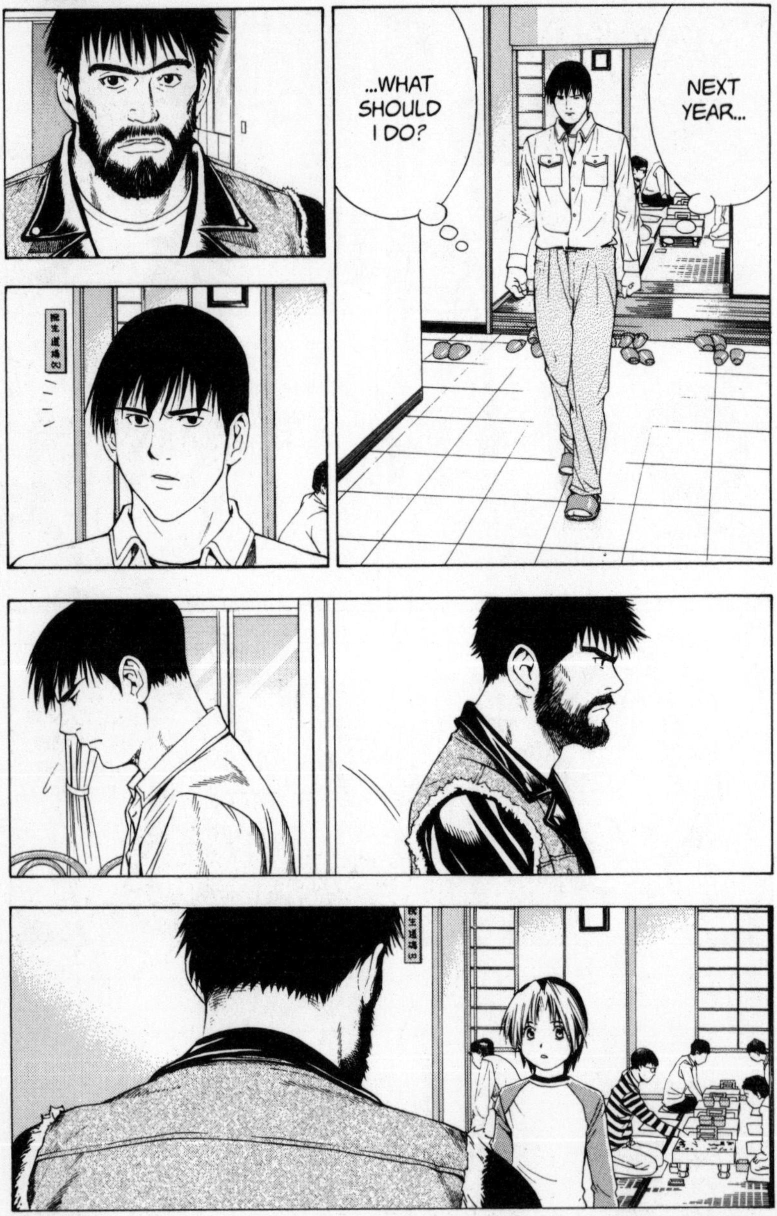
NEXT YEAR...
...WHAT SHOULD I DO?

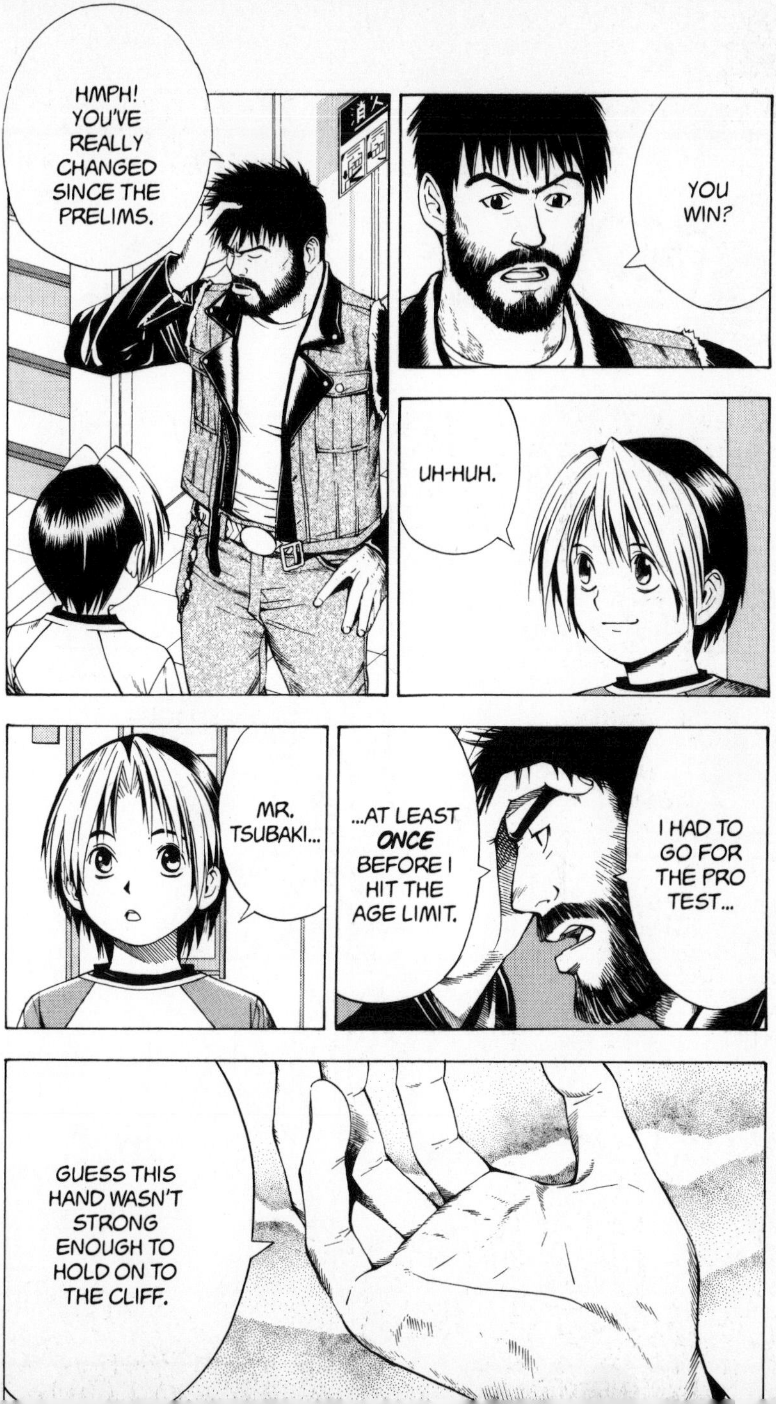
YOU WIN?
UH-HUH.
HMPH! YOU'VE REALLY CHANGED SINCE THE PRELIMS.
I HAD TO GO FOR THE PRO TEST...
...AT LEAST ONCE BEFORE I HIT THE AGE LIMIT.
MR. TSUBAKI...
GUESS THIS HAND WASN'T STRONG ENOUGH TO HOLD ON TO THE CLIFF.

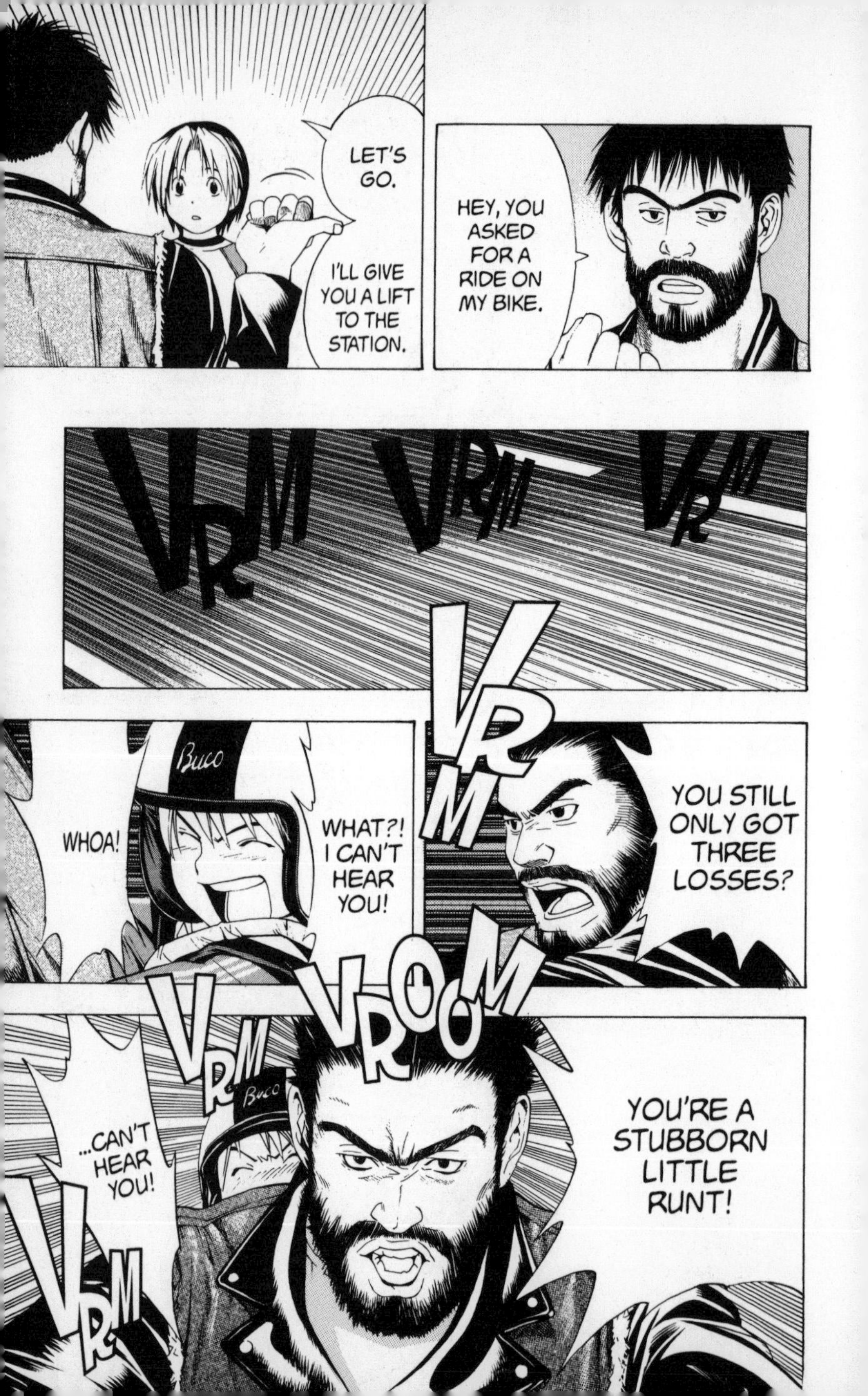
HEY, YOU ASKED FOR A RIDE ON MY BIKE.
LET'S GO.
I'LL GIVE YOU A LIFT TO THE STATION.
VRM
VRM
VRM
VRM
YOU STILL ONLY GOT THREE LOSSES?
WHAT?! I CAN'T HEAR YOU!
WHOA!
VROOM
VRM
YOU'RE A STUBBORN LITTLE RUNT!
...CAN'T HEAR YOU!
VRM

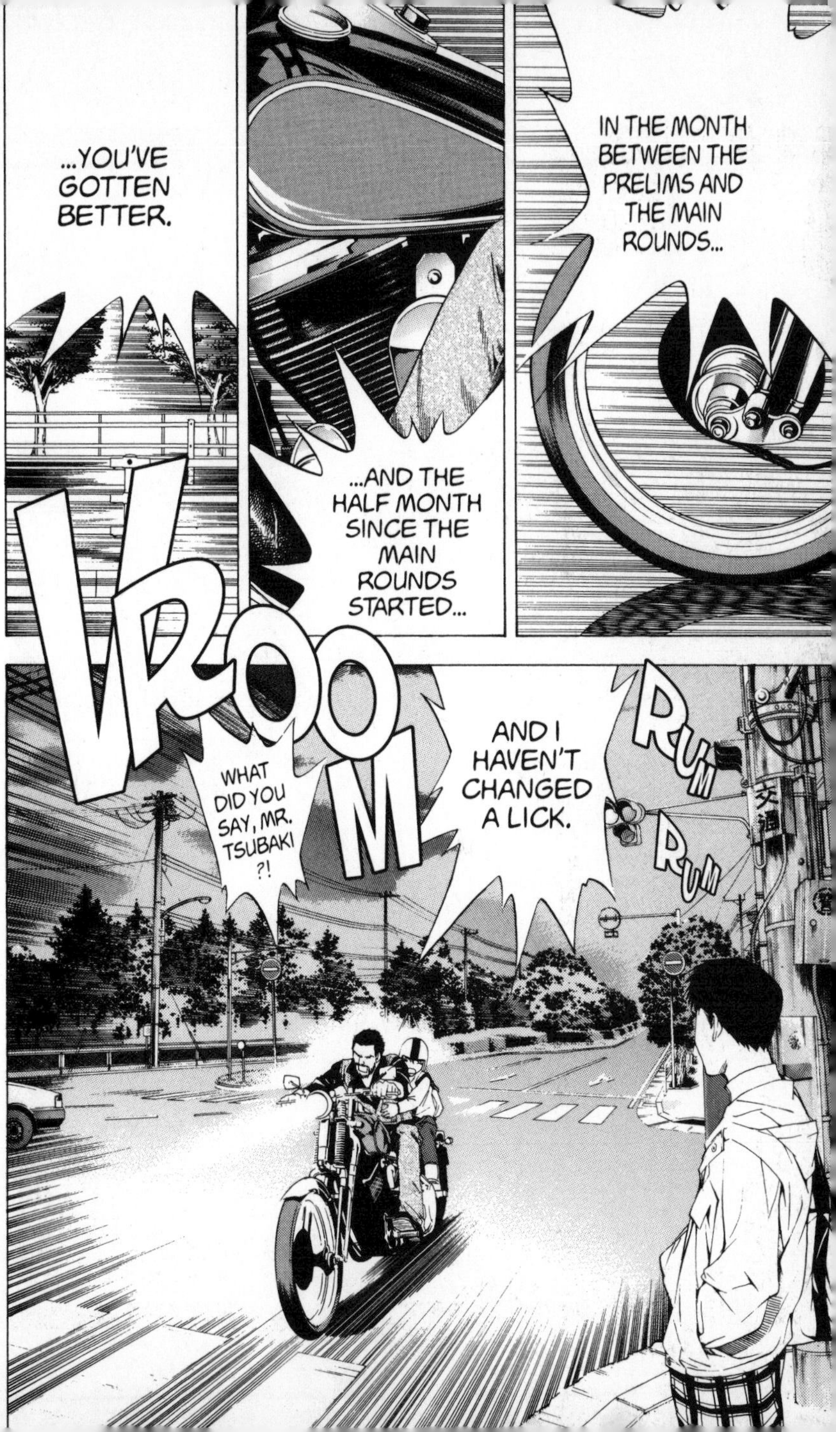
IN THE MONTH BETWEEN THE PRELIMS AND THE MAIN ROUNDS...
...AND THE HALF MONTH SINCE THE MAIN ROUNDS STARTED...
...YOU'VE GOTTEN BETTER.
VROOOM
RUM RUM
AND I HAVEN'T CHANGED A LICK.
WHAT DID YOU SAY, MR. TSUBAKI?!

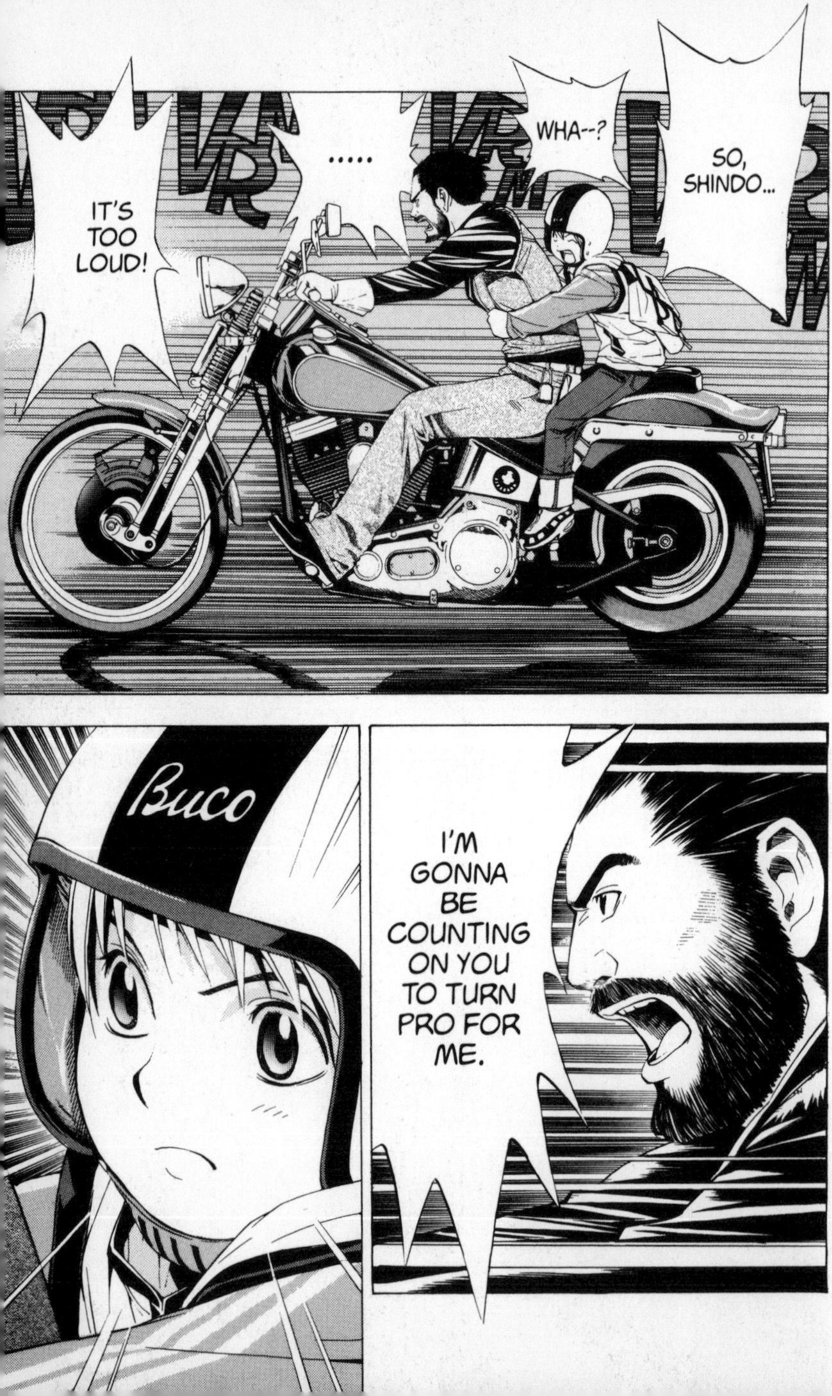
SO, SHINDO...
WHA--?
.....
IT'S TOO LOUD!
I'M GONNA BE COUNTING ON YOU TO TURN PRO FOR ME.
Buco

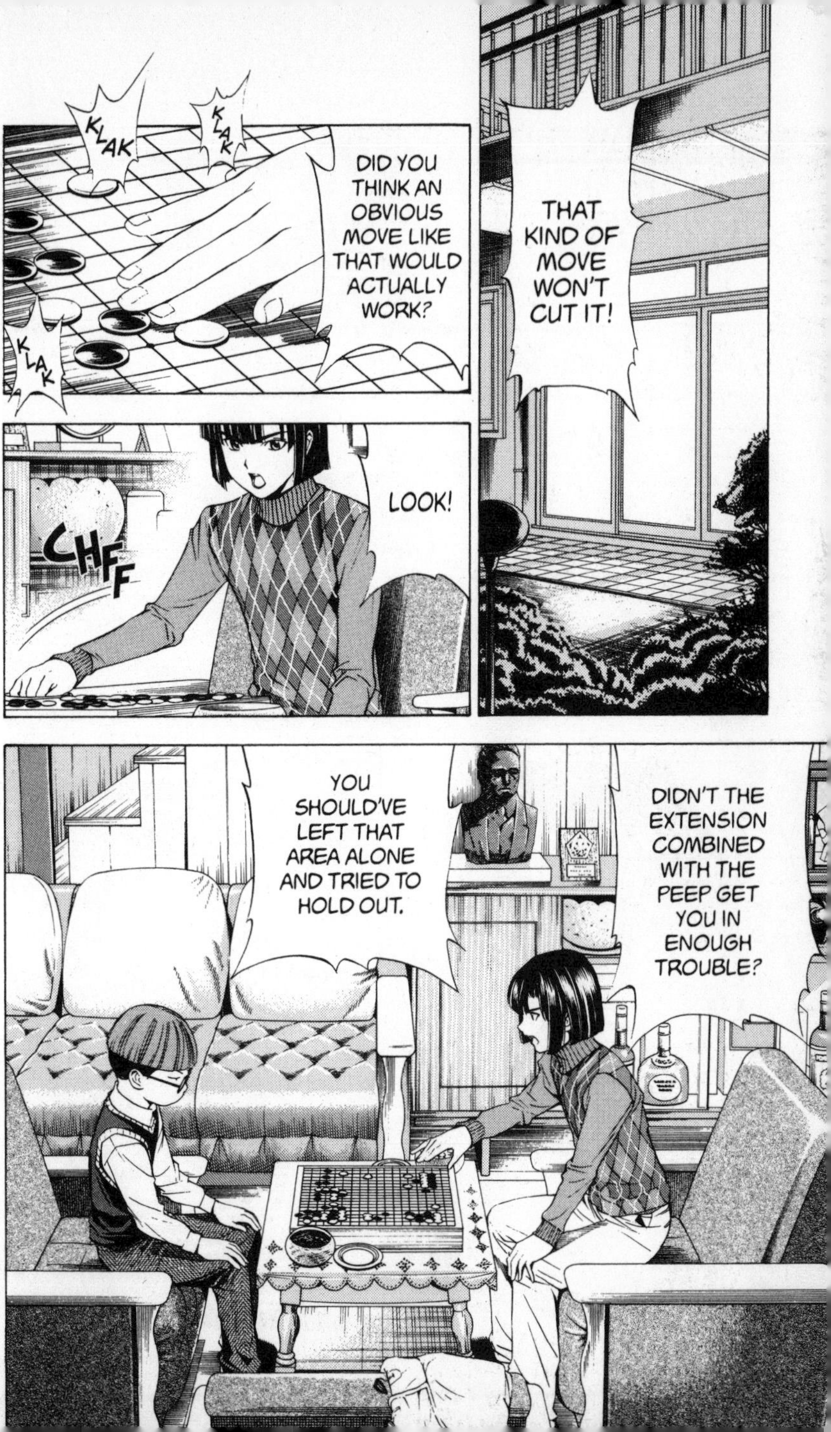
THAT KIND OF MOVE WON'T CUT IT!
KLAK
KLAK
DID YOU THINK AN OBVIOUS MOVE LIKE THAT WOULD ACTUALLY WORK?
KLAK
LOOK!
CHFF
DIDN'T THE EXTENSION COMBINED WITH THE PEEP GET YOU IN ENOUGH TROUBLE?
YOU SHOULD'VE LEFT THAT AREA ALONE AND TRIED TO HOLD OUT.

READ THIS WAY

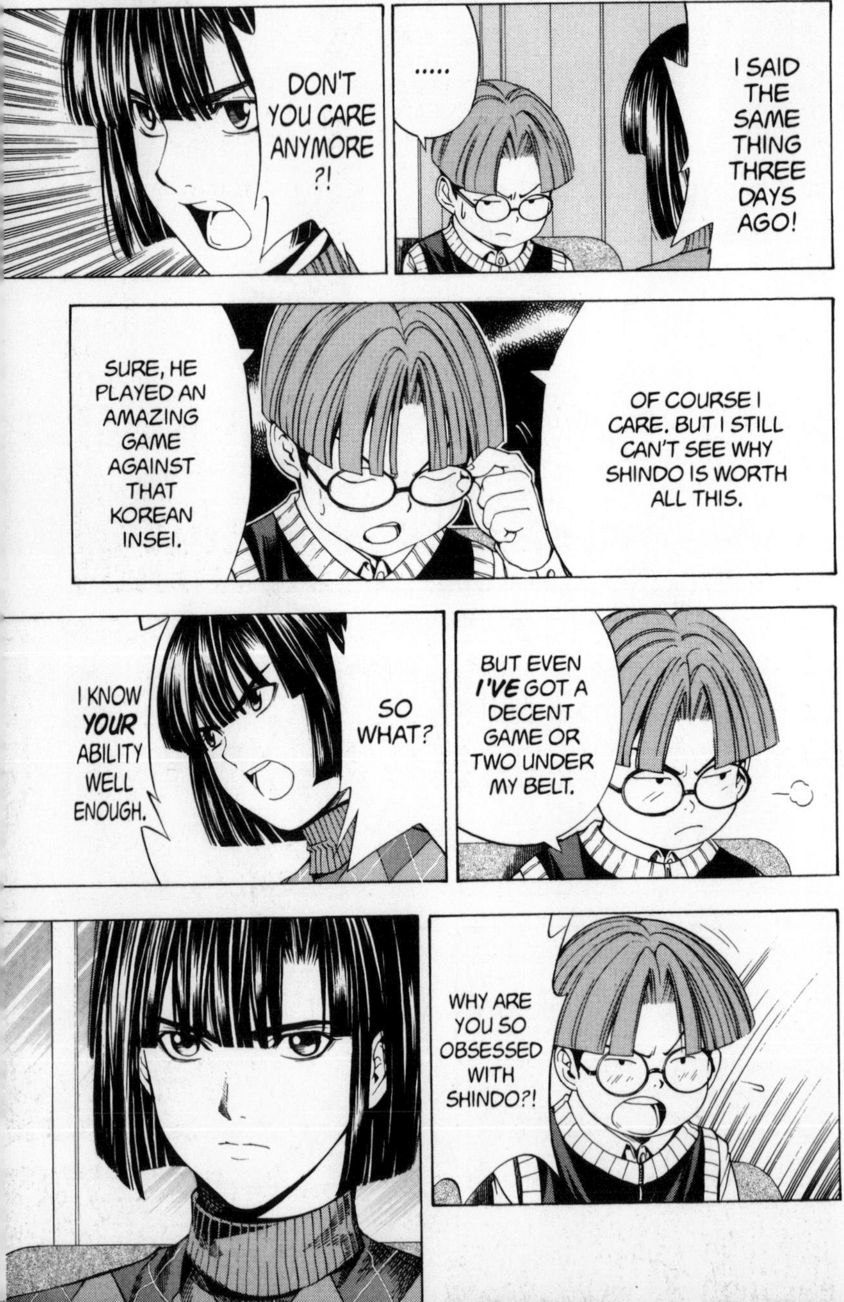
I SAID THE SAME THING THREE DAYS AGO!
.....
DON'T YOU CARE ANYMORE?!
OF COURSE I CARE. BUT I STILL CAN'T SEE WHY SHINDO IS WORTH ALL THIS.
SURE, HE PLAYED AN AMAZING GAME AGAINST THAT KOREAN INSEI.
BUT EVEN *I'VE* GOT A DECENT GAME OR TWO UNDER MY BELT.
SO WHAT?
I KNOW *YOUR* ABILITY WELL ENOUGH.
WHY ARE YOU SO OBSESSED WITH SHINDO?!

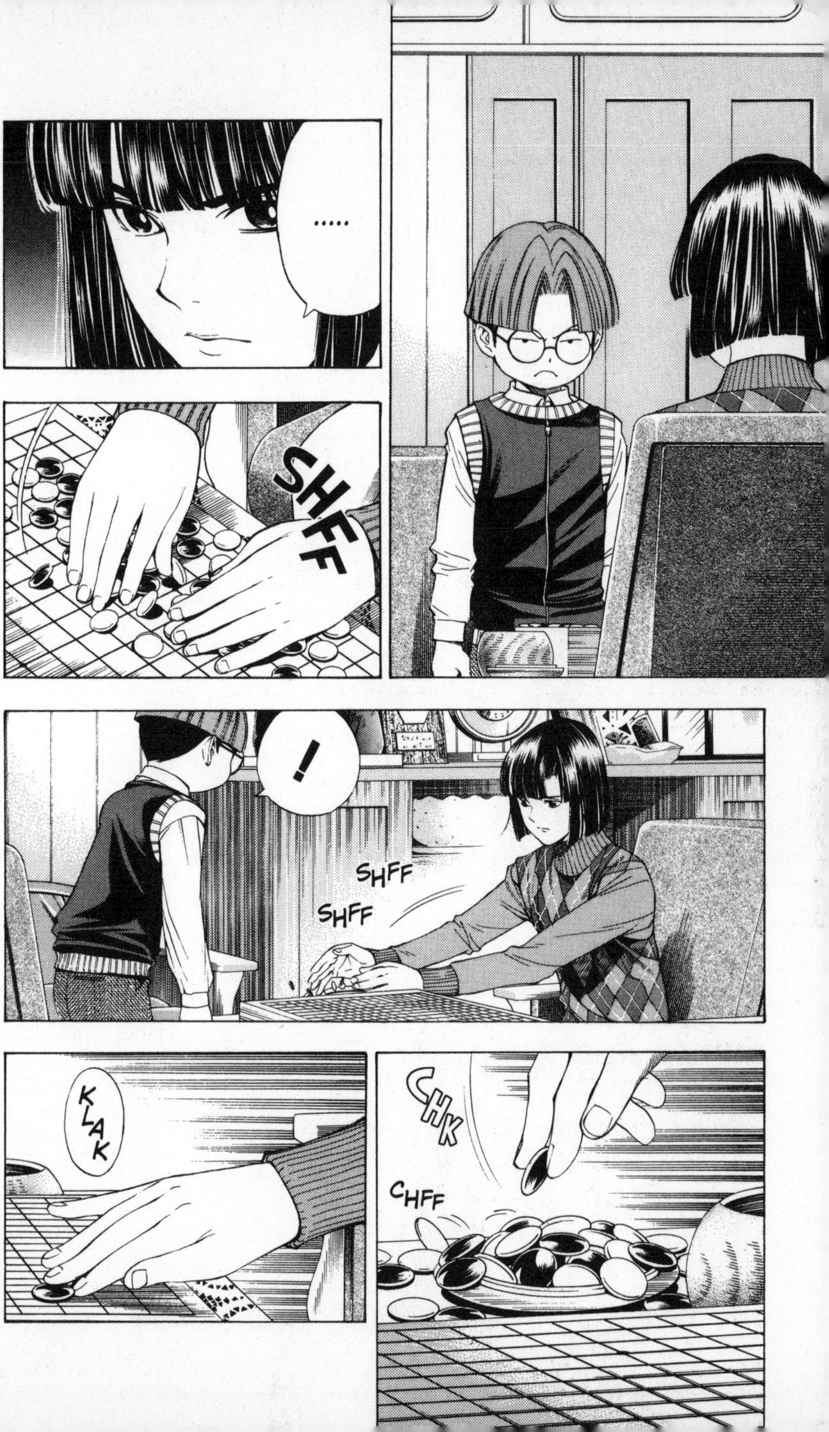
.....
SHFF
!
SHFF
SHFF
CHK
CHFF
KLAK

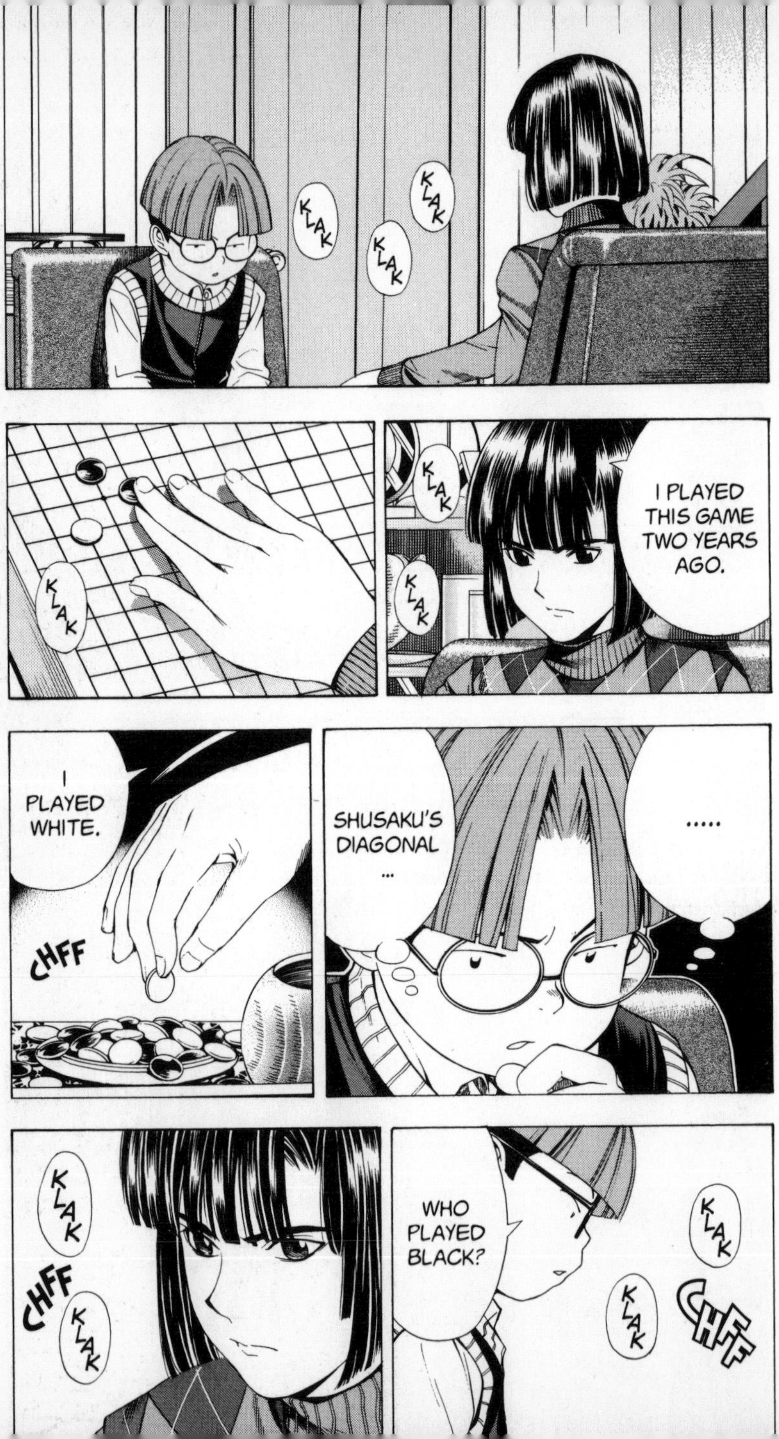
KLAK
KLAK
KLAK
I PLAYED THIS GAME TWO YEARS AGO.
KLAK
KLAK
KLAK
.....
SHUSAKU'S DIAGONAL ...
I PLAYED WHITE.
CHFF
KLAK
WHO PLAYED BLACK?
KLAK
CHFF
KLAK
CHFF
KLAK

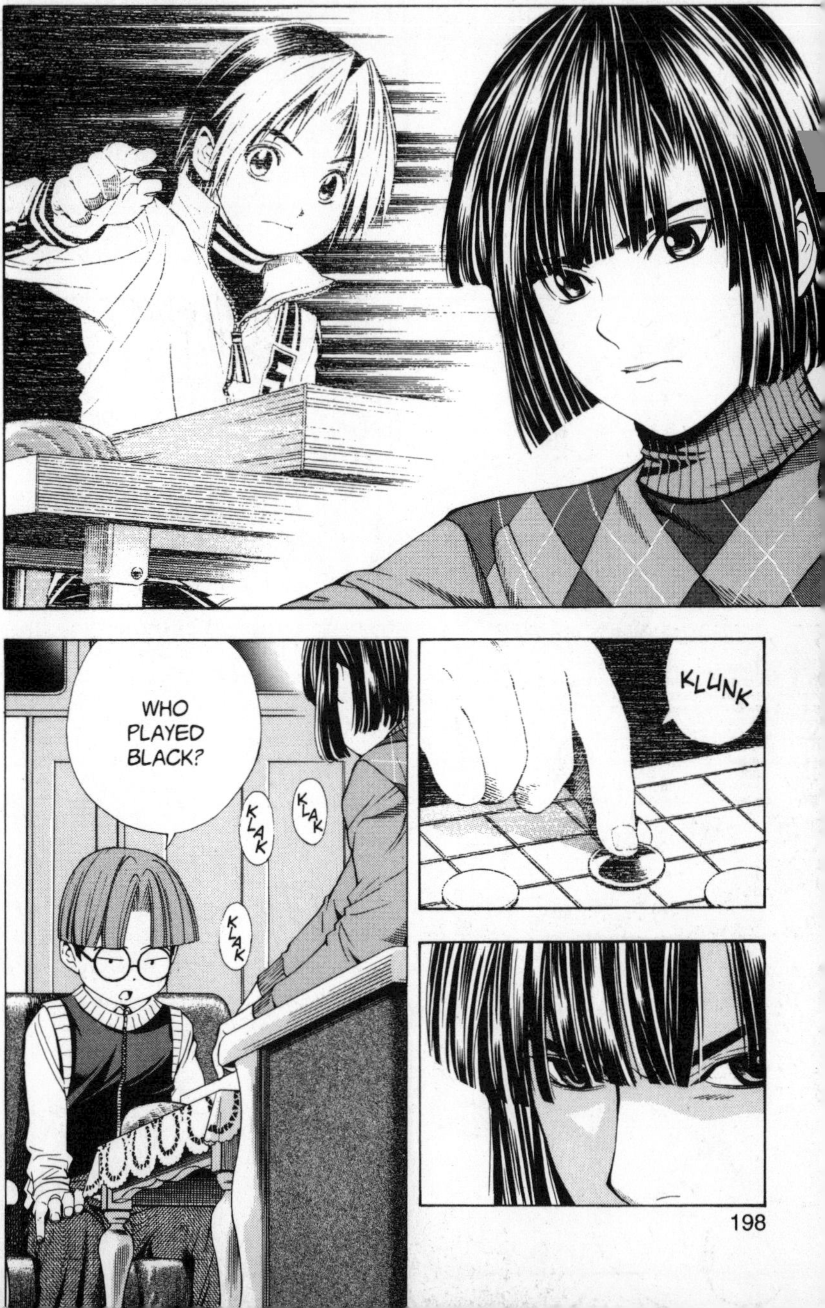
KLUNK
WHO PLAYED BLACK?
KLAK
KLAK
KLAK

READ THIS WAY

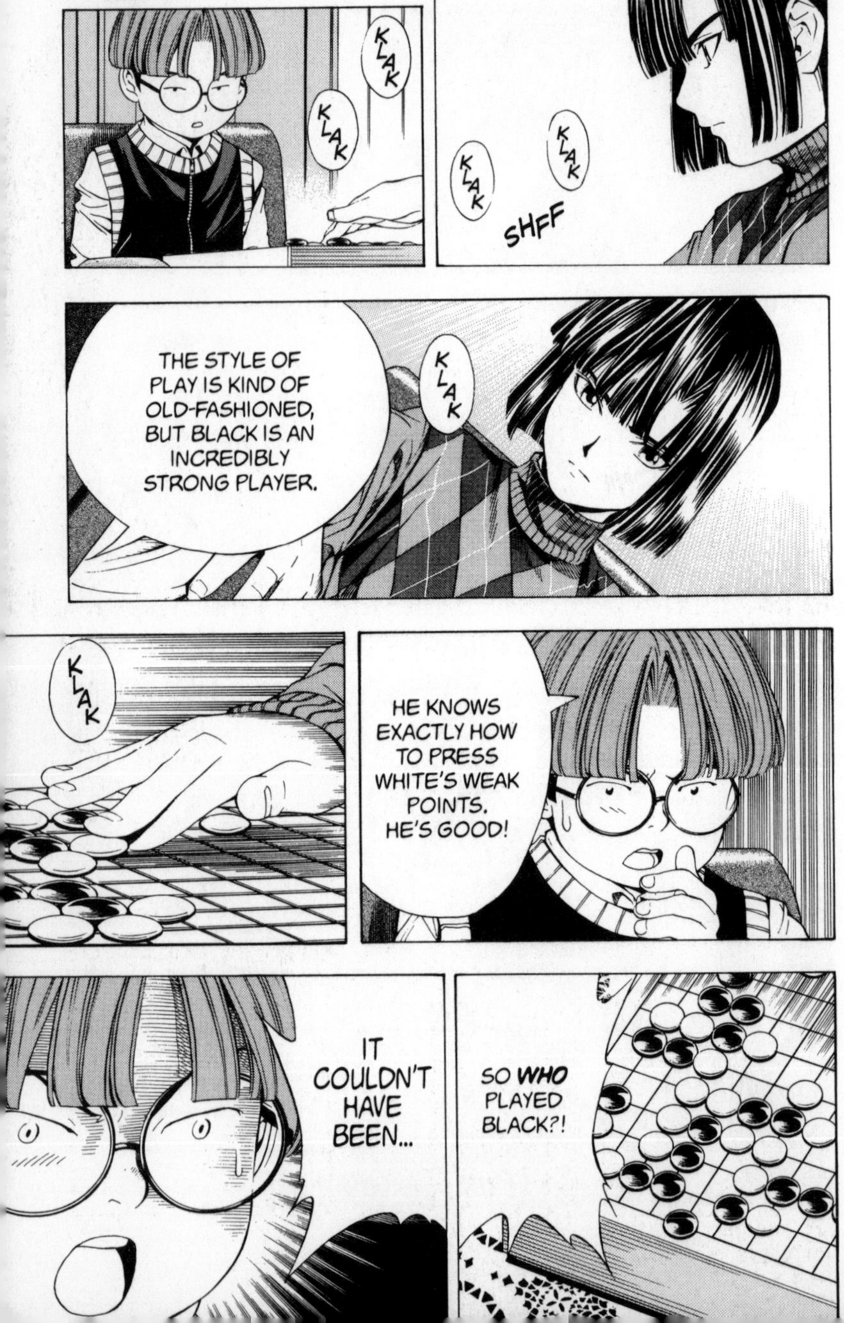
KLAK
KLAK
SHFF
KLAK
KLAK
KLAK
THE STYLE OF PLAY IS KIND OF OLD-FASHIONED, BUT BLACK IS AN INCREDIBLY STRONG PLAYER.
HE KNOWS EXACTLY HOW TO PRESS WHITE'S WEAK POINTS. HE'S GOOD!
KLAK
SO **WHO** PLAYED BLACK?!
IT COULDN'T HAVE BEEN...

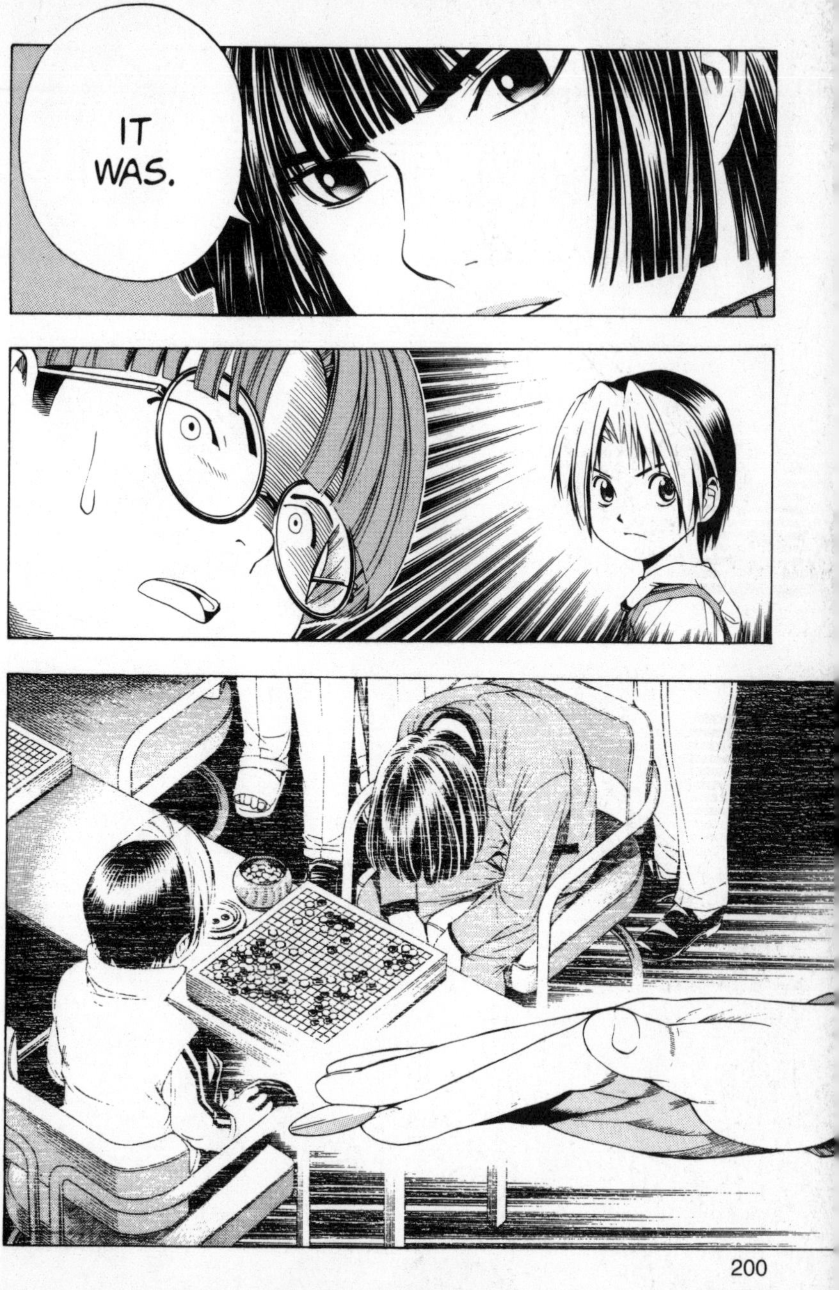
IT WAS.

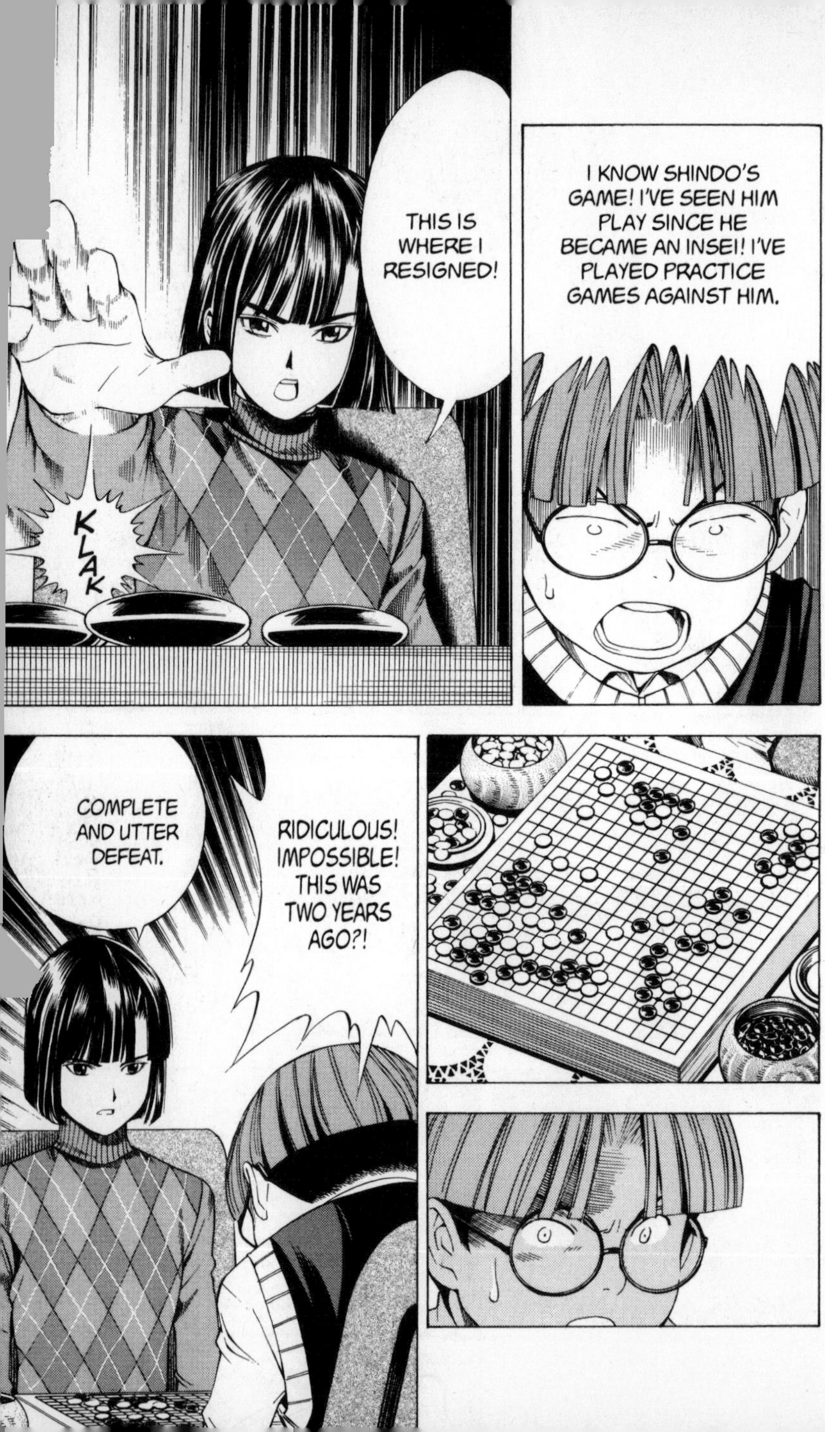
I KNOW SHINDO'S GAME! I'VE SEEN HIM PLAY SINCE HE BECAME AN INSEI! I'VE PLAYED PRACTICE GAMES AGAINST HIM.
THIS IS WHERE I RESIGNED!
KLAK
COMPLETE AND UTTER DEFEAT.
RIDICULOUS! IMPOSSIBLE! THIS WAS TWO YEARS AGO?!

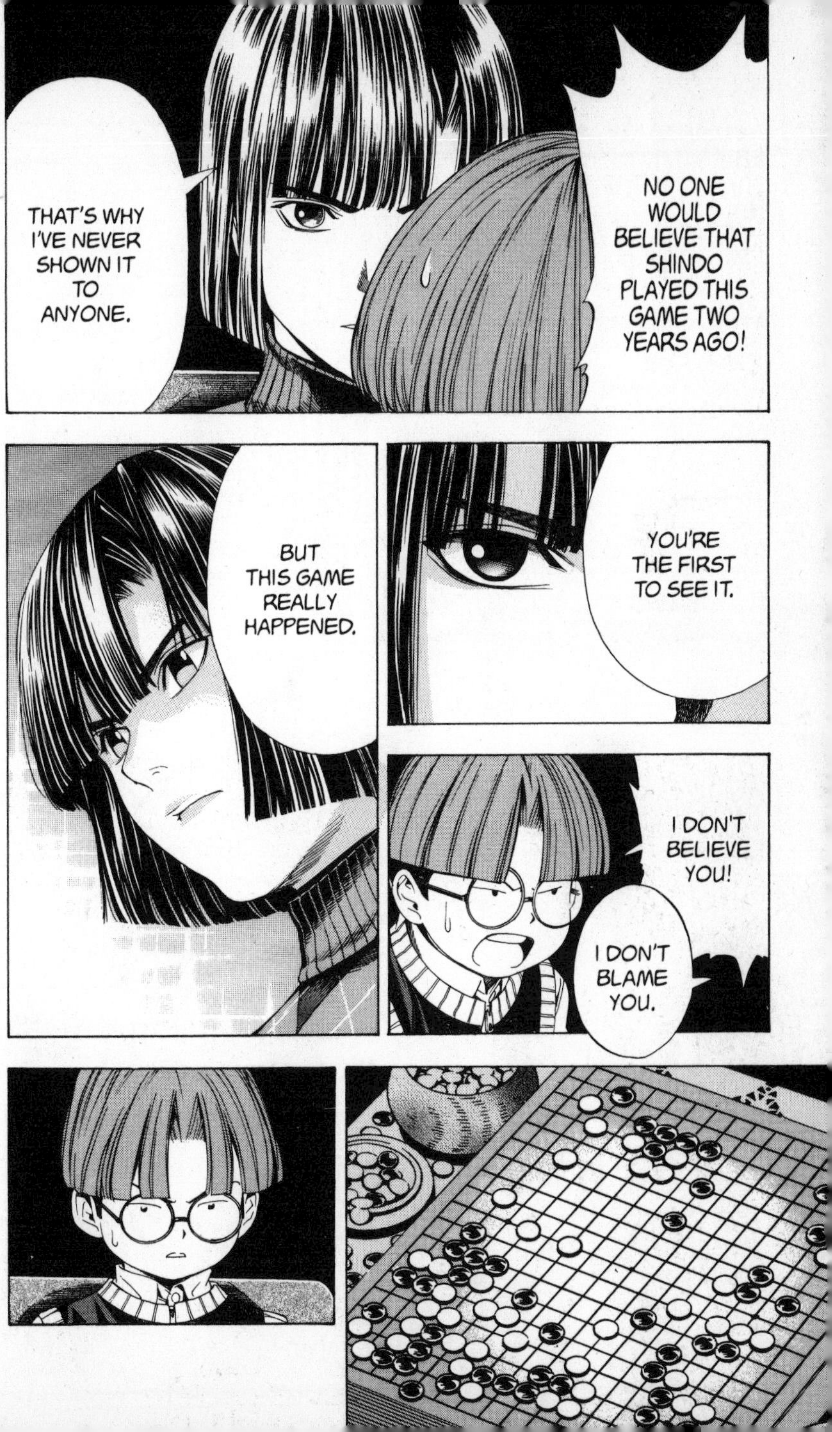
NO ONE WOULD BELIEVE THAT SHINDO PLAYED THIS GAME TWO YEARS AGO!
THAT'S WHY I'VE NEVER SHOWN IT TO ANYONE.
YOU'RE THE FIRST TO SEE IT.
I DON'T BELIEVE YOU!
I DON'T BLAME YOU.
BUT THIS GAME REALLY HAPPENED.

« READ THIS WAY «

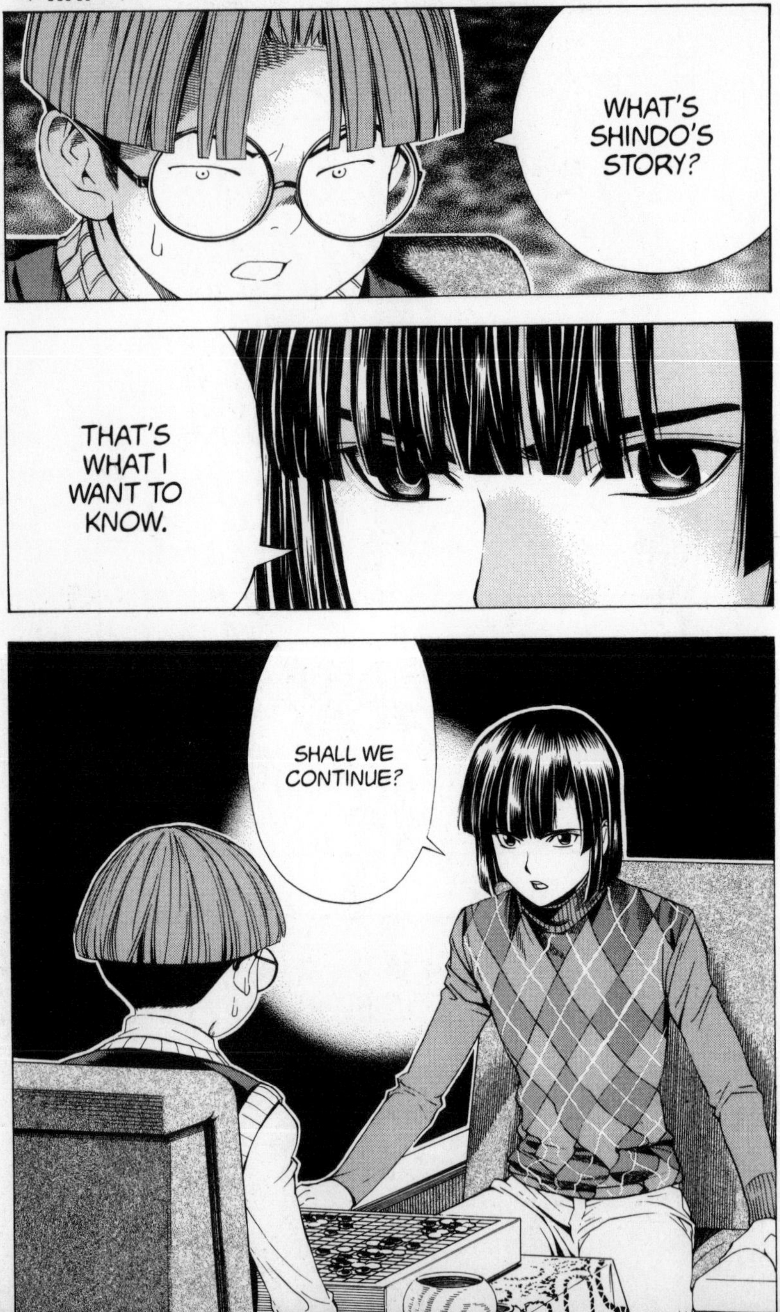
WHAT'S SHINDO'S STORY?
THAT'S WHAT I WANT TO KNOW.
SHALL WE CONTINUE?

Next Volume Preview

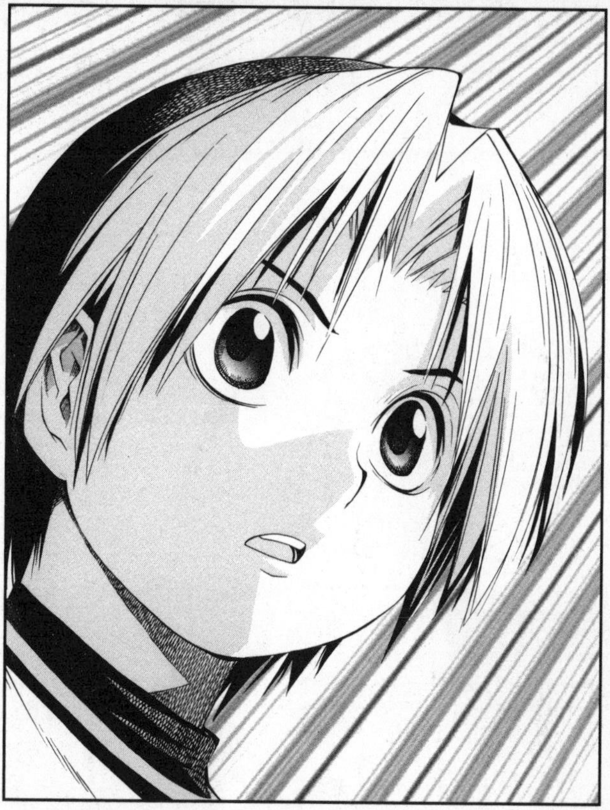

Hikaru gains experience and skill playing games at various go salons, but the 27 main rounds of the pro test are still before him. Only the top three players will move on to become pros…and Ochi, Waya, Isumi and Honda are all vying with Hikaru for those coveted spots!

AVAILABLE NOW

CALGARY PUBLIC LIBRARY
SEP -- 2011